Brass

A Policeman's Log

INCIDENTS FROM A POLICEMAN'S LOG

Bernie Loughran

Brass Buttons

A Policeman's Log

INCIDENTS FROM A POLICEMAN'S LOG

Bernie Loughran

Copyright © 2002 by Bernard A. Loughran

ISBN 0-7414-1300-0

Published by:

PUBLISHING.COM

519 West Lancaster Avenue
Haverford, PA 19041-1413
Info@buybooksontheweb.com
www.buybooksontheweb.com
Toll-free (877) BUY BOOK
Local Phone (610) 520-2500
Fax (610) 519-0261

Printed in the United States of America

Printed on Recycled Paper

Published October, 2002

This book would never have existed if it wasn't for my son Bernie who exercised a great deal of patience while teaching me how to use a Computer, Scanner and Printer.

The human trip is from innocence to experience.
William Blake, poet

You can still walk in this world and make a difference.
Father Daniel Berrigan, activist

PREFACE

I am fully aware that A POLICEMAN'S LOG has no greater significance than a schoolgirl's diary. It isn't about my life but about the things that happened while I was a police officer. When I applied for the job in 1947 I had recently been Honorably Discharged from the Navy along with millions of other World War II servicemen who were searching for a perfect career choice. For me jobs were scarce because the post war boom hadn't kicked in yet and I was one of the last of the World War II servicemen to be released.

I had no desire to be a policeman because I had a taste of similar work when assigned to Navy Shore Patrol duty. At that time I patrolled the downtown streets of port cities on the west coast when thousands of weary sailors and marines returned to await their final discharge. These men fought fierce battles against the Japanese in the South Pacific and they had no intention of taking orders any longer from anyone in the military, especially the Shore Patrol. It was a risky assignment for a nineteen-year-old kid who was waiting for his own turn to be discharged.

I was a police officer during the worse of times for the profession. It wasn't a depression, a war or a sensitive international climate but the prevailing social unrests that made the job extremely difficult. My journal isn't about the department, profession, residents of the township or any officer with whom I worked. There are no references to my family or my social life. It's strictly about my metamorphosis, achievements, derelictions, humiliations, and rigidity as a police officer. It isn't whether I considered myself an excellent officer but how I coped with daily assignments. It is strictly my experiences.

Names are fictional except for my mentor Officer Jim Wentz but if someone recognizes himself and is offended I apologize. I didn't intend to write a negative word about anyone.

Soon after an event occurred I associated a cliché with it and jotted it on my memo pad. A few days later I wrote a draft of what happened and not what I imagined happened. I worked with men who aggrandized their role in an incident to such a degree I didn't recognize the event even though I was present. A teacher warned me that a long drawn-out story could be tedious reading so I purposely stilted my stories to avoid embellishment.

I couldn't include every incident in this book so I sorted through my journal and selected 149. I chose those incidents that could help the average person understand what police work is all about. None of them are spectacular police stories. They are just real everyday occurrences that collectively transformed a giddy kid into a true blue police officer.

The title of each incident was the notation I used to remind me of the event and it is not the sum of the incident. These clichés, germane or not to the subject, I kept.

INTRODUCTION

I don't expect to arouse much interest in my account of the life of a police officer in the Neanderthal Era but I hope my children will be interested in their ancestry. Within these pages they may find a clue to a predisposition. I hope they will enjoy and learn from my musings. These were real situations but they definitely were not amusing at the time. Every incident was a new adventure. Since my training couldn't foresee every probability I often had to grapple for a resolution.

I'm not capable of embellishing or enhancing the facts to garnish an event and it is obvious I have no scholarship in formal writing. I certainly have no talent for creating a yarn nor the skill to cleverly pilfer from another source. If I worked too hard to set the stage or played too much background music it's because I lacked the necessary expertise. One semester in Written Communications isn't enough to master writing prowess. When I had documentation to support an experience I included it hoping there was enough verification through out the book to prove all my accounts are bona fide. Newspaper reports differ from mine because the reporter was not standing in my black shoes and besides they openly admitted they'd *"never ruin a good story with the facts."*

My era was primitive compared to the present day so I tried to portray the thinking in my time. I led a low profile career even though there were times I could have spawned notoriety if I exploited the media but I chose not to take advantage of anyone's grief. My choice of a low profile was also influenced by an event in my father's career as a police officer. His traumatic incident occurred early in his career.

His upsetting incident occurred when freight train boxcars were being robbed with regularity. The boxcars most vulnerable were those in Belmont Hills where the two-way tracks merge into a single track to permit one freight train at a time through the narrow Flat Rock Tunnel. The tunnel was a bottleneck that forced a train leaving Philadelphia to stop and wait until a train entering the city passed through the tunnel. A vice versa situation existed when an inbound train was notified by signal lights to wait until an outbound train cleared the tunnel.

A freight train made up of over a hundred boxcars could be a mile long so a delay at the tunnel might last several hours. Police protection was impossible during these stop-and-waits so thieves were at liberty to break the seals securing the boxcars and take all the merchandise they wanted. The robbers waited for a night when the boxcars were shrouded in darkness and then carried off the contents of a boxcar with the skill and tenacity of marauding leaf ants.

It was after midnight, about 1924, when a passing motorist notified the foot patrolman (my father) on duty at the Green Lane Bridge that a stopped freight train was being robbed. The police force had few patrol cars and they weren't equipped with police radios. Mobile radios didn't exist then. My dad was alone on foot and left to his own devices.

He instructed the motorist to notify headquarters via phone about the robbery in progress and that he was going after the felons. He took off on foot and stealthily crept a quarter of a mile to the open boxcar. Five men were involved. Two were inside the boxcar pitching items to the three men outside who transferred the merchandise to their car. He knew the five men could overpower him if they realized he was alone so he contrived a ruse. He hid on the railroad bank and barked orders to imaginary fellow officers. "Sergeant, I got them covered from here! Bill, you cover them from the left side! Jack, you cover the right side! Are you guys on the other side of the tracks ready to close in? Don't shoot unless they shoot first then let them have it!" His final order was for the five men to surrender because they were surrounded.

The bluff worked without a hitch. He placed four men under arrest and walked them into the arms of fellow officers who by then arrived in the patty wagon. The fifth man was later arrested. This arrest broke up the gang responsible for most of the boxcar pilfering and it discouraged other train robbers. It was a major arrest in its day.

The robbers were shamefully embarrassed because a single officer fooled them into believing they were surrounded by a squad of policemen. If they had known he was alone they would have fled in all directions. On the day of the trial they were being led from the courtroom by guards and they filed passed my father who had just testified against them. They stopped and confronted him and made a serious threat. "We don't like being made to look stupid by your practical joke. When we get out of jail we'll get you." For the rest of his life dad lived a nightmare. He took their threat seriously and feared someday one or more of the gang would ambush him or members of his family.

This was why I chose to tread softly. I preferred to do my duty without reprisals against me or my family. Without neglecting my duty I performed in such a manner I never felt threatened. If someone sought revenge I wasn't aware of it, hence, I never lost sleep over such matters.

I tried not to be harsh on the township. I was conscientious every working day therefore the residents got their tax dollar value. I didn't bring shame or disgrace upon the department or myself. I worked for a minimum wage so the Township Commissioners could brag to their constituency they reduced spending and kept the tax base low.

I worked under the false assumption a pension was deferred wages but my meager pension doesn't begin to cover the hardships I endured on the job and the pain I suffer in retirement due to arthritis. I admit I harbor bitterness toward the Commissioners because they cleverly negotiated a pay raise that stipulated they could deduct half my Government Social Security Benefit each month from my monthly township pension after I reached age sixty-five. No matter how they rationalize their behavior my fellow officers and I were ripped off because they were devious at the bargaining table.

I once read that a retired man earns his pension for the work he does in his dreams. After I finalized an incident for A POLICEMAN'S LOG it was removed from my memory. My pension isn't large enough for me to walk a cold beat or lay on frozen soil in my dreams, consequently, the more I wrote the fewer imaginary working hours disrupted a good night's sleep. I hope my family enjoys this book and they take from it what may be helpful and are proud of their heritage.

CAPTURES 5 SINGLE-HANDED

'Tommy' Loughrey Arrests Gang of Thief Suspects Along Railroad

"Tommy" Loughrey, Lower Merion policeman and former prize fighter, captured single-handed five young men accused of robbing a freight train on the Reading Railway, between West Manayunk and Gladwyn, shortly after midnight.

Another suspect was arrested after he had reported to Manayunk police his motor car, said to have been the one used in the attempted robbery, had been stolen in Fairmount Park. Loughrey identified him as the one he failed to capture.

Magistrate Arthur in Ardmore held them in $1,000 bail. They are [illegible] ████████████████████████████ ████████████████████████████ ████████████████████████████ ████████████████████████████ ████████████████████████████

Loughrey discovered the men piling thick in a motor car. Slipping up quietly, Loughrey confronted the group with a drawn pistol. Two fled. While Loughrey was leading the four away, he saw one of those who had fled running down an embankment. The youth gave himself up when Loughrey threatened to shoot.

The top photo is a newspaper report on the arrest and the bottom photo is an officer pointing to where the arrest took place. My father's professional boxing name was Tommy Loughrey.

TABLE OF CONTENTS:

LOWER MERION TOWNSHIP

Lower Merion Township is a residential community with fine homes, estates, excellent roads, luxury apartment buildings, business districts, department stores, churches, synagogues and first-rate services.

After William Penn received his land from Charles II. In 1681 he persuaded settlers to follow him here. The first to come were the Welsh. The English, German, Swedish, and Scotch-Irish came after them. Many decedents of the first arrivals still live on the land their ancestors purchased from Penn and they adopted the name "blue-bloods".

In 1947 there were many wealthy families and a sizeable percentage of the population served them. It was the land of the chauffeur driven Cadillac. Willie Sutton, the notorious bank robber was asked why he robbed banks and he answered, "That is where the money is." A Lower Merion police officer's primary responsibility was to thwart and capture burglars because Lower Merion Township is where the wealthy live.

Lower Merion police patrol a fairly large area. There were over 40,000 miscellaneous incidents investigated in 1982. It is a busy department and it is doing the job right when in the middle of the night a woman dressed in her pajamas can walk her dog feeling as safe as if she were in God's hip pocket.

GENERAL INFORMATION IN 1982

Population	58,500
Area - Square Miles	24
Roads	280
Highway Miles	275
Parks & Playgrounds	38
Schools	30
Fire Companies	6
Post Offices	7
Hospitals	2
Libraries	7
Banks	49
Dwellings	22,521
Houses	17,718

MY BACKGROUND

On the left I'm in a St. John's High School football uniform. I am 15 years old, 5'6" and 135 lbs. I played on the varsity team in my junior and senior years 1942 & '43 in the Philadelphia Catholic League. On the right is my navy mug shot taken when I was 17 years old, June 1944.

I trained in this Navy Privateer bomber. We were about to fly to the Pacific War Zone when Japan surrendered. This bomber had a nose, tail, top and side turrets. I was an Aviation Ordinanceman and also trained in all the turrets but preferred to call myself a tail gunner. At the end of the war I was assigned to Shore Patrol duty (navy police) for 6 months in several west coast cities until I was discharged.

THE SWEARING IN CEREMONY

One evening a month the Township Commissioners hold their regular Board meeting and conduct the business that keeps the township sailing on an even keel. On the November 1947 agenda there was a nuisance item that had to be dismissed quickly because the doors to the boardroom would be opened in ten minutes to admit the public. Four candidates, including myself, had to be sworn in as police officers.

We stood at rigid attention before the Board members waiting for the moment that would have a profound impact on our future. Two dull incandescent lights hung on a cord four feet from the ceiling over the Commissioners' table. They were the only lights lit in the room until the public was admitted. There were no relatives, spectators, sponsors or reporters present. The room was empty except for the thirteen Commissioners who were preoccupied shuffling papers, the Superintendent of Police and we four police candidates.

The President of the Board seemed irritated when he slapped the papers he was studying down on the table. Without excusing himself or explaining to the other Commissioners what he was about to do he walked double-quick to the front of the table. To him every minute was precious because the doors would soon be opened and a large group of chattering citizens would enter. He had to get rid of this time consuming interruption fast. He stood facing us and in a voice reeking with authority gave the command, "Raise your right hand and repeat after me, I, state your name, do solemnly swear to defend and uphold the Constitution of the United States and the Constitution of the Commonwealth of Pennsylvania."

He was monotone and unemotional so we followed his lead and responded unenthusiastically. After he administered the Oath of Office he forced an insincere smile and thrust his limp lady-soft palm forward to receive a handshake and said, "The Superintendent will tell you when to report for duty." He turned and almost ran back to his seat at the table.

It was a blah ceremony. Even the other Commissioners didn't take notice to what occurred. I asked myself; "Is that all there is? No pep talk? No, 'Welcome Aboard'? No, 'Good Luck'"? I was neither impressed nor thankful I had the job. I could in no way be jubilant over a job paying $2,330 a year for I knew a Philadelphia Union Laborer made more digging a ditch, mixing cement and carrying a hod. Negative thoughts crossed my mind at the moment I said, "I do" but it was the Commissioners' lack of respect for me as a man that caused me to mentally dropout and lose enthusiasm for the job.

The prevailing mood in the room was so grim the Oath of Office lost its relevance. I stood at attention and stoically repeated the words while my mind drifted back to my years in the Navy when I swallowed my dignity and humbly took orders from anyone older than myself. I swore then I'd never wear a uniform again nor would I salute another man or ever stand guard duty again. As our voices droned on "uphold the Constitution of the United States and the Constitution of the Commonwealth of Pennsylvania." I made a promise, "This will be a transient job, one year, two at the maximum.

LOWER MERION TOWNSHIP POLICE DEPARTMENT

MONTGOMERY COUNTY, PENNSYLVANIA

TOWNSHIP BUILDING

ARDMORE, PA.

MAJOR SAMUEL W. GEARHART
SUPT. OF POLICE

November 20, 1947

Bernard Loughran,
167 Old Belmont Avenue,
West Manayunk, Phila. 23, Pa.

Dear Sir:

      Last evening, November 19, 1947, the Board of Township Commissioners appointed you to the position of Probationary Patrolman, at an annual salary of $2330.00, as of December 1, 1947, provided you can make the necessary arrangements with your present employers. If this is impossible, kindly advise me prior to the above date.

      I am enclosing herewith a copy of the Lower Merion Township Police Manual, which contains an article on promotions in the Police Department, and the Police Department Discipline Code. Both of these matters are very important to you as a Temporary Patrolman.

      It is requested that you present yourself at these headquarters prior to December 1, 1947, and procure the necessary authorization to be measured for a uniform.

      Yours very truly,

SAMUEL W. GEARHART,
Supt. of Police.

SWG-D
Encl.

MY FIRST POLICE OFFICER'S UNIFORM

I was not the first former serviceman who wished for a more fulfilling career than police work. Before I joined a half dozen men after being discharged from the service joined the Force but they only tolerated it for eighteen to twenty months. After they resigned they returned their uniform for the next recruit to wear until a new tailored uniform was procured for him.

One fellow jumped ship before he had a chance to wear his new uniform so it was unused when it was issued to me. The only hitch was that fellow was 72" tall and 165 lbs. and I was only 68" tall and 165 lbs. His shirts were size 15" neck and 36" sleeve while I wore a 17" neck and 32" sleeve. His jodhpurs were long and tight yet baggy on me because of their length. His shirts and coats were tight and long.

I think the supply sergeant read my mind and knew I'd only be around a year, two at the maximum.

Visualize a short portly clergyman wearing a cassock that belonged to a tall thin man. That's how I appeared in my uniform. I looked like a helpless guppy out of water. I felt foolish but rationalized if the department wasn't embarrassed by a representative appearing in public looking the way I did then I shouldn't be bothered either.

These mug shots were taken for the department's personnel file the first week I was on the job in December 1947.

PENN STREET VS PENN ROAD

Midnight December 1, 1947 I went forth to protect and serve in my ill-fitting uniform. The night was tolerable only because I was assigned to Officer Jim Wentz. Jim was a fine man. He was only 68 inches tall but built like a gladiator. He was twenty-five years my senior with twenty-five years police experience. He exuded pride in himself, the uniform and the profession. At forty-six years of age he was in his prime. He radiated assurance. His super character was the result of healthy living, having a clean mind and being dedicated to serving his fellowman. I looked like a kid in a Halloween costume next to him and if I stood akimbo I looked like an insulted schoolgirl.

My sergeant knew Jim could tolerate the foolish antics of a kid and would convey the information a recruit must know. Jim was honest as the day is long and could imbue that into a young man. He wouldn't approve of anything that might discredit the profession. He was proud of the fact he "broke-in" every man with a rank. Every Sergeant, Lieutenant, Captain, and even the Superintendent he "broke-in".

He took me to his bosom and in that regard I was fortunate for I was anxious for Jim to approve of me. It was because he showed me respect I felt I could put up with the job for a while. I would absorb all the information he was willing to pass on to me even those tidbits that didn't pertain to police work. There was harmony and bonding during the first two hours. He told me about his unusual experiences and how cleverly he resolved them. I was fascinated. He asked about me but I was more interested in him, then I realized he had to get to know me.

I told him I was in the navy for two years. That impressed him because he never was in the service. He was too young for World War I and too old for World War II. I said I was a tail gunner on a bomber in the Navy Air Force. That infused a little confidence. Since I was a gunner it meant I wasn't gun-shy and was already trained to use my sidearm if the occasion arose.

He asked if I had any radio experience because that would be an asset patrolling in a car. I said as a tail gunner I often used the intercom to talk to the other men on the plane, especially to the pilot, copilot and navigator. On practice bombing runs over small-uninhabited islands in the Caribbean it was the tail gunner's responsibility to inform the pilot and navigator if the bomb we just dropped hit or missed the tiny island. I explained we communicated very formally. After a bomb was dropped I'd get on the intercom, "Tail gunner to pilot and navigator. That bomb was right on but 20 yards late, over." "Pilot to navigator, good shooting. We'll make another pass, over." "Navigator to pilot, Roger." I told Jim we attacked that little piece of real estate until all our bombs were dropped.

4

Time passed quickly as we became more comfortable with each other. We exchanged stories. It was the only means I had for generating credibility. I had to assure him that even though I was young I brought to the job some experiences and at times in the past had responsibilities. I hoped he'd accept me as a man. The average age of the force at this time was over fifty so to the other men I was very immature.

Jim was kind and benevolent yet I knew to tread softly. He was my evaluator as well as my instructor. If he disliked me he could be nasty and put me in my place fast. It was important he communicate a favorable opinion to my superiors for they valued his first impression. Conversation glided gracefully from one piece of trivia to another. Neither of us tried to overwhelm the other. As the saying goes: "Our chemistry mixed well."

At 2:30 a.m. Jim went into an all-night diner to buy a pack of cigarettes and left me in the car to listen to the radio. It was my bad luck that the radio blared out for the first time while he was gone. "Headquarters to Car #6." I responded with a crisp, "Car #6 standing by." "Car #6 investigate the report of a boy tampering with a car parked in the driveway at 1657 Penn Road." I responded, "Car #6, Roger."

After acknowledging the radio message Jim returned. "Jim, headquarters just told us to investigate the report of a boy tampering with a car parked in the driveway at 1657 Penn Street." Jim thought for a second and with doubt in his voice asked, "Barney, are you sure of the address?" I couldn't imagine why he doubted me so I asked what was wrong. "Barney, there is no Penn Street in our township but there is one close by in the neighboring township. Headquarters wouldn't dispatch us there because they have their own police force. I better check." He picked up the transmitter and clicked, "Headquarters repeat that location." Headquarters responded, to my embarrassment, "Car #6, that is 1657 Penn Road."

That was a simple but stupid mistake. Jim said, "Barney you've got to be very careful. There is a tremendous difference between Penn Street and Penn Road."

I felt like a scolded puppy that just soiled a parlor rug. I blew it on the very first radio message. I felt so inept. If Jim lost confidence in me he didn't say but there was a long uneasy silence. I didn't know how to redeem myself. There was no excuse for my stupidity. I wanted so much to be dependable. The silence lasted a few minutes but the memory lasted a lifetime. I was in torment. My first impulse was to flagellate myself then I rationalized, "So I blew it, so what? I'll be around only a year, two at the max."

THE LIQUOR STORE BURGLARY

My first two days on the job were uneventful. Car #6 had only a few miscellaneous assignments. We did routine chores and store checks. As we cruised the streets we continued to share experiences. "Barney, several years ago a transient stopped in Ardmore to catch his legs and while he was here he broke into the Liquor Store by smashing the glass in the rear door. He helped himself to a bottle of cheap wine. The next day the store manager reported the break-in but he couldn't pinpoint what was stolen. He didn't notice a bottle of wine was missing. Three days later the robber appeared at headquarters and confessed to the crime. The investigating detectives asked him why he broke into the store and why he owned up to the theft. He told them on that night he was hungry and after he drank all the wine he threw the empty bottle into the weeds behind the store. He said he knew the police would eventually find the bottle and lift his fingerprints off it and come after him so he decided to turn himself in." Jim and I laughed at the poor fellow's stupidity.

After reflecting on the incident I said, "Jim, do you believe his story or do you think he was looking for free meals and lodging at the county prison for the winter months?" Jim thought about it and said he wasn't sure but the detectives believed him because they put him away.

Jim mentioned a recurring premonition he's had for a month regarding the Liquor Store on his beat. I noticed he gave the store extra surveillance every night. For some strange reason he felt it would soon be burglarized. His clairvoyance became so vivid he felt the following night was the night the break-in would occur.

"Barney tomorrow night I'm off so tell whoever is assigned to this car to give extra attention to the Liquor Store. I'm positive tomorrow night is the night so tell whoever is assigned to this car." The next night I wasn't assigned to Car #6. I was assigned to Car #7 and just as Jim predicted the Liquor Store was burglarized. A truckload of expensive liquors was carted away. When Jim returned to work he heard his premonition became a reality. He didn't say a word to me until we were on patrol and then came down on me like a sledge hammer. He was furious. "Why didn't you warn the officer who took my place?" I told him I wasn't assigned to Car #6; I was assigned to Car #7.

"Barney you still could have warned my relief!"

"Jim", I said. "Please understand my position. I've been on the job only three days. I couldn't take it upon myself to tell a senior officer, whom I don't know, how he should patrol his beat nor could I tell him what to do. To tell the truth I didn't have the guts. I'm sorry."

There was no doubt about it. In Jim's mind I goofed again.

MY BASIC TRAINING

Jim was an encyclopedia chock-full of useful information that every officer must know to better serve the public and to survive. He tenaciously drilled his knowledge into me. His goal was to transform this fledging into a professional like he successfully did with the many rookies before me whom he 'broke in'. "Barney, Route #30 goes east and west, from Atlantic City at the Atlantic Ocean to San Francisco at the Pacific Ocean, and it bisects our Township. Route #1 goes north and south from Maine to Key West, Florida and it is a township boundary. You will come in contact with travelers from all over. (In 1947 the Interstate Highway System didn't exist).

"You must learn about colloquialisms. For example: A person from one part of the country may ask you directions to a State Store another person may ask for the Liquor Store and a third person may ask for a Package Goods Store. They are one and the same store.

"Another example: In this area an officer will stop a motorist for a moving violation and say to a driver, 'Show me your cards' and the motorist immediately will know what the officer wants to see. However, a driver from another State wont know what 'cards' the officer is referring to unless he specifically says, 'Show me your operator's license and registration card.' You must eliminate slang or street jargon.

"Barney, the highest house number in the township is 2200. If someone asks you for directions to a location higher than 2200 it is not in our township.

"The Lieutenant is bound to ask you 'On what street in the township is there concrete Electric Company poles?' They are on Bryn Mawr Avenue, Cynwyd. An Electric Company engineer, who lives on that street, had them installed years ago to study if they had a longer life span than the standard wooden poles. The Lieutenant is checking to see how observant you are." Jim impressed me with his vast knowledge.

He said that at 4:00 o'clock in the morning his eyelids get very heavy. It was a problem most men on the night shift had. He didn't want me to think it was acceptable to sleep on duty but it was imperative he rest his eyelids. To combat falling into a deep sleep he had a simple solution. "Barney sit up straight and place your flashlight between your palms with the glass facing upward and put your hands on your lap. Close your eyes with the intention of resting them but not to fall asleep. If you fall asleep the flashlight will drop from your grasp and wake you."

At 4:00 a.m. Jim hid the patrol car in a secluded location and demonstrated his theory. I can testify it works exactly as he claimed. An hour later my flashlight flopped over onto my lap and startled me. I awoke wide-eyed and bushy-tailed, ready to resume alert patrol.

MY FIRST AMBULANCE ASSIST

My first week on the job was dull. There were no cops and robber chases or to-the-rescue assignments. I was thankful because I was treading in unfamiliar waters and didn't need an initiation into the harsh side of police work just yet. The second week was my first 4:00 p.m. to midnight shift with Jim still at the helm. It was mid-December and approaching the shortest day of the year so at 5:00 p.m. it was black as midnight. A low hanging cloud thick as pea soup blanketed the township when the police radio operator screamed, "Car #6 respond to an auto accident on City Line Avenue. A car struck a pedestrian! The ambulance is responding!"

There was a distinct hint of urgency in the radio operator's voice. Usually he spoke in a calming modulated tone so not to excite the officers in the patrol cars but this time it was apparent whoever reported the accident raised his blood pressure. Jim and I arrived at the scene a few minutes before the ambulance and saw an unconscious woman was lying in the street in the curb lane. The car that struck her was there along with the driver, witnesses and helpful spectators. The witnesses gave us a synopsis of what happened.

The woman was a domestic who had just finished working in a home where she was a cook. She was running to catch a bus that was stopped to load and unload passengers on the opposite side of City Line Avenue. In her anxiety to attract the bus driver's attention and to have him wait for her she stepped off the curb into the path of oncoming traffic. The driver hadn't sufficient time to take evasive action nor could he skid to a stop before striking her.

The incandescent bulbs lighting the street were buried deep in the overhanging tree branches. They were inadequate for this main highway yet they were the best available. The wet roadway and glaring oncoming vehicle headlights reduced visibility to nil. Even though the general conditions were nasty the heavy commuter traffic still raced along at a crisp 40 to 45 mph. The fact the women wore a full-length black raincoat exacerbated the situation. The witnesses corroborated these details even though they were obvious to a trained accident investigator.

The woman lay unconscious on the street. She sustained contusions and lacerations but her most serious injury was an almost completely severed foot a few inches above the ankle. Only a sliver of skin, three inches wide, kept her foot attached to her leg.

Four officers silently and calmly performed like this was just a practice drill. They knew what had to be done and weren't affected by the seriousness of situation. First Aid was administered to stop the flow of blood and to prevent her from going into shock. One officer placed lighted flares on the roadway to alert motorists of the accident while another kept traffic flowing smoothly by the scene. I was impressed by their uncommunicative teamwork.

Officer Madden arrived with the ambulance. He was masterful at taking control and establishing order in the mist of chaos. He barked a single command at me, "Son, hold that foot steady with her leg!" Without a question or hesitation I took hold of the dangling foot and held it tightly between my palms while the other officers on the count of three lifted her off the roadway onto a stretcher. They lifted the stretcher, again in cadence, onto a gurney and slid it into the bowels of the ambulance.

I followed the gurney into the ambulance. My orders were to hold the foot in line with the leg and that was what I would do no matter where the leg went. That sliver of skin wasn't going to rip any farther due to my incompetence. I already looked foolish too many times the previous week.

The ride to the hospital was wild and reckless. The siren wailed a warning to everyone in its path to get out of the way. It swayed at every curve and skipped and bounced over every concrete seam and pothole. Madden knew the woman was losing blood and there was the likelihood of shock, which could be more serious than her injury. He was doing his utmost to get her to professional care as quickly as possible so I didn't criticize his driving. The hospital was seven miles away and a long daring ride in the heavy commuter traffic.

The cramped condition in the patient compartment of the ambulance was insufferable. The space for a stretcher and a passenger was seven feet deep, four feet wide and three feet high. The lack of room was restricting and it forced me to scrunch over on my knees. The temperature gauge was set high for the woman's benefit and I, like a gyroscope, kept her foot positioned as an extension of the leg even though I was being tossed about and unable to brace myself. Holding that foot properly took both hands and required the attention of every muscle in my body.

The smell from the woman's foot was asphyxiating. The odor from the wet silk stocking and wet shoe mixing with the smell of blood was rendered worse by the heat. It was beyond anything I ever endured. When the ambulance jerked to a stop at the emergency entrance I inhaled an intoxicating breath of fresh air the moment the ambulance door was pulled open and the cold night air rushed inside. It was a glorious feeling to stand erect again after I crawled backwards out of the stretcher compartment. Madden and the hospital staff tenderly pulled the gurney out and wheeled it around ninety degrees to enter the hospital. They frantically rushed it into the Accident Ward Operating Room.

Once in the Operating Room the woman was lifted off the gurney onto the operating table. The stretcher was removed from under her by rolling her from side to side. During all this maneuvering I positioned

9

myself out of their way and at the same time kept a steady-on grip on the foot.

A nurse undressed her and prepared her for what was to follow. The woman didn't impede or add to the commotion because she remained unconscious throughout the whole ordeal. I stood at the foot of the operating table while she was rolled from side to side to remove her coat. The rolling continued to cut off her dress. She was rolled, tossed and twisted to cut off her undergarments. A nurse cut off the part of her stocking that was on her leg but left me holding her foot with the stocking and shoe still in place. Another nurse with an orange antiseptic bathed her body.

There was so much noisy excitement and activity going on around me that I was appalled because it wasn't systematic or rhythmic as the police officers at the hectic accident scene. Three more of the hospital staff sprinted into the room and they never noticed I was standing there with the woman's foot between my hands. Everyone was oblivious of my presence yet I was performing a vital task. I was invisible. If I was in their way they skirted around me. At every twist of her body I gently aligned her foot to whatever position the leg was turned and through all this the smelly shoe and bloody stocking was still on her foot.

Thirty minutes passed since I first took a firm grip on that foot and now my mind and body was ablaze from the strain. My back was racked with pain. The muscles in my forearms, biceps and shoulders were as taut as an over-wound clock spring. I was in need of relief so I scanned the room to make certain Officer Madden had left the hospital and only then did I ask a nurse to relieve me.

I cautiously straightened my spine because I was afraid my back muscles might spasm. I took short slow steps out of the operating room and kept walking until I was out of the hospital. Since no one noticed I was in the room I knew no one noticed I had left.

The fresh cold evening air made me tipsy. The blood, exposed bone, torn flesh, pungent odors, excessive heat, the confining ambulance compartment, artificial bright operating room lights and my inexperience ganged up on me. I rushed to the curb and bent over. I hung my head low and had a spell of dry heaves.

Five years after this accident an article appeared in a Philadelphia newspaper. It referred to this case that was first published in the American Medical Journal. It stated a foot was successfully reattached to the leg in the Bryn Mawr Hospital and still functioned. It was a medical breakthrough. Undoubtedly, a future case would be credited as the first authentic limb reattachment and this case will be disqualified because the foot and the leg remained connected by that small piece of skin I struggled to keep from tearing.

THE READING ROOM

It was my third week on the job but my first week on day work, 8:00 a.m. to 4:00 p.m.. Officer Jim Wentz was more at ease with me. At first he guarded what he said and did because there was the possibility his superiors place me with him to be a snitch but he readily shared secrets, like, where to get a discounted meal and where to rest his eyes.

The radio blared, "Car #6, on James Place, in front of Armillio's Men's Store, a man is lying on the sidewalk."

Like a seasoned professional I coolly responded, "Car #6, Roger." Jim punched the accelerator to the floor. With some luck we might get to James Place in ten minutes because this was the week before Christmas and the last minute shoppers were out in droves. This was years before there were shopping mall complexes so everyone shopped in their main street business district.

To get to the sick man we sped through the business district where traffic was bumper to bumper. Cars were double-parked. A delivery truck was parked where it shouldn't be and a bus was stopped in the only through lane. None of this fazed Jim for he did whatever had to be done to sidestep all obstacles in his path. Our patrol car was painted solid black and had no markings or siren. A small ineffectual six-inch flashing red emergency light was on the car roof yet Jim serpentine around every obstruction and arrived at the sick man's feet in seven minutes. I'm sure the spectators expected a quicker response time but if they only knew the wild ride we had they would have marveled at our dedication.

Jim had been teaching me how to first size up individuals and surroundings before rushing brashly into action so when we arrived I made a quick assessment of the man lying on the sidewalk. He was expensively dressed in a full-length black Chesterfield overcoat with a fur collar. He wore a tailor-made suit; a starched white shirt, a club necktie and a Homburg lay on the sidewalk beside him. I could tell he wasn't a bum passing through town. The odor of alcohol wasn't present so I ruled out intoxication. From his complexion and well-groomed white hair I estimated he was about sixty years of age.

Jim knelt beside him while I stood with the spectators wondering what he would do. Jim asked the man, "What's wrong, Mister?" "I'm having a heart attack," the man answered in a barely perceptible voice. "Well don't you worry. We'll have you in the hospital in no time. Who's your doctor? Headquarters will contact him and he'll meet us at the hospital."

"I don't want to go to a hospital. Please take me to the Reading Room." Jim was befuddled. "Mister, you are very ill and should go to the hospital." "No, thank you. Please, take me to the Reading Room."

I had nothing to contribute so I stood back with the rest of the spectators waiting for the outcome of this exchange. I was raised in a 100% Catholic environment and never heard of a Reading Room.

Jim didn't want the man to die in his patrol car unless headquarters sanctioned it so he reached for the radio transmitter and keyed it on. "Car #6 to Headquarters."

"Come in Car #6."

"Headquarters this man is suffering a heart attack but he refuses to go to the hospital or to a doctor's office. He wants to be taken to the Reading Room. What is your pleasure?" There was a momentary delay. Obviously those in authority in headquarters were mulling over the ramifications of their response. It gave me enough time to ask Jim what would the man do at the Reading Room and Jim being an ardent Catholic too shrugged his shoulders like he had no idea.

"Headquarters to Car #6. If the man doesn't want to go to the hospital take him to the Reading Room." As we gingerly eased the man into the rear seat of the patrol car Jim winked and whispered, "Barney, we're going to have a corpse on our hands."

Jim drove and I sat in the rear seat with the man. I politely asked him what would he do in the Reading Room. He gasped and said he would read his book. It was such an effort for him to say those few words I thought it best not to ask what was the title of the book?

I learned the location of another landmark. The Reading Room was on Rittenhouse Place, Ardmore. It is a single one-story brick building. It is a miniature library but furnished more like a comfortable parlor. There was a sofa, several upholstered armchairs, a couple of upright wooden chairs and a desk. Two walls were lined with shelves full of books. The front door was unlocked so we entered.

No one was in the room and that made Jim reluctant to leave the man unattended. He was suffering excruciating chest pains but repeated several times that we had done enough for him and we were under no further obligation. He appreciated what we've done and asked us to leave. That was what he wanted so we left and resumed routine patrol. Thinking aloud Jim said, "Barney I've been around a long time but I haven't seen it all yet."

Jim couldn't get the sick man off his mind. Curiosity and concern got the best of him so an hour later he had to know if the man had died. He drove to the Reading Room to see if he was still breathing and this time we burst into the building in such haste we startled a woman sitting in a plush chair reading a book. The old fellow wasn't there so Jim asked her if she saw a man sitting in the room and what was his physical condition.

"Oh yes, I saw him and he's fine. We talked for a while and then he left."

We went back on patrol. "Barney," Jim said, rocking his head from side to side, "Prayer is a powerful medicine."

TOTAL CONFUSION

During my first three weeks everyone who thought they were being helpful rammed a deluge of information at me but because there was so much all at once there was no enlightenment; only total confusion. It was impossible to absorb it all. I was in a new culture. Nothing I had previously learned fit in this new world.

Jim thought he was reducing the township street directory to a simple equation. "Remember Barney, there is Indian Creek Road, Indian Creek Lane and Indian Creek Drive. There is a Bryn Mawr Avenue in Bala, in Cynwyd, in Penn Valley, in Bryn Mawr and in Wynnewood. There is an East Wynnewood Road, West Wynnewood Road and North Wynnewood Avenue. There is a Haverford Road and a Haverford Avenue. There's a Morris Road and a Morris Avenue. There is an Old Lancaster Road in Haverford and in Bryn Mawr and in Merion." I mentally shutdown after the first Indian Creek. This job was tougher than memorizing the Latin Confiteor when I was a ten year old alter boy. Jim didn't realize it but he sounded like a Franciscan Missionary saying a Litany.

"There is a School House Lane and a School Street in Ardmore and a School Street in West Manayunk. There are several Old Gulph Roads and New Gulph Roads and there is a Berkeley Road and a Barkley Road. There is a Lancaster Avenue, West Lancaster Avenue and an East Lancaster Avenue. Remember the location of the Toll Gate, Three Sisters' Hill, The Guard House, 1690 House and Devil's Den. He droned on and on and after each street he associated an incident or history. I had to know the streets and their location but there were other important things too. What he was saying was meaningful but there was so much it would take years to cram it all in and sort it all out.

A postcard from the 1940s gives a view of downtown Ardmore.

13

THE SICK GREYHOUND BUS PASSENGER

After riding in a patrol car for a few months with different senior officers it came time for me to be sent forth on my own so I was assigned to walk a beat. On the very first day I was standing on the sidewalk wearing my winter uniform in an unseasonable heat wave. I was deliberately minding my own business and wishing no one noticed my presence. It was a stuffy morning and traffic, as always, was bumper-to-bumper and moving at a snail's pace. Nothing could be done to expedite it so I stayed to myself on the sidewalk. It would take a brigade of highway engineers to improve the archaic conditions. In 1948 there was no Turnpike or Expressway. Lancaster Avenue; the Lincoln Highway, route #30, was the only through highway east and west across the country and even then it wasn't an improved highway all the way.

My mind was in nirvana. I saw nothing but a few scantily clad college girls window-shopping. My eyes drifted away from them to an oncoming Greyhound bus. Its destination, San Francisco, was displayed on a sign above the windshield. I returned to reality and puzzled as to why the driver was rolling to an unscheduled stop where I was standing.

I presumed it was more than a coincidence that a cross-country bus should stop in front of a police officer. Undoubtedly the driver needed me. I was praying there wasn't an unruly passenger or one who refused to pay the fare. If I was lucky the driver might want directions and I would simple say, "Straight ahead". I was apprehensive because there were so many nefarious scenarios. I strolled slowly toward the bus because I didn't want to rush into the unknown. The problem would soon raise its ugly head. It was up to me to display professionalism. I had to appear sophisticated and aloof.

The doors of the bus spread apart and the driver stepped out and then turned to assist a woman get out. My first inclination was that the woman was getting off at her destination but then I noticed she was unsteady and quite sick. In this era it was common for a bus passenger to suffer motion sickness or need a restroom. Buses could be unbearably hot and stuffy on a warm day. Smoking was permitted and air-conditioners were not available to cool and clean the air. There was no restroom on a bus then therefore a long ride would be grueling. Kidneys could be jarred to fragments especially if your seat was over a wheel.

I calmly sauntered toward them and was within three feet of her when she threw up. Her reflex action was to raise her handkerchief to cover her mouth and as she did the foul contents of her stomach ricochet off the handkerchief and splashed over the front of my uniform. As quickly as the dastardly deed was done the driver ushered her back into the bus. He yanked on a lever to shut the folding doors and sped off."

The smell was unbelievable. It was something I couldn't hide or tolerate for the remainder of the day so I quickly walked to a Dry

14

Cleaning establishment. A large sign in the show window advertised "SERVICE WHILE YOU WAIT".

I walked into the store where two young men, the owners of the business, were busy catching up on the backlog of cleaning and pressing. I showed them my problem and asked if they would be so kind to quickly dry clean my uniform while I waited. I intended to pay the cleaning bill but they adamantly refused to clean my uniform and in a very insulting tone behaved like a couple of street thugs who had no respect for police. "We're too busy!" "You'll ruin our cleaning fluid!" "Get the hell out of here you're stinking up the store!"

I was naïve, inexperienced and unschooled in the power of my position, but I gambled. I gazed out of the storefront window and nonchalantly pointed to their delivery truck parked in a NO PARKING ANY TIME zone. I barked from the pit of my stomach, "I bet that stupid looking truck will get a lot of tickets for illegal parking!" There wasn't a legitimate parking place anywhere near their store so it was always parked in that illegal spot. They had no choice but to park illegally when they were not loading or unloading.

Without acknowledging my comment, they dropped what they were working on and gave my uniform priority service. I undressed and they tossed the uniform into the dry cleaning machine. After it went through the cleaning cycle, it got a professional pressing. I was out of the store in a shot with a "No charge".

After this experience I always tried to approach a sick person from the side, especially a sick child, but circumstances weren't always in my favor.

FREED FROM BATHROOM
Patrolmen Brady Utz and B. Loughlan were summoned Monday to render assistance at 4 Balwyn Place. Bala. A child locked in a bathroom was rescued.

PRESIDENT HARRY S TRUMAN AND ME

Vice-president Harry S Truman became president in 1945 upon the death of Franklin D. Roosevelt. In the following Presidential election he ran against a formidable competitor so being the tough crusted guy he was he put on the gloves and fought hard. He did most of his campaigning from a private train that criss-crossed the country. At every whistle-stop, village and hamlet he greeted the people from the observation platform on the last car. Our paths crossed for a brief moment due to his unique campaigning tactic.

One night, a few minutes after midnight, a patrol car raced toward me and skidded to a stop where I was walking my beat. The officer shouted through the half open window for me to get in. "The Lieutenant wants all the men to assemble on Belmont Avenue. All walking beats are being picked up. He was secretive so I have no idea what it's about."

Myself and a half-dozen other men stood before the Lieutenant as he explained that the Reading Railroad tracks were blanketed with State Police, FBI, Secret Service, railroad police and Philadelphia police from away up the line right into the city. Truman's train would be coming through and our job was to prevent sabotage. He assigned me to the Flat Rock Tunnel. Why he assigned me, a rookie, to guard the most vulnerable location I'll never know. A determined saboteur would choose the tunnel as a logical place to plant a bomb because there wasn't a hint of illumination or moonlight at that spot and it is far from civilization and detection. If a fellow officer was stationed within a hundred feet of me we couldn't see each other it was so dark.

By 12:45 a.m. I knew it would be a long dismal night because I couldn't locate any shelter. I'd been content if I found a comfortable rock to sit on but it was too dark to hunt for one so I sat on a rail. I figured the rumbling vibrations of the train miles away would travel through the steel rails and alert me that it was on its way.

A damp mist from the nearby river drifted over the area and made the already cold night more miserable. I reached the point where I didn't care if the earth made another rotation let alone worry about Harry.

It was still dark at 5:35 a.m. when the train roared by at 65 mph. It created a vacuum that sucked up the coal dust and cinders and flung the mixture bullet velocity into my eyes, nose, and ears and stung all my exposed skin. The engineer had applied the brakes to slow the train for its entry into the city so the steel brake shoes were pressed solidly against the steel wheels causing them to lock and let out a horrible screech. Multicolored sparks sprayed from each wheel like dozens of birthday cake sparklers racing through a darkened banquet room.

It had been a long, tense, uncomfortable, cold, solitary night. I didn't relax until I saw the observation platform round a curve and go out of sight. I thought, "If a catastrophe befell that train farther down the line I could honestly tell the Lieutenant that Harry was OK when he passed me."

This is the Flat Rock Tunnel. The track on the right is outbound from Philadelphia and the track on the left is inbound into the city. Only one train can fit in the tunnel so the double tracks merge into one through the tunnel. I waited for President Truman sitting on the inbound track.

These train tracks are laid parallel to the river that is approximately a hundred yards away. They generally followed the grade of the river so at this point there is a downgrade, which causes a train to pick up a speed that must be controlled and slowed down considerably before it enters the city.

THE KID AT THE BLOCK PARTY

By May 1948 I had been in uniform for six months and I still didn't feel like an authentic police officer. I looked more like a frightened cub scout in an ill fitting uniform. Even so, I was given a man's job when I was assigned to maintain order at a block party sponsored by an African-American church in the African-American community. This was a new experience for me because I never associated with black people except in a gym. I didn't know if I had to conduct myself differently.

A short street was barricaded at both ends so traffic wouldn't interfere with the carnival stalls set up in the street. I was assigned there because on the previous two carnivals young black hoodlums from out of town disrupted the festivities. They came to the block party just to incite a brawl. My presence was to thwart a similar disaster. I wasn't afraid a hostile gang might show up I just had no idea what procedures to follow or what laws I could enforce. I was wishing the sergeant had given me some instructions.

I must have been a deterrent because for three evenings, Friday, Saturday and Sunday, there wasn't a hint of a rumpus.

Back and forth I strolled. Bored to tears and swearing I was going to search for a different job because I couldn't tolerate this boring one much longer. There wasn't one adult with whom I could wile away the time. No one knew me and I knew nobody. The relationship between black people and police in this era was so unsociable even the church elders who requested an officer to be assigned here looked sideways at me.

However, there was a black boy about ten or eleven years of age who attached himself to me each evening. He was friendly and remarkably articulate and familiar with more police procedures than what I was taught to date. While we paced up and down the street he bombarded me with questions on points of law when he already knew the correct answers.

A typical question went like this: "If my father was beating up my mother and I called for the police and you came to the house could you come into the house and arrest him?" I boasted, "I sure could." My intention was to assure him his world was safe because we police were here to protect everyone. He snapped back, "No you couldn't. You can't come into the house or arrest him unless you saw him hit her."

It was one of many technicalities he knew from hands-on experience and I was to learn many months later in a police course. I wondered what kind of environment did he live in if he knew all the questions and answers. What was he learning at home?

18

MY CATTLE TRUCK LESSON

In 1948 there were no four lane super highways on the outskirts of town to by-pass the through traffic that congested the local business districts. It was because of the absence of expressways and turnpikes and the sudden growth of the trucking industry an unbelievable vehicle logjam developed in every town and city. Most intersections in a populated area are controlled by a traffic signal that is usually red when a burden vehicle approached it. Overloaded tractor-trailers had to lumber through the gears when the red traffic signal finally turned green.

At the slightest incline in the road the lighter trucks and automobiles weren't able to pass a convoy of overloaded tractor-trailers moving at a snail's pace because there were no passing lanes. It is impossible to describe the volume of trucks that appeared on the main roads. It was comparable to a slow moving freight train that had no beginning or end. This condition existed on every road east and west, north and south and as can be expected troublesome problems developed. This particular encounter occurred during my apprenticeship.

On a hot summer afternoon an old-timer, Officer Charlie Sweep, and I were standing on the sidewalk on Lancaster Avenue. He was briefing me on things that can only be learned through an embarrassing experience or from a forewarning; "--- and another thing, when you hear a cattle truck coming east duck into a doorway or hide behind something. You can never trust those 'she cows'."

I had no idea what he was talking about, especially the term 'she cows'. I knew what a cattle truck was. It is a trailer built for hauling livestock from a farm to a slaughterhouse. The livestock is lined up on the trailer in two rows facing the center. Staves are fastened between the animals so they won't lose their footing and fall and possibly be trampled to death. The sides of the trailer are wooden stakes spaced wide enough apart to allow air to flow around the animals.

Just as Charlie made that statement a stake-body cattle truck transporting cows from a Lancaster farm to a Philadelphia slaughterhouse was coming east in our direction. I heard the cows bleating when they were still fifty yards away. We hadn't enough warning to dart into a store so Charlie ducked behind a wide pillar and I followed him. Low and behold a 'she cow' lifted her tail and sprayed urine on everyone walking on the sidewalk for a distance of forty yards.

That was another basic lesson in police work. "Listen for the sound of cows, pigs, sheep or horses being transported in a stock trailer and then waste no time taking shelter until it passed."

THE HEARING

In 1948 a few men arrived twenty minutes before roll call to play a dozen hands of rummy in the Court Room. The wager was a nickel a game and I was one of the fellows who played and enjoyed the comradeship. Ten minutes before roll call five of us were playing rummy when we heard a shuffling commotion outside of the Court Room. We knew a group of people was about to enter so the cards were swiftly swept off the table and each player snatched his nickel to hide the evidence we were gambling. Through the closed doors burst the Justice of the Peace, Captain of Detectives Captain of Patrol, Superintendent, reporters from three newspapers, a photographer and two portly detectives with a handcuffed sad sack between them.

He was a meek disheveled forty-year-old fellow who hadn't shaved in several days. He was out of place among the well-groomed men. He was accused of burglary and was about to have a Hearing. We card players stood silently in the rear of the Court Room waiting for the proceedings to end so we could resume our game. The poor devil's Hearing took less than five minutes.

I had been on the job just a few months so this was my first courtroom experience, however, as I stood there observing the proceedings I was horrified. To me everything was wrong. Everything was deplorably unfair and despicably unsportsmanlike about the ceremony but I couldn't put my finger on what annoyed me. Even though I was uneasy with what transpired the seasoned officers standing beside me were complacent. Maybe they were gloating with pride because someone in the department successfully apprehended a burglar and he was going to receive a punishment to fit the crime.

I felt a sickness in the pit of my stomach but I couldn't logically explain what made me nauseous. I knew whatever injustice was being perpetrated against this individual reflected a stupid judicial system and a very sick society. This defenseless individual was at the mercy of the King's men. It was a demonstration that our civilization hadn't advanced one iota since the signing of the Magna Charta nine hundred and fifty years ago or since the drafting of the Bill of Rights. The King had all the power and his henchmen callously and ruthlessly enforced His Majesty's decrees. These policemen, snug in their positions, cast charges at this hapless person who had no hope of receiving a fair Hearing.

No one was present to speak up on behalf of this milquetoast. No one to defend him or proclaim he only stole to buy a loaf of bread to feed his hungry family. These men of the law and the Justice of the Peace were on one side of the scale and the sad sack stood all alone on the other side. He appeared to have already been incarcerated for several days because the system permitted he be kept locked up for three days if the need existed.

The Justice of the Peace growled, "Are you guilty or not guilty?" The mouse was petrified and squeaked, "Not guilty." "You are to be held in the county prison until your trial in the county courts." The Justice of the Peace snarled as he brought down the gavel to emphasize his statement.

Within minutes they walked single file through the door as fast as they entered. The sad sack was hustled into an awaiting police cruiser and whisked off to the county prison to wait for a trail that might not take place in months. The court system ground slowly. The Hearing was brief and he was out of the detectives' hair until the trial. They returned to their desks and gloried in the day's success.

I couldn't forget that Hearing and the poor helpless fellow. Guilty or not of the charge he was struck by the full impact of the Judicial System. If he was an articulate person he couldn't communicate his innocence with his hands cuffed behind his back. He could only respond to the bland question, guilty or not guilty of the charge of burglary?

The most pitiful player in this whole tableau was the Justice of the Peace. He was a short man, possibly 5'4" tall and afflicted with several uncontrollable nervous disorders. Frequently his arms whipped wildly from his side and a facial tick caused him to continually blink. He constantly flinched and frequently wiped his runny nose on the sleeve of his jacket. His head jerked from side to side and spasms in his back muscles jerked him upright. He suffered from the most visible of all diseases, Tourrette Syndrome and/or Saint Vitas' Dance. It took a recruit several court appearances to become accustomed to his physical imperfections and be able to overlook them.

If I happened to be the one arrested and made stand before this pathetic looking Judge, who had the power to make a judgment call that would affect my future, I would have felt that the Bill Of Rights and the Constitution of the United States didn't pertain to me. Especially since this Judge had no formal training in the Law. He was a mechanic by trade and a politician who belonged to a lucky political party that swept him into office.

Years passed before I knew all the wrongs perpetrated in the courtroom that afternoon. It took the Supreme Court of the United States and Chief Justices Warren (1953) and Burger (1969) to rectify the wrongs. To this day police agencies and arresting officers protest vehemently that their court decisions handcuffed the police. The drama that was so abhorrent to me in 1948 should never again occur in any courtroom because the Supreme Court has since passed many decisions to prevent it. I present a few changes in simplistic terms.

1- Upon arrest a person must be informed of his Civil Rights. If he doesn't know his Rights they are to be explained to him at the time of his arrest.

a) He has the Right to remain silent.

b) He has the Right to council and if he doesn't have council one must be appointed.

c) He has the Right to a speedy Arraignment, Preliminary Hearing, Hearing, and Trial.

2- An Arraignment must be held as soon as possible after being arrested. This means within the hour or within a few hours but never should anyone languish in a lockup.

3- At the Arraignment the person is told the charges against him. He is not asked if he is guilty or not. A Preliminary Hearing date is set and it must be within ten days of the Arraignment. This intermission gives the defendant an opportunity to confer with his lawyer about an alibi.

4- A court trial is scheduled within thirty days of the Hearing or the case is dismissed.

5- At the Arraignment, Preliminary Hearing, and the Hearing, reasonable bail is set. This allows the defendant the freedom to contact his lawyer and the people who can corroborate his alibi. (He cannot defend himself from behind bars and permission to make only one phone call.)

6- A defendant may be appointed a lawyer.

7- At no time during this procedure can the police intimidate the defendant or even talk to him unless his lawyer is present. If they do the case is automatically dismissed.

It took many more Supreme Court decisions for the necessary changes to evolve before I fully understood the wrongs and evils inherent in the old system. Obviously the poor sad sack hadn't any Civil Rights at the time of his Hearing. The wheels of the Criminal Justice System ground much too slow to benefit him.

HE'S GOT TWO MINUTES TO LEAVE

One night I was assigned to the gloomiest walking beat in the township. The business district was in a sorry state of neglect. Most of the stores were vacant and the ones that were occupied didn't have the kind of business that attracted shoppers to the area. There were six saloons on this beat but that wasn't why I loathed the hours I was assigned there, especially the night hours. The neighborhood didn't intimidate me it was the slimy dirty feeling that enveloped me while in this ghetto. The sidewalks are cluttered with trash, the storefronts are sinister and neglected and the street barely lit by primitive incandescent streetlights. The only pedestrians after midnight are the saloons patrons. I'd take a shower as soon as I got home after work I felt so begrimed.

My sergeant drove through every beat during a shift to check on the well being of his men and he expected to see each man every time he drove through his beat. It was already 1:30 the night I'm speaking of and he hadn't been to my beat yet so I stood on this filthy sidewalk, in this bleak part of the township, in front of a squalid saloon waiting for him to speed by. I would salute him and he might return the salute. He wouldn't stop to ask if I was experiencing any problems because he didn't have the time.

I stood in front of a particular saloon because it had a large storefront window. A dirty faded lace drape veiled the window so pedestrians couldn't see the activity inside or recognize a neighbor sitting at the bar. However, the faintly illuminated background helped me be visible to the sergeant when he finally drove by. That was my only concern, as I stood there full of contempt for the job, the surroundings, and for the sergeant.

As I waited I heard the festive drinkers inside. No matter how ugly the squalor may be outside inside a pub the spirit is always gay. I assumed there was an exciting sports event on television because all the drinkers seemed to be involved. Two Irish immigrants who feared the law owned this saloon. Their paramount concern was to prevent any unfavorable reputation from being associated with their establishment. They knew if a significant number of infractions were reported to the Liquor Control Board it would mean the loss of their liquor license. At every meeting with the officer on the beat they curried favor and cajoled him so he wouldn't submit a negative report about their establishment.

I stood in front of the window minding my own business when suddenly there was a loud explosion. The barroom door burst open like it had been blown off its hinges by a bomb. All the patrons were evacuating the building at the same time through the narrow front door. I thought someone for a gag discharged a tear gas bomb inside. I couldn't imagine what else could send them into the frenzy I was witnessing. It was comical to watch all those oversized men with their beer bellies trying to squeeze through the narrow door at the same time. I didn't know what happened but it had to be something serious to drive them out of their wits simultaneously. Perhaps a flash fire raged inside and I should get to a phone and direct headquarters to dispatch a fire department.

I remind you that it had been my philosophy, from day one, to hesitate before acting whenever I saw everyone about me out of control to get a better perspective of what is really transpiring. In a flash I grasped that the patrons were collectively ejecting a single man from the saloon. This was the oddest bar scene I ever saw. It wasn't a case where one customer disagreed with another and the disagreement escalated to a one-on-one scuffle. It wasn't a situation where one group was prejudice against another group and a brawl developed. This one man inflamed a dozen customers so intensely they couldn't tolerate his company any longer so they flared up en masse to physically toss him off the premises.

The agitator was a well-built young fellow, probably thirty-five years of age. It was evident he possessed great strength for it took all the men to accomplish the task. He wasn't threatened by their numbers and successfully put forth a great deal of resistance. The first fellow to exit the barroom door was the young man who was being shoved out but he was not alone. He was dragging a patron in a headlock. The men behind them were pushing but gained only a few inches at a time. The next man in line behind the big guy and the man in the headlock spotted me and sent up an alarm, "The cops! The cops!" Another fellow shouted in a loud hoarse whiskey whisper, "Quiet! Keep quiet!" Another fellow quickly gave the order, "Everybody back inside! Get back inside!" Once the men untangled I heard a fellow inside shout what he thought was a good ploy, "Everybody take a seat!"

After the alarm was sounded they reversed and once again tried to fit through the narrow door and all at the same time. It was a hilarious scene to my sober eyes. Once they were inside they slammed the door shut behind them to keep the cops out but they didn't realize they also closed the door on two men. Abandoned on the sidewalk to confront the cops was one scared Irish owner/bartender and the huge brute. This hulk had been so objectionable and so nasty that to a man all the occupants of the bar wanted him exorcised. I've heard of many barroom fights but never one that was so miss-matched as this one. Nevertheless the fellow was so strong there was no doubt it would take a regiment to get him as far as they did.

The bar owner was scared to death of what the cop on the beat would report so be began with his best Irish Blarney. He talked with a silver tongue but with a quaver in his voice. "You're the new fella on the force. You're Irish, too. Your mother and father came from the same county I'm from. If I can ever help you let me know, etc."

While the Irish owner was giving me a snow job the humongous ox was standing directly behind me. Just in case, I kept him in my peripheral vision. I always gave my opponent my rear side. I knew from my rough school days experiences how to turn what appeared to be a disadvantage to my advantage.

A man in the saloon peeked through a part he made in the dirty lace drape and reported to the others at the bar in his husky whiskey voice, "They're just talking." I probably appeared like a rookie who might call for help. I was frightened but I was taking my time waiting for my next move to develop. After all I was only a meek twenty-two year old kid without any experience regarding the matter at hand. The owner suddenly stopped his blathering and got serious because he had to get back inside and protect his cash register. He asked, "And what are you going to do about him?" pointing a finger toward the big fellow behind me.

As nonchalantly as I could and with my eyes directly on the bartender I spoke up so the big guy could hear. I said, with all the confidence in my ability to achieve the task, "If he isn't gone in two minutes I'm going to lock him up."

I startled the bartender. His mouth drooped and his eyes bulged in shock. He didn't think it appropriate to question me as to how I was going to go about this monumental chore. The young bull was dumfounded too. He thought very hard for six seconds on what he should say or if he should accept the challenge. Perhaps it was due to the booze he consumed that he had difficulty collecting his wits but he decided discretion was the better part of valor. He pulled himself upright to appear sober as a judge and turned on his heels and with a discernible wobble in his stride he staggered up the street as fast as he could and got lost in the black shadows.

The owner thanked me to the high heavens after I assured him there would be no report filed. He returned to his customers with a tale about the rookie cop who was going to stand up against the massive oaf and arrest him. I noticed I received a great deal of respect from the Irishman's customers after that night.

THE WIDE AWAKE COP

One midnight I was assigned to walk the West Ardmore beat. It had been a bitter cold winter and on this particular night the temperature was an Arctic twenty-two degrees. The weatherman didn't compute the chill factor for us those days and it was best I didn't know. It was unthinkable that a person should be forced to endure the polar temperature for eight straight hours yet the sergeant during roll call roared the order that the men on foot patrol must stand out on the sidewalk, out in the open, where the public can see them.

For some unknown reason the frigid temperature sorely affected me this winter. I may have had a virus or walking phenomena and never realize it. Whatever was physically wrong it caused me to suffer miserably from the cold. To get warm this night I sought heat from a Philadelphia Electric Company ventilating grate in the sidewalk. A minuscule amount of smelly electrical heat rose from a transformer buried below the grate. The heat was so imperceptible it wasn't measurable but psychologically it was a tremendous help. For half an hour I stood on the vent forcing myself to stand erect and stay awake. A car drove by me a second time at a slow 20 mph. It went west a few blocks turned around and headed east. It went east a few blocks and west again. It was now 1:00 a.m. and not the hour young men cruised looking for girls to pick up. On their forth pass I jotted down the license number. The three male occupants were satisfied the cop was comatose from the bitter temperature.

Ten minutes after their last drive-by I heard glass break in the Suburban Square Shopping Center that is a hundred yards from where I stood. The broken plate glass window cascading to the pavement shattered the silence and resuscitated me to attention. As I sprinted toward those stores the car that prowled brazenly in front of me sped out of the Shopping Center.

I located the shattered glass on the sidewalk in front of a Television and Appliance store. I telephoned headquarters and gave the switchboard operator the license number of the car I suspected and he checked the Motor Vehicle Registration Directory and secured the owner's name and address. He was an Ardmore resident. A patrol car was dispatched to the address and the officer concealed himself and waited until the car returned and pulled into his garage. The driver was caught red-handed with a portable radio belonging to the Television Store on the passenger seat.

My Lieutenant went ballistic when a burglar was caught by one of his men and he wouldn't let the occasion go unrewarded. He'd give the diligent officer/officers an unauthorized day off. This was an incentive to keep his men alert. I took off the first day that was available on the midnight to 8:00 a.m. shift and it was just what I needed to recuperate and get back in sync.

PLEASE OFFICER, JUST ONE LITTLE SIP.

At a midnight roll call the Lieutenant growled an order to the squad standing at attention in front of him. "Arrest the drunks who sleep in a train station waiting room." To emphasize the order he warned us he was going to inspect every waiting room and personally check if anyone was sleeping in one. This threat was to let us know we weren't to take his order lightly. Every officer knew the railroad waiting rooms were left unlocked for the convenience of their riders but over the years they had become an ideal place for a drunk to take up residence in the wee hours of the night.

There were a disproportionate number of alcoholics in the township after World War II. One particular alcoholic was thirty-year-old Joey. He was a personable fellow but a stoned alcoholic. He'd swallowed every drop of alcohol he got his hands on and then sleep off its effects wherever he found shelter. If the weather permitted he'd sleep on a park bench but more often he'd spread out on a bench in a train station waiting room.

A sleeping drunk is offensive to the riders who board a train. The alcoholic's breath, the foul odor from his unwashed body and the smell of urine and feces is overpowering. The stench permeates the waiting room walls until the room becomes unserviceable. Ventilation can't get rid of the disgusting odor. The only way to get rid of the smell is to demolish the building.

The Lieutenant intimidated me, so I checked the train station on my beat and Joey was snuggled up on the bench so cozy he made me envious and wish I was home in my warm bed. I shook him. "Let's go Joey. You were told many times to stay out of here. Let's go to the lockup." Joey had been arrested several times so he knew the drill; it was best to go along to get along. He knew the scenario. He would be put into a cell for the night to sober up and in the morning he'd be sent to the county prison for thirty days. The time spent in the county prison was a time of cleansing for him. He would be given clean clothes, a clean bed, a daily shower and three good meals. His only deprivation was the absence of alcohol, however, the abstinence would make his first drinks after his release taste more delicious on a cleansed palate.

In the township lockup we were alone. I abided by the department's procedure by removing his belt, shoelaces and tie. There was a long procedure prescribed by the department and the Bureau of Prisons that had to be adhered to before placing a prisoner in a cell. The prisoner had to be thoroughly searched to prevent him from concealing any article he might use to kill himself or a prison guard or use to deface the cell. I placed everything Joey had in his pockets into a Personal Effects envelope. He had done this routine before so there was no need for a lot of instructions. My final act was to hand-search him. As I patted his clothes I tapped a ten-ounce bottle of Aqua Velva After Shave he was hiding in his rear pocket.

Aqua Velva is about 99% alcohol with a strong perfume added that some men splash on their face after a close shave. It burns the sensitive shaved skin unmercifully but that is supposed to be the refreshing part. However, to a penniless alcoholic Aqua Velva is an ideal substitute for liquor. It is much less expensive than a bottle of cheap wine and it contains a more potent alcohol content per volume. I took the bottle from him and threw it into the trash basket.

My shameful disrespect toward good alcohol broke Joey's heart and brought him to near tears. The fluid in that bottle was precious to him and to discard it like trash was sinful. "Please Officer! Let me have one little sip before you put me in the cell. Please! Please!" He continued to beg and implore. I thundered, "Don't you realize you are in a lockup? How can you ask for a drink?" "Please Officer. I need one little sip before you put me in the cell. I need a drink real bad. One little sip and I'll go into the cell quietly." He looked like withdrawal seizures were already setting in. I didn't want him to have the DTs so I gave in to his nonstop beseeching. I had to do my job but I didn't have to be heartless. "OK. Just one little sip," I said

Joey could not have been more appreciative. "Thank you, thank you." He slowly raised the bottle to his lips and what happened next can't be described. I was terror-struck when I found out his throat hadn't a valve. The whole ten ounces drained into his belly faster than a breath of air. The bottle was empty in the flash of a photographer's bulb. It was amazing how the flesh in his mouth could tolerate such a caustic liquid. "Get into the cell!" I shouted. "You'll never get another break from me." I slammed the cell door shut and left him to sleep it off.

A great fear came over me that he might die during the night. If he died an autopsy would disclose Aqua Velva caused his death and there would be an investigation. I wished I never arrested him. For the remainder of the night I prayed for Joey's good health. I prayed Joey would survive and not die in the lockup.

The next morning he was alive and frisky. He wasn't ill or even suffering with a hangover. He passively went to the county prison to spend the next thirty days.

That night the acids in my stomach caused me more harm than what his stomach suffered from the Aqua Velva After Shave.

IT HAPPENED IN LONDON

The first two years on the job I was naïve and impressionable. The unusual things that happened while I was on duty fascinated me so much that when I was in headquarters I'd tell my bizarre experiences to the other officers. They too had amusing anecdotes.

At home I kept abreast of current events by reading the news printed in the Philadelphia Evening Bulletin. I particularly enjoyed the odd news items printed at the bottom of a short column of newsprint. The datelines were always London. I thought it peculiar how so many strange and unusual things happened in London. I figured metropolitan London was spread over a large area and it was so heavily populated anything could happen there.

One evening during this period of my career I returned to headquarters with a traffic citation I had just issued to a male driver who ignored a STOP sign. He was preoccupied kissing his lady friend sitting beside him and wasn't watching where his car was headed. I read the remarks I wrote on the citation to my sergeant to see if he approved of the way it was worded. I wrote; "The vehicle operator failed to stop for a STOP sign because he was engaged in an amorous embrace."

A week later a fill-in item at the bottom of a short column in the Evening Bulletin stated a driver in London received a traffic citation for "Failing to stop for a STOP sign because he was engaged in an amorous embrace." It sounded very familiar.

A few days later I was driving a patrol car with another officer sitting in the passenger seat. He was my partner for the night. For over a mile I followed a car directly in front of us that weaved dangerously from side to side, from one lane to the other, and it even entered the oncoming lane a few times. It was obvious the driver's erratic driving was due to the fact he was more interested in his female passenger. He had his right arm around her and was busily hugging and kissing and fondling. Luckily for them it was 2:30 a.m. and there wasn't any traffic on the road.

When he came to a stop at a red traffic signal I seized my chance and pulled abreast of him. My partner rolled down his window and shouted to the driver in an authoritative voice, "You'd do better if you used two hands!" Not realizing we were police officers the fellow shouted back, "Yea, I know, but I've got to use one hand for driving." Of course my partner was suggesting he place both hands on the steering wheel and pay closer attention to his driving while the fellow had a more thorough fondling of his girlfriend on his mind.

An hour later we were in headquarters and I jokingly told this incident to a few officers. I received an enthusiastic round of applause but eight months later I was shocked when I read in the Reader's Digest an identical incident happened in London.

29

It finally registered. The resemblance was no accident. It dawned on me that a Philadelphia Evening Bulletin cub police reporter was always in headquarters when we told our experiences to one another. That reporter submitted our hilarious stories to his editor who was eager to print them. The editor prudently used a locale that could not be authenticated. The reporter never let on to us he was pirating our experiences.

I never told my fellow officers of my suspicion but I tested him several times. I made sure he was present when I fabricated or exaggerated a silly yarn. He bit on the most idiotic tales. I thought I was pulling the wool over his and his editor's eyes when I read the same thing happened in London but he outwitted me when he was financially rewarded by the Reader's Digest magazine after they accepted his story about the erratic driver.

Police Briefs

Rotton Hamburger Fried And Grilled

Patrolman Barney Loughran stopped a hitchhiker on Lancaster Ave., Wynnewood, about 4:10 p.m. Monday.

"What's your name?" the officer asked.

"Rotton Hamburger," was the reply.

The stranger appeared slightly "fried" and Loughran proceeded to grill him further.

"Look, I asked you in a nice way —what is your name?"

"I told you," the man insisted. "It's Rotton Hamburger."

Sure enough, the man's identification proved he was Rotton Hamburger, 38, of 2123 E. 21st St., Washing: . C.

It is obvious the reporter exaggerated the truth more than I did when he had this yarn published.

I'M THE BOSS!

It was a super summer afternoon in 1948 and I was relegated to pounding the sidewalk in a depressing business district. I was idly strolling by a saloon frequented by black patrons that was on the opposite side of the four-lane highway. It was high noon on a Saturday and all six bars on this beat were enjoying prosperity. Even though it was a boorish day in this ghetto I wanted no excitement. I was rummaging through other career choices as I meandered down the Avenue. Beachcombing beckoned because the sun was smiling radiantly upon me. It was the kind of day a person could be bronzed quickly on a sandy beach.

Two healthy looking black men bolted from the saloon. Their long fast stride wasn't just to scurry across the street between the moving traffic so I sensed they sought to talk to me. The way they were dressed twitched my adrenal gland. They wore white suits with a white shirt, tie and a Panama hat. Their outfits typified the Hollywood gangsters of the period. It definitely wasn't the way the neighborhood men dressed on a hot summer day. They'd be more comfortable wearing a "T" shirt. These fellows looked like "bookies" or "numbers men" or hustlers.

Their menacing approach indicated they had a chip on their shoulder and I suspected their aim was to involve me in something out of the ordinary. It baffled me why anyone who had been drinking would deliberately attract the attention of a policeman. Perhaps there was trouble inside the saloon. Maybe someone was shot for not honoring a gambling debt. After all I was only on the job ten months and not prepared for every emergency.

They stopped me in my tracks without even the courtesy of a casual greeting. I was aghast and engulfed with terror but in no way did I reveal it to them. Without a warning the first thug stood in my face and poked his pointy index finger into my chest and it hurt. By his stance he let me know he was empowered by Divine Right. His first words were, "I'm the boss in this neighborhood and I want you to know it!"

I stood in dazed disbelief. Never had I heard of anyone threatening a policeman like that. It just wasn't done. It fell into the category of idiocy. I hesitated for a moment because I didn't know how the situation should be legally handled. I was disoriented by the shock. The thought came to me it would be best I fluff it off as street harassment yet I didn't want to look like a wimp in a uniform for it would reflect a weak image on all the men on the force. I would give the profession a bad name. God knew this neighborhood needed a strong authority figure but the way these fools tried to intimidate me for the benefit of those observing from inside the saloon infuriated me. Sheepishly I said to the twit with the sharp pointy index finger, "So you're the boss? I'm very glad to meet you. I'm Officer Bernie." I thrust my right hand forward and said,

"I'd be glad to shake the hand of the boss." He went for the ole jujitsu maneuver that is as old as Confucius.

When we clasped hands I squeezed firmly at first and then little by little I added pressure. I compressed his knuckles to the cracking point. I was turning the screw on a vise and when I knew he couldn't endure much more pain without writhing to his knees I jerked him toward me. His eyes bulge in surprise and betrayed a hint of fear. Doubt as to what pain was yet to come flashed like a neon sign across his ugly mug. Just as I knew it would be his reflex reaction was to violently pull backward to break my grip and to convince me he was still in command. It was his show of machismo but all the while my clutch pained him beyond his tolerance threshold.

With his hand firmly gripped within mine and with his additional help I took one step forward to his right rear and added a downward thrust. It is difficult to explain how easily this jujitsu stratagem works but as I planned the poor sap did a flip and landed flat on his back on the filthy sidewalk in his clean white suit.

My back was to the second fool and he thought he had an advantage so he gave me the ole classic "bear hug from behind". I don't know what he had in mind; maybe he wanted to keep me from booting his buddy while he was lying on the sidewalk. That was the style of street fighting those days but I'd never reduce myself to utilizing any such foul tactic. Maybe he wanted to restrain me until his friend got on his feet and proceeded to punch me senseless. I had no idea what he intended but I knew my next move and it was simple too. I held his arms firmly against my chest so he couldn't break loose. He was trembling with fear of the unknown. I made a less than half knee bend and bumped my rump and he flipped over my head.

He landed like a felled tree. The idiot landed on the sidewalk and bounced like a wrestler on a padded mat. I wasn't a bit surprised both maneuvers worked so well but was thrilled I caught them both off guard. These were jujitsu moves I practiced often on the rough kids in Pretzel Park after school. Just like those kids these bums weren't hurt. Correction, their macho egos were gravely bruised.

I reached down and picked my police hat off the sidewalk and nonchalantly dusted it off like I was more concerned about it than whether they were injured or if they were going to join forces and attack. Slowly and deliberately I placed the hat on my head and adjusted it. If they knocked it off again there would be no holds barred. With aplomb, yet decisively, I authoritatively said without looking directly at either one, "When I'm on duty I'm the boss around here and don't you forget it! If I ever see you creeps again I promise you will not be able to walk away from me! Be very careful I don't come looking for you!"

They stood for a moment groping with the idea they should do combat rather than return in disgrace to the bar from whence they came.

They'd rather be handcuffed and jailed than be mocked by their peers. I sneered at them like an annoyed bull pigeon.

They didn't say a word. They took but a few seconds to mull over their options then turned on their heels and fled back across the street. I didn't watch where they went because I wanted to demonstrate aloofness to the spectators behind the dirty curtains even though I was still petrified. Luckily I never saw either of them again.

I made it sound like it was so effortless and that I wasn't afraid of those bullies but I was very apprehensive. I had no way of knowing what to do once the clash became physical and I wasn't positive my tactics would be successful. If my handgrip didn't fit perfectly or if it was too weak and if I didn't jerk and push with perfect timing they both might have thrashed the beachcomber dream out of me.

I was never a tough kid nor did I ever look for a fight but these two maneuvers I pulled on the bullies that toyed with me after school in a public park. Every day I was confronted by a group of boys from a different school who enjoyed harassing me because I was always alone. Out of necessity I perfected a few tricks that would subdue more than one opponent very quickly without hurting them or getting hurt. I used these two stunts so often they became effortless. They didn't require great strength, just timing and coordination.

Nevertheless, I agonized over that confrontation. Legally I should have arrested them because they attacked an officer on duty. That was the appropriate action. I worried someone saw what took place and would inform headquarters of the police brutality they witnessed. Even if those two goofballs didn't report me an onlooker might be happy to swear the policeman attacked first. I expected to be fired for mishandling the incident.

Uneasiness consumed me for I couldn't bear the shame of being Dishonorably Discharged and drummed off the Force. Who would hire me with that mark on my résumé? I finally rationalized it was foolish to worry because I wasn't married and had no responsibilities. All along I barely tolerated the repulsive job and the ill-fitting uniform and now I was hoping to save them both. Be that as it may, I considered it discreditable to lose a job for such a stupid reason. My mind was heavy but fortunately I was never questioned about it. I often wondered what the fellow with the pointy finger was the boss of and should I have waited for an explanation.

That experience convinced me jujitsu worked and I could rely on it. More importantly, I now possessed the confidence necessary to do police work under any threat. I patrolled my beat knowing I had the strength of Samson if I used my brains. I kept in mind there were men tougher than I and physically cleverer than me so I never walked with a chip on my shoulder.

AT ALL COST BE A LADY

I was a police officer less than five months but I already learned how to brace myself and accept the pathetic with the macabre. At 1:30 a.m. on a gloomy night my mind was turning over the eerie line, "On a midnight dark and dreary". I had six and a half more hours to keep the peace in the business district I was assigned too. What a joke.

My trance was disrupted by a large frightened middle-aged man frantically running toward me shouting, "Ossifer! Ossifer! Come quick! There's trouble at the Club!" This fellow was healthy enough to handle any trouble better than myself, that is, if he was sober. He was referring to an after-hours club twenty-five yards from where I stood. The only calamity that might take place in an after-hours club that would cause a member to get as excited as this fellow would be a free-for-all or a shooting. Either situation was far beyond my expertise at this stage of my career. Perhaps, if I delayed the problem might rectify itself. Moving slowly gave me time to pray for Divine assistance. I subscribe to the belief that a suave moving man reflected self-confidence and in control of his domain.

Within twenty seconds we arrived at the Club. I was shocked to find his problem was a huge, intoxicated; disheveled Amazon sitting on the step at the front door to the club. Her appearance was hilarious but it was no laughing matter because I hadn't a clue as to what had preceded my arrival. I assumed she fell when leaving the club and was seriously hurt. Maybe she had a broken fibula or a fractured hip or was knocked unconscious. She sat upright on the single step with her legs stretched straight out in front of her. Her extra-large buttock filled the door. It was as far as the club bouncer and the doorman could get her after a fierce struggle to eject her from the building. The doorman and the bouncer were shouting expletives at her and commands to me. Of course at that hour of the night it can go without saying everyone present was well into his and her cup.

"Officer, get her the hell out of here!"
"She's drunk!"
"She didn't get her load here!"
"She's not a member!"
"We don't want her kind in here!"
"She got her load somewhere else!"
"Get her the hell out of here, Officer!"

It was obvious these two fellows had no respect for this kind of women. I hadn't shown any involvement yet because I wanted to let each party know I was impartial and that I was in complete control and knew exactly how to address this situation as soon as they simmered down. Actually, I was calculating how to pick up an obese intoxicated woman without putting my spine out of alignment. Obviously the doorman and the bouncer, and probably others, tried unsuccessfully to get her on her feet.

The doorman and bouncer continued their vilification on her and were about to turn on me because I hadn't shown enthusiasm equal to theirs. One thing I would not tolerate and that was disrespect for my profession from a drunk so it was best they didn't start on me. They had lost their patience and were about to get physical with her so it was the time for me to take overt action, good or bad, right or wrong. I bent over her slightly, enough to whisper acerbically in her ear, "Madam, at all cost be a lady for you shall be treated according to the way you conduct yourself."

I utilized that pronouncement for whatever it was worth. I had no idea where I heard it before but I'm sure it wasn't in a Shakespeare reading. I straightened up and turned my back on her to question the bouncer and doorman. I needed some data if it became necessary to ask headquarters for more manpower and transportation to take her to the lockup. I needed answers to questions like; "Who is she?" "How did she get here?" "Is she alone?" "Where does she live?"

Before I had time to formulate my first question she rose to her feet, shook like a wet hen, pulled down her slip and skirt, adjusted her bra and blouse and staggered away oblivious of the commotion she caused. Her motor coordination needed fine-tuning but I wasn't going to get involved with that. Getting her on the move and away from the Club was all that was asked of me. Down the street she waddled. Navigating better with each step into the foggy dark night. I wasn't worried she might be raped or mugged; if the doorman and bouncer couldn't budge her I was sure a rapist or mugger couldn't.

This incident burned twenty minutes off the long night and now I wished for something else to occupy the remaining hours but I hoped nothing as frightening would happen.

I chuckled every time I thought of those men asking each other if they overheard what the cop whispered in her ear?

A TREE AND A BARKING DOG

At roll call the sergeant called out my assignment for the following night and every night thereafter until notified. It was another burglary detail in the dead of winter. I was to dress in warm old civilian clothes and stakeout an estate in Villanova. Three other men were also picked from the men standing at attention. There was a mix of cursing and sighs of relief because we all knew how the temperature plummets during the night in January.

None of the men liked to work these details considering the hours pass so slowly. This particular assignment was disliked because we'd be abandoned in the center of a medieval forest. Houses in this remote area were old mansions built for absolute privacy. The only trees removed from the property were those necessary to make room for the building. The area was unknown to the public but at the same time was an ideal place for burglars. This neighborhood after dark was a vacuum; without life, traffic, pedestrians, birds or animals. There was nothing to relate time or space to. It was another dimension; a twilight zone.

My comrades weren't afraid of the dark or the loneliness because we cruised this area many nights. I'm sure a city police officer would shiver in his boots if he was assigned to this wilderness for one night and likewise I'd cringe if I had to walk a street in a city ghetto.

The following night a patrol car dropped us off a quarter mile apart on separate estates. No post was sweeter than the other. It was so godallful dark without street lights, house lights or moonlight. Before I walked deep into the estate I looked around for some shelter away from the main house. A vacant stable or a gardener's tool shed would do fine. It would be better if I weren't close to the house in case I stumbled and created a noise and woke the occupants. I dreaded the thought I'd activate an intrusion alarm and wake the whole neighborhood and compromise the police effort.

My greatest fear would be if the homeowner let out his guard dog for the last time and it sensed my presence. The barking and snarling would be impossible to stifle. A senior officer once instructed me to shine my flashlight into the eyes of an attacking dog to blind it and stop it dead in it's tracks. Well, that theory remained to be proven by me. How could I explain to a homeowner's satisfaction that I was a genuine police officer when I was dressed like a bum in my oldest clothes?

Before my eyes completely adjusted to the dark I bumped into a low tree limb that blocked my path. At a closer inspection I saw this was an unusual tree and one that may not be indigenous to the area. It had a gigantic girth and each limb was massive. The branch I bumped into jutted from the trunk seven feet above the ground and curved downward under its own tremendous weight and then struggled upward to reach the sun. The curvature was a natural hammock and wide enough to balance myself upon even if I happened to doze.

It was an awkward and cold place to lie but at least I wouldn't be standing or sitting on the frost covered the lawn. I was troubled by the thought that large black ants might be parading up and down the limb and they might eventually find their way into my clothes but I was already too cold and too tired to fret about ants. I climbed onto the limb and laid comfortably into my private hammock.

I was cozy for less than twenty minutes or until I heard a dog barking way way off in the distance. My nerves tingled and my brain calculated every element of that bark. It could barely be heard it was so far off but because it wasn't a friendly bark I surmised the dog confronted an intruder, maybe one of the other officers. It was too far away to concern me even if the intruder was the burglar I was waiting for. I figured I'd never see the burglar anywhere but in the hospital if that dog ever got hold of him.

There was nothing else to reflect upon so I studied the bark and judged it came from a large leather throated dog. It definitely wasn't a lap dog. It might be a German Shepherd or a Doberman Pinscher? Both dogs were bred to attack a man. I was thankful it wasn't stalking me. It might be a Mastiff. That breed was bred to charge and bowl over a horse and its heathen rider during the Crusades. No matter which bred I hoped it would never sense my presence and bowl me off my perch. I lay stone still and slowed my breathing.

I tried to pinpoint the exact location of the savage beast. At first it seemed way off in space but now it could possibly be on the far side of the mansion I was watching or in a nearby estate. Suddenly there was no doubt in my mind the dog was on a beeline toward me and at a fast gallop. The barking grew desperate and homicidal. It never zigzagged off target. I couldn't fathom how it knew I was trespassing on his turf but anything was possible in this remote jungle.

The dog pressed down upon me even faster as it got closer. It leaped yards each vault forward and it never ceased it's diabolic barking. I wished it was chasing a burglar but no human could run that distance and sustain that speed. There was no place for me to hide even if I had the time so I lay still hugging the limb with all my might. If I rolled off now it would be a dead giveaway and I couldn't get at my flashlight from the way I was perched. It became a bloodcurdling nightmare.

The bark was primal like a banshee howl alerting me of impending death. If it's timbre was an indicator of the size of his bite I would be destroyed in a single snap of its jaws. It kept charging like a kamikaze pilot insanely focused on a mission while squirrels were playing tag in my stomach.

To my utter surprise it ran with a full head of steam on the opposite side of the tree trunk and sped on until the bark tapered off to a faint sound in the east just like it rose in the west. I can't imagine what the dog was chasing that could sustain that speed for such a long distance. It couldn't be a deer because deer don't run in a straight line, rabbits serpentine from side to side and a youthful burglar couldn't run at that breakneck speed. If it was a burglar he probably never heard the theory about shining a flashlight into a dog's eyes to stop it from charging. It had to be an animal with night vision and great speed and endurance because there were many bushes, hedges and trees to avoid. The only animal with the capability to compete with the dog was a fox. If it caught whatever it was chasing I hoped it wasn't rabid.

I was so thankful the dog didn't return to his home base via the same path for he surely would have caught me if he meandered by this tree.

Kaffirboom coral tree

The tree looked similar to this one. It had a massive trunk and huge bulky limbs. The limb I laid on was on the right side just like the one above but the downward curvature draped lower and within easy reach. The sharp dip and upward sweep was like a rear yard hammock. The dog ran passed me on the left side of the tree.

DON'T DISMANTLE THE CAR

A **NO PARKING BUS STOP** regulation is posted in front of the entrance to a busy bank; however, some of the bank's customers assumed this restriction was a cunning trick the bank vice-president arranged to reserve parking spaces for his prized clientele. Should an officer issue a ticket for violating the regulation it became common knowledge the recipient could hand the ticket to the bank vice-president. He in turn would telephone a higher authority in the police department and have the ticket voided.

The fine for the violation was one dollar. Maybe it wasn't the money but the principle, plus, the vice-president had an opportunity to demonstrate to his customers he had enough clout to intimidate the cop on the beat and whoever fixed the ticket.

The bus drivers on this route complained to their supervisor that they couldn't safely pull to the curb to pickup and discharge passengers because there were always cars parked in this bus stop. It was a sensitive situation so their supervisor went to the president of the bus company. He in turn wrote a tactful letter to the Superintendent of Police requesting stricter enforcement at this bus stop for the safety of the riders, pedestrians and the free movement of traffic.

The Superintendent wasn't tactful. He issued an order that the **NO PARKING BUS STOP** regulation was to be vigorously enforced.

On a cold nippy afternoon a car was blatantly parked in the **NO PARKING BUS STOP** so I proceeded to issue a ticket. The procedure was to place the ticket under the windshield wiper on the driver's side of the car so the driver would see it when he got behind the steering wheel. It was to be placed under the wiper blade so it wouldn't be blown away by a gust of wind or when the driver drove off.

Routinely I picked up the wiper arm to slip the ticket between the blade and the windshield but to my surprise and consternation the wiper blade fell off the wiper arm. I made several attempts to attach the blade to the arm but I couldn't get the two pieces to fit together. My fingers were too cold to manipulate and hook them together. After several tries I left the ticket and the blade on the hood of the car and vanished.

The bank vice-president was on the telephone and contacted the Superintendent personally about that ticket and the stupid cop on the beat who issued it. The next day at roll call the sergeant told the whole squad, "When you put a parking ticket on a car don't remove the windshield wiper blade." I let the remark slide.

From that day forward I kept the bank vice-president busy calling headquarters to have parking tickets squashed. He telephoned so often his complaints were soon dismissed as crank calls and he was looked upon as a nut case.

THE FIRST TRAFFIC TICKET I WROTE

The first traffic ticket I gave a driver was for reckless driving and the young man who received the ticket turned around and sold his prized souped-up hot rod to spite me. I couldn't figure out his logic but that is what he did.

It happened on a beautiful Sunday afternoon when I was pounding a sidewalk. For most of the five hours that day I stood in a statue-like pose striving to appear utilitarian. I was only on the job six months and very insecure. The volume of vehicle and pedestrian traffic was lighter on Sundays so there wasn't a thing to worry about except for the supped-up hot rod that brazenly sped back and forth in front of me. The driver raced eastbound for a mile then turned around and raced by me again. He made a detour or two but generally sped by me every fifteen minutes. His antics wouldn't normally annoy me but he gunned the motor to make excessive noise when he was abreast of me. He drew my attention and the attention of the adults and the college students promenading in the business district.

The posted speed limit in a business district is 25 mph yet he drove in excess of 45 mph. To maintain this speed he was forced to weave in and out of traffic. He jeopardized his car and passengers, pedestrians and the other motorists. His erratic behavior continued for an hour. He was proud of his car and the modifications he made on it and he wanted to present them to the youths on the sidewalk but his disrespect for the law became a personal embarrassment. He deliberately and wantonly flaunted his recklessness in the presence of a police officer. On his fifth time around I signaled him to a stop. I reminded him of the posted speed limit and told him I was going to give him a ticket for reckless driving. There was no conversation and no denial and since he didn't question my judgment I considered the case closed.

Four days later a friend of his walked up to me while I was standing on the same sidewalk. "Officer," he said. "Do you remember the speeding ticket you wrote last Sunday? Well, the driver wanted me to tell you that he got back at you. He sold his car to spite you. You won't be able to give him any more tickets."

The subject was too mundane to pursue so I walked away without dignifying it with a comment. I never understood how he got revenge by selling his prized car. He did, however, teach me an important lesson I long remembered. He taught me that issuing a traffic ticket shouldn't be done irresponsibly because it can impact some people in a very strange way and cause very odd behavior.

Years later I stopped a man for running a red light. He jumped out of his car and yelled uncontrollably. His wife whispered, "Officer, He's having a nervous breakdown." I didn't know how erratic he'd behave if I gave him the ticket so I ate it.

THE RIVER ROAD FLOOD

One spring morning in 1948 I drove through a cloudburst to be on time for the 7:40 a.m. roll call. It was seasonal weather; continual rain for over a week. Farther up state the rains were torrential but locally it was a steady heavy downpour. It was a spring we knew all our lives. We accepted rainy days and hummed "April showers bring May flowers". The Weather Bureau tracked the rain clouds and repeatedly broadcast optimistic reports over the radio. The forecasters reported the rain would soon ease up. Each news report assured us the river would crest within the hour but instead it kept overflowing its banks.

When there is exceptionally heavy rain in early spring the solid frost in the ground prevents the water from soaking into the soil so it runs off into the gutter and through the sewer system into the Schuylkill River. An extended rainy period causes the creeks and rivers to swell and overflow their banks. Tributaries rise and there is serious flooding. Those who live on higher ground are accustomed to the slight inconvenience created by large puddles at some intersections but the swollen river tragically affects the houses built on the banks of the river.

This spring the heavens sprung an irreparable leak. Of course the subsequent flooding was not just the result of the continual downpour. It was a combination of factors; heavy rain, the early spring thaw of the ice and snow in the mountains upstate and the frost in the ground. Another component in this equation was the fact the riverbed hadn't been dredged of all the silt that was washed down from the upstate coalmines.

At roll call the sergeant barked, "Loughran, McLister and Prengel go to River Road. Two houses are under water and a few residents are trapped inside. A rowboat is there for you to use to get the people out. Patrol cars will be there too. You three get the people out of the houses and the cars will transport them to the firehouse where they will receive shelter until they can safely return home."

Just like that. "There's a rowboat." No questions like "Were you guys ever in a rowboat?" "Can you guys swim?" "You guys go home and change into a bathing suit." It is unbelievable the excess baggage we were wearing. Beside our heavy uniform and equipment there was the heavy rubber covered canvas raincoat and rubber boots. Our wet uniform weighed forty pounds, enough weight to drown us.

I had no experience in a rowboat and neither did the other two officers. Officer Prengel sat in the center position expecting to use the oars. Officer McLister sat in the front and I was in the back. With the help from the men standing at the side of the road we pushed off into the flood waters to reach the houses a hundred and fifty feet away. The ground sloped sharply from road level to approximately nine feet below the road at the front of the houses. The first floor of three single houses was under water. I couldn't understand why people stayed in these

41

houses until it was too late to evacuate. Maybe they believed those forecasters who predicted the river would soon subside.

I was thankful the water wasn't flowing as forcefully in front of the houses as it was in the rear. It was mild compared to the rear of the buildings where a mad raging river raced by. The current was swift and flowed with such force it uprooted trees and telephone poles along its path. The debris floated on the surface at the velocity of a runaway freight train. Huge gasoline tanks, oil tanks and oil drums by the dozens sped by every minute on a current that would dump them into the Delaware River and eventually take them to the Chesapeake Bay and on farther to the Atlantic Ocean.

If our rowboat was drawn into that maelstrom the debris would capsize us within a heartbeat. The river had more rubble than a bowl of vegetable soup. We would be knocked unconscious and drowned within seconds. There was no chance of survival even if we weren't wearing our full uniform and equipment and were Olympic swimmers. A person going over the Grand Rapids in a canoe had better odds than we had if we got sucked into that catastrophic torrent.

There were no safety precautions. There were no safety ropes or lifelines tied to the rowboat and each of us. There were no life jackets or flotation devices or an escape plan if the worse case scenario should occur. We were expendable.

Our rowboat drifted passed a ranch home that was abandoned a few days earlier. Only its roof was visible. The oars were useless so by hand we inched forward by pulling on tree limbs. Prengel used an oar to push off a fence post and I grabbed a clothesline but before I jerked too hard I prayed, "Sweet Jesus, don't let this clothesline be dry rotted." McLister tugged on a clothesline post protruding a few inches above water.

We finally positioned the boat below a woman's bedroom window. The difficulty was holding the boat snug against the house while she squeezed through the bottom half of the open window. There wasn't anything on the outside wall to cling to and steady the undulating boat. We rocked back and forth and rolled side to side at the whim and mercy of the choppy current. After a frustrating struggle McLister abandoned all courtesy and yanked her into the boat.

During this whole ordeal no one broke silence except Prengel. He asked himself out loud, "When the hell did I join the Coast Guard?" McLister and I laughed because we knew he meant it to be a joke. It eased the tension. Cautiously we tugged on a clothesline, shrub, hedge and tree limbs to get to the road and safely deposit the frightened woman into the hands of those waiting for us.

This was an extremely stressful operation but fortunately no one in the boat panicked. It was all in a day's work. Three police officers, a few volunteer firemen and some spectators stood anxiously on the road waiting for us to return. No one shouted instructions or helpful hints. There was absolute silence because our lives were at stake.

Our triumph bolstered our confidence a wee bit so we pulled and pushed our way back to the second house. A girl in her late teens and an old lady were at an open bedroom window. The girl shouted and waved her arms appealing to us not to overlook them. As we got closer she said the old lady wasn't ambulatory and she couldn't help herself a lick.

The outside wall of this house had a smooth plaster finish. I hunted for something, anything, to cling on to hold the boat still. There was a hairline crack in the plaster so I reached for it. The tips of my fingers pulled to draw the boat against the house but without warning the plaster fell off. The suddenness of the falling plaster gave us all tremendous jolt of fear. For a few seconds we expected all the plaster would fall off the side of the building and land in our rowboat. The weight of it would surely sink the boat. I prayed, "Jesus, Mary and Joseph don't let the river topple the house onto us."

A two-foot square hole was opened in the plaster. Where there once was plaster now lath was exposed. Between two laths there was a half-inch vacant space where I jammed my fingertips and took hold. I prayed over and over, "Sweet Mother of Jesus don't let the lath break." With a fingertip hold on the thin strip of wood I held the boat against the side of the house no matter how it wanted to oscillate.

I don't know how they managed to get the old lady into the boat because I was preoccupied steadying the boat close to the wall under the window. I felt I'd be blamed if the old lady and the girl fell into the river and drowned. The old lady was no help but I didn't fault her because she had no muscle or fat, only a thin skin and bones. The transfer bruised her painfully yet she never whimpered. She knew the two officers and the girl were doing their darnedest to be gentle. She had a perfectly good reason for begging to remain in her bed until the very last minute.

The return trip to the road was extra hazardous because the boat was now crowded and sat lower in the water plus my fingertips were raw. I ignored the pain and groped, pulled and pushed until we reached the safety of the rescuers on the road.

Our mission was accomplished. No one applauded or said, "Job well done O kind and faithful servants." Four hours remained in our workday so Officers McLister, Prengel and I went our separate way on routine patrol in our wet uniforms to finish our eight-hour tour of duty.

THE MISCHIEF NIGHT NIGHTMARE

It is my firm belief that children have a lot of nerve going door to door on Halloween asking for treats when on the two previous evenings these same grubbers prowled the neighborhood spreading havoc and destruction to private property.

October 29th is Soap Night, the night every car parked on the street or in a driveway is fair game to these demons. The little goblins carry a bar of hard soap and scrape it over the body of a car and in many cases destroys the finish. No car owner who is a victim of their prank thinks this is amusing child's play.

October 30th is Mischief Night, the evening when the real havoc strikes. Some parents deserved the destruction that comes to their personal property because they themselves irresponsibly implant destructive thoughts into their child's head. "When I was a kid your age on Mischief Night I did this and we did that."

October 31st is Halloween, when the same imps go door-to-door as innocent as you please pleading for handouts. No wonder they dress in a costume and wear a mask. They don't want to be recognized as the brats who inflicted damage to your property on the previous two evenings.

To minimize the amount of damage caused by vandals on Soap Night and Mischief Night the police department reinforced the personnel on duty with off-duty officers. After working a full day the men return to work 6:00 p.m. until 10:00 p.m.. There is no compensation for the extra hours they work and that too made the assignment objectionable.

On my first Soap Night I was assigned to walk in a three square block area. It was a Gothic neighborhood where the residents are affluent and the houses are large single homes with spacious lawns planted liberally with trees, shrubs and hedges. A well-manicured bush or two serve to mark the property lines and the streets are lined with trees that make the streetlights ineffective because the globes are buried deep in the low branches. A gentle breeze caused shadows to dance everywhere. A shadow might be a child darting from behind a bush to a hedge. It was spooky for a novice cop in strange surroundings because that darting figure might not be a child but a burglar.

I caught a glimpse of a boy crouched behind a bush waiting for me to walk by. I was proud of my ability to pick him out from among the shadows. I called for him to come hither and asked for his name and address. He lived a few houses down the street. There were the routine questions; "Where are you going? What are you doing out? What are you doing with that bar of soap?" He brazenly lied "I have no soap." "Well, what are hiding behind your back? Take yourself and the soap home immediately and stay in the house for the rest of the night. If I see you out again tonight I'll lock you up!" The kid scampered home.

The procedure was to telephone headquarters every hour on a police call box so when I made my first call to headquarters the sergeant ordered me to go to that boy's home because his father telephoned headquarters and demanded I apologize to the boy. Suddenly the sap flushed from my spine. I'm on the job less than a year and I'm in trouble again. I made an oath that from this day forward I'd see no evil, hear no evil and speak no evil. I'd blindly walk the streets and do nothing. Headquarters wont receive any more negative reports about me.

An order is an order so I went to the boy's house. I hesitated before stepping up to the front door. The affluent and the imposing mansion intimidated me. Mansions were indicative of wealth, influence and clout. I barely completed knocking when a man yanked the door open. Without a greeting he yelled, "How dare you accuse my son of having soap? How dare you confine him to his home? He was on his way to the movie theater and now he is too frightened to go out of the house. I demand you apologize to my son."

The child was about eleven years old and looked so meek cowering beside his domineering father. He was more intimidated by him than I was. He was between two flame throwing dragons. I was in an awkward position too but his was more desperate. I looked into the boy's eyes and sensed his mortification. I thought, "He's only a child let him save face. Nothing would be gained if I defended myself. I'll let him learn about truthfulness from someone else at another time."

I apologized for my stupid error and reached out and shook the boy's hand. Then I turned to his father and said "Mister, I am very sorry this happened." I purposely didn't shake his hand. I quickly turned and walked to the street and got lost in shadows.

The next evening was Mischief Night. I reported to headquarters to receive my assignment and the sergeant snapped, "Loughran! You are to patrol the same area you had last night. I have a note from the Superintendent and he wants you to go back to the same house tonight. That man wants to apologize to you because his son admitted he had soap and was soaping cars." I returned to the area but avoided the house where the boy lived. I didn't need an apology. I wasn't getting paid so why should I be aggravated.

Soap Night rolls around every year and a vivid memory of that incident returns to haunt me. I have guilt feelings because I didn't return and accept the man's asinine apology. I wonder if I caused an irreparable strain in that father-son relationship. Probably every year both the father and the son recall that night and are overwhelmed with shame. I hope "that police officer" gave them both an opportunity to become men on their own.

MY FIRST COURT APPEARANCE

Ben and Mary Yancy lived on River Road, a hundred yards west of the Green Lane Bridge. Mary was a tall Amazon with a loud leathery voice and a nasty disposition when she was drinking, which was often because she seldom was sober. Ben was the opposite. He didn't drink and was a gentleman. She walked upright while he flip-flopped on flat feet. When I was a kid I avoided eye contact with Mary and scooted to the opposite sidewalk. Mary was always punching and kicking Ben and I was afraid she might attack me for watching. Ben was the personification of spousal abuse.

I was twelve years old the afternoon I walked across the bridge and saw my dad, who was on duty, speaking into the Police Call Box that was strapped on the telephone pole located at the foot of the bridge. Ben stood beside him with both palms under his chin. Blood oozed between his fingers. I thought he was holding his head on his neck. Mary cut his throat with a switchblade. She came running from her house toward us looking more irate than a provoked hornet. I never heard my father be forceful but he roared a direct order to her. "Mary, I just called for an ambulance to take Ben to the hospital and if you don't turn around and go home I'll call for the wagon to take you to jail." She hesitated a moment to mull over her options then wheeled around and went home.

I stood by in case Ben keeled over but my father issued another order and that was for me to leave. I left because I didn't relish seeing Ben's head fall off which I expected it to do at any moment.

Ten years later I was a witness in courtroom 'A' in the Norristown Court House. I was to testify as a police officer in my first court case. The only prepping I received on how to conduct myself on the witness stand came from my peers and they knew very little. Their brainless advice was, "Don't volunteer anything. Answer questions with a yes or no. If you inject anything else the lawyers will reduce you to chopped liver. It's their ball field. They went to Law School specifically to learn how to twist a cop's testimony. Just respond with a yes or no."

While I waited in the courthouse corridor I was told the judge assigned to courtroom 'A' was Judge Jurdon. He had garnered a reputation for being an ill-tempered grizzly that delighted in brutalizing lawyers with his caustic wit. He was an old curmudgeon who over the years tired of young lawyers who waxed eloquence in his courtroom. Lawyers learned not to joust with him because his sense of humor could slay a brash lawyer and destroy his credibility and case. Most lawyers feared him and knew better than to get flippant with him.

Hearing these words of caution only made me doubly timid when I stepped into the witness box. The District Attorney opened the case in his most professional timbre. He began his interrogation by asking me a simple warm-up question. "Officer, state your name and where you are employed."

"I am Bernard Loughran. I am a police officer on the Lower Merion Township Police Department."

Judge Jurdon raised his gavel to interrupt the questioning. "Are you, Tommy Loughran's son? Tommy was a fantastic fighter. I saw many of his fights. He is an excellent police officer and an incredible witness. I enjoyed his testimony in all the cases he had before me." I felt it was my fault the judge wavered from protocol to hold a private conversation with me in the middle of a trial. In the least he was prejudicing the case but neither lawyer had the nerve to object. I didn't know how to react so I faced him and politely said, "Thank you, Your Honor. I shall tell dad what you said about him."

He didn't stop there. Talking only to me he mentally sorted through a file cabinet full of cases searching for a particular one. Then he continued. "There was a case when your father was on the stand testifying against the defendant, a Mary Yancy. She jumped up and interrupted the proceedings. She shouted out, 'Your Honor, that's the officer which punched me! He done knocked me out! He punched me, Your Honor! He done knocked me out! Arrest him, Your Honor!'"

Judge Jurdon continued. "I turned to your father and asked if she was telling the truth and Tommy said, 'Your Honor, you saw many of my professional fights and you saw me get punched by the toughest professional fighters. I withstood stout punches thrown by strong men but when Mary struck me my knees buckled. I never received such a stunning blow. When she charged to strike me again I had to stop her so I knocked her out with one punch.'" The judge laughed uproariously like he just heard a good joke in the judges' chamber. He returned to the present after glancing at the two lawyers who were obviously annoyed by the delay. I had a strange feeling they'd workout on me for causing the interruption but he looked at me and gently whispered, "Officer Loughran, Good Luck on your new job." Then he banged the gavel down like it was a ten-pound sledgehammer and started the trial again.

The District Attorney resumed with a mollifying voice, "Officer, tell the jury what you saw when you arrived on the scene."

I was trembling more now than I was at his first question. "When I arrived on the scene I saw the victim lying----."

The Defense lawyer saw I was a rookie and intended to shatter my nerves immediately. He sprang to his feet and with a thundering voice shouted, "I object!" He was quiet effective in rattling me with this upheaval. I knew then this was going to be a painful ordeal. I hadn't finish my first sentence and I blurted out the wrong thing, whatever that was.

"Your Honor, the witness referred to the deceased as a victim and that implies my client is a guilty villain!"

Judge Jordon turned to me and spoke as softly as a pre-elementary school teacher, "Officer Loughran you may use names."

"Thank you, Your Honor," I said disguising a tremor. From then on my responses were an unemotional yes and no. I'm sure I was the dullest witness Judge Jordon ever heard but I didn't want to be embarrassed again. When I was dismissed I couldn't wait to get off the hot seat but as I was about to step out of the witness box the judge stopped me. I was terror-stricken. I didn't know what to expect. Perhaps I made another blunder.

He turned to me again and said, "Good Luck to you on your new job, Officer Loughran." Then with a parental concern whispered, "Be very careful. It's dangerous out there."

I looked appreciatively into his gentle eyes and said, "Thank you, Your Honor. I will be sure to tell dad what you said."

This photograph of me was taken in 1951, three years after the above incident. I am 25 years old and a police officer only four years and I already have a casehardened stare.

TAKE COVER!

While in the Navy I attended a Navy Gunnery School in West Palm Beach, Florida. While there I met a sailor who recently returned to the States from the Pacific War Zone. He was a battle weary tail gunner who earned a rest but it was during the height of the war with Japan so there wasn't time for him to relax. He was assigned to teach us new tail gunners the survival skills he learned in combat and especially those skills on how to accurately track and shoot at a fast moving enemy airplane.

He and I were walking down a palm tree lined residential street one afternoon when a passing automobile backfired. The explosion shocked us both. He reacted by diving under a parked car. In the War Zone it was expedient to take cover after an explosion because an enemy bomb usually caused it. I remembered that moment because it taught me to be prepared to take cover while on foot patrol.

One night I had just completed checking the stores on my beat and was pounding the empty sidewalk. It was 2:00 a.m. and my nerves were still edgy after being startled by an opossum that scampered over a trash can lid when I was checking behind a store.

My thoughts were on plans of spending a delightful day with my family at a local church carnival when suddenly there was an earsplitting explosion that sounded like a gunshot. My mind whirled. Someone might be shooting at the cop and I had better take cover. Maybe I was being shot at because I happened upon the commission of a major crime I wasn't aware of. I looked around for cover but there wasn't a parked car to dive under. There was no shelter or barricade or anything I could use as a shield.

I rapidly surveyed the area to pinpoint the source of the noise and quickly discovered it was a tire blowout. The car with the flat tire was slowly rolling to a stop where I stood. The driver was a handicapped gent with two women passengers. He felt fortunate there was a police officer close at hand that could help them.

The driver got out of the car to determine the extent of his problem. He saw a rear tire had a large gapping hole that made it impossible for him to drive ten more feet. He approached me and asked, "Officer! Will you please help us? Where is a telephone I can use to call a garage? Do you know a garage I can call? I can't fix a flat nor can the ladies." I explained there were no all night garages in the area. There wasn't even a gas station open and if there were the lone attendant would not close the station to answer a road service call. The only alternative was to call the home of a tow man who might respond but it would take a couple of hours for him to get out of bed and walk to his garage to get his truck. The service call would cost twenty-five dollars. I asked if he had enough money to cover the bill and he said he didn't have that much on him.

It was too late for me to vanish so I was obliged to volunteer even though there was a department directive forbidding such physical activity. There were officers who incurred serious injuries; especially back injuries, doing this type of good deed.

"Not to worry," I said.

I opened the trunk and grabbed the spare tire and bumper jack. In the speed of light, so the sergeant wouldn't catch me, I jacked up the car, spun off the lug nuts and dropped the wheel with the flat on the road. I hoisted the spare wheel and tire onto the lug nut posts. On went the lug nuts and I kicked the hubcap in place with the heel of my shoe. Down went the jack and I loaded it into the trunk along with the wheel with the flat tire and down went the trunk lid. You would have thought the fellow made a pit stop at the Indianapolis 500. It took me fewer than ten minutes to do the deed.

The old gent reached into his pocket and pulled out a single dollar bill. He thought he was being generous when he made the motion of handing the money to me. I could see his fingers were tightly clenched on his end of the bill indicating he was reluctant to part with his big tip. "Here," he said, "Get your uniform cleaned." My mind clicked, "Mister if I called a tow man he would have charged you over thirty-five dollars. I jeopardized my job for a lousy buck." With a false smile on my face I said, "No thanks."

He didn't offer the dollar a second time. If he did I would have accepted it and my kids would have had an extra ride on the Ferris wheel.

In this photograph I'm on the Pennsylvania State Police Academy pistol range in the summer of 1948. I'm 22 years old.

THE PENNSYLVANIA STATE POLICE

From the very beginning of my career as a police officer my aim was to get the job done without a confrontation, violence, or a nauseating aftertaste. The Pennsylvania State Police taught me it could be done and it was their influence that made me determined to be a clever street cop.

I was appointed to the police force in December 1947 and by rotation I was sent to the Pennsylvania State Police Academy, Hershey for the months of May, June and July 1948. Our Superintendent was a retired State Police Major and he knew the strings to pull to get his men the best training available.

The municipal officers were boarded at the Academy along with the State Police cadets. We received a three-month basic training version while the cadets continued on for a total of six months. The training was intensive and by the time we graduated we knew every ramification of the job. We could recite Articles and Sections of the Motor Vehicle Code and the Penal Code pertinent to everyday police work. Theirs was a super course. We were taught everything a municipal police officer must know to work successfully on the street.

The last day was for unwinding after the pressure of daily tests. A senior sergeant leisurely gave us a history of the State Police and its origin. He took us back to the Iron and Coal Police era when every coalmine, iron mill and railroad hauling iron and coal had its own private police force. These men were usually hired thugs and strike breakers who were guilty of so many atrocities they were despised by every miner. It was because of their felonious crimes these evil men were legislated out of existence and replaced by the newly formed Pennsylvania State Police. However, the mill and mine workers didn't immediately accept the Troopers. They weren't trusted because they too could be oppressors with a different name and a uniform.

The Pennsylvania State Police was the first State Police Force in the country. The famous Texas Rangers were already established but they weren't a state police force. In many ways they differed. Some Rangers had been gunslingers that were sworn in and issued a silver star and sent forth on a horse to enforce the law as they saw fit. The Pennsylvania State Police by contrast were educated young men who were already respected in their own community before they joined the force. These fellows received intensive training and a handsome uniform so they could be easily identified. Discipline was a paramount factor. They weren't similar to the original Texas Rangers in any way.

At the onset the Troopers were not welcomed by the oppressed upstate Pennsylvanians who worked the mills and mines. There was the ever-present suspicion the Troopers were a tool of their evil employers. The Troopers had a tough time earning the miners' trust. Each Trooper gained respect on his individual merits. Considering the caliber of men

51

that was selected for the job and their training and discipline their acceptance came quickly. Miners, at this time, had lost family members at the hands of the former police authority. Miners were murdered and many wives and daughters raped by the Iron and Coal police so they were justified in their suspicions."

The sergeant told the class this incident involving the Troopers in the early formative days of the State Police. It occurred when there were frequent uprisings at mines. He pointed out how the Troopers used brainpower and psychology instead of brute force. Through some clandestine means the State Police obtained information an attack was planned for a particular coal region. Mine shafts were to be blown up and all the oppressive foremen were to be killed. The mines were to be totally destroyed. A date was set for a Monday when the attack would do the most damage and be most effective.

Alerted by this information the State Police assembled a contingent of twelve Troopers and dispatched them to the town. They arrived on Saturday morning two days before the scheduled bombing. They boldly rode into town on their beautifully groomed horses. The community was suspicious. They were too uncertain to greet the Troopers but instead hid behind shuttered windows and watched. They were impressed by what they saw for the first time. They never witnessed such a resplendent display.

The townspeople couldn't help but be impressed by the strong, handsome, fearless young men in their immaculate uniforms. Their polished brass glistened as they trotted in military formation on precision trained horses fitted with highly polished leather that shone brilliantly in the sun. It was a shocking contrast to the bleak squalor in the community and from what they expected. These men were nothing like the Iron and Coal Police to which they were accustomed.

Suspicious organizers peered from behind drawn shades to see the next move of these interlopers. They didn't know if the Troopers knew their plans, nevertheless, all was ready and the attack would come off in spite of them. The horses were quickly stabled and the men filed through the entrance of the hotel to their rooms on the second floor. They locked the doors behind them and that was the last they were seen.

The organizers posted spies to watch the rooms where the Troopers were sequestered. They hoped to observe a clue as to how they planned to thwart the attack on Monday but the Troopers never gave a hint. The spies couldn't detect if the Troopers were going to side with the mine owners or with the miners or stay barricaded in the hotel rooms until the bombing was over for they communicated with no one. Word was sent to the organizers that the Troopers never left the hotel, however, there was strange activity going on in one room all Saturday night. They couldn't tell if it had anything to do with the miners' plans.

On Sunday morning the Troopers emerged from the hotel in their handsome uniforms and marched in formation down the main street to the Catholic Church. They marched in pairs down the center aisle of the church and genuflected before they took their places in the first three pews. The miners were aghast. Instead of preparing for the bombing scheduled for the following day they allowed themselves time to attend Sunday Mass.

The church was packed with curious townspeople. All eyes were on the handsome young men in their magnificent uniforms. The congregation never saw such a glorious sight in their church. The Troopers rose in unison to stand. They knelt as one. They stood at attention to hear the Gospel. They bowed their heads when the Host was raised and they struck their breast in cadence at the ringing of the bell. They marched to the altar rail and received Holy Communion and with their head bowed returned to their pew. When the Mass ended they genuflected in cadence and marched out of the church without even a glance toward those who stared in awe. They went directly to the hotel and secluded themselves in their rooms once again. The Irish Catholic miners were bewildered.

The organizers called an emergency meeting to discuss and analyze what took place. They finally decided to call off the attack. They weren't going to harm these fine Catholic lads. Public sentiment would be against the miners if one of the innocent Catholic Troopers were injured.

The sergeant concluded this story by telling us only two men in the contingent of twelve were Catholics. The two Catholic Troopers repeatedly performed a mock Mass in the hotel room on Saturday night. Throughout the night the men rehearsed when to stand, when to genuflect, when to sit and how to receive Holy Communion.

This story impressed me. To me it was a clever approach to a volatile situation. Without a word spoken a catastrophe was avoided.

The sergeant, who was old enough to have been a member of that contingent, mentioned other incidents. He didn't moralize. Each student benefited from them in their own way. Some students were exhausted and slept but he didn't care. He saw many students come and go and some eventually became good police officers. He had my attention.

He assured us a single Trooper sitting upright on a groomed horse could trot into a strange town and by his deportment quell a riot. By the Trooper's demeanor he could exude confidence and convince the frightened citizens he was in complete control of any situation.

That was profound information. If it was possible for one man to subdue a riot by the aura he radiated then why couldn't I have the same effect upon people when I patrolled my beat? I left the classroom that day convinced if I diligently pursued it I too could have that effect. If I studied and worked on it I could possess that power.

I finally possessed that confidence but it took eight years to acquire the necessary self-assurance. I had no mentors or lecturers or professors who knew the formula. I learned by trial and error because I wasn't gifted at birth with street smarts. I had to develop brains over brawn. It took years to learn how to use the authority vested in me and not my mouth.

Municipal Police Graduating Class, August 1, 1948. Pennsylvania State Police Training School, Hershey, Pennsylvania.

Sitting, L. to R: **Bernard Loughran**   **Lower Merion**
              Jacob MacKeown   Narberth
              Elwood Loehler   Lancaster

Standing, L to R: George Dramis   Lower Merion
              Joseph McCann   Lower Merion
              Gilbert Deen   Lancaster
              David Dommel   Lancaster
              Robert Sherts   Lancaster

THE GIFT SHOP BURGLAR

In the middle of the night, around 2:00 a.m., an officer was completing his first store check. He was about to try the doorknob of a gift shop but first looked through the store window and saw a man inside holding a gun. He returned to his patrol car and notified headquarters via radio of the store burglar and requested assistance. Within minutes the fellow was handcuffed and spirited off to the lockup.

The following morning at a Hearing before the Justice of the Peace the young man pled guilty to all charges and since he couldn't post bail he was remanded to the county prison until his court trial. He was charged with Burglary: *Anyone who enters a building with the intent to commit a felony is guilty of Burglary, a felony.*

After the Hearing another officer and myself was assigned to transport this burglar to the county prison. I sat in the rear of the patrol car handcuffed to him as a preventive measure. I was to keep him from escaping during the thirty-minute ride to the prison.

This was during my first year on the job and my first face-to-face meeting with a burglar so I decided to pick his brains. This was an opportunity to study a felon's psyche. I wanted to know why he ventured into a life of crime. Since burglars march to a different drummer he might clue me as to what that beat was. He told me his strange story.

He said he was twenty-six years old. At birth he was abandoned on the doorstep of a state institution without a name or background. He never knew a relative and was never adopted or placed in a foster home. He was raised by the State in various institutions until he was twenty-one years old. At that age he reached his majority so the system released him to go forth into society and fend for himself.

He told me he tried to live outside of an institution but it was impossible for him to adjust to managing his own affairs. He worked industriously at a job and had an apartment of his own but he couldn't cope in an unstructured environment. Routines like paying rent, buying food, clothing, paying an electric bill, phone bill and water bill or doing his laundry were beyond his comprehension without someone to teach him how these things were done.

These necessities had always been provided without him ever questioning how they came about. Since they were now unattainable he didn't know how to secure them or solve simple every day tasks. Through all his formative years he had his meals prepared and waiting for him to respond at the sound of the dinner bell. His laundry was washed and ironed and never was he concerned about shopping or making choices between brands of food. The lack of responsibility and experience made him as helpless as a queen bee. Crossing a busy street confused him. Heavy traffic and street noises made him light headed and dizzy. It was difficult for him to grasp his menial job.

He decided it was hopeless for him to adapt to the outside world so he returned to his last institution and explained his dilemma to his former supervisors but was told the State regulation was unyielding. Once a child reached his majority he must leave the system. He begged and pleaded until a caring administrator relented. He was permitted back into the institution as an employee but for only two years. He was given a temporary job on the campus to circumvent the law.

When the two years was up he was forced to return to the real world where he again struggled to adapt. He even fell in love with a beautiful girl and they set a date to marry but at the last minute he confronted reality. He realized he wasn't mature enough or capable of adjusting to married life. Life outside an institution was too complicated and confusing. He couldn't support and care for a wife and family when he couldn't even take care of himself. The only way for him to live out his life was in the sterile sheltered world in which he was acclimated.

To solve all his problems he had to get back into an institution. The only way for him to accomplish that was to commit a serious crime. After much reflection and planning he decided to break into a building and be apprehended. He didn't want to be hurt or injure anyone so he selected the gift store at an hour when it was closed.

He waited in the shop for three hours for a policeman to come by and catch him. While he was waiting he passed the time examining all the unusual artifacts on display. He considered himself very lucky that he happened to be inspecting an antique pistol when the officer saw him. It was because he was holding a gun he was presumed to be armed so the charges against him were graver and the penalty more severe.

The gun he held could not be used except to deceive someone. The barrel had been deliberately plugged with lead and the firing pin had been removed. It wasn't his gun but one of a pair of civil war flintlocks made into bookends and placed on a display shelf. He wouldn't explain all that to the arresting officer or to the Justice of the Peace because he preferred to be guilty of the greater crime.

I said, "So, you planned your capture so you would be arrested and sent to jail?" "Hell yes! Don't you understand I'm going back home. I'm returning to my friends who are my family. It may be impossible for you to comprehend but I am returning to the place where I was raised. I'm going back to where I fit in. I'm going home."

After we deposited him into the custody of the county prison guards I sat pensively on the return trip to headquarters. Many times I envied men who were raised in an environment enriched with the finer material things in life but that burglar gave me a new perspective and the vision to see beyond the superficial. He awakened within me a deep appreciation for my home, family, parents, siblings and my extended family.

THE PANTS BURGLAR DETAIL

In 1948 Charlie excelled at his profession. For five years he plied his skill as a burglar in the township. His method of operating was unique. He operated close to the Pennsylvania Railroad tracks. At night he'd walk westward out of the city into the suburbs using the railroad tracks as a path to the affluent homes. He seldom wandered more than a few hundred yards on either side of the tracks in search of a victim. After he selected a house he'd climb up the side of the building using a rainspout or portico and enter through a second story window. Once inside he would go directly to the master bedroom and while the occupants slept he'd pick the pockets of the man's pants that were usually draped over a chair. He'd leave the house without disturbing anyone. That's why he was dubbed The Pants Burglar.

In their infinite wisdom the detectives suspected Charlie was the culprit by his method of operating. They hadn't proof until one midnight in late November he was seen entering the township by way of the Pennsylvania Railroad tracks at the Overbrook train station. My Lieutenant longed for an opportunity to catch a burglar so he seized this chance to capture slick Charlie. He took every man off his regular assignment and posted him along the tracks the length of the township.

Patrolman Rundolf and I were staked out where Charlie was seen entering the township. It was hoped he'd exit the township where he entered. I respected the Lieutenant's logic but it was a horrid place for human beings to spend a cold harsh night.

The bitter cold gnawed at Rundolf and myself as we sat silently on a discarded railroad tie lying on the railroad bank. The dampness froze us until we reached the depth of despair. A dense fog clung to us like a wet horse blanket. We didn't dare smoke or break silence. The misery we endured for five hours was too painful for words. By 5:30 a.m. neither of us could tolerate another minute yet there was still two and a half more hours until the end of our night.

Rundolf was the first to break the silence. "I can't take this any longer! I'm quitting this job! I'm walking back to headquarters and turning in my badge! No job is worth this kind of suffering!" He didn't influence me because I too was so cold I nurtured the same thoughts for the past five hours. I made up my mind around 1:00 a.m. that this job was definitely not for me. I planned to turn in my badge after we were picked up in the morning. I was so cold it wasn't possible for me to walk the three miles to headquarters.

Together we rose from where we had been sitting so the circulation could return to our extremities. We stood erect for less than two minutes, waiting for mobility, when Charlie walked within five feet of us. It was early winter and before daybreak plus the dense fog reduced visibility to within five feet. The conditions were such that it was impossible to see one another and that is why Charlie could walk as close to us as he did.

The three of us were equally startled but the bitter cold hadn't fuse Charlie's limbs. He had been walking all night to find the house he favored. He immediately sensed we were policemen because he had walked that route hundreds of mornings and never met anyone here. If he hesitated to do a double take he would have seen we were in uniform.

Without squandering a second on a double take he whirled around and took off like a scared rabbit. I made an attempt to run after him but when I was less than fifty feet from were we sat I noticed Rundolf wasn't in pursuit. He was frozen stiff and couldn't move so he did what he thought was the only other way to stop Charlie. He unholstered his gun and pointed it where the dense fog had been disturbed and fired. When I heard the gun reports I turned around and saw two brilliant flashes leave his gun barrel. The red-hot lead piercing the darkness narrowly missed me as they whizzed by.

I was so stiff I could barely walk on the railroad ties but since Rundolf was shooting in my direction I hit the ballast. I lay there until he shot the last bullet in the cylinder. Later he apologized and said he hoped he might scare Charlie enough to stop him. I survived so I didn't think it necessary to chastise or accuse him of recklessness. I allowed the fog was so thick he didn't see me. Charlie vanished into the thick of it.

Rundolf and I recognized him from mug shots in that brief instant when we were face-to-face so on the strength of our credibility in the courtroom Charlie was sentenced to serve five years in prison. During his stay in prison he lost his agility and yearning to live on the cutting edge. He had grown too old to climb the side of a house like he once could do very easily.

The truism: *You can't teach an old dog new tricks* applied in Charlie's case. He was too old to learn a new modus operandi.

MY ACHING BACK

It was in my second year on the job that I acquired a back injury that plagued me for the rest of my life. It happened in a blink of an eyelash but I'll never forget the moment. I had been well tutored and practiced in the proper way to pump iron and power lift but there came a time when I didn't do by the book what had to be done.

There was a call for help from a woman who fell in her kitchen and fractured her hip. She was an overweight person who by sheer will power raised herself into a kitchen chair to use the telephone. After my partner and I arrived in the kitchen we saw there was more than her weight to contend with. She couldn't be placed on a stretcher and maneuvered through the narrow hallway between the kitchen and front door so we decided it was best to carry her to the ambulance sitting in the chair.

My partner gently tilted the chair back and I gripped the front legs and began a proper power lift. Her excessive weight drew my face forward and deep into her crotch so I twisted my torso to avoid this embarrassing position. For an instant my spine wasn't aligned. My back muscles went spastic and twisted my spine out of shape.

There were many times thereafter I lifted a person onto a stretcher or from a gurney to a hospital bed. I did what had to be done due to the urgency of the situation but for weeks thereafter I paid dearly with another painful back spasm. It took a single improper lift to leave me with a fragile spine that tortured me forever.

I am at the Pennsylvania State Police Academy, July 1948.

FIRE! FIRE!

One midnight I was assigned to the Haverford Station Road Shopping Center because someone had been breaking into a different store every night. There were only ten stores and the Haverford Train Station in this shopping center. I was taken there shortly after midnight and was to be picked up at 7:55 a.m.

Immediately I searched for an ideal place to carry out the surveillance and luckily found a spot where I had a full view of all the stores yet I wouldn't be seen. I always bundled up before I left the house for work but there are only so many layers of clothes I could pile on. The night started out pretty chilly but it grew colder by the minute. My teeth were chattering and I shivered uncontrollably. The freezing temperature chiseled at my will power. It was crucial I find shelter soon. I was no longer concerned about my visibility or the burglar. Three hours had crept slowly by and I was agonizingly numb. This assignment had turned into a nightmare.

At 3:10 a.m. I abandoned the surveillance and looked for a place where I could thaw. I found refuse in the Haverford Train Station waiting room. It was a cold drafty glass enclosed wooden addition to the main building. It had a cast iron potbelly stove in the middle of the room. Either my luck had changed or my prayers were answered. I was ecstatic. The stove was ice cold and there was no telling the last time it held a fire but on a bench was a discarded daily newspaper.

I tore the paper apart sheet by sheet and rolled each sheet into a tight ball and stuffed them into the stove until it could hold no more and set a match to them. The stove quickly became warm and radiated a heat that filled the room. My clothing absorbed the warmth and it worked its way inward to my body. Each joint slowly defrosted. I savored the delicious heat and was proud of how clever it was of me to roll the paper into balls that would burn slowly and thus give off the heat of a burning log. I sat on the bench five feet from the stove and placed my flashlight between my palms and closed my eyelids to rest my eyes. I plunged into a coma.

After thirty minutes the heat seared my face and wrenched me from my sound sleep. I freaked out when I became fully aware the iron stove had turned white hot from the heat produced by blazing paper balls. I never saw white-hot iron so I expected the stove would soon melt and ooze onto the floor like molten lava. Then I had another paralyzing shock. Above the top of the stove extended a smoke stack. The five foot galvanized sheet-medal stack stretched up to the ceiling and through the roof. By convection the whiteness of the stove already crept up the stack to the ceiling. My fear heightened when I saw the redness touching the flashing on the wooden roof.

I groped furiously for a solution to this problem short of calling for a fire department. If I summoned the fire department it would be known I had been sleeping on the job. Investigators would deduct it was I who burned this historic building to the ground. With precious little time to waste I collected my wits and summoned a presence of mind to close the damper on the stack and to close the door at the base of the stove that supplied the draft. The air feeding the fire was snuffed out and the flames died down in time to prevent a major disaster.

Hysteria gripped me as I focused on the hot galvanized smoke stack. The red leading edge sluggish descended from the roof. I closely examined the ceiling for smoldering hidden embers but there were none. The rust color gradually came back to the stack and then to the stove. The newspaper balls were totally incinerated. Every trace of them disappeared. The stove and the stack cooled to the touch and soon became cold.

I tarried in the waiting room until I was satisfied the building was no longer in jeopardy and then fled to where I was to be picked up by the patrol car. The terrifying events of that night I kept secret.

HAVERFORD COLLEGE STATION of Pennsylvania Railroad on Station Rd. in Haverford. Built about 1871.
(Bob Swartz-Lower Merion Historical Society Photo)

A glass-enclosed waiting room was added to the right side of the building.

HIEL HITLER!

June 1950 was five years after VE Day, four years after I was discharged from the Navy and two and a half years after I joined the police force. The war with Germany became history and everyone was struggling to adjust to the post war era.

I was ordered via radio to proceed to a supermarket. "Car #15 the manager has a shoplifter in custody." I hurried to the store because I didn't want the thief to escape the manager's grip and at the same time I was apprehensive because I was alone and hadn't experience dealing with shoplifters.

As I entered the store an employee whom I knew from our school days was standing on a tall ladder. He was hanging an advertising banner from the ceiling at the far end of the first aisle. To catch my attention he waved his arm and gave a loud "Hi Bernie!" Automatically I responded by raising my right arm and angled it upward and returned his greeting with a softer "Hi".

At that moment an elderly Jewish gentleman bent with crippling osteoporosis halted his shopping cart directly in front of me. He made a sharp turn to face me and snapped to attention. In a singular reflex he thrust his right arm upward and gave me a snappy "Hiel Hitler".

He realized he embarrassed me and was very apologetic. He explained what happened in his past that caused him to do that. He said during the war he was confined in a concentration camp where every moment of every day he anticipated a thrashing and death. Whenever a Nazi guard appeared he had to give a subservient Nazi salute. To him my uniform looked like a Nazi SS uniform and it brought on an involuntary salute. It was a conditioned reflex.

Until that moment I was proud of my uniform. It was nothing like a city police officer's uniform. It was styled after the Pennsylvania State Police uniform that I admired and always thought garnered respect. My uniform consisted of black leather leggings (putties), Jodhpur trousers, black leather Sam Browne belt, holster, handcuffs, peaked hat with a hat piece, shiny brass buttons and a badge. To this former concentration camp inmate I looked like a Nazi SS Storm Trooper and I couldn't blame him because there were many similarities.

Maybe to some Italians I looked like a Brown Shirt Trooper and to some Asians I may have appeared as a Japanese Manchurian invader. To Hispanics I might have looked like a Franco Fascist and it is possible to extrapolate this further and suggest that some young Americans, because of my uniform, saw me as a military oppressor rather than a protector of their public safety

WHAT SHOULD I DO?

In 1951 I was still in my formative stage when I was Joe Forney's partner. On a lethargic Sunday afternoon he parked our patrol car on the apron of a closed gas station to savor a brief pause after an hour of nonstop cruising. On the opposite side of the street was a sixty-year-old man mowing his front lawn with a hand push-pull mower.

Joe nudged me. "See that fellow over there, he's an atheist." Joe didn't say how he knew that but I couldn't detect any telltale signs in his behavior. I marveled that Joe could cleverly identify an atheist from his outward appearance. I wondered if after many years as a cop I would acquires that same skill. Undoubtedly Joe at some time had a serious conversation with the fellow.

Joe had just finished saying the day was too hot and humid for pushing and pulling a mower when the fellow keeled over and hit the lawn face down. We were stunned and jumped from the car and ran to his side expecting to administer mouth-to-mouth resuscitation and first aid for heat exhaustion but the fellow was undeniably dead as a doormat. His heart made its final beat before his face touched the tallest blade of grass.

The man's daughter bolted from the house to see what happened. Joe was accomplished with soothing words in delicate situations like this so he took his time comforting her. When he felt the time was right he asked a series of routine questions. "Which doctor do you want us to notify so you will get a Death Certificate? Which undertaker do you wish us to transport the body to?"

Even though Joe had forewarned me my idiotic contribution was "Do you want us to notify a clergy?" Her response was a hard scowl. Joe was right the man was an avowed atheist and so was his daughter.

A month after that experience I was assigned to a walking beat. I stationed myself on the sidewalk at a safe distance from all pedestrian traffic. I refused to be bored by idle chatter. I stood motionless so not to attract attention and was wishing the time would pass faster. I saw a gent eighty some years of age leisurely strolling toward me. I studied his unusual slow gait. He came to within sixty feet of me and collapsed like a burst balloon. By the manner in which he fell it looked like the person who was manipulating the strings that held him upright had suddenly cut them. I had been studying his every step and knew he didn't trip or stumble or lie down. He just crumbled. I ran to his side and gave him a superficial examination and decided he was beyond resuscitating. I went to a police call box strapped on a pole on the opposite side of the street and advise headquarters to dispatch an ambulance.

Four evenings later this man's wife met me as I stood on the same sidewalk. She came up to me and snapped, "Officer, did you say the Act of Contrition or the Lord's Prayer into my husband's ear as he lay on the sidewalk?" I said "No." She was furious and raised her voice and scolded me. "Don't you know that the soul lingers in the body? You should have whispered prayers into his ear. His soul would have repeated them before it left his body!"

She wept and I felt lousy and stupid once again. I was taught by the nuns in grade school to do that very thing but while a crowd of spectator surrounded me I felt they expected something more traditional from a police officer.

I had to learn how to recognize a person's religious persuasion by their outward appearance. This was another skill I must develop.

Man Cutting Grass Collapses And Dies

As Patrolman Bernard Loughran was passing ▓▓▓▓▓▓▓▓▓▓▓▓▓▓▓▓▓▓▓▓▓▓▓▓, Sunday afternoon, he saw ▓▓▓▓▓▓▓▓ ▓▓▓▓▓▓ of that address being carried into his home by a neighbor and a passing motorist.

▓▓▓▓▓▓▓, 60, had been mowing the lawn and collapsed, according to his daughter, ▓▓▓▓▓▓▓▓▓▓▓. The police ambulance and a physician were sent for, but efforts to revive the stricken man were in vain.

▓▓▓▓▓▓▓▓▓▓ said her father had apparently been in good health. Dr. Charles R. Tatnall, who pronounced ▓▓▓▓▓▓▓ dead. stated that a coronary occlusion was the cause of death

My account and the newspaper reporter's details differ again. I found reporters to be very creative. I wouldn't believe the Lord's Prayer if a reporter printed it.

TAXI! TAXI!

At 7:45 a.m. I was driving slowly toward headquarters. I was gauging my speed so I'd arrive no earlier than 7:55 a.m. and in time to report off duty. The radio was brought alive by the sleepy voice of the radio operator. "All cars be on the lookout for a young man who just escaped from the Ludlum Sanitarium." It was too close to quitting time for me to get involved so I noted the escapee's description on my note pad. At exactly 8:00 a.m. my relief, without a lengthy adieu, slid behind the steering wheel and drove off. He had received the information about the escapee at roll call. I went into headquarters and saluted the sergeant good-bye and went home to bed.

At midnight that same day I returned to work to begin another eight-hour tour. I forgot about the escapee and proceeded to carry out other responsibilities and routines. That message was already sixteen hours old and yesterday's news. I expected the fellow would be in another county or state by now.

At 1:00 a.m. I was cruising from one chore to the next when a young man darted from the shadows. He startled me even more when he leaped off the sidewalk and into the path of my patrol car's headlights to flag me to a stop. He was in such a hurry I thought he wanted to tell me about an emergency situation where a police presence was needed immediately. As he approached the patrol car I critically checked over his overall demeanor to determine what sort of person he might be and what he might be getting me involved in. He could be drunk or victim of a crime or a raving lunatic. In any case I was confident in my ability to handle any physical situation so I opened the door on the passenger side so he could tell me his problem. He quickly eased into the seat.

He began by stating where he wanted to be taken when suddenly he noticed the police uniform. He was shocked to see he put himself into a patrol car. He apologized and said he thought he hailed a taxi but before he could get out of the car I told him I knew he was the escapee and that I had to return him to the sanitarium. He laughed heartily at his unlucky twist of fate. He was a total gentleman and accepted the inevitable. He didn't resist or plead for a compassionate break.

The next day I learned a little more about the fellow. He was a lawyer with a prestigious Philadelphia law firm. He possessed a great potential but when under rigorous pressure he resorted to liquor to pull himself through. He was susceptible to frequent binges and nervous breakdowns. When he had a relapse the firm didn't dismiss him but instead institutionalized him until he recovered. On this occasion the young man saw an opportunity to walk off the sanitarium grounds without permission.

THE AFFLUENT MAIN LINER

The Pennsylvania Highway Department mailed an ultimatum to the Township Manager that stipulated "If your Police Department cannot enforce the **NO PARKING THIS SIDE** regulation the Pennsylvania State Police will be assigned the task." The Pennsylvania Highway Department was referring to the area in front of a popular news agency.

This was a slap at the integrity of the Lower Merion Police Department. Action had to be taken so the buck was passed down through the ranks to the patrolmen who walked the beat. I happened to be one of them.

Coincidentally, the letter was sent a week after my father underwent surgery in the local hospital. He was a police officer too.

On the morning the stern order from the Superintendent was read at roll call I was assigned to walk the beat and as usual motorists stopped in front of the news agency in violation of the **NO PARKING THIS SIDE** regulation. This store attracted motorists twenty-four hours a day and every driver assumed he had the right to park at the entrance to the store. Motorists on their way to work habitually parked in violation of the regulation and dash into the store to buy a newspaper, cigarettes and a carton of coffee and then rushed back to their car. A slow line at the cash register or a brief conversation with a friend that turned into a gabfest frequently delayed an errand that should take thirty seconds into ten minutes.

Since this was a favorite place to shop a solid line of violators was present all day. As one vehicle pulled from the curb another was double-parked waiting to take its place. The state's major artery <u>Route 30</u>, <u>The Lincoln Highway</u>, <u>Lancaster Avenue</u> had a bottleneck. Instead of it being a through two-lane highway into the city it was backed up by the same drivers every day. The Highway Department was justified in demanding the obstruction be eliminated. I accepted my responsibility without question or instructions and posted myself in front of the store. As each motorist prepared to park I advised them of the posted regulation and that the department no longer intended to overlook violations. Some drivers graciously drove off while others were so eager to get their necessities that they drove around the block and returned to park in spite of my warning. They promised, "I'll only be a minute."

In the first hour I issued six tickets but I could have written many more. One driver parked on the opposite side of the street occupying two parking meter spaces without putting a penny in either meter. He saw I was issuing tickets but chose to ignore me. I couldn't overlook his blatant violation and strictly enforce another because a vengeful person might be observing and for maliciousness report me for showing favoritism. I wrote a ticket for improper meter parking while the man was in the store and placed the notice under the windshield wiper blade.

I had not yet moved away from the car when he walked across the street with his daily paper.

He was wearing a double-breasted pinstriped business suit that mirrored a man of means and education. He definitely wasn't a blue-collar worker. He scowled as he yanked the ticket from under the wiper blade. "That's the thanks I get after operating on your father. You'd better hope I never have to operate on you."

In a huff he got into his car and slammed the door shut. He yanked the gearshift so roughly I thought it might snap and without checking to see if it was safe he pulled from the curb and sped off before I could respond to his nasty remark. If he had given me a chance to thank him for taking excellent care of my father I would have taken the ticket back and tore it up. I could have easily done that.

I never met him before so I didn't know he performed the operation. I am certain it wasn't free because dad had health insurance that paid the surgeon and the hospital the going rate.

I often thought about that meter ticket incident and I could never justify why a surgeon on the staff of a prestigious hospital would bust on a young cop doing his job. He not only complained about a <u>one-dollar</u> parking meter fine but also made a diabolical threat.

Many times I practiced over and over in my mind a variety of survival tactics I might use to escape a threatening deranged individual who had a weapon but when I weighed the surgeon's warning, the inference in his tone and his facial bitterness, I worried how inappropriately serious he was. His declaration, "You'd better hope I never have to operate on you" was a guarantee I wouldn't survive and no one would suspect a thing.

With the type of job I had I could be under the bright operating lights in his hospital any day and he might be the surgeon hovering over me with a scalpel between his teeth. If it should really happen I'd be anesthetized and strapped to the table and unable to tell anyone of my fear.

THE HAZEE

Before the Schuylkill Expressway construction began in 1950 a road was in its place appropriately named River Road because it ran parallel to the river from Belmont Avenue, West Manayunk to West Conshohocken. It was ten miles long; a narrow two-lane road without curbs, sidewalks, or soft shoulders. A weak incandescent streetlight appeared every quarter-mile but even so it was a dangerously pathetic main artery.

There was a cluster of six houses every mile. Some were so close to the river they were submerged up to the second floor during the flood season. Some stretches of the road were level with the river and at the river's edge while other places it was high on a cliff overlooking the river. A flimsy cable guardrail, which was ruptured in dozens of places as a result of many automobile accidents, offered no protection for an unfamiliar driver. In the history of the road there were times when vehicles went out of control and landed in the river.

The most dangerous spots were the sharp curves. These curves were narrow and barely wide enough to accommodate two cars. If there was an advance warning one driver would pull to the side of the road before he got to the curve and wait for the oncoming vehicle to squeeze by. At night it was an eerie ride its whole ten miles. A motorist didn't look for an oncoming vehicle but scanned far ahead for headlight beams. He'd frisk the pitch-black void for a bouncing headlight beam to peek around a curve long before the vehicle arrived. It was also an ideal place to dispose of a dead body or for a fatal auto accident that wouldn't be stumbled upon until daylight.

The first night I was assigned to patrol the beat that included River Road I was alone in the police car. It was 1:00 a.m. when I cruised on the road. I drove slowly and cautiously through a heavy fog that always appeared after midnight in the low spots. I didn't expect to meet oncoming traffic and I certainly never expected to see a lone pedestrian. At a place where the road is straight and not covered by the fog I accelerated to cover a greater distance quicker. Without any warning my headlights glistened on a ghostly figure forty yards away walking slower than a zombie. I applied the brakes expecting to come upon a dreadful automobile disaster.

As my car coasted closer I made out the figure of a boy carrying two two-gallon galvanized buckets. A bucket dangled from each hand. The bright headlights of my car blinded him and caused him to stagger in a daze. He was bare-chested except for the remnant of a torn shirt draped over his shoulders. It looked like it was violently torn apart. He wore shredded trousers and tattered sneakers. His skin was smeared with dirty oil and red paint that from a distance looked like he was covered from head to toe with blood. He was a hideous sight. He emerged from this black funnel appearing like the lone survivor of a tragic mishap or the type of accident that often befell strangers unfamiliar with the characteristics of this poor excuse for a road.

It didn't take long for my adrenaline to acclimatize me to the terrifying sight. I stopped the patrol car and rushed to the poor fellow's side to assess the immediate First-Aid I could administer. I asked a group of questions all at once. "What happened? Was anyone with you? Where did it happen?" I was more scared than he until he unfolded this stupid story.

He was a freshman in a local college and was being hazed. The students in the fraternity he hoped to join outfitted him this way. They doused him with motor oil and axle grease and smeared his body with red paint to appear like blood. They drove him a mile west on River Road and abandoned him with instructions to walk all the way back to the fraternity house. A departure from this mandate would result in severe penalties. He was warned that observers were stationed alone the route to make sure he complied with the orders. He had three more miles to walk to the college.

He was equally afraid I might arrest him or insist he get into the patrol car and be taken to face the college provost. Actually, I was glad he refused my offer to drive him closer to the fraternity house. I didn't insist because I knew how important it was for a student to be accepted by his peers. In fact, I was pleased he stubbornly declined a ride. He would have left a dirty oil stain on the upholstery that would've been impossible to remove.

As I drove away I had to laugh, "That kid's daddy is paying tuition for a course in Stupidity 101."

I'm on the State Police Academy rifle range, July 1948.

THE RUNAWAY PRIEST

By 1952 I was twenty-six years of age and on the job four years but I still hadn't learned much in the way of police science. A major reason for my slow progress was due to the fact most of my working hours were spent walking alone on a foot beat or patrolling solo in a cruiser. I couldn't benefit from the experiences of other officers. What I learned was from hands-on experience and not from what other men shared with me.

As the years moved sluggishly along I imagined the eight hours would be more interesting and enjoyable if I was a celebrated detective. I read a few detective stories that stirred a yearning to have investigative mastery at a high level. I wished to be a clever interrogator and an expert interviewer but I never had an opportunity to develop the skill. To be superior at any endeavor demands practice and experience and I had neither.

At 5:00 p.m. one November afternoon I was leisurely cruising in a patrol car when I came upon a seventeen years old boy thumbing a ride. Hitchhiking was a common practice among teenagers and college students. I must mention in this era a child was legally a minor until he was twenty-one years old. It was a cool time of the year yet he wasn't wearing a jacket or sweater so that aroused my suspicions. The nights grew very cold after sunset so I assumed he wasn't traveling far. If he was a local lad I could make him a friend by giving him a ride home. I pulled abreast of him and opened the door on the passenger side and said, "Hop in, Pal. Where are you from?"

"South Philly" he responded without hesitation and in a friendly respectful tone.

"Where are you headed?"

"Germantown P A."

That was not the right answer. A kid from South Philly would have said "Germantown" but not "Germantown P A." He betrayed he was from out of state, plus, he was thumbing away from Germantown. I was aglow with my deductive prowess. I was correct on several deductions. Sherlock Holmes couldn't have been more accurate. I was excited now that I had someone to interrogate. This was my opportunity to hone a necessary talent if I wished to be a detective. I would skillfully practice on this boy.

Alas, my inexperience caused me to plunge into the interrogation impetuously. My stupidity turned what could have been a piece of cake into a disaster. I went headlong into direct questioning, which is a self-destruct technique. It took me three hours to achieve what an experienced interviewer would have accomplished within minutes. I thought I was in the catbird seat. He was sitting in the passenger seat of my patrol car and that was like sitting in my office at my desk. He was

70

on my ball field and I had the rulebook. I was comfortable while he was on unfamiliar territory.

"Listen son," I threatened, pointing a finger at his face. "One thing I'd hate is to put myself in a position where anyone could point a finger at me and say, 'You're a liar!' Now tell me, where are you from and where are you going?" The boy took the cue. I wasn't going to make a liar out of him and I didn't intimidate him either. He elected not to answer any questions and thereby he wouldn't be a liar. His lips were sealed and they would remain so forever if the need be.

I was helpless now that he wouldn't talk. It was obvious he ran away from home. If I complied with the department's procedures I should take him to headquarters and place him in a holding cell. After a few hours in the smelly cell he would be eager to tell what we wanted to know. I didn't think that method was professional yet that tactic was the traditional tried and true procedure. But, if I transported him to the lockup I wouldn't be much of an interrogator and I'd blow an opportunity to develop myself.

The evening was quiet. I wasn't given any radio assignments so that was a break. I could take all the time I needed to deal with this lad. We cruised for an hour and all the while I talked about unrelated subjects. Despite my change of approach he persisted in his refusal to communicate. He was uncanny. I thought if I showed a kindness he might trust me so I gave him a dollar and sent him into a drug store to purchase a couple of bottles of soda and two packs of crackers. It was now 6:00 p.m. and my dinnertime. The drug store hadn't a rear door or windows so he couldn't escape but he didn't know that.

He returned to the car and we snacked and cruised. Every few minutes I'd ask an unrelated question he might answer but he wouldn't speak. Another hour passed before he finally realized I wouldn't turn him lose without some satisfaction. I had the tenacity of a bulldog so he finally decided to talk but with stilted replies. He broke his silence hoping I'd release him. "You are like my mother. You're doing the devil's work!" After another five-minute pause he said, "I have a Vocation and a Calling from God to be a priest and she doesn't want me to respond to that Calling."

There was a ten-minute pause again and he was close to sobbing. "You are stopping me too! You're the devil's advocate too! But I will not be stopped! I won't be stopped! I will fulfill what God has ordained for me! I have a vocation and I shall be a priest!"

He irritated me and I lost my patience after he called me the devil's advocate. For all I cared he could respond to the call of the wild. He broke the law by running away from home while he was still a minor. My job was to obtain his name, address and phone number and contact his parents and notify them to come pick him up. Since he refused to give me that information I was about to take him to the lockup at headquarters.

71

I took a few deep breaths and got a grip on my temper. I reminded myself I was breaking all the cardinal rules of an interrogation. An interrogator shouldn't become involved in anything an interviewee says. He mustn't condone or condemn, approve or disapprove. An interrogator listens and listens some more. An interrogator repeats what is said and waits. An interrogator knows nature abhors a vacuum and if he waits long enough the interviewee will break the silence and talk. A good interrogator repeats the last sentence the interviewee said.

I regained control of my wits. "So your mother and I are the devil's advocates?" I repeated what he said and waited to see what would happen. The wait was painful for us both. I hoped I chose the right question. Maybe something else should have been added. After an unbearably ten minutes he added another piece to the puzzle.

"I was in a seminary for a year and a half. The seminarians there were predominately of an ethnic group of which I don't belong so that made me a minority. I was the butt of all their jokes and pranks. I had to leave because I couldn't mediate on Holy thoughts and it was impossible for me to pray due to the harassment they constantly dished out."

I felt he had more to say so I waited and waited. "Today I left home without my mother knowing it to join the Trappist Monks. There I can concentrate on my Calling. You are like my mother, the devil's advocate, if you prevent me from going. Please, let me fulfill God's Will." His reluctance to talk now made some sense. He was on his way to join the Trappists, an Order of Monks who take a vow of silence. It was clear he was practicing on me and I was just another obstacle he had to overcome before he would eventually be a priest.

He relented very little but the fact he began to talk in spurts took me by surprise. He was so sincere and I knew the Catholic Church could use every priest it can get. I felt guilty because his logic seemed sound. I wondered if it was possible the devil was using me to prevent him from becoming a priest? My conscience was bothering me and I became the silent one. I mulled over the big question, was I really the devil's agent?

I was about to defer to the boy's logic when I became aware that this was not a good way to start out to be a priest. Suddenly I was inspired. I maneuvered my interrogation toward a friendly conversational tone. I knew in which direction my interrogation should go. Delicately, I asked him a series of questions about a Bible story. He responded with the same answers I had been taught in grade school but all the while he had no idea where I was heading until the very last question.

"Would you agree a boy seventeen years old today would be comparable to a boy twelve years old in Jesus Christ's day considering the shorter life expectancy then?"

"Yes."

"Did you know that Jesus left home without his parent's permission when He was twelve?"

"Yes."

"Do you know for how long?"

"Yes. Three days."

"Do you know where his parents found Him after searching for those three days?"

"Yes. In the Temple."

"Do you know what He was doing in the Temple?"

"Yes. He was teaching Scripture to the High Priests."

"Do you know His mother's first words?"

"Yes. 'Son, why have you done this to us?'"

"And what was His reply?"

"'Don't you know I am about my Father's business?'"

"And what did His mother say?"

"'Son, come home with us.'"

"Who did Jesus obey? His mother or the Calling from God?"

"His mother."

"So He went home with His mother and stayed with her and waxed in wisdom until he was thirty years old. What does that tell you?"

"I must return home."

I trusted the boy since he intended to be a priest so I gave him the rest of the money I had in my pocket. It was less than a dollar but the bus fare to the 69th Street Bus Terminal in Philadelphia was only ten cents. I drove to a bus stop and told him to take the bus to the end of the line and from there he could telephone his parents collect. "Tell them you are at the 69th Street Bus Terminal in Philadelphia and ask them to come and pick you up." I purposely didn't ask the boy his name or address because I wanted him to know I trusted him.

That night a blizzard blanketed the Tennessee Valley. I doubt he would have survived unless he got a direct ride to the Kentucky monastery. A month later headquarters received a letter from the boy's mother addressed to "Officer Bernie". She had to do some investigating to find out my name and where I worked.

"Dear Officer Bernie,

Thank you for sending my son home. He has a fervent desire to be a priest. He was in a seminary for a year and a half but suffered a nervous breakdown. He hasn't fully recovered but when he is well again and if he still wishes to be a priest, I will not stop him. Etc. etc. etc.

Thank you."

I wonder if there is a priest somewhere who could verify this incident.

THE NIGHT WATCHMAN

During the early months of 1952 an office building was in its initial construction stage. The concrete foundation was poured and rapid progress was being made until a union dispute halted all construction jobs throughout the area. Several weeks went by and only the steel framework outlined a building that eventually would be four stories high, a hundred feet wide and seventy-five feet deep. If it weren't for a few sturdy steel cables tying the girders together the fragile structural framework would collapse in a mild breeze.

A hundred feet to the rear of this steel skeleton was a loosely thrown together guard's shack. It was an eight-foot cube made of plywood sheathing with windows cut out on three sides and a door on the fourth. A bunch of kids could build a more palatial bunk than this shack. Shortly after 2:30 a.m. on a cold night I drove by the area with the specific intention of checking on the construction site. Vandalism and thefts sometimes accompany union disputes so I hoped that a police officer's show of interest in the area might thwart any damage to the property. At the same time I'd check on the well being of the night watchman in the shack.

I stopped my patrol car beside the shack and tooted the horn. The guard took every precaution to make sure I wasn't a troublemaker before he came outside. I opened the patrol car door and he slid in beside me. "My it's toasty in here," he said.

"Don't you have an electric space heater in the shack?"

"Hell no. I don't even have an electric light bulb. The only thing in there is a stool and a telephone."

"What do you do all night?"

"I mostly sleep but every hour I take my time-clock and I punch sixteen keys. There is a key on each corner of the building on each floor. I go to each corner and insert the key hanging there into my time clock and it registers that I was there."

"Does anyone ever check the time clock?"

"They sure do. One night there was an electrical storm and it lightened something fierce. I wouldn't take a chance walking on those steel girders cause I could be electrocuted. Two weeks later I was called to the front office in center city. The security boss wanted to know why I didn't make my rounds that night."

"Seems like a lousy job. Why do you stay with it?"

"It ain't too bad. I have a regular job during the day. I'm sending two children to college and I need the money for that. If it weren't for the mud I have to walk through to get to the building it wouldn't be so bad. Some nights it is really cold and windy and there is only a few twelve-inch wide wooden planks stretched from one girder to the next. When the frost sets on those planks they are mighty slippery. I climb ladders to get to and from each floor but I can do the whole routine in twenty minutes if the conditions are good. After I finish a round I come back to the shack and sleep till the next round. In the morning I'm rested and ready for my other job."

"Aren't you afraid you will oversleep and miss a round?"

"I haven't missed yet. I wake up in time. The worse part of this job is my day off. In the middle of the night I wake up and to go back to sleep I must get out of bed and walk around the room before I climb back into bed." I could relate to that. There were nights I was so tired on duty I'd doze off. On those nights I prayed that I'd wake up in precisely one hour, in time to check with headquarters over a police call box. I never made it a habit of it; consequently, those few naps never kept me awake on my night off.

This photograph was taken in September 1952 when I had a walking beat. I was 26 years old and a police officer four years. My sergeant hated to see me wearing sunglasses. He never actually ordered me not to wear them but sarcastically always asked, "Where's your tin cup?"

THE DETECTIVE SERGEANT

At 2:30 a.m. I decided to check on the night watchman I met a few nights earlier at a construction site. A substitute watchman came out of the guard shack and identified himself and told me it was the regular fellow's day off. I don't know if this substitute watchman had sleeping problems too because I never asked him. This guard was a congenial fellow about fifty-five years of age. He was proud of the fact he was a retired Philadelphia Police Department Detective Sergeant.

He was eager to share his police experiences with another police officer and started right off by telling me how he built a successful career on his uncanny ability to solve major crimes that occurred in the center city district. He produced several newspaper clippings about himself as proof of his expertise. He was a nonstop talker but I didn't blame him for blowing his own horn because he seemed to have had an impressive career. He was helping me stay awake at a late hour on a monotonous night.

He told me the most bizarre police story I ever heard but before he shared it with me he made me promise I wouldn't reveal it to anyone. He didn't want his former colleagues to know his source of information. I must preface this story with a few comments to help make it believable.

His story could only happen in an intercity police district. I remind the reader there is a portion of our society who when burdened with guilt go to another person and tell them all about it. The listener has the spiritual authority to absolve the person of their wrongdoing and in so doing disposes of the guilt feeling. If this is unbelievable think of Roman Catholics and their Confessor.

There is a segment of society that refuses to go to a doctor for medical treatment even when they have a fatal illness. They seek council from their Practitioner. The Practitioner assures the sick person he will get well if he does not falter in his faith. He recommends more diligent praying. Some of these people are Christian Scientists.

There are people who cannot function before they consult their Therapist and Scientologist depends on their Auditor. There are people when in need of counseling telephone Dial-A-Prayer, Suicide-Hot-Line, True Confessions Hot Line or whomever.

On a TV show a man who bought a 300-year-old map for $3.00 was being interviewed. A collector offered him $500,000 but his Prophet advised him not to sell. Following his Prophet's advice he expected to make $2,000,000 and still own the map.

The United States Government admitted it employed Psychics and President Ronald Reagan was known to consult an Astrologer when pressed for a major decision. Even police investigators have employed Psychics to help them solve complicated crimes.

This retired Detective Sergeant may have scoffed at the idea of a Confessor, Practitioner, Therapist, Auditor, Prophet, Astrologer and Psychic but he had a fervent faith in his Gypsy Fortune Teller. To him she had a special gift for peering into the future. He wasn't referring to an after lunch tealeaf reading entertainer. He was talking about the real thing. A genuine Gypsy Fortune Teller who resides in the intercity, behind a dirty curtain, in an abandoned store, in a depressed business district. That's where you locate the really gifted Gypsy.

Need I say more to sway you to accept the fact there are people who believe and trust Gypsy Fortune Tellers. Who among us has heard a respected friend say, "Go to my fortune teller, she is fantastic, she knows everything. She can predict your future with surefire accuracy."

I listened as he told his story and I assured him I wouldn't betray his confidence. If no one on the Philadelphia Police Department knew his secret I certainly wasn't going to tell on him, however, promises have a statute of limitations.

When a burglary of grand proportions was committed in his district, like a company safe cracked and a payroll stolen, he rushed to confer with his Gypsy Fortune Teller and she not only told him who committed the crime but had precise instructions on how to arrest the perpetrator. "Be at Al's Deli Saturday evening at eight o'clock. A fellow named Joey will be in the last booth. Tell Joey you have witnesses. Tell him to own-up to the crime and you will plea bargain on his behalf with the District Attorney and the Judge. Tell him he will only get a year suspended sentence. Tell him to keep the loot because the Insurance Company already paid off the loss. Make sure there is no one with you. There is to be no violence and no guns."

The Detective Sergeant would follow the Fortune Teller's instructions and make a banner arrest. Another major crime was solved and another Commendation was placed in his Personal File. He paid the Gypsy for her information with money set aside in the Department's Informant Fund.

Joey also visited the same Gypsy Fortune Teller and sought counsel. He told her "I did a safecracking job and got away with the loot? I want to know if I'm going to get caught and will I go to jail?" The Gypsy told him to follow her instructions or he will go to jail for a long stretch. "Be in Al's Deli Saturday evening at eight o'clock. A Detective Sergeant will join you and offer you a proposition. He will have you dead to rights. Cooperate with him and he will plea bargain on your behalf with the District Attorney and the Judge. He will get you a suspended sentence. Don't give up any money. Tell him you spent it on expenses and to pay off huge gambling debts. Don't resist. There is to be no violence and no guns." Joey would follow her instructions and get off free and easy except he had to pay her fee with some of the loot. She was a slick opportunist who worked both sides of the street.

The Detective Sergeant proudly admitted he caught many criminals in the act of committing a crime just by following her predictions. I'm sure there were times she had a sacrificial lamb. There was always the admonishment, "No violence and no guns."

Probably there were times when a burglar confided; "My gang is going to rob the Grand Warehouse on Friday night. Will we get caught?" She accurately predicted they would not be caught because on Friday night, without the criminals knowing it, she'd dispatched the Detective Sergeant and his men to the opposite end of the district to apprehend an insignificant criminal she deliberately lured with her advice.

The bad guys she traded off to the Detective Sergeant one week received preferential guidance and probably more lucrative advice on their next visit. She cleverly worked both parties with her insights into the future. Both sides had faith in her and paid handsomely for her predictions. Neither side suspected she was gouging them. The Detective Sergeant believed her.

How can I be so sure of what really was going on? Well, he talked so fast and told so much anyone could figure it out. He never listened to himself for if he had he would have figured it out. His faith was so intense he couldn't or didn't want to know he was duped. He only accepted what was beneficial to his career.

I never met him again. That was the nature of his job. He was a relief man who was moved to a different location every night. I wished we had met again so he could tell me more about his unusual investigative technique.

THE SNIPER

During the summer and fall of 1952 a sniper terrorized Philadelphia. From ambush he took potshots at unsuspecting people. For months he kept the Philadelphia police busy searching for forensic clues. Glaring headlines kept a count of his attacks. Several people were injured and one person was fatally shot. Philadelphia newspapers printed a running account of the sniper's activities and soon a pattern developed. He usually shot through a kitchen window or rear door window at a woman working in her kitchen. It was while she was preparing supper or washing the dinner dishes. Sometimes he shot through a picture window in the front of the house but it was always at a person in the house and not just to break the window. The city grew tense because it was not known where he'd attack next.

On one occasion the Sniper operated within the boundaries of Lower Merion. A Philadelphia Transportation Co. 'E' bus traveling south on City Line Avenue at Monument Road, Bala was the target of the Sniper. It happened on a fall evening, about 6:00 p.m., when it was dark outside but the interior of the bus was brightly lit. The Sniper shot through a window on the right side as the bus lumbered slowly up a steep grade. A woman was sitting in the middle of the bus at a window seat and the bullet shattered the glass but narrowly missed her. The flying glass slashed her face pretty bad. The Sniper shot at the bus from a position on Monument Road in Lower Merion. This section of the township was undeveloped and Monument Road was a lover's lane type of road with little reason for through traffic.

The Philadelphia police mailed liaison reports of the most recent findings to the surrounding police departments. They kept neighboring departments informed of every clue they obtained from the evidence found at several scenes. They uncovered evidence that the sniper used a .22 caliber automatic pistol and a .22 caliber rifle and that the ammunition and guns were merchandise sold by SEAR.

At 11:30 p.m., four months after the bus shooting, I was patrolling Monument Road. It was a dark night with a light drizzle. Sixty yards west of City Line Avenue and where the bus shooting occurred I came upon an occupied parked car. I quickly assessed my known facts: The ground was wet under the vehicle so it arrived at this spot after the drizzle began to fall; therefore, it wasn't here long. As I drifted closer I saw a man was behind the steering wheel so I parked the patrol car behind the car and cautiously approached the driver.

"Good evening sir. Why are you parked here?" I asked.

"Officer, I had a strenuous day at work and I stopped to rest my nerves and to unwind before I drove home."

"Step out of the car, please." As he stepped out of the car I accidentally on purpose brushed against him. I felt a heavy object in his sport coat pocket.

"What do you have in your pocket?"

"That's a -----" and he was about to reach into the pocket.

"Never mind! I'll get it! Put your hands behind your head!"

I reached into his pocket and withdrew a SEAR brand .22 cal. automatic pistol.

"Put your hands behind you. I'm going to handcuff you." I put his pistol into my pocket and in a flash had my handcuffs on him. I ran my hands over his body for a thorough field frisk. I shone my flashlight into the front seat area of his car and there was nothing on the seat or the floor. I looked into the rear area and on the seat was a folded blanket. I opened the rear door and pulled off the blanket. Under the blanket were a SEAR .22 cal. rifle and a box of SEAR .22 cal. ammunition. I associated the ammunition and the guns with the Sniper and was positive I had captured him. The citizens of Philadelphia would rest easy after they read about it in the morning newspapers.

I asked headquarters for assistance to transport a "man with guns" to headquarters for further investigation. A detective arrived so I placed the man in the detective's car and followed them to headquarters. I never searched the trunk of the man's car because I assumed detectives would conduct a through search at their leisure. It was after 1:00 a.m. when we arrived at headquarters and there was no need for me to stay around. The investigation was now in the capable hands of the Detective Bureau. It was far past my quitting time and I wasn't being paid for overtime so I retrieved my handcuffs and left. There was no need to alarm my wife if she was still awake and worrying about me.

On my way home I gloried in all the praises, kudos, and civic awards that would be showered upon me for my outstanding capture. I rid society of a dangerous menace.

The following day I was working the same 4:00 p.m. to midnight shift and as I drove to work I still had that elated feeling. I expected my peers would greet me and ask for the details. But when I arrived at headquarters no one was there to greet me. I thought that was strange. On a desk a copy of the morning paper was spread out so it would catch my eye. I couldn't believe the bold article that was on the front page. The reporter made a fool out of me.

The reporter said I deprived an innocent citizen the right to practice his trumpet in a secluded section of the township. I couldn't believe there was no reference made of the Sniper. The newspaper account had this fellow with his sheet music spread out before him and his trumpet to his lips. It had to be a ploy. It had to be a trick calculated by the detectives to get this fellow to relax and betray himself.

Not one detective remembered the liaison reports. No one in the newspaper newsroom questioned the reporter's facts. No one from the Philadelphia Police Department related this stupid article to the sniper and delved into it. Was I the only policeman trying to solve the sniper problem? There wasn't a trumpet and sheet music in the passenger compartment of the car. Maybe in the car trunk but I never looked there. I was never asked the reason the man gave me for being parked at that location. I should have inquired into the investigation and the newspaper articles. This incident left me with a much lower regard for the detectives and I lost my yearning to join their ranks. This case along with several others convinced me they were cement-heads.

A concluding word that comforts me; the Sniper was never heard from again after that night.

Trumpeter Needed Gun For Protection While Practicing

As Patrolman Bernard Loughran was making the rounds in Bala Friday night, he came across a young man practicing on a trumpet in a car parked on Monument Rd.

"What goes on here?" asked the officer.

The trumpeter, who said he was [redacted] 25, of Philadelphia, explained that he was not permitted to practice at home.

Loughran frisked him and found a .32 colt automatic in his pocket. "And what's this for?" the officer asked.

"I'm afraid of the dark," the man replied, "so I took the gun along for protection."

McGhee was held in $300 bail for violation of the uniform firearms act.

No Peace for McGhee

Solo Trumpeter Throttled As Bala's Brass Horns In

THE [illegible] that once through Bala's woods [illegible] all the birds awake was stilled last night, and [redacted] who was armed to the teeth against anti-trumpet fanatics who might seek to throttle him, was in bad with The Law.

[redacted] stood there yesterday at his hearing before Justice of the Peace Edward S. Murray, Jr., in Lower Merion township as living proof that nobody could practice on the trumpet, anywhere, any time, without being molested. It is a wonder trumpet players do not become extinct.

For the place where [redacted], a 25-year-old electrical engineer, chose to blow the trumpet—a little patch of woods near Monument and Glen rds. in Bala—was as remote as he could get, short of leaving the State. And the time he chose would bother nobody but the chickadees—11 o'clock Thursday night.

* * *

BUT as he sat there in the back of his car, with the [illegible] shining down on the [illegible] stuck in a potable [illegible] attached to the front [illegible] car rushed up the [illegible] of the bad place [illegible] Patrolman Bernard Lochran jumped out to demand what it was all about.

"I am just practicing [illegible] the trumpet," [redacted] replied meekly.

"A likely story," replied the [illegible] liceman. "Let us see your driver's license."

And then Lochran spied a rifle propped beside John.

"Ah, ha!" he said triumphantly. "What have we here?"

* * *

"IT'S for protection." [redacted] replied, but he was lost, and he knew it. People may say they would like to kill trumpet players, but none has ever been known to go far enough to require the hornist to go around armed. Lochran did a quick frisk, and found a revolver in John's pocket.

The unhappy [redacted] went on to explain more fully. He lives, he pointed out, in a rooming house on Pomona st. near Germantown ave. He knows an embryo trumpet player is not loved, so when he got his trumpet two years ago, he decided to blow. Rather than wait to be asked, he went to the great outdoors to practice. For a while he practiced in the dead of the night, far from human habitation, on a Ridge [illegible] One night a police car came along [illegible] The police didn't search him, [illegible] they were skeptical anybody would be blasting the air at that time of night.

"They made me play a piece to show them," he said.

It was no use. Patrolman Lochran locked him up and yesterday Murray held him in $300 bail on a charge of violating the firearms act.

Mad Sniper of 1950s Still Free

By ASH___. ? HALSEY 3d
Of The Bulletin Staff

He used a .22-caliber carbine (a rifle) not as awesome as "Son of Sam's" .44-caliber revolver, but equally capable of killing, maiming and plunging a large city into fear.

The unknown man, who wore a slouch hat pulled down over his eyes, terrorized Philadelphia more than 25 years ago, yet in retrospect, he rates only as a minor-league terrorist. He killed one person and wounded s__ __hers.

Yesterday morning, the latest city terrorist, New York's "Son of Sam," struck down his 12th and 13th victims (five dead and eight wounded), giving him a deadlier reputation than his earlier Philadelphia counterpart.

But, even so, in the more tranquil time of the early 1950s, before terrorism became commonplace, the man in the slouched hat produced about as much fear in Philadelphia as "Son of Sam" has in New York.

Unlike the New York slayer, who supplies cryptic notes, the slouch-hat killer let his actions speak for themselves. Since he wouldn't give himself a name, the police found one for him — they tagged him the "Mad Sniper."

He may still walk the streets of Philadelphia, for despite a massive manhunt, he has never been caught.

Claire Cohen, a 28-year-old mother of two toddlers, was washing dishes in her parents' comfortable Oak Lane home when the Mad Snipers' bullets cracked through the kitchen window pane and ripped into her back and stomach.

She screamed and staggered into the living room where her husband and parents sat.

"Something burst inside me," she shouted as she slumped to the floor.

Claire Cohen died less than an hour later. It was eight days before Christmas in 1950.

Mrs. Cohen, the wife of a junior high school teacher, was the sniper's seventh and final victim, and the only person shot to death by the sniper. The six others struck by his bullets survived.

It was the murder of Mrs. Cohen that opened the floodgates of fear.

Mayor Bernard Samuel ordered Safety Director Samuel Rosenberg to use "every facility at your command" to track down the sniper.

Rosenberg launched one of the biggest manhunts in the city's history, sending 180 policemen to the area where the people had been shot. Squad cars patrolled the streets and a policeman was assigned to patrol each block in the neighborhood.

The police were joined by 50 vigilantes who cruised the streets, tailing suspicious looking cars and peering into back alleys.

While "Son of Sam" has been selective in his search for victims, appearently seeking out long-haired women, the sniper seemed to choose his victims at random. The six people he shot in the month-long spree prior to the murder of Mrs. Cohen included two men, two women and two boys.

A 26-year-old man shot in the arm while working in the yard of a Cheltenham Township steel tube company.

The wife of a rookie policeman was hit in the ankle by a bullet as she waited for a bus at Broad st. and 66th st.

A housewife was wounded in the hip as she walked down Chelten ave.

A 22-year-old Oak Lane man fell wounded on the sidewalk.

The sniper's two youngest targets were a 16-year-old high school student and an eight-year-old Elkins Park boy. The younger boy was shot in the arm while riding his tricycle.

None of his victims could describe the shadowy figure who had shot them.

Following the murder of Mrs. Cohen, police appealed for help in hunting the sniper. They were swamped with tips as many fearful city residents began to see a gunman behind every sign post.

There was momentary relief in the city when a suspect was arrested two days after Mrs. Cohen's murder. But his alibi stuck and he was released after questioning.

The police kept coming up empty-handed.

The tension began to wane with the passing weeks as the sniper failed to strike again.

From time to time a possible lead would hit the headlines, but each quickly faded.

"One of the men the officers bring in will be the right one," said a confident detective lieutenant working on the case. "He can't fight shy of us forever."

But, apparently, the "Mad Sniper" has done just that.

A Philadelphia Bulletin Staff member wrote this article more than twenty-five years after the night I came upon the questionable trumpet player. By then I was retired ten years.

THE ITINERANTS

Officer Charlie Sweep grew crotchety waiting for the forced retirement age. He already gave forty of his best years to serving the public. Those less acquainted with him may have thought he only had serrated edges but I thought he was an exceptional man. He was sixty-four years old and I was twenty-two. We worked the same hours but only met on the hour at the police call box to make a pull.

Lancaster Avenue in 1948 was the only route connecting the east coast with the west coast and because of the vast number of travelers on this road there was bound to be bizarre happenings. A subculture of impoverished people was always in transit. They hitchhiked or drove old dilapidated Junkers and were constantly on the move.

Mobile farm workers following the crops used this road. One day they were on a New Jersey farm and weeks later they'd be on a farm somewhere in the west. After one crop was harvested they moved to wherever another crop was ready to be picked. Transients on foot were seldom a police problem. They were innocent people exhausted by hard work. They were tired in body and spirit and down on their luck. Cold, penniless and hungry they stopped wherever there was a dry niche to sleep in for the night.

One scorching summer afternoon Charlie and I had just met at the police call box when two cars traveling east on Lancaster Avenue stopped for a red traffic signal. A frail frayed rope tied to the rear bumper of the first car pulled the car behind it. When these cars came to a stop at the red traffic signal the engine in the towing car stopped dead and refused to start again. This was the worse calamity that could occur on this busy main highway. The driver cranked the motor but it refused to turn over. A major traffic jam was rapidly developing.

I had no idea what a policeman could do to correct this problem nor a clue as to what Charlie might be planning. These cars were old relics. The lead car was a LaSalle that was once a large luxury limousine but out of production for years. It was towing a Hubmobile that was also a large luxury car out of production. The car being towed acted the role of a trailer. Every possession this family owned was in or strapped on the two cars. Chairs, tables, clothes, rugs and boxes were tied on their roofs. These were monstrous cars and capable of bearing a heavy load when they were in their prime.

In the lead car was a young couple; itinerant farmers with two beautiful children under the age of seven. They were the poorest looking kids yet the cutest I ever saw. Their clothes were tattletale gray after being worn too long without a good scrubbing and their adorable faces were unwashed. Their hair was filthy and matted but golden and would become soft as silk if shampooed and brushed. The driver looked like a frightened turtle pulling his head back into his shell when he saw two policemen hovering over him. His young wife looked like a life of stress and arduous work had sapped the prettiness and youth from her face. This was a real life "Grapes of Wrath" scene. Anyone of us would look that ratty if we traveled a great distance under the same conditions.

From a policeman's perspective the vehicles were health hazards and shouldn't be on the road. They wouldn't pass inspection, the license plates had expired and the tires were tread bare. These people couldn't pay the fines if all the violations were levied against them. They would be financially bankrupt. They never possessed the sum of money needed to pay all the fines. The parents would be committed to the county prison and the children placed in foster homes.

I hadn't an inkling of what we should do. Charlie didn't rush to where the cars were stopped and I walked slowly beside him. When we came to the lead vehicle, where the family was seated, Charlie put his head through the open window on the passenger side and after a few soothing words withdrew. He took a step back and slyly removed three one-dollar bills from his pocket. He surreptitiously bent forward to fit his hat through the window again and slid the money into the man's palm. Tenderly he said, "Here Mister, buy the children an ice cream cone." No one saw Charlie's good deed but me.

Charlie stepped back and for the benefit of the nosy spectators and the drivers in the cars stopped in the traffic jam he made a wide arm gesture like a cop does to get slow traffic to pick up the pace and roared, "Get these cars out of here!!!" The haggard young driver was frightened by the cop shouting at him and in desperation pushed the starter button once again. I would have bet 100 to 1 the car wouldn't start but it kicked over. The driver eased the gearshift into low gear and limped away to New Jersey or wherever.

Some observers may say the motor started up on Charlie's command or it was a miracle or a reward from the angels for his generous gift but it was none of that. It was in compliance to the laws of physics. The motor in the lead car had struggled for hours and for many miles with the laborious task of propelling two large cars that were heavily overloaded. On a hot day an engine that is forced to labor for an extended period will become overheated and stalled by a vapor lock and an old battery quickly loses its energy when it is urged over and over again to start a vapor locked engine.

The solution is time. The motor must rest and be allowed time for the vapor lock to dissipate, also, after a brief rest the battery will rejuvenate enough to start the motor. This is what happened in the few minutes it took Charlie and me to stroll slowly to the cars plus the time it took Charlie to perform his generous deed.

This was one of many lessons I learned from Charlie without him even being aware he was tutoring me. From that day on I was an easy touch for every destitute traveler in need of a few shillings for something to eat.

SNOW CHAINS

Hardly is there a person alive who recalls installing snow chains on an automobile tire during a blizzard when their fingers were frostbitten and caked with snow. What a nasty struggle it was. If ignored an improperly installed chain would severely damage a fender. Most motorists today have no idea what snow chains are or their function because over the years snow chains were replaced by snow tires. After a few more years snow tires were upgraded to studded snow tires and after a few more years All Season tires outdated them. Except for utility vehicles, emergency vehicles and snow plows chains are rarely available in auto supply stores.

I used to look forward to the nights it snowed heavily and traveling without chains was almost impossible. Even experienced drivers were stalled on an unplowed road. Automobiles easily skidded into a snow bank or were stranded at the foot of a hill. Chains were a necessity if a driver was to negotiate a grade covered with snow and ice.

I cruised the streets in search of stranded motorists. It wasn't my duty to help them because the department policy forbids an officer to do anything physical with a disabled car. The department didn't want a man injured and laid-up with a long-term disability. However, I was forced into being an opportunist because my salary was less than $3,000 a year. That was damn little even those days.

I had "putting on chains" down to a science. If conditions were right I could install them within ten minutes. Some motorists hadn't the dexterity required to do the job, especially young girls, women and infirmed men. Some drivers never learned how to install them and others might battle for a long time and never adjust them properly.

It was impossible to get a mechanic to respond in the middle of the night for a motorist stranded in a snowstorm. If one was located he demanded twenty-five dollars for the service call plus a hefty fee for installing the chains. Some tow men refused to jeopardize their equipment in a snowstorm.

After I installed a stranded motorist's chains I'd refuse any gratuity but after a brief insistence I'd graciously accept whatever was offered. I expected more than enough "to get my uniform cleaned."

Believe me there was no worse sensation than being stranded in the snow late at night in the middle of nowhere. If the motorist couldn't fix the chains himself then both of us I benefited. Unfortunately not every stranded motorist was generous and appreciated my services. Many thought it was my duty to help them. If I was lucky I came across one, two or three stranded cars a night. I never asked a motorist for money. If none was offered that was Ok too. I felt I did a good deed. But, if the snow continued for two nights I was able to keep the big bad wolf away from my door until the next snowstorm.

TASHU

In Manayunk there was a boy whom I knew by the name Tashu. I first saw him during my elementary school days. We were about the same age but he looked more mature. That may have been because he never wore kid's clothes. He looked strong and tough and older because he wore men's clothes and never took time out to play. He never carried schoolbooks so I assumed he didn't go to school. His gait was peculiar, stiff as a military academy cadet, and my assessment of him was that he was quite strange. My classmates who lived in his neighborhood said he was mentally challenged and that was why he had no schoolmates, playmates or friends.

He walked alone dragging a small wagon on the streets of Manayunk. He was forever in search of discarded refundable soda bottles and beer bottles, old rags, old newspapers, scrap metal and whatever could be sold at a junkyard for small change. My friends said this was the only source of income he and his sick immigrant parents had. No one actually knew his situation because he didn't confide in anyone and since he was a very private person he became mysterious.

He was easily agitated so everyone was afraid to walk near him. He believed anyone who ventured close to his wagon intended to steal his treasured possessions. If a stranger or pedestrian accidentally got close to his wagon he'd fly into a rage and threaten violence. He wandered for miles to find what he could convert to money. His days were long considering a six and eight ounce bottle was redeemed for two cents. A twelve ounce and quart bottle was worth a nickel. Rags and newspapers were pennies a pound.

Our paths never crossed until we were twenty-five years old. I was a police officer three years and he was still pulling his wagon. I was surprised to see him outside of Manayunk and pulling the same wagon on my beat in West Manayunk. He purposely walked within a few feet of my parked patrol car. I couldn't escape so I said, "Hi Tashu."

It was the first time I heard him talk so I braced myself should he fly off the handle. I was stunned when he started on a lengthy tale about himself. It was obvious he was slow but no one said they ever heard him talk. It was a very chilling experience because we were only three feet apart. He stood rigid as a zombie and his eyes were focused over my shoulder on something in infinity. He rarely blinked and paused after each word. He was different but not stupid and he realized he had limitations. I was uneasy only because of the fear my schoolmates instilled. They instructed me to avoid him at all cost and now I was wishing there was more space between us. I didn't want to arouse him so I froze my face so I wouldn't make him mad. Why he told me about himself I don't know but he told me this.

"I once was a beautiful child. I went to school and I was a good student. One day I was on my way home from school at lunchtime. I was crossing the street near my home when a Philadelphia police car sped around the corner and ran into me. The two cops picked me up and drove me home. They hollered at my parents for not watching over me better. My parents don't speak English and didn't understand. They were told they couldn't sue the city for my medical bills. Six months later my parents got a bill from the city for the damage I did to the police car. I was in the third grade. I went to school but the nun asked my mother to keep me home because I scared the other kids."

That explained why he was different and it reinforced my thinking that I must give him a wide berth the next time I see him, that is if I'm in uniform. There was no way I could check the validity of his story so I accepted it as the truth. I do remember being taught that the city could not be sued. English Common Law stipulated "The King could not be sued nor could he be held responsible for the misconduct of his representatives." That isn't the law today because the city of Philadelphia is frequently sued for the wrongful acts of its police officers.

I never expected to meet Tashu again but a long separation was not to be for our paths crossed a week later. It was on the construction site of a high-rise office building. I patrolled by that building project and noticed the construction progressing. I saw the concrete foundation and sub-basements being poured and I saw a huge crane raise the steel girders that were to be the skeleton but I never saw Tashu on the premise collecting the soda bottles that were discarded by the workmen.

The steel girder erectors saw that Tashu would go to great lengths to salvage a discarded soda bottle. These men after years of training, practice and conditioning became accustomed to great heights and they knew how to walk on the narrow I-beams. It took them years to be able to guide girders into place and fasten them together. However, instead of them throwing their empty soda bottles to the ground they purposely set them on the highest girder in plain view for Tashu to see.

Every few days the steel framework rose another floor so Tashu had to climb higher and higher. He must have amazed the professionals. At this stage of their skill there was no need for ladders, planks or safety nets. Tashu had no girder climbing training yet he forged ahead ignoring all safety precautions just to garner another precious two-cent bottle. The construction workers didn't exercise good judgment when they toyed with him. They just kept testing to see how high he would climb.

The General Foreman saw what the erectors were up to so he approached Tashu intending to chase him off the property but Tashu was not to be deterred. After daily warnings to stay off the girders the intimidated General Foreman took the only recourse left to him, he called the cops. It was my beat so I was dispatched. The radio operator's message was brief, "Car #15. There is a trespasser on the Jacobson construction site."

As I drove to the site I imagined all sorts of scenarios and how I would conduct myself in each case. If it is a union dispute such as a union boss shutting down the job, what should I do? If it is a fired employee refusing to leave the job, what should I do? I was on my own in a patrol car with no experience in these matters.

The General Foreman greeted me at the opening in the cyclone fence that surrounded the property. At the same time I saw Tashu standing akimbo about a hundred feet behind him. Tashu had the meanest and most vicious scowl I ever encountered. His non-blinking eyes pierced us like laser beams. My first thought was, "Oh my gosh! Tashu! I'm in for a challenge. This means real trouble."

The foreman explained that Tashu was climbing on the girders to retrieve the empty soda bottles. He tried to chase him off the property but Tashu refused to leave and returns every day. He was afraid for Tashu's safety because he climbed over the I-beams with his arms full of bottles. The beams were up to the fourth floor and it seems he would be around when the structure reached the eleventh floor. The Foreman said Tashu ignores his warnings so he resorted to requesting police assistance.

As the Foreman spoke my thoughts strayed. Did Tashu crawl on all fours across the I-beams or did he walk upright as he saw the construction workers get around? I pulled my thoughts together and asked myself how was I going to get a message across to him. It would take tact, diplomacy and self-control if I were to remain in command of the situation. Without a trace of hostility I told the General Foreman not to follow me. I walked to where Tashu stood snarling at us. I knew he had prepared an argument but I threw him off balance. Instead of yelling at him I said in a calm friendly voice, "Good afternoon Tashu. The General Foreman told me you are trespassing on private property. He said nobody but the workers are allowed inside the fenced area."

Tashu exploded, "I don't have to listen to you!"

I didn't react. I remained composed and sympathetic. "Tashu, if you don't stay off this private property you will be arrested and you will have to pay a fine or go to jail. If you go to jail who will take care of your sick mother and father?"

He was so incensed I feared he'd attack me. His chin quivered from hate as he shouted, "I know you cops. You want the bottles and get the money for yourself!"

I didn't say another word because I figured I gave him enough to think about. Instead I turned around and walked back to the foreman. The foreman knew how vicious Tashu's reaction could be so he had stayed far away from us. He didn't want to be involved in anything that could get him hurt.

I wanted to act like an experienced police officer so I didn't give him an explanation I just assured him, "He won't be back." Then I said loud enough for Tashu to hear, "If he comes back give headquarters another phone call."

I glanced up to the fourth floor and saw the steel workers standing upright on the narrow I-beams wondering how I handled the situation. They were too far away to overhear what was said. Maybe they were jeering among themselves because I was a spoilsport. They looked like ugly gargoyles annoyed because I put an end to their fun. I tried to get a feel as to whose side they would be on if Tashu decided to tussle.

I took my time getting into the police car because I wanted to give my remarks time to assemble into Tashu's thoughts. I coasted out of the fence enclosure and eased down the road waiting to see what was going to happen. I took a sly peek in the rearview mirror and saw Tashu and his wagon leaving the construction site too. Case closed.

Headquarters required a status report so I keyed on the radio transmitter and said, "Car #15 to Headquarters. The trespasser left the property." I never saw Tashu again.

THE MARINE PFC.

Just after dinner on a day in October 1952 an excited radio voice ordered me to respond to a report of a shooting. I drove the patrol car as fast as I could to the address and met a man who said his neighbor, a marine home on leave, was shooting a deer rifle at his family. He pointed to the marine sitting on the doorstep outside the front of his home and he had the rifle across his lap. Within minutes several backup officers arrived on the scene.

It was already dark so I took the half-mile-ray light from my patrol car and got two more from the other patrol cars. I positioned the beams directly into the fellow's eyes hoping the bright spotlights would blind him. If he was blinded it would give us police officers an advantage and it would also provide some protection for the spectators gathering on the sidewalk. He was about a hundred feet from the street so before his eyes adjusted to the lights I crawled on all fours behind a low hedge and slipped behind him.

I entered his house through the rear kitchen door and tiptoed to the front door. In the light of the half-mile-rays I saw him sitting on the doorstep with the rifle across his lap. Seconds counted so without hesitating I lunged through the open door. I gauged my leap to take me above him and calculated my landing would pin him and his rifle down. If I was quick and if he didn't see me my plan would work. But he did see me when I was in mid-flight.

He had been facing the street but upon seeing me flying through the air he spun the rifle around with the intention of shooting me down like a clay pigeon. He was intoxicated and his sharp reflexes were sorely affected. He pulled the trigger prematurely the moment his rifle was pointing at his own chest and as I fell upon him. The blast from the rifle was ear piercing and the bullet shattered his heart. He was dead before he inhaled another breath of the cool night air.

The rifle blast shocked me but I quickly collected my wits and rose to my feet to assess my own physical well-being. There was a tremendous amount of blood splattered over the doorway and over the both of us. My uniform, hands and face were covered with his blood. I was so close to the blast and there was so much blood I couldn't help but think I was struck by the bullet. I padded my torso to be sure.

The marine was still sitting upright with his eyes open wide. He had a fixed gaze that seemed to regret what he had just done. Ten feet from him lay his wife and father-in-law whom he had killed minutes before his neighbor telephoned the police.

The police report read, "Double murder and suicide."

Berserk Marine Veteran Fires At Relatives And Neighbors As Lower Merion Police Close In

The final curtain will descend tomorrow on the scene of one of West Manayunk's most sorrowful tragedies.

Funeral services will be held today and tomorrow for ███

All three met their death early Saturday night as the West Manayunk soldier and former Marine went on a shooting rampage which ended when he took his own life with the deer rifle used in the double killing.

███████████████████████ left parentless by the tragedy. They are now being cared for by their 89 year-old grandmother, who was widowed by the shooting.

The mad spree started as the family prepared to go to the movies. ███████████████████ had gathered at the elder ███████ home at ███████████████ for a cup of dog food while the others waited in a car parked outside.

███████████ who was home on a three-day pass from Fort Smith, Va., was inside the house. After a few moments young Kenneth came running out crying 'Daddy won't be mommy go?'

At ███████████ went into the house and was leaving with the ███████ Army man picked up a rifle and shot his wife in the back. She fell on a small front porch of the bungalow.

███████████ and her husband then fled to the safety of their home as bullets pelted their house. ███████ was taken into a nearby house during the shooting.

Meanwhile, the elder Marshall started up the ████ steps to his daughter's aid. He was killed at close range by a single shot fired by the expert rifleman.

By this time, the neighborhood was in an uproar and ███████████ telephoned Lower Merion Township police. Squad cars were despatched to the scene led by Sgt. Francis Pyle. Patrolmen Bernard Loughran, George Drash, Russel Raffa and Herbert Dupee surrounded the house. Loughran and Dupee forced their way into the kitchen as Pyle, Drash and Raffa closed in on the front.

███████ shouted at Loughran and Dupee, "I hear you back there." As the officers drew closer ███████ ran to the front porch, propped the stock of the gun against the railing and put a bullet into his left breast. He died instantly.

No adequate explanation could be given for the soldier's mad outburst, although it was precipitated by his suspicion over his wife's insistence on going to the movies.

Capt. William H. Shaffer, head of Lower Merion Township Detectives, closed the case with the notation, double homicide—no prosecution because of suicide or murderer.

███████ who is now caring for the two parentless boys, said, "I have these two little children, I hope and wish, God's help I will do it."

She said her son-in-law was a changed man after his return from the Pacific where he spent three and a half years with the Marines during World War II.

"He was moody at times and wouldn't go to church as he did formerly," she added. He used to tell me 'They preach in churches 'Thou Shalt Not Kill,' and then during the war we were told to go out and kill."

During the week when ███████ was at camp the family lived with the elder ███████████. When he returned on weekends they lived in their own home across the street.

On World-wide Communion Sunday, October 1, ███████ became a member of First Presbyterian Church in Manayunk. She took an active interest in the affairs of the church and on numerous occasions was in charge of the nursery of the church held in conjunction with the morning service.

With the two recent wars as background setting for the tragedy, neighbors also revealed undertones of marital difficulties between the couple during the past six months.

As the excitement died away on Saturday night, a shocked silence prevailed over the community of West Manayunk.

███████ days later ███████ commented, "It just doesn't seem possible that what has happened has actually happened, it is more like something you would read about in a book. It is so unreal."

A combined funeral will be held for ███████████████ and her father, ███████ Sr., at 1 p. m. ████████████████ Chestnut street. Dr. Chris DiPietro, pastor of First Presbyterian Church, Manayunk, and Dr. John O'Hara, former pastor of the Ashland Ave-

THE ARSONIST

The Autocar Truck Factory fire was the larger fire but in terms of property damage the Bryon and Carlo Moving and Storage Warehouse fire was far greater. Flames fed by the flammable contents stored in the warehouse raged on for two days. A volunteer fireman high up on a ladder was overcome by smoke and fell to his death. Investigators suspected arson but they couldn't conceive who would do such a dastardly deed.

Four hours after the first alarm was sounded I received a radio message directing me to investigate a prankster tampering with a police call box on River Road. As I sped to the call box I expected I'd apprehend a juvenile vandalizing the equipment but instead a weary man was standing there waiting for me.

He said he was Mr. Bryon and it was he who set the Bryon and Carlo Warehouse on fire. He told me he had wandered aimlessly for hours pondering the consequences and the rationale of his act. He grew exhausted and decided to telephone the police. On our drive to headquarters I informed him he didn't have to tell me anything but if he did I would repeat it in court if I were asked. He released me of any confidentiality. By sharing his burden with me he hoped he might get some emotional relief. He unveiled this story.

He began by saying he was the son of the deceased cofounder of the storage business. Over a long period of time he had become distraught because young Mr. Carlo, son of the other deceased cofounder, was introducing new business tactics he couldn't accept or condone. Young Mr. Carlo was ruthless with their faithful customers and scurrilous toward him. Mr. Carlo had already initiated steps to take over the business and force him out altogether.

Mr. Bryon said he was burdened with thoughts of vengeance and retaliation. For months he couldn't eat, sleep or go to church knowing he harbored this hate. His anger and contempt ate away at him and drove him insane. He'd rather terminate the business than have the family's reputation besmirched. He knew of no other way to end the partnership and at the same time get revenge.

I placed him under arrest and charged him with the crime of arson, a felony. Based on his voluntary confession on our ride to police headquarters he was found guilty and sentenced to five years in the county prison.

Million Dollar Revenge Blaze Roars; Suspect Surrenders in W. Manayunk

A .... walk from Bryn
Mawr to ..... Manayunk while
a .... he allegedly
.... behind him gave
.... to of San Mar-
.... Bryn Mawr, time to
.... upon the revenge that
....

At ..... of a mile hike
.... River Rd. he
.... and his flight He
...... quietly into a gasoline
.... conducted by
James .... at Belmont
...... Jefferson St.

The ...... may lubrica-
ting an automobile, didn't see
the .... present was
..... by .... Jusly Waters
of 48 Rd., who were seated in
their car. ....
.... won the pedestrian
.... stood in the office of
the ...... station.

The ...... made to the pro-
...... a moment later was the
.... most startling he
...... heard in his years of op-

erating a sense station.

"Do me a favor, will you?"
implied the stranger.

"What is it"

"Call the police and tell
them I'm her. They are looking for me."

Pleads for Police

.... pressed
for a reason, he said ......
peared nervous and depressed,
declined to say why he was
wanted by police. He also refused to give his name, but he
was adamant in his desire to
be taken into custody.

The service station operator
subsequently obliged.

...... finally decided to disclose his reason for wanting to
be taken to headquarters when
he was arrested by Patrolman
Bernard Loughran, son of
Thomas Loughran, 187 Belmont
Ave., a veteran Lower Merion
patrolman.

Police said that ...... apparently crossed Lancaster Ave.,

wandered around until he
reached River Rd., north of
Flat Rock dam, and then walked along that quiet road until
he arrived at Belmont Ave.
There, looking for a place to
telephone police and give himself up, he saw the lights of
the gasoline station.

...... who has been op-
erating the station at that corner for six years, said, "Nothing
like this ever happened to me
before."

The accused man told police
he "wanted to give the Christ-
ies a headache."

Charged with arson and lar-
ceny, ... was committed
Thursday by Magistrate Robert
Riethmuller, Ardmore, to the
Montgomery County prison in
Norristown to await action of
the Grand Jury. The defendant
pleaded not guilty.

Faces New Charge

Lower Merion detectives said
that ...... will also be re-

Continued on Page Six

I CAME ACROSS MANY STRANGE NAMES

I asked so many people to identify themselves it can be certain I came across many non-traditional names. One example was the fellow I stopped for speeding and he produced a driver's license, registration card and an automobile insurance card that proved his name was Seldom Banks. Odd names became routine and I accepted them after the person produced proof. I often wished I kept a list just for laughs. I also came upon a man who never had a surname.

He was a black man from the Deep South. It was 1954 and I met him at the scene of an accident. He drove a truck hauling lumber to a construction site. The General Foreman instructed him to unload the lumber in a place where it was awkward for the truck to get to. The truck became bogged down in freshly excavated soil but the driver kept trying to extricate the vehicle. No matter how he tried to prevent it its wheels only spun wildly and sank deeper into the mud. Finally the truck slid erratically out of control down an embankment and into a huge crane. There was damage to the equipment and to the truck so the General Forman called for the police. It was on my beat so I was dispatched.

The first step in my investigation was to ask the driver to produce identification.

"I don't have any, Sa," he said.

"Do you have a driver's license?" I asked.

"No, Sa."

"What is your name?"

"Henry, Sa."

"Henry? Henry who?"

"That's the onliest name I got, Sa."

"What is your last name?"

"I aint never had no last name, Sa."

"How old are you?"

"I'm ninety-three years old, as best as I knowed, Sa."

He could easily be ninety-three years old. Even though he had a strenuous job driving a lumber truck his face and body were proof he had lived through many tough decades. His body was agile and his mind was sharp and clear as a bell so there was no reason for me to doubt he wasn't ninety-three years of age.

I did some mental calculations and if he was ninety-three he was born before the Civil War began. Slaves didn't have family names until after the war ended and then they adopted any surname they chose. It was possible this fellow's family never took a last name. Evidently he never needed one or didn't know how to obtain one. Apparently he got along fine without a last name until now.

I wasn't going to encumber myself with an additional investigation to ascertain if Henry was telling the truth unless I wanted to nail him to the wall.

My professional inclination was to prosecute the lumber company for allowing an unlicensed person to drive their truck but after some soul searching I felt they should be given a Humanitarian Award for giving a man ninety-three years of age a job.

Something Rotten About This Story Of Cop's Plight

Patrolman Bernard Loughran was patrolling Lancaster Ave. in Wynnewood Monday afternoon when he spotted a man walking along the highway.

Loughran decided to make a routine check of the fellow and pulled his patrol car alongside the man.

"Hey buddy," Loughran called, "what's your name?"

"Rotten Hamburger," the stranger spoke up.

"All right, wise guy," Loughran said, "I asked you a simple question, how about giving me a simple answer. Now, what's your name?"

"Rotten Hamburger," was the fellow's laconic reply.

"Before I take you off to headquarters for insulting the dignity of an officer of the law," the indignant policeman snorted, "let's try once more. What's your name?"

"Rotten Hamburger."

"Prove it," Loughran snapped.

The stranger dug into his pocket, produced a wallet and withdrew identification. Sure enough, his name was Rotten Hamburger, a resident of Washington, D. C., bent on hitchhiking his way back home.

I FLEW THROUGH THE AIR

One night (1956) I was driving my patrol car south on City Line Avenue and came upon a car parked between W. Wynnewood Road and Lancaster Avenue. I could see the driver was slumped behind the steering wheel. It was 3:00 a.m. so there were numerous possibilities. The driver might be drunk, he may be asleep, he might have had a heart attack, he may be ill or he could be a burglar with an accomplice prowling the neighborhood. I decided to investigate.

I pulled my patrol car to the curb in front of the parked car but before I opened my car door I checked on the flow of traffic. There was a cluster of headlights a half-mile away traveling toward me at a reasonable speed so they were no threat to my safety. I exited my car and walked back to check on the driver. As I arrived at his front door the cluster of cars sped passed where I stood. There were five cars and all the drivers evidently saw our two parked cars and me because they gave us a wide berth. That is, all but the fifth driver. He plowed into the left rear fender of the parked car with his right front fender. The impact slowed him down but the momentum kept his car moving forward and it hit me and tossed me up into the air like I was pizza dough. I came down on the hood of the car while it was still in motion. I slid off the hood onto the roadway and lay there flat on my back. I was helpless and scared waiting for the car to come to a stop over me.

Lady Luck was with me. I hadn't any broken bones or bruises and miraculously neither driver was injured. I had to submit an accident report so I asked the driver of the car that struck me why the accident happened. He said he was following the cars in front of him but didn't realize he was asleep at the wheel. When the cars in front of him veered away from the curb lane to the center lane to avoid the parked cars he didn't react because he was asleep.

I asked the driver of the parked car his reason for being parked at this location. He said he had been driving for three hours and grew eye weary so he pulled to the side of the road to take a short nap. He said he assumed he would be safer on a main thoroughfare under a streetlight.

CALL A PLUMBER

At 3:30 a.m. one January night in 1957 I was dispatched via radio to a three-story mansion address. The lady of the house telephoned headquarters and reported the hot water tank in the basement was leaking and she didn't know how to turn off the water. She said she tried everything. She even telephoned a plumber but he bluntly told her he didn't make house calls in the middle of the night and she could call back in the morning. She was desperate so she called the police. Police officers aren't plumbers yet they are expected to have the solution to every emergency in their hip pocket and the right tools in their arsenal.

Because of the urgency I responded quickly. She explained her husband was a salesman out of town on business and that she had shut off the main water supply valve but the water kept flowing out of the boiler onto the basement floor. I diagnosed the problem and ascertained the source of the water was from the hot water heater like she said. The cellar floor was covered with two inches of water and like most cellars it was used for storage so there were many items floating about.

As fate would have it I didn't bring my boots to work because moisture wasn't predicted in the weather forecast so I removed my shoes and socks and rolled up my pants and went into the shallow lake. It was a large house so a confusing number of pipes hung from the joists and were strapped on the walls. All old houses had many pipes added over the years to accommodate a new powder room or a new appliance. It was difficult to determine which valve controlled what because there were so many.

It suddenly dawned on me that the water was draining back into the tank through the hot water pipes that fed the radiators on the upper floors. I quickly closed the valve that let the cold water into the boiler and the one that let the hot water out of the tank. To my surprise, and the woman's relief, the leaking water stopped. That took care of her problem until a plumber came in the morning.

She asked me to help her get the water out of her basement but I told her that would take all night. It wasn't an emergency and it didn't have to be done right away nor did I have the time. I was sure the plumber would have a suction pump that could remove the water quickly and without much effort.

I put my socks and shoes on and returned to routine patrol but before my feet were thoroughly dry I was dispatched to the scene of a house fire. I took up a post at a busy intersection to detour traffic but since my feet and socks were still wet I caught the worse head cold I ever had in my life. I didn't take any days off sick but I had a persistent cough, runny nose, fever and headache that patent medicine couldn't relieve. I was wretchedly sick until mid summer when I gradually began to feel like myself.

THE COAL PILE

On a nasty February afternoon in 1958 my partner and I began our tour of duty patrolling in #15 Car. At 4:00 p.m. we started out in a light snow shower but by 6:00 p.m. I was driving through a blizzard. It was impossible to cruise the streets because the car's headlights reflected back off the white blanket of snow like there was a huge mirror in front of us. Driving was tedious and dangerous because the roadway markings were obliterated and the curbs outlining the width of the roads were obscured. The prudent thing was to park the car and not move unless we were dispatched on an emergency. I selected a safe spot on Old Belmont Avenue facing the Reading Railroad tracks. The tracks were ten feet above the road on an earthen bank and on the far side of the tracks were three silos used by the Glen Willow Coal and Ice Company to store coal.

We were snug as bugs in a rug in our warm patrol car for less than ten minutes when I spotted a man standing on the tracks about sixty yards from us. He was almost impossible to see through the falling snow but obviously the fellow had a nefarious reason for braving the foul weather. Pedestrians never used the tracks so thinking like typical policemen we assumed he was up to no good. He could be a lookout for an accomplice burglarizing the Glen Willow office on the opposite side of the railroad bank and out of our line of sight.

Reluctantly we left our cozy car and stepped into the cold, white, wet night. We began our investigation by clawing our way to the top of the snow-covered bank to the tracks. Climbing the bank was extremely difficult because every time we were about to reach the tracks we lost our footing and slid on our bellies down to where we started. This was repeated several times but we persevered and together we reached the top. I cautiously slinked to where I first saw the man but he had disappeared.

My partner followed footprints going in the opposite direction that were left by an accomplice. The telltale footprints in the snow rapidly filled up or blew away so we had to hurry. I ran as fast as I could to close the gap between the lookout and myself. His trail led me to each door and window around the office building. He was looking for an easy way to enter but didn't find one. His wet footprints led to beneath the coal silos. They were visible on the dry concrete but suddenly vanished.

The silos were built on stilts so a coal delivery truck could be driven underneath and be loaded from above by opening a trapdoor that held the coal in the silo until it was needed. However, there was a mountain of coal in the shape of a volcano eight feet high below one silo. The trapdoor was purposely opened to let all the coal fall out onto the cement apron. I searched the perimeter of this coal pile for footprints but there were none. The rascal couldn't disappear into thin air so he had to be hiding in the center of the volcano.

I never climbed a coal pile before but I quickly learned it is not easy. It is similar to climbing a sand dune. Every time I advanced upward a few feet the coal collapsed and I slid back down to the base of the volcano. Eventually I reached the top and there in the center of the crater was the man I was looking for. I placed him under arrest and charged him with the theft of coal and trespassing on private property with the intent to commit a felony.

Before we spotted him he had unlatched the trapdoor and let the coal fall out of the silo so he and his brother could leisurely steal it by the bucketful after he burglarized the office.

During the bitter depression, not many years before this night, coal was a precious commodity. The families who lived near this coal company were so impoverished they swallowed their pride and picked the coal that spilled off the coal cars traveling into the city from the upstate coalmines. Often a compassionate freight train fireman would toss a shovel full or two off the train as it sped through a poor village. The grateful residents would pick only the coal that was lying along the tracks. That coal was for the taking but no one blatantly stole it by the bucket.

My partner caught up to my man's brother and without any guilty conscience we placed them both under arrest because there was no need for them to steal coal any more. The depression era had passed and they were not destitute. They both, and their father too, had jobs with the township just like my partner and me.

This is a 1952 Chevy sedan patrol car; notice the 6" emergency light on the roof. It didn't have a siren. The lettering on the front doors states it is a police car. Officer Joe Crooks is 53 years old and a police officer for 30 years. I am 25 years old with 3 years experience.

A BARN IS ON FIRE!!

The year was 1952 and it was 3:00 a.m.. I was cruising solo in a countrified area of former small farms. Rarely does anything happen in this corner of the township but what does occur usually is of a serious nature because after dark this area is off the beaten path. A murder could be committed on one of these unlit rural roads and no one would know about it before daylight. Burglars hunt for neighborhoods like this because there is open space between the houses. A car thief could dismantle a car or take one from a driveway without disturbing a soul.

I was alert as any twenty-six year old policeman could be at three o'clock in the morning. I was wishing for an interruption that might have a hint of excitement but without a lot of fuss. I hadn't enough experience to handle all possibilities yet a little adventure would be a welcomed interlude in the monotonous cruising.

My wish was granted when I spotted a flickering flame in a barn that was two hundred feet from the road. It was almost impossible to see from a moving car. If there wasn't a full moon I might not have even seen the barn but it was a clear bright moonlit night and the barn was silhouetted. It was only a faint shimmering glow but I knew flames and barns are definitely incompatible. Without wasting valuable time investigating the source of the flame I picked up the radio transmitter and informed headquarters, "The barn on the Ramsey Estate is on fire. It's going pretty good. Send the local fire department. Telephone the house and alert the owner and occupants, if they are home. The house is listed in the vacant house file."

The owner is a popular politician so headquarters and the fire department knew the location without me giving them an address.

I drove up the long driveway and parked a safe distance from the barn. I didn't want the paint on the police car to be scorched or pitted by falling embers. I hurried into the barn to see what might be in there. It was the first time I rushed into a burning building and I found it a frightening experience that I wouldn't want to repeat.

The barn was small, about twenty-five by thirty-five feet. One side of the floor and loft was chock full of bales of hay and loose straw. Lying in a straw nest was a hen and her chicks. There were two piglets, two young goats, and a cat with a litter of kittens. All the animals were awake and staring at the burning embers that dripped from the rafters like raindrops. Straw and dust crackled everywhere, especially overhead on the rafters.

A spark shower is an amazing phenomenon. I never saw or heard of anything like it. It reminded me of Fourth of July sparklers. The animals were in awe too because they made no attempt to leave their nests. My thoughts ran in all directions. I didn't panic but I didn't know what I should do first. I shouted at the animals, "OK, everybody up! Hit the deck! Let's go, everybody out! Fall out!"

A few animals strolled leisurely out the door followed by their young but they weren't fast enough to satisfy me. I picked up the little piglets and carried them outside. I hurried back in and chased the goats and the hen and chicks out. Some of the animals I had already chased out returned to their nest. It was a losing battle.

I gave up on the young animals because they weren't paying attention. Besides them there were the two horses standing quietly in their stalls. The dripping embers didn't alarm them because the flames hadn't reached their side of the barn yet. I grabbed a bridle and tugged hard but the horse refused to budge. I slapped its rump a few times but to no avail. I went to the second horse and tugged away at it but it was just as stubborn. I couldn't get either of them to stir. The flames and the smoke terrified me so I abandoned the horses and when outside for a breath of smoke free air. I stared at the barn feeling powerless and incompetent because I didn't know how to save the helpless animals.

It didn't take long for the fire trucks to come roaring up the long driveway. I marveled at how quickly they responded. Half dozen vehicles arrived with enough manpower to squelch a raging forest fire. I salute them for their loyalty to the citizens of the township at that hour of the night. I shouted to the firemen hanging onto the side of the first truck, "Two horses and some small animals are in there!" Two fearless firemen jumped off the moving truck and ran inside the barn. Within seconds they were leading out the two horses. I was impressed!

There was an above ground swimming pool in the yard near the barn and that water was used to douse the fire. Their training was evident because the fire only burnt a few the bales of straw. It could have easily destroyed the barn and spread to the house. Their quick response and heroic effort saved the property and the animals. The wood construction and dry straw could have gone up like tissue paper.

While the firemen collected their hoses and equipment I talked to the Fire Marshal. I asked, "Jim, how did those firemen get the horses to leave their stalls when I couldn't budge them?" "Bernie," he said. "When a horse is out in the pasture and it is frightened by an electrical storm he runs to the safety of his barn. His barn and stall is his haven of safety, his sanctuary and place where he feels safe and secure. When the fire was burning the horses didn't realize it could consume them. They believed they were safe in their stall. To get them to leave you must first cover their eyes with a blanket. That way they do not know why they are being led out of their stall and they will follow you."

I recalled seeing the firemen leading the horses out of the barn with a blanket covering their head but I thought it was to protect them from the falling embers.

After the fireman left calm was restored in the barn. I returned to cruising my beat with one more piece of information in my memory bank. Before this night all I knew about horses was which way the jockey faced. Would I ever use what I just learned? I hoped not.

101

SAY GRACE

On October 30, 1954 I had already worked my tour of duty from 8:00 a.m. to 4:00 p.m. but it was Mischief Night and I was ordered to return and work overtime in the evening (without compensation). I was assigned to cruise a quiet residential area. Luckily the evening was uneventful until 8:00 p.m. when there had to be that one solo incident.

It was a dry fall evening, unseasonably warm with an invigorating breeze. A few days earlier the leaves had fallen from the trees in great abundance after a heavy shower and had collected in the gutters along the curbs and on the sidewalks. A thick blanket of dried leaves covered the lawns. A whirlwind every few seconds whipped a bunch of yellow and orange leaves into a frenzy and danced them from one yard to the yard next door. It was a fall phenomena that is pleasing to the eye along with the changing of the colors.

The street I was driving on has beautiful sprawling trees lining both sides for a quarter of a mile. Every yard had several trees for esthetics. The heavy rain a few days earlier burdened the leaves and brought them crashing to the ground in one cascade. After the rain subsided a warm breeze tossed and turned each leaf over many times until it was thoroughly dry and crisp.

As I drove down the street my headlights picked out a glow from a small flame in the gutter fifty yards ahead of me in the right hand curb. I conjectured how that small flame could quickly ignite the leaves on the lawns and be blown by leaps and bounds toward the houses. I envisioned a fire that would easily escalate into an inferno. Conditions were present this evening that could create a firestorm. The whole community could flare up like a dried discarded Christmas tree. As I approached the fire I saw four boys, fifteen years of age, nonchalantly sauntering away from the flame. They acted like they knew nothing about the burning leaves.

I jammed on the brakes and jumped out of the patrol car and faced the boys. I barked authoritatively, "OK fellows, you had better stamp out that fire. If I have to call the fire department you are in deep trouble!"

They rushed to the burning leaves and furiously tapped like they were doing the Mexican Hat Dance. They pounded and thumped each flicker of light until there wasn't a hint of a smoldering leaf. They admitted to having a can of cigarette lighter fluid that they sprayed on the leaves to get a good blaze started.

Before going on patrol that evening the sergeant instructed us not to bring any mischief-makers into headquarters. Instead we were to take names, addresses and phone numbers. He said the Superintendent would telephone the child's parents and arrange a meeting in his office at a later date. At that meeting he would lecture the child and the parents.

I was surprised these boys gave me their correct name and address because I didn't ask for identification or verification. If they weren't honest kids and were less respectful of authority they could have given me a fictitious name and address. They could have even run off in four directions and I would have never caught them. I submitted the information to the sergeant at the end of the night.

I considered the incident closed and forgotten; ancient history that would never be remembered. Many incidents in my past taught me that a street officer's relationship with a case is a truncated one. The officer will make the initial arrest but others in the system take over. However, this event was to rise fifteen years later like a phoenix from the ashes on the occasion of the Superintendent's retirement banquet.

The Superintendent was a highly regarded person whom everyone in the community respected and liked. On the evening of his retirement party a large banquet hall was filled to capacity with his friends and guests. At the head table was the pastor of the Presbyterian Church he belonged to, a Rabbi of a local Temple and an Irish Roman Catholic Priest. Everyone knew the Superintendent was a proud Mason, an Orangeman and a Presbyterian so it was strange the Catholic Priest would be called upon to say Grace.

The young priest rose to say the Grace Before A Meal. Before he began the prayer he announced he first had a few personal words he'd like to say. He stood humbly before the guests that embodied every dignitary in the area; businessmen, doctors, lawyers, commissioners, township department heads, judges, police officers, police chiefs of surrounding departments, family, friends, guests, et al. He spoke of the profound influence the Superintendent had on his Vocation and his direction in life. He confessed that one Mischief Night, when he was a teenager, he and three friends without malice or forethought of arson or setting the town on fire, set dry leaves lying at the side of the road on fire. They were promptly apprehended by a police officer cruising by. A few days after their foolish prank he and his parents were notified to report to this Superintendent's office for a private conference. He said he remembered every word of that lecture.

There was mention of a serious charge of arson because of the hazardous conditions that existed that evening when the area was an ocean of dried leaves. He spoke of the disappointment and shock I gave my parents and how I discarded my future potential and betrayed all those who expected more from me.

"It was at that moment, as I stood before him listening intently to every word he said that I made up my mind to be a priest. I am profoundly indebted to him."

THE BEATIFIC NUN

It was the day after Labor Day in 1958 and it was hot enough to fry an egg on a shady sidewalk. I received a radio message to respond to an auto accident that happened in front of a gas station. Since it occurred in front of a gas station I assumed the attendant notified headquarters and gave full particulars. Since I was the only officer dispatched it implied it was a simple two-vehicle accident without injuries. As I approached the scene I saw the two damaged vehicles and a man exchanging information with two nuns of the Immaculate Heart Of Mary Order. I knew that because it was the IHM nuns who guided me through my eight elementary grades.

My technique for learning who was driving which car without asking was to instruct the operators to drive their car off the road so they wouldn't obstruct the flow of traffic. That was how I learned the man drove the car that struck the nun's car. I asked for their operator's license, registration card and insurance card and assured them I would make a carbon copy of all the information. After I compiled the facts I gave each driver the opportunity to verbalize his or her opinion as to how the accident happened. I asked the man for his version first.

He said he had pumped gas into his car at the self-service island and unknowingly stepped on spilled gas or oil near the pump. He didn't realize it until he drove to the edge of the driveway and applied his brakes. His slippery shoe slid off the brake pedal onto the accelerator and his car lunged forward into the side of the passing car. He accepted responsibility and apologized. I thanked him and sent him on his way.

The nun who was a passenger was well into her eighties. The ravages of time wrecked havoc on her frame. The devastating pain over many years wrinkled her face and the acute angle of her spine indicated years of suffering from osteoporosis. The nun who was the driver was in her early twenties. She was beautiful, without a wrinkle or frown. In a religious habit she was a vision of Holiness. She patiently stood by radiating an aura of a person who never had an evil thought about anyone. She was fully devoted to the service of God. All her adolescent life she must have groomed herself to be a nun by constant prayer and meditation. She must have prayed relentlessly for a religious calling for she appeared serene and pious beyond description.

She stoically endured the brutal heat without complaint. She waited for her turn to give her version of the accident. She wasn't ruffled by this trial. She stood in her heavy woolen habit laden with yards of large rosary beads draped over her cummerbund. She waited in the sweltering sun without a crease in the habit or a bead of perspiration on her brow while I showed visible signs of discomfort on the back of my shirt and under my armpits. She was an apparition of a spirit not of this world. I couldn't help but admire her demure and pious radiance.

It wasn't necessary for the nuns to be exposed to the eyes of passing motorists so I had them sit in her car. They sat in the front seat and I sat in the rear seat. I didn't want her to feel discriminated against or have the impression I thought her input wouldn't be credible because she was a nun. Soothingly I asked, "Sister, would you please tell me in your own words how this accident happened?"

I was shocked senseless when her language wasn't consistent with her appearance. She began slowly and softly as if she was saying the Memorare but due to stress she quickened her pace and became intense. "I was driving west about 25 mph when that dumb sonavabitch came out of the goddamn gas station right into the side of the damn car." It was a great surprise because she had remained so calm all along. She stopped talking and cried hysterically. The old nun tried to comfort her, "Sister Patrick, don't be upset. Don't be hard on yourself. The accident was not your fault. You couldn't have avoided it."

"Officer," the young nun sobbed. "You don't understand the ramifications of this accident. Our pastor refuses to allow nuns in his parish to drive a car. He will not allow the convent to own a car even after a parishioner was willing to donate a new one and pay the insurance and maintenance costs. Our parish is in a remote section of the suburbs where transportation is difficult to come by yet he is of the old school and adamantly against nuns driving a car."

After another crying spell she continued. "Sister Joseph is very ill. She is so sick and she is in so much pain it was impossible for her to keep her doctor's appointment today. She couldn't travel into the city via train or bus because of the agony she is suffering so I begged the pastor to lend me his car so I could drive her to her doctor's office. You'll never know how I pleaded for Sister Joseph's sake. I actually knelt and begged on my knees to get the use of his car. Now that stupid sonavabitch ruined everything not only for me but also for all the Sisters. I feel so goddamn horrible for the position I'm in because of that clumsy bastard. How am I going to explain to the pastor that the damage to his car was not my fault? He won't accept that. How am I going to convince him it wasn't his fault because he let me use his car? How could I explain to that sonavabitchen driver he did more than dent a goddamm fender?" She cried some more and vented her emotions with a few more expletives.

What could I say that Sister Joseph hadn't already said? I waited until the sobbing subsided to inject a few words that must have sounded very insensitive. "Sister Patrick, my name and the department phone number are on the fact sheet I gave you. If your pastor wants to he may telephone me. Rest assured I will let him know there was no way you or anyone else could have prevented this accident and in no way did you contribute to it."

Back to patrolling I went and out of my life went the most angelic nun I ever saw.

THE BRAIN CONCUSSION

A woman was driving home on a residential street but somehow failed to negotiate a sharp curve and drove head-on into a tree. I was still a novice but I knew how to collect information for a report.

My job was complete after I arranged for a local garage to tow away her disabled car. The only injury the woman sustained was an enormous lump on her forehead. I recommended she have it examined but she refused to go to the hospital. She lived only two blocks from the accident so I volunteered to drive her home. Before she got into the police car the Lieutenant arrived to see if I handled the investigation correctly.

Immediately he doubted my assessment of the woman's condition. He noticed she staggered and her speech was slurred so on the basis of those symptoms he ordered me to place her under arrest and to charge her with "Driving while under the influence of an intoxicating substance." I disagreed but complied without any challenge because he had the silver bars, the expertise and the authority.

Months later she and I faced each other in the county courtroom. I, being the arresting officer, was the heavy while the Lieutenant sat in as a spectator. What made this unusual was the fact the woman's attorney called on the County Coroner to be an expert witness in her defense.

The Coroner doesn't usually testify in a routine automobile accident case. He is called upon on deaths where there are suspicious or unusual circumstances; homicides, suicides or rapes. It is highly irregular for him to take the stand in a mundane case such as this and he usually corroborates the prosecuting attorney's arguments against the accused. In this trial he was offering testimony in defense of the accused.

It was because he is highly respected in the courthouse he was given liberties on the stand. He wasn't confined to answering questions with a simple yes and no. He began with a thorough explanation of a brain concussion. It was his belief that the woman suffered a severe concussion that was caused by the blow she sustained on impact with the car's windshield. She was unbalanced and incoherent during the police interview at the scene due to the trauma to her head. She was not intoxicated or under the influence of drugs or medicine.

He was a brilliant witness. He patiently guided the Judge, the jury, the lawyers and me through the anatomy of a brain concussion. To illustrate he cupped his palms together and explained that the brain floats freely in a fluid like it would float in a soup bowl. A thin layer of bone called the skull covers the bowl. The brain is constantly pounded against the sides and top of the bowl and each time it strikes a side there is a slight concussion. He said every step we take causes a slight concussion. When we walk down a flight of steps there is a series of concussions.

When we bounce along in our car on a rough road and even as we walk on a smooth level sidewalk we cause faint concussions.

He continued with his explanation. When the brain strikes the sides of the bowl there is a bruising and a healing. The healings form adhesions. Adhesions upon adhesions can build up and affect the brain's ability to perform. This is what occurs to a professional fighter who sustains many critical blows to the head and the adhesions aren't given sufficient time to heal before he takes another pounding. We know the fighter to be Punch Drunk and recognize him by his awkward gait and slurred speech.

No one felt he was talking down to us. The Judge gave him all the latitude he needed to complete his testimony. The jury and I were willing to learn something new.

The Coroner stretched his arms straight out and gently swayed his cupped palms to and fro, side to side, and rotated them in a small circle. We were to visualize a brain floating in a bowl of nature's jelly then he jerked his arms to a sudden stop. We could almost see a brain bouncing violently against his thumbs. "That is what happened to her brain," he said. "The sudden impact caused a concussion or a severe blow to her brain."

The jury acquitted the woman. It didn't matter one way or the other to me but the Lieutenant was miffed. Especially since the Coroner defeated the State's case.

I never forgot the Coroner's demonstration and I applied his theory every day thereafter. After that lecture I first considered if a person could be debilitated by a head injury more than by the alcohol or a medicine consumed. From that day forth I concentrated on keeping my brain steady and from bouncing violently and frequently against the sides of my soup bowl.

SAY A PRAYER FOR THE DECEASED

Officer John Madden, me and Joe Algio.

I'll acknowledge I never had a resolute desire to be a police officer. I accepted the job with the intention it would be a temporary arrangement, one year, two at the max. Deny it as we may we are a product of our environment and it was because of my unwholesome city environment I had a negative assessment of the police profession. My irreverence was acquired from my associates during my teen years. In a large city there are many demeaning stories and nasty rumors of police degenerate integrity. Blatant contemptible behavior, often in full view, convinced us youngsters that a policeman's priorities were, graft, women, alcohol, and sleeping on the job, but not necessarily in that order nor for every officer.

On several social occasions I met policemen who reinforced my negative beliefs with their crude boasting. I avoided them because if there was the slightest difference in opinions or if there were a personality clash I would definitely emerge the loser. It was after I was on the force a very short time I had a major attitude adjustment.

I got to know policemen from a different perspective. I heard their concerns and saw how they reacted under stress. In sensitive situations they were caring and spiritual. These were moments my social friends knew nothing about. These moments banished the ugly ideas I carried onto the job. One such occasion was the time Joe Algio and I were assigned to a patrol car and responded to an accident at a train station. An electric commuter train was halted at the station so obviously it was involved. As we walked toward the coach where a conductor was waiting for us a hideous sight struck us. On the railroad ties lay a man's head. There was no blood or body in sight only a cleanly severed head. At first glance I thought it might have fallen off a mannequin.

The conductor said the train had stopped to pick up and discharge passengers but when it slowly started out a man raced after it. He was a half second late so he made a dash in an insane attempt to get on board. He may have lacked the expertise necessary for boarding a moving coach or the train jerked as he adjusted his grip on the handrail. Maybe he tripped and fell beneath the wheels. Exactly how it happened will never be known because he was decapitated. His head was left behind while he and his clothing were tangled on the undercarriage and dragged twenty feet down the track.

Officer Madden arrived with the ambulance so Algio and I prepared the stretcher and gurney. We worked swiftly so our activity wouldn't attract spectators to the gory scene. We opened the rubber body bag and were about to remove all traces of the accident so the train could get back on schedule. A detective collected statements from witnesses while another detective photographed the scene. The photographer focused on the position of the coach and the body underneath it and their relationship with the head lying on the tracks.

The department's policy put the ambulance driver in charge at incidents where the ambulance is needed so it wasn't difficult for Joe and me to take orders from Officer Madden. He had twenty-five more years of experience than we had. As he led us to the edge of the train station platform Joe and I purposely started toward the decapitated head because it was the most macabre segment of the grim scene and it might cause a queasy spectator to become ill. In that case we would create additional problems for ourselves.

Algio and I were about to step off the train station platform and onto the ballast to begin the sickening task of picking up the head when Officer Madden called us to attention. He sharply exploded with an order. "Just a moment men! First bow your head and say a prayer for the deceased."

A STORE IS ON FIRE!!

I finished checking all the stores in the business district but there was one more store in the residential section of my beat. After I checked it my first round would be done and I could leisurely cruise the streets. The last store was a Feed and Grain Store that catered to small farms and large estates. The building was once a four-car garage without windows or a rear door. Inside was a desk with a potbelly stove beside it. Large bags of fertilizer, seed, and animal feed were stacked against the walls. Bulky merchandise was also piled neatly in the yard in front of the garage. These items were protected from thieves by a six-foot cyclone fence that surrounded the property.

From outside the cyclone fence I saw a faint glow through the grimy glass in the front door. I dismissed it for a night-light but then intuition told me there were fluctuations in its intensity and color. To ease my mind and to be certain I climbed over the security fence to examine the faint glow because it might be a burglar's flashlight. I pressed my face against the dirty glass. I saw bales of hay were stacked close to the potbelly stove and one was smoldering. That was the flickering light I spotted from the street. It wasn't a blaze yet but it soon would be if left on its natural course. It might soon burst into a spontaneous combustion.

It was 2:00 a.m. and I was alone. My only means of communications was the radio in the patrol car so back over the fence I climbed. I wasn't as agile as a gymnast or maybe I panicked, whatever, I tore a twelve inch gash in my pant leg on a wire barb.

The volunteer firemen did an outstanding job considering they were roused from their bed by a siren on the roof of the firehouse and did a foot race to the firehouse to get to the equipment. If they had dawdled a raging fire might have consumed the surrounding buildings because there was the kind of fuel present that could quickly roar out of control.

No accolades came my way for discovering the fire and saving property. I did what I was paid to do. My discovery proved that checking stores served a worthwhile purpose. I thought that preventing a major fire was as important as catching a burglar so I expected an extra day off but it wasn't forthcoming. The indignity of it all was that I never got a replacement pair of pants until the next routine uniform issue that came eight months later.

THE BIG CATCH

It was just before the 5:00 p.m. closing time when two men entered an appliance store and snatched a 20-inch portable television set off a display shelf and ran out of the store. The manager saw the men steal his merchandise and ran after them. He was quite portly but even so he had the advantage. The TV was heavy and awkward to carry while running. However, being portly placed the belt holding up his pants under great stress. It snapped and his pants fell to his ankles and sent him tumbling to the sidewalk. It gave the thieves time to sprint out of sight. The manager returned to the store and telephoned headquarters.

It was my beat so I was dispatched and I arrived within minutes after the theft occurred. The manager offered no clues or identification or any information that could be helpful except that the men fled on foot in "that direction". I began my investigation by walking in "that direction". I peeked into every parked car along the way. I hoped I'd come upon the stolen TV in a parked car. The men couldn't lug it all the way to their destination but would have used a car for transportation.

The manager didn't see a car speed away so it was possible the car was still parked close by and the men would return for it when the coast was clear and the theft forgotten by the police. My hunch was right on the money. I located the car with the TV on the rear seat. It was parked seventy yards from the appliance store.

I telephoned headquarters and told them of my find and the detective sergeant laid a plan to make a catch. The car and the TV were to be left undisturbed and I was to take a surveillance position in a store where I had a clear unobstructed view. The car was only fifteen feet from my lookout position. The bait was left in the car waiting for the fish to bite.

Time passed slowly. All the stores in the area had closed for the day and all the consumers and merchants had left. By 7:00 p.m. the regular commuter traffic was home and there wasn't another car parked anywhere nearby. It was a summer evening and the sun continued to shine brightly.

It was 1956 and I was still young so my patience was wearing thin. I hadn't the patience of a fisherman. I wanted to leave my post and return to routine patrol, yet, I felt strongly the bait would lure them back. I also felt they wouldn't give the "dumb cops" enough credit to look into their car. They planned after a sufficient time lapse to return when the police were preoccupied with something else. They expected to nonchalantly drive their car away.

At 7:30 p.m. a car occupied by two men cruised slowly by. The men looked around for anything suspicious, especially for signs of a police presence. They hesitated for a long few seconds and then the passenger got out of the car. He was six foot five inches tall. To me he looked like Goliath the Philistine. My first thought was for my own safety. "What if he turned on me?" There was no way for me to know the size and character of his companion.

I dared not act hastily or prematurely expose myself. I nervously waited in the store until the giant approached the parked car. He casually glanced into it to see if the TV was still there and then walked passed it. By the way he scanned the surroundings he revealed he was the culprit I was waiting for. He walked forty feet passed the car and then returned. His friend watched and waited on the opposite side of the street sitting behind the steering wheel of the car that brought them. Their behavior was so amateurish there was no doubt they were the thieves but I preferred to wait until there was positive proof they were connected with this car.

Goliath swallowed the bait! He inserted a key into the door lock on the driver's side and yanked open the door. He slid into the seat that was already adjusted to accommodate his long legs and inserted the ignition key. He was about to give it the twist that would start the engine when I stepped out of hiding and stood abreast of him. In the deepest and harshest voice I could muster I barked loudly, "Don't move or I'll shoot a hole in you head!" My hand was on my gun grip but it wasn't out of the holster.

An unnatural thing happened that was even more startling than seeing Goliath for the first time. My loud growl bounced off the surrounding buildings. My voice was so strong it echoed like a shout in the Grand Canyon. It sounded like a detachment of marines had the area surrounded. If I was shaken by the strange loud voices just imagine what must have gone on in the head of the thieves. They jumped out of the two cars and stood at attention.

The second fellow was six foot, which made it awkward handcuffing them together but headquarters was within walking distance so it wasn't difficult marching them to the lockup. My fears had dissipated and I felt no need for backup. As we were walking the tall fellow asked, "Where did everyone else go?" I lied, "Keep walking straight ahead. They're behind us."

I caught a few others in my time, and other cops caught a lot, but I bet this was a record-size catch.

U.S. SENATOR JOE McCARTHY

In the early 1950s U.S. Senator Joe McCarthy (R Wis.) drew worldwide attention to himself by warning the American people about the danger America faced from the communists who had infiltrated the Government. To combat this perilous problem and to effectively weed out these communist subversives he had legislation passed mandating all government employees take a Loyalty Oath.

One morning after roll call my Captain called the squad to attention and ordered us to take the Loyalty Oath. "Raise your right hand and repeat after me, I, state your name, do solemnly swear that I am not now and never was a member of any organization that intends to overthrow the government of the United States or the Commonwealth of Pennsylvania." That was the loyalty oath and to prove we took it and swore it was the truth we signed the paper on which it was printed. The signed paper was salted away in our Personal File.

It behooved me that I was expected to believe that anyone engaged in subversive activities would betray themselves by refusing to take that oath. I didn't believe it had a deterring effect nor would it shake any spies out of the trees. I raised my right hand and took the oath with a clear conscience and went on about my job and my life. I didn't know any communists nor did I know what the Communist Party espoused. But I did have a core feeling that I did not subscribe to the Senator's egomaniacal political tactics. I totally ignored his probe into everyone's loyalty even after he got me involved with his stupid oath.

Twenty years later the media continued to tell us the 'cold war' was a threat. Despite that danger new menaces surfaced to preoccupy us. The communist threat from within subsided after the Senator died and a new wave of priorities bathed the country. The new Damocles swords came in the form of protests, boycotts, sit-ins, demonstrations, marches and riots. The country's largest and most intimidating demonstrations and marches were held in Washington DC.

During a seminar sponsored by the FBI local police departments were forewarned of the emerging new public enemies and how treacherous they were. These new enemies were the demonstrating protesters. We were told large demonstrations were a daily occurrence in front of the Capitol in Washington, DC. It unsettled me because I never heard of an impending demonstration in our area. Even more unnerving was the fact that each demonstration was accompanied by counter demonstrations and often there were as many as five layers of demonstrators at the same time.

The instructor gave us this example: The African-American group might be demonstrating for Civil Rights legislation and their demonstration would attract a counter demonstration by the KKK. The KKK would draw the Jewish Defense League into the mix.

113

The FBI instructors said the logistics for these demonstrations were horrendous. Police manpower, barricades, paramedics, FBI, Secret Service, fire department personnel, motor scooters, patrol cars, canine units, ambulances, motorcycles, helicopters, mounted police, SWAT teams, army reserves and police reserve units on standby blocks away from the actual demonstration site. There were so many details requiring attention including the conveniences that had to be provided for the health and safety of the demonstrators. They required essentials like a sufficient number of PORT-O-POTTIES, lunch kitchens and First Aid Stations.

Until I attended the FBI seminar the only information I had concerning a demonstration was what I read in the newspapers or saw on television. No one in my department or anyone from the surrounding suburban police departments had hands-on experience. Our Township Manager and Superintendent didn't overtly show interest or concern; yet, several major cities didn't weather well from some form of protest. At every instance the police officer on the front ranks emerged the villains. The negativism toward the police came about because neither the individual police officer nor his superiors received training on how to respond objectively to these displays of social unrest.

A few months after I attended the FBI seminar an Anti-Vietnam War protest of considerable magnitude was scheduled for Washington, DC between the Washington Monument and the Lincoln Memorial. My interest was aroused by the FBI seminar. In my endeavor to learn I arranged my days off so I could attend the demonstration, **as a spectator.** My intention was to gather helpful information I could present to my superiors in the event there should ever be a demonstration planned for our township. I went to Washington, DC without the department even being aware of my interest.

The enormity of this demonstration was beyond description. I couldn't estimate the tens of thousands of people in attendance. The ranks and defensive formations exhibited by the Washington police were astounding. The behavior of every police officer was above reproach. This may have been due to the vast number of experiences of this nature they faced in the past or it could have been the result of firm discipline. I returned home befuddled and proud of my profession for the way they handled themselves under that ominous climate.

The following year another Anti-Vietnam War protest was scheduled for Washington, DC and I arranged my schedule again so I could attend. At the first protest everything was so awesome I was bewildered by the excitement. There was so much activity I assimilated only a few notable highlights. The second time around I wouldn't be so naïve. Perhaps this time I could comprehend and better evaluate what I saw.

The second Anti-Vietnam War protest was held on the day President Richard Nixon was inaugurated for his second term in office. The inauguration parade was held on a street parallel to the street where the protest march was held and only a few blocks away. Naturally some demonstrators went to see the inauguration parade. I followed them to see if they would behave respectfully and if they didn't I was interested in what counteraction the police would employ. I was tremendously impressed by the power of the masses when they band together to demand a social change and equally impressed by the drills the National Guard and the police executed to thwart any intrusion by the Anti-Vietnam War protesters. The police and the Guards had their hands full but judiciously and without drawing any attention they prevented the protesters from causing a disturbance or confrontation.

When I returned to my office I wasn't hailed as a student of human behavior nor a sergeant with ideas to be implemented before the big clash struck the township. Instead, I was tagged as a protester against the President of the United States, the government's policy on the Vietnam War, Pro-draft dodging, Pro-Civil Rights Movement, and Pro-Equal Rights Amendment.

These were flammable issues and unpopular causes in conservative circles. To take a stand on any one item would bare a nerve and ignite heated arguments. Negative rumors concerning my loyalty circulated throughout the police building. As with all rumors the facts were not known but instead were distorted and exaggerated.

From time to time FBI agents collaborated with the local police on cases they were called upon for assistance and on one of these occasions an alert FBI agent overheard the water fountain gossip. Ferreting out this kind of information is a fundamental responsibility of the FBI. There remained the remnants of the fear anyone could be a communist ready to overthrow the government. An alert agent reported to his superiors what he learned about this police sergeant.

I worked under a shadow of suspicion and scorn for a few years. I never argued with or tried to convince those who were incriminating me because it was a sad time in this country for those who went against the grain. I would only magnify my problem with an adamant denial so I let the rumor run its course and die a natural death.

If I were really interested I'm sure I could obtain from the FBI files, under the Freedom of Information Act, a file with my name on it, and I firmly believe, if it was not deleted, there's a document on which I am classified a "COMMUNIST SYMPATHIZER".

MY FIRST MOTORCYCLE CHASE

Here I am on my Harley-Davidson police motorcycle.

My first day on a motorcycle the Lieutenant assigned me to enforce the 35 mph speed limit on a rural road. I lacked experience driving a motorcycle; yet, I wanted to project a favorable impression. The Lieutenant ordered, "Go get 'em, Tiger! I want results!"

I arrived at the location ready to greet the onslaught of commuter traffic. The same motorists used this route every morning and evening because there aren't any traffic controls to interfere with their high speed. When the first car came racing down the street I slipped from my hiding place and shifted into pursuit. That was the precise moment when I lost control of the cycle. This was a typical rural road with bumps, depressions, potholes, dips and ruts. When I drove over a bump or depression I was hurled high into the air off the motorcycle seat. My feet were off the brake and clutch.

As I was lofted into the air I tightened my grip on the handlebar where the accelerator is located and twisting it only made the cycle surge forward even faster. For a fraction of a second I peeked at the speedometer and it indicated 85 mph. I don't know if that was actual speed or airborne speed for the wheels were whirling off the road more often than they were on the road.

Somehow, but without any deliberate help from me, I regained control of the cycle. I couldn't care less that the speeder escaped. My nerves were devastated for the remainder of the day and for several days I only thought about surviving.

That experience taught me a single powerful lesson; *I must do a reconnaissance job on the road before I travel at breakneck speeds. I must first ride over the road several times and study its characteristics.*

PLEASE DON'T DRIVE OVER MY HAT!

I was on my police motorcycle and engaged in a high-speed chase behind a speeding taxi. Both of us were flying low because the cabby had no idea I was clocking him. This highway has two smooth lanes in each direction and there are no obstructions so we were tooling way above 65 mph in a 35 mph zone. For me to catch up and overtake him I had to bump up my speed at least 10 mph faster than his so I poured on the petrol. I almost did a wheelie but I wasn't going to let him get away. After following him for a mile it was time for me to close in. Just as I was about to pull abreast of the cab and show myself the wind got under the brim of my hat and picked it off my head.

I looked around to check on its whereabouts and saw it bounce, tumble and roll down the street like it was doing its utmost to catch up to me. After bouncing thirty or more yards it lost momentum and stopped in the curb lane.

My hat was a five-pointed clothe cap without a chinstrap to hold it securely on the head. It had a hidden medal rim sewed into the seam to help it keep its shape. This was in 1955, many years before crash helmets were developed.

I made a snap decision to abandon the pursuit and to turn around and retrieve the cap before some wise guy came along and snatched it up for a souvenir. At the speed I was traveling I couldn't make an immediate U-turn so I slowly brought the cycle to a near stop to make the turn. I slowly cruised back to where the hat lay. As I drove closer to the hat a driver came speeding toward me. He was galvanized by the sudden appearance of a motorcycle cop when he came over the crest of a slight grade. He suddenly took notice to his speed and realized he was exceeding the speed limit. He panicked and froze at the steering wheel. He was too scared to think about avoiding the strange looking object in the street. At his speed it looked like road-kill so he drove right over it. My hat was totally crushed.

This was about the time when every department in the township had to bear the brunt of an austerity program so the motorcycle hat wouldn't be replaced. In that regard it was a priceless item because there wasn't another in the police department's supply closet.

The wire rim that gave the hat its shape was fractured in two places. It now sat cockeyed on my head. I always preferred my uniform hat sit square and military like on my head but now it was tilted in such a way it gave me a jaunty rather than a professional appearance. I had to wear it. I had no choice.

MY MEAT IS SPOILING!

Early one Sunday morning in June 1955 I parked and purposely relaxed sitting on the seat of my police motorcycle. I was in plain view for all to see. My mind was blank but to passing motorists I appeared to be as menacing as a junkyard dog.

A fast moving tractor-trailer with squealing brakes and smoking tires came to a screeching stop right where I was parked. Since I was daydreaming I heard the truck before I saw it. The driver exploded from the cab and dashed up to me. I expected the worse from the wild way he was waving his arms. "Ossifer! Ossifer! I need a synagogue! Where is a synagogue? I have to get to a synagogue!" The poor fellow's eyes bulged from their sockets. He looked rabid as he shouted insanely for a synagogue. My first impression was he was nuts. I would have thought the same of him if he were shouting for a confessional, however, there were no synagogues in the township and I told him so.

"I need a Rabbi! I need a Rabbi right away! Please! Get me a Rabbi quick!"

He was actually in tears. He was in a sad pathetic state. Whatever troubled him had to be tremendously important and something I didn't understand. I told him to calm down and tell me his problem. Perhaps there was a chance I could be of some assistance. Between sobs he said, "Ossifer, my trailer is loaded with kosher meat worth twenty-five thousand dollars. It will be spoiled and worthless if a Rabbi doesn't renew the Kosher Blessing. The old Blessing will lapse in fifteen minutes."

I had no idea what he was talking about but judging from his wild behavior it had to be desperately critical. I got on the police radio hoping someone in headquarters might have a solution for his dilemma but all the time I knew no one in headquarters was Jewish. I felt stupid talking about it over the air because every citizen with a scanner could receive my message.

"Headquarters, I've got a truck driver here who needs a Rabbi to renew the Kosher Blessing on the load of meat he is hauling. He has only fifteen minutes left on the old Blessing. If it isn't renewed in time his valuable load is worthless. Any suggestions?"

After a brief pause the radio operator in headquarters responded, "Take him to the SUNOCO gas station. I contacted a Rabbi in Philadelphia and he will meet you there."

The truck driver and I were at one end of the township and the gas station was catty-corner at the other end so I turned on my emergency lights and siren and escorted the tractor-trailer at breathtaking speeds toward the rendezvous location. It was a Sunday morning and there was very little traffic. Luckily those people who did leave their homes were in church at the moment. I was traveling at a fast clip and all the while I failed to consider the tractor-trailer couldn't be maneuvered like a motorcycle. The truck driver had enough on his mind trying to keep up with me and not letting me get out of sight. He couldn't worry about the time schedule too.

A Rabbi was at the gas station waiting for us. The driver pulled into the driveway and was out of his seat in a flash. He dashed to the rear of the trailer and jerked the large doors open. The Rabbi climbed in amongst the load of carcasses draped from the ceiling and the walls. He dragged the gas station owner's water hose in after him. The water hose was the one the gas station attendant used to wash cars.

It suddenly dawned on me why headquarters directed me to this particular gas station. All the gas stations in the township are closed on Sundays including this one but this station is the closest to the city limits and to a Rabbi. The radio operator also sent us to this station because he knew the outdoor water valve was always left turned on and the garden hose was always connected. Many officers, when off duty, brought their personal car to this station late at night to wash it. It was a gratuity extended by the station owner for the added security. The radio operator knew water and a hose would not have been available at any other gas station in the township.

This was another piece of information the nuns didn't teach me. They taught me a great deal about religion but this particular situation was all too mysterious for me to understand. The significance of a chant and water being sprayed on a truckload of meat was never explained but there had to be something beautiful and gratifying about it for I never saw a happier truck driver.

A friend took this photograph of my wife Evie, my son Bernie and me when we weren't looking.

119

SENATOR JOHN F. KENNEDY

The year (1955) I drove the police motorcycle was chock full of excitement. Since the cycle itself offered no protection I was hot in the summer when exposed to the direct rays of the sun and dreadfully cold in the winter when the north winds blew. Yet, there were enough pleasing experiences to compensate for the harsh conditions. One bitter cold morning I took a post in front of an Elementary School. I intended to issue tickets to speeders who ignored the 15 mph school zone speed limit. I became so cold standing on the sidewalk I climbed back on the motorcycle and went for a ride to warm up.

I sensed when pedestrians on the sidewalks were in awe as the handsome police officer on his shiny iron horse rode by. It was an egotistical ride leading a parade and so was escorting dignitaries and escorting an oversize vehicle through traffic on a main highway. Dignitaries always seemed to operate on a tight schedule and were always behind the timetable on their itinerary. The Jewish Mayor of Dublin, Ireland, Mayor Briscoe was a half hour late for his lecture at the Villanova University. I was his police escort from the city limits to the University and I was expected to make up some of those lost minutes.

Escorting Senator John F. Kennedy was a harrowing experience. It happened one evening when he was flying from Boston to Washington, DC. He purposely made a brief layover at the Philadelphia International Airport just so he could visit his sister who was a student in residence at Rosemont College twenty some miles from the airport.

His aide contacted the Philadelphia Police Department and they consented to have their motorcycle squad escort him as far as the city limits. They in turn notified the Lower Merion Police and requested an escort from that point to the College. It was 7:00 p.m. on a fall evening and already dark. Officer Algio and I were patrolling on motorcycles so we were dispatched to escort the Senator the final five miles. We met the Philadelphia Motorcycle Squad and his car on the fly on Lancaster Avenue at City Line Avenue, Overbrook.

The sight of a dozen police motorcycles coming toward us at a break-neck speed was awesome. We never saw so much excitement created by bright headlights and blinking red emergency lights. The roar of their engines and screaming sirens was scary. They came to a sudden stop at the city limits and without a nod or wave we took over for the next leg of the trip.

Kennedy's chauffeur drove recklessly fast so we drove furiously too to keep ahead of his car. He drove so dangerously close to us I thought he might drive up our backs. Joe and I leap-frogged from one intersection to the next. Our insignificant red emergency lights were flashing and our sirens wailed a weak high pitch sound. We were near hyperventilated from blowing our whistles to attract the attention of drivers on the side streets. It was a daredevil's ride and we both took to foolish risks.

The Senator's sister was expecting him and was waiting on the campus driveway. The college nuns and students ogled from dormitory windows at the young handsome Senator. They exchanged a few words and then kissed good-bye.

Before Algio and I had enough time to collect our runaway wits his aide shouted loud enough to be heard at the far end of the campus, "Let's roll!!" Off we sped on another terrifying flight back to the city limits. The Philadelphia Motorcycle Squad was waiting where we left them and were ready to take over the race back to the airport. Algio and I were more than happy to turn the welfare of the Senator over to them.

By the time we reined our bikes the Philadelphia cycles were already blocks away. We took a deep sigh of relief. We weren't worth a plug nickel after that wild experience so we drove to a diner for a cup of coffee and to settle our nerves. We took enough risks for one evening.

PATROLMAN LOUGHRAN

This is a newspaper photograph of me directing traffic around a motor vehicle accident. It was in 1955 when I was 29 years old.

TWEET! TWEET!

One of the items issued to me the day I received my first uniform was an ancient second-hand whistle. This whistle was unusual because it had a plastic sheath. The purpose for the covering was to keep the user's lips from freezing to the metal on a cold day. It was a practical idea considering pulling skin off a lip is very painful. The down side of the plastic application was it reduced the effectiveness of the whistle. It wouldn't emit a loud commanding blast and it took a pair of young lungs to get a fair toot out of it. I didn't know the difference when I was issued it and I thought it was the same as any other whistle. It was in service long before I got it and after using it for seven years I became accustomed to blowing it forcefully. Through all the years it was in service the little pea inside gradually wore down and out of round.

One afternoon I was directing traffic through a construction site and the loud noise of the jackhammers and bulldozers overrode my whistle so I had to blow it with all the gusto I could muster. For an hour I was blowing my lungs out and waving my arms like a windmill. At a critical moment I gave an extra hefty puff and the pea flew out of the whistle. It was useless now so I turned it in to the supply sergeant and requested a replacement. The replacement didn't have a plastic sheath similar to the one I had so I foresaw a cold day when I might lose some lip skin. Since it was summer I didn't object.

Before I tested the new whistle and heard what it sounded like I was assigned to enforce the 15 mph speed limit in a school zone. I arrived at the school and parked my motorcycle in a private driveway and stood at the curbside ready to teach a few errant drivers the law. While waiting for a speedster I studied a house painter on a porch roof directly across the street from where I was standing. He was on the top step of a six-foot ladder and dangerously stretching as far as he could reach with the paintbrush the gable on the upper roof. He was so intent on keeping his balance he wasn't aware of my presence.

A woman driver came barreling down the street. I was sure there wouldn't be an argument about my judgment call. Once I told her the posted speed limit she'd have to admit she was exceeding it by a wide margin. I stepped off the sidewalk and blew my new whistle for the very first time. I gave it my all like I had been doing on the plastic covered whistle but my new Alarmer-Thunderer didn't need much heave. The shrill blast startled me because I never expected such a loud sound.

The noise startled the house painter so badly he toppled off the ladder onto the porch roof. The gallon of white paint he was holding spilled over the black tar roof. The ear-piercing blast also terrified the driver. She jammed on the brakes and screeched to a stop farther down the street.

I intended to issue a speeding ticket to the woman but she was crying hysterically. The blast unnerved her so badly she was trembling. I made an attempt to soothe and calm her but she wasn't even cognizant of my presence.

I created a horrible chain of events. I couldn't console the woman nor could I help the house painter clean up the paint stain. There wasn't a thing I could do but make a quick getaway so I hopped on my motorcycle and scrammed from the weird scene that was my making.

Twenty minutes later I was curious so I returned to the scene of my crime. I saw the painter busily mopping and scrubbing the white paint off the tar but I knew there was no way he could remove or cover the white stain. He probably was wondering what made him fall off the ladder. The woman driver was still sitting behind the steering wheel and sobbing like a child. She too would never know what happened. I pulled up beside her and asked if she was ok and she assured me she was. I asked if she needed any medication and she said no. I asked if I could help her in any way and she said no. Since she repeated it so often I was satisfied she was ok, just frightened. I shifted into gear and rode away like nothing unusual happened.

I never again blew my new whistle with that much gusto.

This is a newspaper photograph of me directing traffic around a motor vehicle accident. It was taken in 1955 when I was 29 years old. Check my fractured cap and notice my trusty Alarmer-Thunderer hanging from the button on my right breast pocket.

MR. ED PRENDALL

For eight years I hunted for a flawless method I could use when I issued a traffic ticket for a moving violation. This incident assured me I was on the right track toward achieving my impossible dream. It happened when a quiet street suddenly became a major artery and at the same time a nettlesome thorn in the township's side. It was once an unruffled residential street tucked safely in a corner of the township.

Historically it was a forgotten road devoid of traffic except for the few vehicles that belonged to the people who lived on the street. The macadam was their sidewalk and a playground for their children. But, after the construction of an office building, TV/Radio station and hotel complex the little community lost their private driveway. Overnight it became a highway for commuter traffic and a shortcut for those who worked in the new commercial area.

There were only a dozen homes; six on each side of the street, but the area is overrun with preteen children and they weren't adapting well to the fast moving traffic driving through their playground. For their safety action had to be taken. The residents band together and appointed a spokesperson to confer with the Township Manager. He referred him to the Police Department Traffic Safety Officer.

The Traffic Safety Officer immediately had the highway department sign crew paint a solid white line down the center of the road. This was to inform motorists this was a road and not an airport runway. Within a few days the community spokesperson complained the line was ineffective. The Traffic Safety Officer's next approach was to have four bold white SLOW letters painted on the blacktop in both directions but they had no effect either. His third attack was to alternate four large yellow SLOW and WATCH CHILDREN signs on both sides of the road but they too were a waste of the sign crew's time and the township's money.

The neighborhood representative demanded aggressive police patrol. He demanded an officer be assigned to the street twenty-four hours a day and he was to issue a ticket to every motorist traveling at an unsafe speed. The speed he had in mind was an unrealistic 10 to 15 mph. The characteristics of the street lent itself to greater speeds.

It is a straight road that ended in a T-intersection at both ends. The driver's visibility was excellent and he usually was alone on the road plus there weren't any parked cars to impede his progress. The negative features were, it is a high crowned narrow twenty-four foot wide road, it has no curbs, soft shoulders or sidewalks, the houses are almost up to the curb line and there is an abundance of young children.

A patrol car would have difficulty enforcing the speed limit legally. The Motor Vehicle Code stipulates a violator must be clocked for three-tenths of a mile and this street was only five-tenths of a mile long. A patrol car couldn't pursue a car, attain the necessary speed, clock the speeder and come to a safe stop within the five-tenths of a mile.

My Lieutenant, who happened to be the Traffic Safety Officer snapped, "Loughran! I'm getting a lot of heat from the Township Manager, the Superintendent and the people on that street! Issue tickets! Stop all violators! I don't want any excuses!!"

Fortified by intimidation I drove my motorcycle to the street in question and immediately doubts abound as to how I was going to tackle this assignment. I cruised the street several times to get the feel of the road. It hadn't been resurfaced in years so it would be a bouncy ride. There was a pronounced slope toward both curbs to promote rainwater run-off, which meant riding dead center would be the safest, except the freshly painted white center line is slippery as ice for a motorcycle even on a dry day.

On my test runs I saw the eight bold SLOW letters on the road and the eight SLOW, WATCH CHILDREN signs and the two red STOP signs. All that effort by the sign crew was for naught. It was now Show Time! It was the time to bring up the big gun to get the job done! Loughran to the rescue! After a few bumpy test runs I got wise to the road surface. I found a place to hide the bike and myself under the drooping branches of a Weeping Willow tree located at a T-intersection. I hid and waited for a speeder.

At 4:10 p.m. the first speeding car raced up the street unconcerned about his speed so I sprang out of my lair. The operator wasn't mindful of any reason why he couldn't drive at a comfortable 50 mph while I was doing catch-up at 65 mph. At the four-tenths of a mile marker I signaled for him to pull over. I was hoping he'd glance at his speedometer and see how fast he was traveling.

An observer may assume it doesn't take any skill to apprehend a speeder. Some people may regard a motorcycle cop to be the highest paid unskilled laborer in the country so I'll run through the mechanics of a typical motorcycle chase. A motorcycle officer must be as ambidextrous and coordinated as a double-jointed contortionist. He must select a positive offender. He must catch up to the speeder first and then clock him for three-tenths of a mile. The chase must be carried off in an inconspicuous manner or the driver might notice he is being followed. If the officer is spotted the driver might jam on his brakes and if that happens the officer must act quickly and employ evasive action.

After speeding behind the driver for three-tenths of a mile the officer must attract the attention of the violator. He does this by turning on his red emergency lights and his headlight with his left hand. This has to be done quickly because the left hand controls the front brake lever. With his left toe he depresses a pedal that pushes the siren against the rotating rear tire and activates it. His left heel depresses the clutch to disengage the gears.

His right hand is busy controlling the accelerator grip on the right handlebar. He also uses this hand to motions to the driver to pull to over. The hand signal must be seen, must be affirmative and it must be quick because if the accelerator is left unattended the bike will automatically accelerate. In these desperate split seconds the officer doesn't wish to go faster but wants to bring the bike to a stop before it is too late to do it safely.

The right foot at the same time is depressing the rear wheel brake pedal. It is imperative the front brake lever on the left handlebar and operated by the left hand and the rear brake pedal operated by the right foot be synchronized with the same amount of pressure or the cyclist will be bolted out of his seat.

That is a list of the maneuvers that must be coordinated to bring the violator and the motorcycle to a safe stop. The situation is compounded when there isn't sufficient distance to perform all these functions. At 60 mph a motorcycle travels a hundred feet per second so even if I failed to explain it thoroughly believe a motorcycle officer is as busy as a one-legged soccer player when pursuing a speeder.

When the first speeder appeared I threw the bike into gear and took up the chase. The sound of the siren attracted the residents and they dashed from their houses to witness something that never occurred before on their private playground. The spokesman that demanded the police action was among them.

After I completed my business with the speeder I pulled to a stop in front of the spokesman and said, "Charlie, please get these people off the street and back in their house. This isn't a smooth ride and if I bounce off this cycle some kids could get hurt. I don't have complete control of the bike all the time, and not only that, if a driver sees a crowd he will slow down and I won't be able to do the job you want. While I'm going back to my hiding place you get them indoors for me. Thanks."

The next time I roared up the street they were peeking through the curtains.

At 6:25 p.m. I sensed I was pushing my luck so I figured one more chase and I'd call it quits on this street. I'd cruise my regular beat until quitting time to relax my frazzled nerves. I took up the chase of the last driver. It was no different than the previous ones. All the rides were hairy but I didn't have to vary my shtick one word.

After I stopped the car I got off the cycle and walked to the driver. I tipped my hat and said, "Good evening sir. I am Officer Bernie Loughran. May I see your driver's license and owner's card, please? I stopped you because you were driving too fast for the conditions of this street. There are numerous warnings devices advising you to slow down. There is the solid white center line, four painted SLOW signs and four posted yellow slow signs and watch children signs. I am issuing you a warning ticket that will be placed in my department's files. If you ignore this warning and you are stopped again the second time will automatically be a citation. Please cooperate with my department and me in our efforts to make the highways safer and slower. Good day sir." I tipped my hat again and turned to go back to my cycle.

"Officer!" the man called out. I returned to him expecting to hear a complaint. "I'm Ed Prendall and I work at the TV/Radio station down the street. My job is to read the evening news and make advertising tapes. I also have a radio talk show between 6:00 p.m. and 6:15 p.m.. I comment on contemporary events of the day and I would like your permission to speak about the traffic ticket I just received."

I was unsure he might vent his resentment over the air.

"Sir, only the Superintendent can authorize a press releases or public relations message. Would your remarks be positive or negative?"

"Officer, I can only say good things about the way you performed your duty."

"In that case I'm sure the Superintendent wouldn't object so say whatever you wish. Be objective and subjective."

"Thank you Officer."

That would be the end of this story except there were relevant happenings going on in the background during these same hours of which I had no knowledge. A dozen fellow officers get together and play softball two evenings a week. There is no established league or uniforms. One evening the opposing team may be the telephone company female switchboard operators and on another evening schoolteachers, or bartenders, volunteer firemen or whomever would like to challenge the police.

For the policemen it is an opportunity to keep fit. Spectators are welcome to watch the games and mix with policemen in a casual setting. Those who meet policemen out of uniform for the first time are taken by surprise. They didn't think of police officers as average men because they appear Herculean in uniform. They aren't as tall or muscular and threatening looking. Spectators often expressed themselves, "You fellows look like regular people and you even have a sense of humor."

Unbeknown to Mr. Prendall and me the game scheduled this evening was with the TV/ Radio station employees. The employees and the police officers worked until 4:00 p.m. and the game was scheduled for 6:00 p.m.. The TV/Radio station players traveled on the street I was patrolling to get from the station to the baseball field. They drove fast so they'd have time to warm up before the game. On the surface it looked like my enforcement effort was planned entrapment, however, my Lieutenant wasn't aware of the game either or he would have picked another day for the enforcement.

Each TV/Radio station player I stopped showed up at the baseball field and let it be known he received a speeding ticket. He hoped it would be fixed and removed from his record by the policemen in the game. One officer telephoned headquarters and told the switchboard operator to radio a message to Loughran and tell him to knock it off with the tickets. The switchboard operator came right back with "No way. Don't fix any of the tickets. The Lieutenant and the Superintendent are listening to the radio and the news announcer is broadcasting every time he issues a ticket."

The TV/Radio players were relaying the news to the station. A news broadcaster announced the baseball score several times during the program; "The station staff is beating the police on the baseball field 3-0 but the police are winning on the street. Another player received a speeding ticket on the way to the game. That score is 13-0."

By police radio my Lieutenant ordered me to contact him on a police call box. He asked, "Did you patrol the street I assigned to you and what is your count?" "Of course I did. I always comply with your orders, Lieutenant. The count is ten warning tickets for speeding and three Faulty Equipment Slips for faulty brake lights." "I want to see them when you report off duty." He wanted to make sure the tickets didn't get lost in a "fix".

This should be the end of this anecdote except a few days later I was sitting at a desk in headquarters just outside the Superintendent's office. I was concentrating on an accident investigation report I was writing when a woman came charging into the building like a raging bull. She loudly demanded to see the Superintendent and was promptly escorted into his office. Through the thin office wall I overheard her shouting. I listened because I was curious as to what made her so raving mad and how the Superintendent would appease her.

A discourteous police officer made her furious. "He shouted at me, 'I don't give a goddamn if you just went into the store to get change. The meter had expired and you're getting a ticket. Now get the hell out of here or I'll lock you up for Disorderly Conduct.' I heard Mr. Ed Prendall talking on the radio about how polite Officer Bernie Loughran was when he issued a speeding ticket. You should have Officer Loughran teach that unmannerly officer how to talk to people."

I was euphoric. It was nice to know I was being praised behind my back and of all people the recipient was the Superintendent himself. I worked hard and studied long the difficulties of issuing a traffic ticket and I obviously developed a pretty good technique. It was gratifying. It was the encouragement I needed.

MY MOTORCYCLE ACCIDENT

In the fall of 1954 I volunteered for duty with the Motorcycle Squad. There were only four men in this squad. It wasn't a prized assignment because it was cold in the winter and hot in the summer but there were rewards that justified my volunteering. The midnight shift was eliminated and that was compensation enough because I dislike that shift. The motorcycle squad didn't patrol on Saturdays, Sundays and Holidays or after 7:00 p.m. and I didn't have to work any more burglary details. These were the incentives that lured me.

My peers saw the motorcycle duty as extremely hazardous and jeopardizing oneself unnecessarily. They believed whoever volunteered for it had a death wish. In spite of this criticism the squad was considered elitist and I relished the prestige associated with belonging to a select group. It was an ego trip.

During the 1955 Fourth of July holiday week I leisurely patrolled the main arteries to be visible to the holiday motorists. Occasionally I issued a traffic ticket but I mainly was just a deterrent. One afternoon I intercepted a radio message from a patrol car that was dispatched to a home where a baby was having convulsions. The officer informed headquarters that the baby was not responding to his First Aid treatment so he was going to transport it and the mother to the hospital. I decided to escort the car to the hospital so at E. Wynnewood Road and Lancaster Avenue I took up the lead. My red lights were flashing and my headlight was on high beam and the siren was wailing.

I was directly in front of the patrol car whisking along at 60 mph. The speed itself was no threat because the highway was smooth and in excellent condition and it was a straight run. As we approached a major intersection the traffic signal went into a changing phase. It had changed from green to amber and it would remain amber for five seconds. Traveling at 60 mph I could cover a great distance. I even sped faster anticipating I'd be in the intersection before the light turned red. At 60 mph I couldn't jam on the brakes because I had now passed the point of no return.

I had eye contact with the motorists stopped for their red signal and they seemed to acknowledge they were apprised of my presence and were willing to give me the right of way. However, a woman who was first in line on my right had other ideas. I stared into her eyes but mistakenly assumed she too was going to give the patrol car and me the right of way. Without any hesitation she darted into the intersection the moment the traffic signal turned green for her. I plowed into her broadside. Her car and my motorcycle were demolished.

The officers behind me said my cycle was catapulted over the top of the car and my body shot straight up into the air. On the way up my face struck the top of the car's front door jamb and I landed unconscious twenty feet from the impact. I sustained a shattered left elbow and the right side of my face was squashed. The woman suffered a broken hip and a fractured pelvis. Both of us were transported to the hospital.

The officer who investigated the accident interviewed her to get her version of the accident. She said she saw the motorcycle and the emergency lights coming toward her but she didn't associate them with an emergency situation. She said she didn't hear the siren because she was not wearing her hearing aid. The battery was dead. She was on her way to a drug store to purchase replacement batteries.

The patrol car with the baby continued on its way to the hospital but it wasn't admitted. The convulsion had ceased.

WAS FILLING MERCY CALL—Patrolman Bernard Loughran, who was riding this motorcycle to escort a car rushing to Lankenau Hospital with a sick child, was badly hurt Tuesday when an automobile crossed his path at the intersection of Lancaster Ave. and Clover Hill Rd., Wynnewood.
—Both Photos by Fuller

Motorcycle Cop Escorting
Sick Child Badly Injured

A motorcycle escort was requested Tuesday noon to clear the way for a sick child being rushed to Lankenau Hospital and Patrolman Bernard Loughran was assigned to the call.

Fellow officers are carrying my motorcycle to the sidewalk because it was totally damaged in the accident.

WHAT'S HE KNOW ABOUT FIRST AID?

When I woke up in a hospital bed I had no idea how much time passed since my motorcycle accident but I had complete recall of the events leading up to the impact. My left arm was in a cast, my face and head were wrapped in gauze and I was in a hospital gown. There were no hospital personnel in the room so I figured whatever emergency care I required was rendered and I was left to sleep and heal on my own. I was in a cerebral fog yet I could tell by all the treatment I received a great deal of time had gone by.

What woke me was an excruciating pain at the back of my neck. I hadn't assessed all my injuries because I was still under the effects of the anesthesia but there was an intense pain at this one spot. It persisted like a Chinese torture. My whole body was anesthetized except for that one grinding neck pain.

I opened my eyes and recognized a man who delivered flowers for a local florist standing beside my bed. He was also a volunteer fireman who had a police and fire radio in his delivery truck so he would always be available for emergency fire calls. He heard about my accident over his radio and since he had flowers to deliver in the hospital anyway he took it upon himself to check on my well being. I also knew he was a certified First Aid Instructor.

The dreadful pain aroused me from my unconscious state like an out of breath swimmer frantically kicking his way to the surface of a pool. I had to stop this horrendous stabbing ache. I saw the cloth arm sling that held my fractured left elbow stable and knew immediately it was the knot in the sling that pressed on a vertebra at the base of my neck. I made a feeble attempt to untie the knot with the fingers of my free hand but was unsuccessful. I asked the First Aid Instructor to untie it but he staunchly refused. He argued that the doctors knew what they were doing when they put the knot there. In my semiconscious state I wasn't fully cognizant of the magnitude of my injuries but I did know for certain I couldn't tolerate the intense pain any longer.

I pleaded and begged him to untie the knot and relocate it but my beseeching was to no avail. Finally, in my most authoritarian tone said, "If you don't untie that knot now I'll kick the hell out of you when I get out of here!" I had to be nasty to get his attention. He took the threat seriously and untied the knot and left the loose ends hanging. The pain subsided immediately. He was so afraid a nurse might catch him he fled from the room like a naughty child.

I was still under heavy sedation when a student nurse came to my bedside with a critical problem. She said, "There is a crowd in the hall outside your room. They are waiting for an opportunity to visit you. They refused to leave and they are very demanding and they are arguing with the nurses. The doctors instructed us not to allow any visitors into your room but the first fellow in line is very persistent. He insists I let him in. He won't leave until he sees you. His name is Shultz. What am I to do?"

I was too drowsy to be concerned with what was going on outside the room but I knew Shultz. I told her to let Shultz in and then close the door and put a NO ADMITTANCE sign on it.

I was happy to see Shultz. Our friendship went away back to the rainy night I played poker with him in an underground telephone vault. He was one of the telephone wire splicers. I thanked him for visiting and then asked him to do me a favor. I asked him to order the people waiting outside my door to leave because I was unconscious and too sick to see anyone. He was a large tough take-charge fellow so I knew he could be forceful and convincing. The nurse never complained again so I guess he got the people to leave.

Motorcycle Cop Escorting Sick Child Badly Injured

A motorcycle escort was requested Tuesday noon to clear the way for a sick child being rushed to Lankenau Hospital and Patrolman Bernard Loughran was assigned to the call. The car bearing the child, ▬▬▬▬▬▬▬▬ of the ▬▬▬▬▬▬▬▬, ▬▬▬▬▬, was met by Patrolman Loughran. The little girl appeared to be strangling.

At the intersection of Lancaster Ave. and Clover Hill Rd., a motorist tried to cross the Pike with the green light in her favor. She was ▬▬▬▬▬▬▬▬▬▬▬ ▬▬▬▬▬▬ Rd., Wynnewood. Being somewhat hard of hearing, according to police, she did not stop for the officer's motorcycle, which was headed eastward with siren screaming.

CYCLE HITS CAR

The officer's motorcycle crashed into ▬▬▬▬▬▬▬▬ and Loughran, who is 29, was hurled to the pavement. He suffered a severe head injury, a fractured arm and bad contusion of the shoulder. ▬▬▬▬▬▬▬▬ suffered contusions of the thigh.

The child's trip to Lankenau hospital was completed in a commandeered car. She was treated and discharged.

Officer Loughran was removed to the same hospital, where his condition is said to be satisfactory in spite of the severity of his injuries.

132

DID YOU EVER SEE YOUR BOSS CRY?

After the First Aid Instructor and my friend Shultz left I lapsed into la-la land. When I woke again I saw the Superintendent and the Captain leaving my room. I murmured, "Superintendent, did you want to see me?" They were surprised to hear my voice because I was still under the effects of anesthesia.

They returned to my bedside and the Superintendent said, "Yes, Barney, I wanted to know the extent of your injuries and to see how you were." I said, "Superintendent, I'm very sorry if I embarrassed you and your Department." I couldn't say more before my eyes closed but for a brief moment I saw the Superintendent was genuinely concerned about me. He had tears in his eyes.

Believe it or not, policemen are a very sensitive lot.

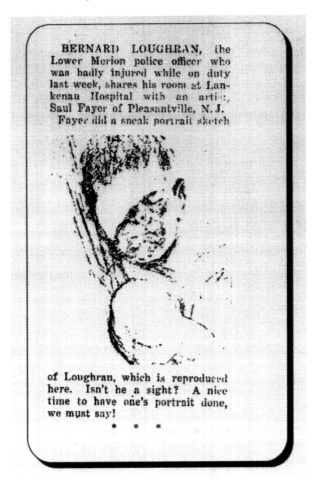

BERNARD LOUGHRAN, the Lower Merion police officer who was badly injured while on duty last week, shares his room at Lankenau Hospital with an artist, Saul Fayer of Pleasantville, N. J. Fayer did a sneak portrait sketch of Loughran, which is reproduced here. Isn't he a sight? A nice time to have one's portrait done, we must say!

* * *

DOCTOR OKIE

On my second day in the hospital an uncouth boorish looking doctor plopped heavily on the side of my bed and woke me. The mattress tilted and in my mental state I was afraid I'd roll out of the bed. He was by no means a traditional sophisticated doctor with bedside manners. He was unkempt, uncombed and he wore a blood stained hospital gown. He told me he was the hospital's plastic surgeon and explained that the sinus sack under my right cheek was shattered and it had to be repaired.

He explained a procedure he experimented with when he was in the service during World War II. He'd drill a small hole in the roof of my mouth and insert a Foley Catheter tube into the sinus sack. He would inflate the catheter with water and use it as a form to hold the tiny bone fragments in place after he slid and pushed them where they belonged. The pieces would be left to set until calcium growth glued them together into a single solid bone again. After a few days he'd open the catheter tube and let the water run out so he could remove it from the sinus sack.

He made this analogy: It was like putting a balloon inside a shattered egg shell and working each fragile piece into place like a jigsaw puzzle. After the broken shell mended he'd remove the balloon. He said he developed this procedure when he was stationed in a service hospital in a city in California where sailors and marines were stationed. Each serviceman was loyal to his own corps and defended it against disparaging remarks. Fights erupted and a fist or a blunt object shattered many sinus sacks. This occurred so often it was incumbent upon him to find a way these injuries could be repaired quickly and accurately so the serviceman could be returned to his unit and sent off to war.

I related to what he was saying. When I was in the Navy Shore Patrol in California I broke up several of those confrontations. To assure me we were brothers in the saddle he added that he drove his motorcycle across the country after his discharge. That was quite an accomplishment in those days so it did engender a great deal more confidence in him.

The procedure he mentioned sounded like barnyard surgery and his general appearance was farmer like. His fingers were thick and massive as a gravedigger's and not the tools for delicate operations. When he finished explaining what he would do to my face he asked for my permission to perform the surgery.

"By the way," he said. "I'm Doctor Okie."

In my semiconscious state he had secured my trust in him and his unique procedure but after he said his name I pictured an Oklahoma farmer (an Okie) operating on me. But I had no choice because I didn't know another plastic surgeon. In desperation I consented. It turned out to be the wisest decision I ever made. There were no complications and every piece of the sinus sack shell was in its proper place when he was done and it healed quickly

NO THANK YOU

I was still heavily sedated after my sinus operation so I wasn't having dreams, nightmares or flashbacks about the moment of impact but when I did wake up it was the most traumatic event of my career.

I was stirred awake by loud voices in my hospital room. In my semiconscious state it sounded like an argument was being rehashed over and over. It was such a silly row that I forced myself to leave my safe twilight zone to find out who were the participants and what was their problem. I was surprised to see my father at the foot of the bed talking to a teenage student nurse. She was assigned surveillance duty in my room. She was to watch over me until I was out of danger and to keep all non-family visitors out of the room. I knew my dad meant well but he was insisting she accept a gratuity for being so concerned about his son's welfare.

He urged her over and over to accept the money he held out to her. "Here, take this. You have been very helpful to my son." She said, "No thank you." Again he thrust the money at her and repeated, "Take it." She tried to show appreciation but again replied, "No thank you!"

His insistence was annoying her and me. I couldn't understand why he couldn't comprehend that she wouldn't accept a gratuity. I was about to butt into the conversation when the nurse gave her final and definite "No!" and added, "No thank you. You will take the pleasure out of being a service."

Dad relented and put the money back in his pocket. I felt sorry for him for he truly wished to show his appreciation for all she and the others in the hospital did for me but he knew of no other way to convey his sincere thanks. It hurt me that this child who had wisdom beyond her years embarrassed him.

Hundreds of times I repeated her words. Whenever a person wished to demonstrate their appreciation for a good deed I performed I said those fabulous words that expressed it so succinctly, "No thank you. You will take the pleasure out of being a service."

I included these words in every lecture I gave to new recruits and encouraged them to adopt them as their own. After I retired I hoped the men who heard my lecture passed these words along to other recruits.

PATROLMAN BERNARD Loughran, who was injured in that collision on Tuesday, has room 628 in Lankenau Hospital.

At times the switchboard at Police Headquarters was swamped with calls asking about his condition. It appears he has many friends.

* * *

Cycle Hits Car, Policeman Hurt

Thrown from his motorcycle in a collision with an automobile while escorting a police car to Lankenau Hospital shortly after 1 P.M. yesterday, Bernard Loughran, 29, of the Lower Merion township police force, was seriously injured at Lancaster pike and Cloverhill rd., Wynnewood.

He was taken to the same hospital to which he was bound as escort of the car carrying an ailing child. His condition was reported "improving" last night, although he had suffered a fracture of the right arm, dislocated shoulder and possible concussion. Police said the car that he hit was driven by ███████████████, of ████████████████████., ███████████.

136

HE'S A FLIRT

Eliciting a favorable reaction from a person after I accused them of committing a motor vehicle violation became a passion. I struggled incessantly to find an unassailable technique. One day, very early in my career, I issued a speeding ticket to a motorist and he turned around and complained to my superior. He didn't question the validity of the charge but complained about my brusque attitude. My Lieutenant took me aside and told me I was too gruff and abrasive and that my approach was too harsh. He advised me to lighten up.

The Lieutenant knew from his personal experiences that it is almost impossible to accuse a person of breaking the law and expect that person to accept the criticism gracefully. I found out from his lecture that embracing censure is not natural so I accepted his advice and promised I'd try my best to improve.

Six months later I was ordered via radio to return to headquarters. As I entered the Lieutenant's office I noticed a man nodding to him. I sensed his visit was to complain about something I did wrong. I overheard the man say, "You're right. It couldn't be."

When the man left the office the Lieutenant told me the man's wife, whom I stopped for speeding the day before, claimed I only stopped her to flirt with her. I could kick myself. Again I failed to perform this function without generating flack. The man's wife was fifty-five years old and unattractive to this twenty-eight year old kid. In my leather motorcycle jacket and puttees I appeared strong and viral. To these mature minded men it was obvious if I were prone to use my uniform I'd hustle attractive girls my own age.

These accusations didn't offend me as much as I was tortured by the frustration at not knowing how to deal with people. I had been wrestling with the problem for eight years. I discussed the subject with my peers but they were grappling with the same problem. When things didn't go smoothly for them they rationalized. Some men solved this problem by avoiding people or did their job only when forced into a situation they couldn't escape. Other officers sought assignments that removed them from having to encounter the public. Men who regularly dealt with people resigned themselves to the fact that some encounters would be successful and an equal number would have negative results. My contemporaries had no suggestions that might make the task easier. They were convinced there was no formula and resigned themselves to the fact a policeman's lot was not a happy one.

I experimented with many possibilities but kept coming up with glaring errors in something I said or did, yet, I believed an officer could deal successfully with people every time if he only knew what the gods knew. Since I couldn't find answers from hands-on experience I sought the answers from formal education that is obtained only in college. I studied Psychology; the study of human behavior; Logic; the art of thinking: Metaphysics, Epistemology, Educational Psychology, Written Communications, Public Speaking, and every subject offered in the Humanities. The more college courses I took the more I became aware there was much more to be learned. I took seriously the saying, "He who thinks he knows Toto knows nothing."

I had to learn why people behaved the way they do and what I must do to have them behave the way I wanted them to. I thirsted for information and registered for five and six subjects a semester. My desire to hone an ideal technique sustained me through ten years of evening college. I sacrificed my days off, vacations and holidays just to attend classes. I skipped lunches and nights out with the boys so I'd have the money for the tuition.

Gradually I came to understand my role as a police officer and why the public had an attitude toward me in that role. I was less critical of people and more understanding of various personalities. I finally achieved my objective when I confronted a person. I could have that person willingly cooperate with me when I phrased the suggestion correctly. After all the evenings I spent on college courses, seminars and conferences that dealt with police skills I finally became competent at my job. No matter how complicated the situation it was minuscule for me and I resolved it quickly.

I became especially accomplished at a motor vehicle accident scene. It matter little the number of vehicles involved or how seriously injured the occupants. If the drivers were hostile toward each other before I arrived I calmed them by displaying confidence. I cared for the injured and collected information in a professional manner. Proof of my ability was in my investigation reports. They left no reason for a discussion. The few cases that were settled in a courtroom were civil cases. These were cases where all Insurance Companies denied financial responsibility. I'd testified in court with such clarity that my testimony was accepted as the words from a traffic accident-investigating expert. I learned how to deal with people under stressful conditions. I could accuse a motorist of a violation and never feared a reprisal. I could arrest the most heinous felon single handedly and never be threatened.

I once arrested a burglar who had the potential to subdue me and escape but I threw him into a state of uncertainty when I tipped my hat and calmly said, "Good evening sir. You are under arrest for trespassing on private property. Please cooperate for you shall be treated according to the way you conduct yourself. Please get into the police car. Thank you."

The difficult situations became simple and the impossible became trouble-free because I had scaled mountains to learn the correct and proper way to do this job.

THAT MAN IS SICK

It was a Sunday afternoon in 1958 and I was enjoying a casual cruise around my beat when I was directed via radio to go to a hospital, "An intoxicated man refuses to leave the accident ward." The message didn't stir my adrenaline because it sounded like a routine complaint. However, as I pulled up to the accident ward entrance I thought it strange that a doctor and a nurse would be greeting me outside the hospital and they would be supporting a man who hung limp between them. They were visually perturbed which I thought was highly uncharacteristic of their profession.

The man was about sixty years old and even though his clothes were old I didn't see him as an indigent but rather a man who possessed culture and pride. I noticed he respected people with authority. I thought it odd that he couldn't talk or move a limb nor could he stand erect without assistance. It was difficult for him to place one foot in front of the other. There were other indications that made me think this person was not intoxicated but very ill.

In unison the doctor and nurse shouted unethically, "Officer, lock this man up! He's drunk and he won't leave the hospital!" I hoped they were trying to intimidate the man and not me. I don't like people to show disrespect for the police uniform.

I studied the man some more and said, "This man isn't drunk he's sick." I realized I was trespassing on their field of expertise even though they were positive of their diagnosis. Angrily they yelled, "He is not sick he's a drunk! Lock him up! Take him to the lockup!"

I studied the man again as if to thoroughly examine him. "This fellow isn't drunk he's sick. I refuse to arrest a sick person." Of course I had no idea what ailed him but I had a gut feeling he was very ill. Maybe he suffered a stroke or a heart attack. It could be anything.

The doctor and nurse started to intimidate me. "Officer, this man is a drunk! We know him! He sleeps in the hospital boiler room! Lock him up! Get him out of here! We have sick patients inside to care for!" I grew more sure I was right and that they weren't thinking clearly. Their diagnosis was clouded because they wanted him ejected from the hospital and out of their hair. I said, "You may know him as a drunk but he is very sick now. I'm not going to lock up a sick man."

They became fanatical and disrespectful. The nurse shouted, "If you don't take him off our hands and lock him up I'll call headquarters and have them dispatch someone who will lock him up! I'll call your Superintendent at his home and tell him you refused to do your job! Then I'll press charges against you for neglect of duty!" That language was strong enough for me. They were representatives of the medical profession and of the hospital. The onus was on them. They were the experts in the medical field. I had no medical knowledge. I was only a dumb cop with a nothing to support my suspicions.

I took the gentleman by the arm and said, "Please get into the car sir." I looked into his sick and partly drunken eyes and I read his mind. He was begging me, "Officer stand your ground. I'm not drunk, I'm sick. Please do not give in to them. You are my only hope." I had no other recourse but to take him to the lockup. I was uneasy when I helped him into the cell to dry out. He couldn't talk yet his eyes seemed to be pleading for help but I was forced to defer to the doctor's and the nurse's opinion.

The next day I reported for work and learned my prisoner died in the cell during the night. I felt terrible and the acids tore at my stomach. I should have stood my ground. I should have insisted they treat him as a sick man. No matter, that was all hindsight.

The Superintendent had me on the carpet to question me on the matter. He demanded to know, "Why did you put a sick man in the cell? What were you thinking?" I was frightened I might lose my job or even be socked with criminal charges but I told him outright that the doctor and nurse insisted the man be taken to the lockup. I said I told them several times he was sick but they insisted otherwise. They said they examined the man and found he was only drunk. I told them he wasn't drunk but very ill but I had to defer to their expertise. I told the Superintendent how they threatened to bring charges of neglect of duty against me. I acquiesce to their diagnosis when they said they were going to telephone him at home and report me for not doing my duty.

The Superintendent was furious and banged his fist on his desk to emphasize the predicament he and the department were in now. "If you were so sure he was sick why didn't you take him to a doctor's office for a checkup?" I asked him, "Where could I have taken him? It was a Sunday. Where could I find a doctor with office hours? If I had taken him to a private practitioner and he was found to be intoxicated who would pay the doctor's bill? You would have been upset that I contradicted the hospital staff."

He sharply dismissed me without giving me any indications of what he was thinking. There was a Coroner's Inquest but I wasn't called as a witness. I don't know if the doctor and nurse were questioned. In cases where a prisoner dies in a cell the Pennsylvania Department of Prisons conducts an extensive investigation and if the police department is found negligent a heavy fine is levied and the lockup might be permanently closed.

I heard no more about the incident and I thought it more prudent if I didn't inquire.

THE FAKE ACCIDENT INJURY CLAIM

By the time I had fifteen years experience I was a virtuoso at investigating a motor vehicle accident. Forensic evidence never escaped my eye. A witness never left the scene before I obtained a written statement. No injured person languished at the scene without getting immediate attention and no operator left without all the pertinent information his insurance carrier needed.

At a glance I knew which vehicle did the striking and with how much force. From the direction of the skid marks and their length before and after the impact I estimate at what speed they were laid and where the vehicles traveled out of control after impact. From the kind of material used for the road surface I read the evidence deposited there like I was an Indian scout. The dirt and dust shaken from under a fender pinpointed the exact point of impact.

My Public Relations training helped me calm the operators, the injured, and the spectators. I scrutinized everything amid the swirling chaos. I say I was a superior investigator not to be braggadocio but to illustrate how finely tuned my accident investigation skills had become. My system was impeccable but even though I handled dozens of accident with grace and ease it was inevitable that when my ego became inflated something embarrassing always cropped up to bring me back to earth.

I was performing at my peek the time I investigated a routine accident at an uncomplicated intersection. A taxi and a car collided at an intersection controlled by STOP signs. There was barely any contact. There was hardly a noticeable scratch on either vehicle. I collected the necessary information and gave a carbon copy to each driver. The cabby and his three passengers insisted they weren't injured and refused to go to a hospital for a checkup. There were no onlookers, however, I obtained witness statements from all five individuals involved. The investigation at the scene was completed in twenty minutes and I submitted a formal report that was available to any insurance underwriter who purchased a copy.

Three weeks later my Lieutenant called me into his office and asked me if I noticed anything suspicious about that accident and I confidently said I saw nothing unusual. He said the Insurance Fraud Investigators were checking on the cab driver. It was his fifth accident where he and the same three passengers submitted inflated injury claims.

I hadn't a clue there was a scam going on nor did my investigation uncover one. I was good but not that good. My Lieutenant said he was only passing the information on to me for my edification and suggested I be alert and suspicious in the future.

That was another skill I had to develop.

THE GREENHILL FARMS DETAIL

For ten days a burglar harassed a section of the township boarding City Line Avenue. This person wasn't a real threat to anyone. He was just hungry and wanted something to eat so he'd enter an unoccupied house and raid the refrigerator. He didn't ransack the house in search of money or valuables but after he ate he left a very untidy kitchen. Each night he entered a different house.

The detectives in their clever analytical fashion theorized the burglar was either a young boy from the neighborhood who was having a terrible time getting through puberty, or, an itinerant on his way through this part of the country who happened upon a temporary place to pause and rest. It doesn't matter who it was; a serial burglar of any sort unsettles a community. To date he hadn't confronted anyone but if he were cornered his temperament might change. It is a fact that every burglar leaves his victims with a physiological trauma that last forever.

At midnight roll call my sergeant barked an order, "Loughran, take a post on the corner of 67th and City Line on the city side. There is a vacant lot there and from that vantage point you will have an unobstructed view of the area. Be on the lookout for whoever is hitting those houses. The beat car will drop you off and pick you up at 7:45. He is not to return to you at any time during the night."

Oddly it never entered my mind to protest or refuse an assignment. It wasn't done during this era. The current attitude was that this night it was my misfortune to draw the short straw. Some days the bear eats you and some days you eat the bear. No matter how unreasonable the assignment you bit the bullet and carried on. Our attitude was formed during our military service when you either obeyed the order to charge over the hill or you were shot.

I wasn't the first man assigned to this detail. The man assigned a few nights earlier told us how unbearably cold the night was. How other men coped with the inclement weather we never knew because they never shared their secret. Whatever scheme they used might have brought neglect of duty charges against them.

This particular area is unique because a central heating plant located in the city heats the homes on both sides of City Line Avenue. Hot steam is generated in the central heating plant and forced through underground pipes to the houses that subscribe to the system. Police officers knew where the underground pipes were laid because the steam on its way to the houses leaked from vents and pipes under the streets. Some steam rose out of the culverts at the side of the road. Snow melted first on the surface of the road heated by the underground pipes and after a rain the same road surface dried first.

The officer assigned a few nights earlier told us he became insanely cold and climbed into a heated culvert to thaw. He was so desperate he

142

stood in a culvert that may be occupied by foxes, rats, opossums, raccoons, wild dogs, stray cats and other wild creatures. We patrolled those streets at night and we often saw a wild animal, frightened by the patrol car's headlights, scurry into a culvert along the curb.

I could never be so desperate that I'd share a residence with wild creatures. After all I'd be invading his territory therefore the animal would have every right to bite me with rabid and diseased teeth. I might carry diseased lice home on my clothing and contaminate my house and family. What fears other policemen had I never knew but I'd rather confront a vicious felon who might resort to any means to avoid capture than climb into a culvert.

I dreaded not finding a comfortable place to sit or shelter from the harsh weather. Without some kind of comfort the night would be unbearably long. Unidentifiable shadows were scary and there was the insufferable silence and solitude. I dread the thought I might startle a passerby or a homeowner. These were my primary concerns. The possibility death may be stalking me was at the bottom of the list.

At midnight the beat man deposited me on the designated corner with a foreboding, "I'll pick you up at 7:45." The inference was, "If you are not here at 7:45 I'm returning to headquarters without you." As he sped off I darted into the vacant lot before I would be observed. The weeds weren't a foot high so they didn't offer any cover or shelter. There was a single tree in the center of the lot so I leaned against it. The weeds at its base was trampled flat by the other officers who were assigned here. A burglar clever enough to prowl a neighborhood undetected would find more shelter than this tree.

The temperature quickly dropped to freezing. The cold in the ground worked on my toes and crept up my legs. The little bit of heat in my shoes thawed the ground frost and created a wet puddle. Every minute seemed like ten. I examined my wristwatch often to make sure it was still ticking. Checking the time only made it pass slower. My feet froze and my legs became so numb I couldn't stand still any longer. I jogged in place and skipped rope until I was exhausted. When I rested legs cramped and my knees locked. I no longer cared if the burglar ate his way through the whole township. I couldn't stand any longer so I sat on the damp ground. I abandoned all caution as the dampness eased up my spine. I knew my future would to be cursed with piles. My choices were culvert or piles and I opted for piles.

I stopped checking my watch because time wasn't my enemy. The bitter cold and dampness was. I couldn't sit upright any longer so disregarding the consequences I rolled on my side and got into a fetal position. Eventually I fell into the euphoric deep sleep the early trappers experienced on the Klondike when they were lost in a blinding snowstorm. I was alone against raw nature.

I awoke in a panic. "What time is it? Did I oversleep? Is it after 7:45?" A horrible fear overtook me. Did the beat man leave me behind because I wasn't at the designated spot at the agreed time? Was a search party sent to look for me? Will I loss my job for sleeping on duty?

Then a new fear struck. I couldn't move my arm to check the time. I've had an arm or leg fall asleep before and it was no big deal. I've awakened in my own bed with a leg cramp but now I was in a total state of paralysis. I couldn't move a limb. I got a grip on my wits and commanded the blood to flow to my fingers, then to a forearm, then to a biceps and finally to my shoulder. I concentrated on the other arm. I dared not proceed too rapidly for I might cause a muscle cramp. I feared my bones were so chilled they were brittle and any sudden jerk might cause one to snap. I rocked onto my stomach and after a few seconds rest I slowly raised onto my elbows. I gave the command to my left leg to move under me and then gave a similar command to my right leg. My panic diminished somewhat when I was on my elbows and knees. If I moved very slowly everything would be OK.

I hesitated and took stock, "What time is it? It must be late because the commuter traffic started to roll. People were walking toward a bus stop and it is near daylight." I hugged the tree and worked my way up the trunk to a standing position. I pushed back my sleeve and looked at my watch and it was 7:30. I was safe, time-wise. I had my gun and equipment so no one crept up on me while I was in a coma. I did slow calisthenics to circulate the blood and by the time the beat car arrived my flexibility returned. I was in good shape considering how my body was thirty minutes earlier.

I entered the car and felt a blast of warm air from the heater. "Hi Pal. Any excitement during the night?" What I really asked, did I miss anything I should have observed? Were there any reported burglaries? Was there a fire or an auto accident in the area that I would have known about had I been awake and alert?

"Not a thing. The radio was dead. A couple of guys asked for radio checks to be sure their radio was working. It was an exceptionally long boring night." "I concur."

My arthritis never let me forget that horrible night. Flashbacks are the eternity I spend in hell. I have nightmares that my spine is permanently fused and I'm a paraplegic with no one to care for me.

The burglaries ceased so I was the last man assigned to that detail. The fellow who sought refuse in the infested culvert never wanted to be that cold again so he quit the force and became a successful automobile salesman.

THE SUICIDE

One morning I received a radio message to go to an address. The radio operator said a houseman reported a loud blast came from the basement. Two other officers were dispatched also. Together we questioned the frightened houseman. He said just before the loud explosion he saw the mister go into the cellar but he had no idea what happened and he was too scared to go down alone and find out.

The three of us cautiously walked down the cellar steps. We didn't know what we'd find but suspected a suicide. Our first setback was the cellar light switch didn't function and the cellar was in total darkness. There wasn't a single ray of natural light down there. We walked into a black cavern not knowing what kind of monster was lurking in a corner. The basement was cluttered with odds and ends. I groped around for a light cord and when I felt one dangling from the rafters I tugged on it but the bulb didn't glow. It was frustrating until an officer fetched our flashlights from our patrol cars.

We flashed the beams around the ceiling and located three cords dangling from the rafters but each socket was without a bulb. The bulbs had been shattered by the concussion. The darkness absorbed the faint light from our flashlights and made them less effective than penny candles. We needed light from several bulbs so the houseman removed three from the lamps in the living room and handed them to us.

While I was searching in the darkness for a hanging light cord I slid several times on the cement floor. I lost my balance and almost fell because the floor was damp and I was stepping on small objects lying about. I couldn't imagine what I was walking on. My major concern was to get the lights on. We removed the old light bulb brass bases and inserted the new bulbs and finally had the light we needed to look around. I checked to see what was on the floor. The floor was covered with pieces of flesh and bones and a coating of coagulated blood. Lying at the foot of his workbench was the mister, minus the top of his head, and the shotgun he used to commit suicide.

I had been stepping and sliding on fragments of the man's brains and skull. It was enough to make a weak man sick but like a true soldier I pulled myself together and joined the others collecting all the pieces. We combed the floor for the tiniest spec of brains, skull and flesh. Every piece was placed in a bag and saved for the coroner. After the detectives completed their investigation we helped the undertaker place the corpse into a body bag.

NOTE: There was no such thing as plastic gloves for any assignment even assignments as gruesome as this in this era.

WHAT'S THE WEATHER FORECAST?

On the morning of March 11, 1956 Lou and I were riding together on the day shift. Snow flurries began to fall at 8:00 a.m. when we started out on patrol in Car #24. The snow never let up but even after two hours we didn't have to adjust our driving habits. It didn't look like it would become a threat yet it was an odd snow. It wasn't the type of snow that appears on Christmas cards. It was fine as sugar and as solid as white rice.

In mid March snow usually falls in large flakes called "onion snow". Onion snow comes down in a heavy shower and blankets the roadways and lawns but melts rapidly leaving little trace of it after forty-eight hours. This definitely was not onion snow. Instead of lying on the highway it sailed ominously across the blacktop like sand being blown over a desert dune. It vacillated from one lane to the other depending on which lane had the last moving vehicle. Like confetti it swirled and floated in the air and didn't pause long enough to get the road wet.

Over the police radio came an urgent message from the Lieutenant who wasn't familiar with this freakish snow. He was inside headquarters and could only evaluate what he saw after looking out a window. When in doubt every Lieutenant called upon an officer on patrol for a status report. This time he believed he was conferring with a weather expert when he asked Lou for his assessment of the snow. "Car 24. Lou Milo, is this snowfall going to amount to much?"

Lou and I looked at each other. He took us by surprise. It was really dumb to ask us that over the radio. He should have asked us to call him from a police call box. We both laughed. I jokingly suggested, "Lou tell him to call the Weather Bureau." Lou said, "I can't do that. He probably did that already but now he wants my opinion." Lou didn't have an answer. It wasn't a stupid question but we felt it should have been discussed over a phone.

The Lieutenant had grave responsibilities when it snowed. There was a checklist in the event of a heavy downfall. He had to notify all fire company housemen. He had to notify the Township Highway foremen and they in turn contacted their men and instructed them to install snow chains on the snowplows, dump trucks and refuse trucks. Dump trucks had to be loaded with cinders before the snow got out of control. He had to notify the Township Manager and the Superintendent of the emergency. He coordinated the township department supervisors and they conferred with each other through him. He was responsible for the successful attack on a heavy snowfall.

In a crisis, such as a heavy snowfall that might paralyze the township, he had to make sure all the cogs were moving and meshing. Sometimes it was difficult to make a decision based on his limited information. For help in making major decisions he called upon the one man he thought had natural instincts in evaluating the weather.

His assumption was not without foundation because Lou was an outdoorsman. Single-handedly he built a hunting cabin in the mountains and he was an avid hunter and fisherman. He was a Marine for six years during World War II and survived by his wits in the fierce South Pacific Island battles. Lou could survive in the wild just by reading nature's signs; therefore, he was a creditable person to rely on for a weather prediction.

Over the radio the question came for the third time, "Car 24. Lou, does it look like this snowfall will amount to much?" Lou didn't like being put on a spot where everyone within earshot of a police radio will listen and heed his critique of this freakish snow. He became more tense every second he delayed. He hoped the Lieutenant wouldn't call him again but instead call upon another officer in another car.

"Bernie, how does he expect me to know how much of this stuff is going to fall?" I laughed but he was panicking. The question was begging for an answer. I considered the facts. It was in the middle of March and snow usually melts quickly this time of the year. If the snow became threatening an adjustment in the decision could be made in time for the various tasks to be performed. Lou was at the point where he had no opinion of his own so I told him all the things that I considered and concluded with, "Tell him this snow may not amount to much but we will have to wait and see."

Lou repeated what I said into the microphone and the Lieutenant took his advice and delayed putting into effect the township's emergency plan. The two-hour delay turned out to be crucial. When the Lieutenant finally sounded the alarm it was too late because it developed into the worst storm the township experienced in modern times.

On March 11, 1956 it snowed a record 8.9 inches for that date and if that wasn't enough of a hardship five days later, March 16, 1956 there was another record 11.8 inches that compounded the existing problem. Not one flake was onion snow. It snowed heavily and drifted so high that the township was snowbound for three weeks.

The businessmen couldn't wait for the snow to melt. They demanded it be removed and their business restored at any costs. People had to shop for food and necessities. Employers wanted their employees to return to work.

The township had to reinforce its own overtaxed highway personnel to get the major roads open. Under political pressure the Township Manager hired a construction firm to add manpower and equipment to the overburdened township laborers. Bulldozers, front end loaders, road graders, plows, dump trucks and various heavy equipment was rented at the exorbitant cost of $250.00 a day for each machine and operator. The construction firm plowed and carted the snow away.

Motorists drove in ruts worn so deep the high mounds of frozen snow damaged the undercarriage of the cars. The hired construction workers toiled around the clock to open the main roads. Ten days passed before the business districts were accessible but two weeks later the ugly snow still remained piled high along the curbs where it was plowed and left to melt. Finally the contractors hauled it away too. It was a horrible month.

Lou's credibility went down the chute. It didn't bother him too much except the Lieutenant glowered at him when their paths crossed. Lou knew the Lieutenant was in a pressure cooker and in near panic when he repeated the question over and over on the radio. But his conscience was clean. He didn't intent to be malicious even though the Lieutenant suspected Lou might have deliberately sabotaged him.

Lou and I had two options and just by the flip of the coin I opted for the wrong one. History will record the volume of snow the township experienced on these dates and I'll remember them as the dates I made my worse decision.

The pistol team (1959) is posing with the trophies won over the previous five years. From the left Brady Utz, Chester O'Shell, Joe Algieri, Frank Wilson, and me.

THE TREE TRIMMERS

. 10, 1958   Telephone: IVy 2½¢ 3-7¢¢   5 CENTS
GM Main St., Phila. S. Pa.

Grocer Talks Abductors Into Releasing Him

Two 15-Year-Old Boys Accused; One Hurt in Flight, Taken to Hospital

A Manayunk grocer was seized by two youths at 11 A. M. yesterday on the Schuylkill Expressway, forced at gunpoint to drive them through the Main Line and was left stranded in a woods near Belmont Hills.

The youths were captured by Lower Merion township police, one of them running away from the grocer's car, wrecked against a tree, and the other after being flushed out of another woods in Wynnewood.

Joseph Sokoral, 42, of 131 Dupont St., told police he saw two youths hitch-hiking as he approached the Belmont entrance of the Expressway. He picked the boys up.

In 1958 the Township Commissioners were zealously frugal. The spending crunch affected every purchase including the scheduled Capital Improvements just so they could boast to their constituency they didn't raise taxes. An impressive bottom line would influence voters so spending was pared to the bone.

In their endeavor to cut costs there was the notion a sizable savings would be realized if the amount of gasoline used by the patrol cars was reduced so automobiles with a smaller engine were purchased. The vehicle's overall dimensions and weight was the same but the engine's horsepower was far less. Instead of the powerful eight cylinder engines the new cars had only six cylinders. The reduced horsepower used less gas but it was reflected in insufficient power, slower speeds and a feeble pickup.

This cherubic idea was from the mind of a man who had no concept of police work. It turned out to be penny wise but pound-foolish. The maintenance costs soared because the smaller engines couldn't withstand the torturous all-seasons-twenty-four-hour workload.

The first clue came when an officer drove upon a burglary in progress. Two men were loading the contents of a gas station into their truck. They spotted the officer approaching at the same time the officer saw them. They jumped into their truck and speed off. The officer accelerated his patrol car to pursue them but when he applied the gas the small engine stalled. He tried desperately to start the car but it wouldn't kick over until the burglars were long gone and far away. Other officers began to report similar horror stories. I hadn't any such problem until the afternoon the very same thing happened to me at a critical moment.

At noon on a chilly damp afternoon I went on duty. I drove from headquarters in a six-cylinder patrol car that was parked overnight in the cold outdoors. I got two blocks from headquarters when there was a radio alert to all cars. I happened to be stopped behind traffic waiting for the red traffic signal to change so I took this opportunity to jot the details on my clipboard.

The radio message was urgent. "All cars be on the lookout for a green Chevy station wagon Pa license 123-456. Two boys stole the car. These boys were hitchhiking on the Schuylkill Expressway at the Green Lane Bridge. They pulled a gun on the motorist who picked them up. They walked the motorist into the woods in Gladwyne and forced him to undress. They tied him to a tree and fled with his payroll and his car."

I took my eyes off my clipboard to check the status of the traffic signal because I didn't want to hold up the traffic stopped behind me. There was the Chevy station wagon in front of me waiting for the same red light to change. I saw the driver looking into his rearview mirror and from the startled look on his face I could tell he realized there was a policeman behind him. Without waiting for the light to change to green he raced off. I started to chase after him but when I punched down on the accelerator the six-cylinder engine stalled and refused to start.

I radioed headquarters and informed them of my dilemma. At the same time other patrol cars overheard my radio message and in what direction the car was traveling. Many valuable seconds were lost before my engine started up. When it finally did kick-over I took up the chase but the Chevy was a half-mile ahead of me. I accelerated to a reckless speed even though my car hadn't a siren or emergency lights to alert the traffic around me. I wasn't gaining on the Chevy but another six-cylinder patrol car came in on the chase from a side street and closed the gap a trifle.

The fleeing car would have easily escape if the driver stayed on the main highway but to shake us off his tail he made a right turn into the first side street. In a long race he would have out-distanced us even on the side streets because our cars couldn't accelerate on command at every intersection like his. Our cars might even stall if we pushed the pedal too hastily. But our advantage outweighed his. We knew the side streets like the lines in our palms and he didn't.

The street he turned into was a dead-end street that had a large ancient tree at the end of it. At the speed he was traveling he was unable to bring his car to a stop before plowing into it. His passenger was catapulted through the windshield and sustained a broken leg but the driver ran blindly down an adjacent street with me running after him. The two officers in the other chase car stayed at the accident scene to assist and arrest the injured passenger. I was no match for the kid who ran from the crash because my police clothing and equipment were a heavy restricting burden that weighed me down.

The kid and I ran neck and neck for a hundred yards before I realized I'd never catch him in a foot race. I was so out of breath I decided to threaten him with a show of my pistol. I hoped it would bring him to a halt before I had to abandoned the race altogether so I could catch my breath. I pulled my gun from the holster and pointed it at him. In my most authoritative voice I roared, "Stop or I'll shoot!" He didn't stop so I pointed the gun barrel toward the clouds and let a bullet fly into the tree branches that overlapped in the center of this bucolic road. The kid was so tense and scared he actually believed I shot him in the back. He fell to the macadam and withered in pain.

At the time I was on the police department's pistol team and I was positive I didn't shoot him but I was pleased with the results of the warning shot. All I had to do was walk up to him and put him in handcuffs. However, I was so exhausted and out of breath it took me a few too many seconds to reach him. Those extra few seconds was all he needed to collect his wits and realize he hadn't been shot at all. He jumped up off the road and continued his dash to escape.

I figured if shooting the gun worked once I'd give it another try. I gave the command to stop and let another shot off high over his head. This sounds like an exaggeration but once again he collapsed in pain. He again thought the bullet hit him. He could feel the sting of hot lead in his back. He twisted and crunched into a fetal position in the middle of the road. I got within grabbing distance when he jumped up and sprinted off into a wooded area and got lost in the underbrush. Every officer on duty was brought into the area to beat the bushes. It took a half hour to locate him.

I walked back to where I left my patrol car. Along the way I saw the Township Shade Tree personnel up in the branches overhanging the street. They were busily pruning the dead branches. There was no sign of them when the chase was on because they parked their trucks on a side street. They advanced down the street trimming one tree after the other. I shot twice into those trees and I could have shot a tree trimmers.

Every day I learned something different.

151

PROSPECT HILL

All winter I lay on a cold bare ground that had a frost in it that was two feet thick. I was assigned to Prospect Hill, an isolated godforsaken nine-acre plot, to wait for a burglar to walk by me. The odds he'd ever cross my path were astronomical. It was the dead of winter without even a faint sign of life and in that black silent emptiness I waited for Godot.

I was the department's response to the demands of the residents for beefed up police protection. To prove the Detective Bureau was concerned it produced statistics indicating there were X number of officers posted in the area for X number of hours and for X number of nights. However, the clever Detective Bureau never assigned a detective to sit on outposts like the one I was assigned because they protected their own. They argued it was economically sound to assign a patrolman because there was a nickel an hour difference in the salaries. This method of policing was used in the Neanderthal era and these flatfooted detectives collectively couldn't think of a new approach. They couldn't comprehend that if by chance the burglar did walk by me I'd be too frozen to pounce upon him and shackle him. An hour after lying on the cold ground I'd be too stiff to chase an opossum or raccoon that was curiously sniffing me.

I went on the assignment each night with a negative attitude. I was living the life of a hermit. In the morning I'd go home and stand under a hot shower until I thawed and then I'd hunker under the blankets to store up enough warmth and energy to sustain me through the following night. My body had to be recharged every day. I saw my wife and children for a few hours during the day but I was too fatigued to enjoy them. At 10:30 p.m. I ate my dinner and prepared for the long cold night by layering bulky underwear and clothing that provided no protection from the north winds. At midnight I was transported to my post where there wasn't a soul within a hundred yard radius. If I got into a predicament I wouldn't know in which direction to shout for help.

The average person might think being isolated in a place blacker than an anthracite mine with the possibility of confronting a felon was by far my primary fear but it wasn't. My cautions centered on nocturnal animals and insects that foraged in total darkness. Warm-blooded animals might want to snuggle against me to get warm. Wild animals are often rabid and a single tooth penetrating my clothing could be fatal because there was no way I'd get immediate treatment. A snake or an infected fly or crawling insect could inject a poison under my skin that had no known cure. There is a fist full of fears I might encounter:

(1)   Confronting the burglar.
(2)   Enduring the relentless cold temperature.
(3)   Chasing off a mad animal.

(4)   Having an attack of diarrhea. The frigid weather might bring on a severe case of the runs. I was never a boy scout so being in a vacant field without a modern convenience would be a major dilemma. A run-in with a felon was not my main concern.

Burglars don't have to be an Indian scout to smell cigarette smoke a hundred yards away so I dare not smoke all night. That was a dreadful deprivation.

Within minutes after being dropped at my post I was bitter cold in spite of the layers of clothing. I felt like a fish caught in a trawler's net and about to be quick-frozen. The cold didn't gradually creep upon me it instantly swaddled me. My toes were numb and pained and my knees vibrated like a palm sander. My ears burned with frostbite and my nose ran until it was raw from wiping it on my coarse coat sleeve. There are colder jobs and men who beg for relief from the excruciating cold but few jobs demanded a man stay his post for eight hours without some compassionate relief. A detective doesn't have to be a genius to know that planting a man in an open space was heartless and then to expect a burglar to promenade by him was an exercise in stupidity.

Incidentally, Grace Kelly, the Princess of Monaco, owned this nine-acre field in Prospect Hill. She was basking on a toasty Monaco beach while I was freezing. This land was her financial investment and my hell but I didn't fault her because she hadn't a clue about what was happening on the property she was paying taxes on.

My outpost had an unobstructed panoramic view of West Conshohocken, Conshohocken and Bridgeport. These communities are only a mile away as the crow flies. In the darkness the scenery is beautiful. Lights glowed in the houses built on the hillside and outdoor lights twinkled like stars in the heavens. Streetlights outlined the roads and traffic signals rhythmically changed colors every thirty seconds. In one corner of the landscape bright stadium lights illuminated the Allen Wood Steel Mill that was spread over sections of each of these towns.

Before dawn every day an explosion at the mill sent a shock wave rumbling toward me. It was like a clap of thunder following a flash of lightning. The sound reached me with vibrant clarity. The explosion was the dynamite charge that blew open the furnace to allow the molten ore to gush forth. The black sky above the mill burst briefly into brilliant red and after the scarlet glow touched the low clouds it leisurely receded.

I heard the blast and saw the phenomenal red flash rise and fade in another world where it was very warm. I studied the boom and flare-up and saw additional details every night but after seeing the spectacular light show every morning for two weeks it became a common occurrence and no longer held me spellbound.

The explosion and flash of light only marked a point in the night reminding me there was three more freezing hours to go until I was on my way home and under a hot shower.

THE AUTOPSY

After ten years on the force I gradually grew callous and somewhat insensitive. The change in my outlook was the result of frequent exposure to shocking sights and deplorable situations. Always in the nick of time something pops up to remind me I am a human being inside this veneer of brass buttons and blue cloth.

A wake up call came when I was investigating a fatal auto accident. The driver was killed under strange circumstances. The coroner was suspicious so he decided to perform an autopsy. His objective was to determine if the man ingested medication, alcohol, drugs, had a heart attack, blacked out or whatever before the collision.

My report wouldn't be complete until I included the coroner's autopsy report. I needed to interview him so I telephoned his office. His secretary said he was out for the remainder of the day and he was leaving on a two-week vacation. She added he was performing an autopsy at the local morgue and I could reach him there. His information was critical so if he was leaving town I had better see him while I could. If I nailed him down at the morgue my investigation report would be wrapped up.

I caught up with him just after he scrubbed up and was about to enter the operating room. He invited into the operating room if I wished to observe an autopsy. I considered it a unique experience so I accepted his invitation. Not many officers have this opportunity.

With a flourish he yanked the sheet off the cadaver lying on the table. The sight of a naked body shocked me even though it was a male's and he was dead. As he performed the procedure he explained his every move into a recording system. For a moment I thought he was explaining what he was doing to me until I saw a dainty microphone dangling from the ceiling over his head. Later his secretary would transcribe the tape into a formal typed report.

His first move was to cut a full circle around the top of the man's head. He then picked the scalp off by the hair to expose the skull. It reminded me of a chef lifting a lid off a pot. After a series of passes behind the ears and under the chin with the scalpel he peeled the skin off the man's face in one piece. It was like a child removing a Halloween mask. I couldn't peel the skin off a freshly roasted turkey that easily.

At that point I decided I learned all I needed to know about an autopsy. I sensed the nauseating operation wasn't going to get any better. The coroner's commentary and procedure were bound to get more grisly and I wasn't as hardnosed as I thought. I gave the coroner a courageous hand signal and lip-synched, "I've got to go, Doc. I'll get in touch with you later, thanks." He nodded without interrupting his conversation with the microphone.

I exited the room double-quick before I had an embarrassing accident. If I had stayed any longer I would have lost my lunch.

THE FENDER SKIRT

Because I solved this difficult Hit and Run automobile accident I came up smelling like a gigantic bouquet of roses. In 1959 I had been a police officer for eleven years and beginning to strut in high cotton. This accident happened on the first rainy night after a long drought. The roads were slippery and slick from an accumulation of oil drippings.

A speeding car slid off a narrow suburban road and struck an iron rail fence. Two six-foot wide by three feet high sections were twisted out of shape and tossed twenty feet from their posts. The rails were rusted and decayed and I assumed of little monetary value. Their sole purpose was to define the property line and was probably erected when Indians roamed the township. The fence wasn't visible to anyone passing by because it was hidden under a heavy growth of vines and weeds that were neglected and never cut back. If these two sections weren't replaced they would never be missed.

The owner, however, thought the rusted rails were priceless antiques so he visited the Superintendent's office every few days to ask what progress had been made on the investigation into who destroyed his fence. The officer who investigated the accident detected a speck of green paint on one rail so he reported the striking vehicle was green and since the rails were mangled he assumed the vehicle suffered extensive damage on the right side. That was the extent of his expert investigation.

After three weeks everyone but the property owner forgot about this accident. He continually harassed the Superintendent. He demanded the culprit be found and made to make restitution. As an incentive he offered a reward to the officer who located the driver who destroyed his precious fence.

The fence owner's constant pestering annoyed the Superintendent so in frustration he went to my Lieutenant and directed him to reopen the investigation. My Lieutenant assigned me to go to the accident scene and collect whatever information the first investigator may have missed. Three weeks had passed since the accident so I didn't expect any additional forensic evidence would be still at the scene and any effort on my part would be a demonstration of futility.

Since the irritating fence owner persisted in haranguing the Superintendent maybe a few additional manpower hours on the investigation might appease him. Be that as it may from the Lieutenant's tone of voice I interpreted the assignment as an order to solve the crime so I drove to the location post haste with that in mind.

At the scene I was surprised to find that the twisted sections were hidden deep in the underbrush. I wondered how the driver extricated his car after being entangled in all the overgrowth. I tried to fathom why the owner generated so much fuss over something that had no monetary or esthetic value.

While trampling through the weeds and vines I was afraid I'd be infected with Rocky Mountain Fever from a tick bite. I applauded the officer who located the rails and the faint paint marks for his tenacity but my main concerned was for my personal safety. I cautiously searched around for snakes slithering in the weeds and for a wild animal den when a black fender skirt suddenly peeked through the dense vegetation.

For the reader who may not know what a fender skirt is I'll try to describe it. It is a decorative piece of sheet metal that covers the rear wheel well of an automobile. The rule of thumb is that the fender skirt is the same color as the car but here was a hand painted black fender skirt that came off a green car. The first investigator was absolutely right because I saw the traces of green paint on a rail too. I didn't fault him for not finding the buried fender skirt because I was just lucky to see it.

Here was a telltale clue that eliminated all automobiles with matching colored fender skirts. It proved a car with a green body and black fender skirt combination was the culprit. I proudly submitted my report an hour after being assigned. The Lieutenant posted a notice on the bulletin board directing all patrol officers to be on the lookout for a green car with a black fender skirt missing on the right side.

I reported off duty at 7:00 p.m. that evening and went home. A note from my wife was posted under a magnet on the refrigerator door. She asked me to pick her and the children up after work at a Hospital Spring Fair. I quickly changed into civilian clothes and drove to the fair.

On the way I was almost involved in an auto accident with a vehicle that ignored a STOP sign. I jammed on my brakes in the nick of time and avoided a collision. The car crossing my path was a green car and the right side was severely damaged. Chimes went off in my head. This may be the car that struck the fence.

I followed it until I had an opportunity to pass it on the left. I was ecstatic when I saw a black fender skirt covering the left rear wheel well. I memorized the license number and drove to the fair.

The next day I obtained the name and address of the owner from the Bureau of Motor Vehicles and presented the information to my Lieutenant. He assigned another officer to go to the owner's address and arrest the car owner on a Hit and Run charge.

The Superintendent was euphoric when he was told he could notify the fence owner that the Hit and Run driver was apprehended and restitution was forthcoming.

The Police Pension Fund was enriched by a hundred dollars and I received shinny Gold Brownie points.

MERRY CHRISTMAS

After a few years on the job an officer sharpens his awareness and observation acumen to a remarkable clarity. I'll give single example of how keen an officer can be. An officer was cruising by a Social Club on an evening when the Club was holding a gala black tie affair. Parked in the parking lot and on the surrounding streets were the finest luxury automobiles. The members were society people who arrived in Buicks, Cadillacs, Lincolns, Continentals, Oldsmobiles, etc., all hallmarks of society and symbols of wherewithal.

A single dirty vintage car parked among the elegant cars was out of place. It aroused the officer's curiosity so he parked in the shadows and watched it. After a brief wait his patience was rewarded. A burglar darted from behind shrubbery and jumped into his getaway car. Before he could drive off the officer was upon him and made an arrest. I'm not suggesting I am that clever. I am just giving an example.

One blustery Christmas Eve I was cruising through a shopping center parking lot an hour after closing time. I was giving the stores a final visual check. The lot was littered with debris discarded by the shoppers over the previous weeks. On this evening the Holiday shopping season finally came to an end. The mannequins in the store windows looked exhausted and the window trappings lost their brilliance.

During my tour in the Navy Air Force I learned how to judge the speed of the wind. Pilots must know the speed of the wind and from which direction it is blowing in the event an emergency landing had to be made. The speed of the wind is estimated by studying the leaves and litter dancing across the ground. If the debris doesn't move there isn't any wind or there is only the whisper of a harmless breeze so the airplane can be landed unaffected by it. If the debris is whipped in whirlpools and leaves race over the fields and if the trees are bent or bowed the wind is judged to be a strong force and a factor to be considered.

As I slowly cruised in the parking lot I studied the debris. The wind was brisk and the trash was tossed vigorously across the blacktop. As I scanned the area I noticed one object didn't budge so being an inquisitive cop I investigated. It turned out to be a crushed gift box containing a new Angora sweater that was intended to be someone's Christmas present. The box protected the sweater from the traffic that rode over it. There was no sale slip or identification of the giver or the receiver in the box. It was as black as tar and more expensive than any I could afford. Now it was mine because there was no way to trace the buyer, receiver or the store where it was purchased.

My wife and I were on a very tight budget and couldn't afford gifts for each other but when she opened the new box I wrapped the sweater in she sprang to her feet and placed it against her body and screamed, "Thank you! Thank you! Merry Christmas!"

ROW THE BOAT

When I was fourteen years of age I stood on the bank of the Schuylkill River and watched three policemen in a rowboat dragging the river bottom for the body of a swimmer who had just drowned. What disgusted me was the heckling the three officers put up with from the spectators. I thought the policemen earned a lot of credit and on the occasion of an accidental death the victim deserved sympathy and a silent prayer, yet the spectators were reveling.

Fifteen years later I was in a rowboat, in a police uniform, dragging the same river for a body not far from the earlier location.

For an hour I rowed an aluminum rowboat against the currant while two officers in the boat with me dragged grappling hooks along the river bottom. The blazing sun beat unmercifully on us and heated the metal seats to stovetop temperatures. There isn't any shade in the center of a river yet we remained gallant sailors and stayed our post. It was a painful mission that had to be done. I rowed on and on without complaint even though my aching back was killing me.

The companions of the ill-fated swimmer pointed to where their friend was last seen so I did my best to hover over that spot but the current insisted on drifting us downstream. A spectator or two shouted we were nowhere near the place where they pointed. They didn't realize the grappling hooks sometimes got snagged on debris or a rock on the bottom of the river. I rowed the boat around in circles until the hooks became free. All this time there was nonstop shouting from the spectators that we were fishing in the wrong place.

I was cursing them under my breath. Here I was in a lousy tin boat in the center of the river and our efforts were not appreciated. I was close to getting seasick and on the verge of a stroke or sun poison at the very least. I would gladly turned the job over to one of those jug heads but they couldn't do better if they were suffering with my back pain.

In the meantime a scuba diving club was contacted and six volunteers arrived on the scene. They swiftly donned their wet suits, goggles and oxygen tanks and slipped into the water. They swam to the spot where we were grappling. In a precision grid pattern they combed the river bottom and within ten minutes located the body.

I preferred the divers find the body rather than one of our grappling hooks. A hook can ruthlessly tear a body to shreds when raising it to the surface.

THE LOUD HOUSE PARTY

It was a sultry Saturday evening in August years before a home or car air-conditioner became common appliances. I was cruising in a sweltering car with all the windows rolled down so I could get a breath of air but if I were sitting on a cake of ice it wouldn't have helped. This had to be the hottest August day on record.

An order from headquarters came over the radio, "Car 18. Go to 1069 Hilton Road. There is a loud house party. Quiet it down."

On the way to the address I ruminated on how I should approach the homeowner. How can I delicately tell people who are enjoying a festive evening they are a neighborhood nuisance? I was in a quandary as to what choice words I could use that might persuade them to cooperate and at the same time not create a neighborhood feud.

When I arrived at the house I heard the noise and it definitely was an exuberant affair. A five-piece combo played popular War songs that got everyone singing at the top of their voices. I didn't fault whoever called the police because it was 11:00 p.m.

I was hoping for an inspiration but nothing came even as I was knocking on the open front door jamb. I peeked inside and saw wall-to-wall people. Everyone had a beverage in one hand and a cigarette in the other. A guest answered the door and before I could stifle her she shouted hysterically, "Someone get Tom!! Quick!! The cops are here!!" "Hurry up, get Tom!" That didn't help a bit because now everyone's attention was focused on what I had to say.

Tom rushed to the door. I tipped my hat and politely said, "Tom, Good Evening. You are having a fantastic party but it is much too loud for this nice quiet neighborhood. Maybe if you close the doors and windows you could keep most of the music and singing inside. The noise would be muffled and no one could say you didn't take appropriate measures to control it. Why don't you try it and see if it works. Thanks, Tom. Have a great time. Good Night."

Maybe it was because I was so polite, yet authoritative, that made Tom willing to cooperate. He and his guests accepted my suggestion and closed the doors and all the windows.

About forty minutes later I drove by the house and was shocked to find the place was vacant. I never in my wildest dream planned what would be the result of my suggestion. I didn't realize it but when Tom closed the doors and windows it broke up his party. The house became a Bessemer furnace full of thick cigarette smoke. The guests became so uncomfortable they left.

I picked up the radio mouthpiece and without any explanation I said, "Car #18 to headquarters. All's quiet at 1069 Hilton Road."

THE RADAR TRAP

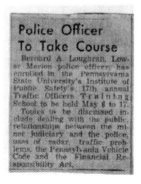

In 1957 I attended a two week Traffic Safety Course that was held on the Penn State Campus, Center County. It was a course designed for officers assigned to traffic control. For a one-hour period a factory representative extolled the virtues of a new technology for accurately enforcing the speed limit, the Radar Speed Detector.

The subject interested me even though the navy already taught me all about radar. The Radar Speed Detector employed the same principles as in the navy radar application. In the navy I installed radar equipment on airplanes and I used the instrument and interpreted what appeared on the monitors.

Before the instructor concluded I asked a mundane question just to give him and the sponsors of the course the impression I was enraptured by his lecture. "Sir, the navy taught us to be extremely cautious around radar because direct exposure to the rays could cause sterility. Could this be the fate of a police officer who used your machine on a daily basis?" He laughed and said, "I don't know. You should ask Trooper John Quinn of the Ohio State Police. He has eight kids." The class was amused but I was embarrassed.

I envied that representative because he was quick with an answer, right or wrong. I couldn't compete with anyone that sharp. I wanted to say, but didn't, "I know Trooper Quinn and he had those kids before your radar speed machine ever existed." The lecture ended on that note.

Two days after the course ended I read an item in the daily newspaper about a radar installer who was cooked to death by radar waves. The article stated there wasn't a trace of any physical injury on his flesh but the organs inside his body were burnt to a crisp

Man Stands in Radar Beam And Dies Within 2 Weeks

Los Angeles, May 31—(AP)—The death of a 42-year-old man who stood in front of a radar transmitter for less than a minute is reported in the current issue of the California Medical Association monthly.

"As far as I know," said Dr. John T. McLaughlin, author of the article, "it is the first case of death from radar ever reported."

Delay in Disclosure

Dr. McLaughlin, a Glendale, Calif., surgeon, said the man was a technician in a radar manufacturing plant in the Los Angeles area. He died in 1954, but for plant security reasons the case is just now being reported, the doctor said.

As told in the magazine, "California Medicine," the man stood directly in the beam of a radar transmitter, within ten feet of the antenna, while at work. In ten seconds he had a sensation of heat in the abdomen. In less than a minute the heat became so intense he had to move away.

No Marks on Body

The man was hospitalized and died within two weeks. Although no marks appeared on the surface of his body, his "insides were cooked," Dr. McLaughlin said.

Dr. McLaughlin urged immediate research to determine safe doses of microwave radiation, which, he said, "must be treated with the same respect as nuclear radiation."

He said the microwaves emit-

NOTE: In the mid-1990s police officers from departments around the country refused to use radar speed machines. They argued that statistics suggested the machine had induced side effects. They contend that the cumulative effects of the radar waves caused cancer.

161

THE CAR WITH A CAVITY

I was involved in several accident investigations that were not the run-of-the-mill. They didn't attract the media but they did impress my superiors. Some Hit-Run accidents were difficult to solve but when I submitted my final report I couldn't help being proud of myself. This particular case doesn't seem significant because it loses its suspense in the writing. On the surface it seems like it took very little effort and a lot of luck but until it was solved the Superintendent was in a pressure cooker.

The accident happened on a large estate. The estate owner was an influential wealthy person who had a tremendous amount of political clout. The estate consisted of acres and acres of the most valuable and picturesque real estate in the township. The owner recently had his property enclosed by a rustic wooden split rail fence. The new fence was in place only a few days when he reported to the police that two rails were broken during the night. He was furious and wouldn't tolerate this transgression and vandalism to his property so he personally visited the Superintendent's office and demanded every officer be deployed to apprehend the scoundrel.

Two weeks passed and the officers who may have been interested at the time of the accident gave up all hope of locating the culprit because there wasn't a clue to go on. Even so, there never was more than superficial interest in the case because the damage was infinitesimal. The monetary loss to this wealthy man was so ridiculously small it was easy to dismiss this accident and to get on with currant assignments.

For the Superintendent it was an entirely different story. The fence owner visited his office almost daily. He blasphemed him and his men. He accused us of incompetence and denounced the Superintendent for being the biggest incompetent of us all. He reminded him he didn't have Civil Service protection but was only an appointee who may be out of a job real soon. He hounded the poor Superintendent for two weeks and demanded he get results.

It was no secret he was harassing the Superintendent because the shouting was heard throughout the building. The troops weren't intimidated or motivated because they had civil service protection. For them this accident soon became ancient history. Each day presented them with more pressing problems.

The Superintendent couldn't casually dismiss the owner's threats so he went to my Lieutenant for help and my Lieutenant fell on me. The Lieutenant ordered me to go to the accident scene and conduct an in-depth investigation. I was to find out who damaged the fence.

Naturally, because the Lieutenant always frightened me, I hastened to the scene to find some clues. I looked over a field of acres and acres of dry grass over a foot tall and was aghast that such a wealthy man could reduce himself to be upset by such a mundane problem. The whole fence, maybe five hundred yards, cost tens of thousands of dollars to install but to replace these two rails wouldn't cost twenty-five bucks. His maintenance man could easily purchase and install them.

I saw nothing that wasn't already reported by the initial investigator yet I paced back and forth over the area until I was about to give up. It was a cloudy day with a heavy overcast. It was about to shower soon when suddenly a hole opened in the clouds and for a few seconds a bright sun glistened upon a three square inch piece of chrome that was concealed in the tall grass. If it had rained or if I stood at a different angle I would never have seen it. I knew it didn't belong on the farm or the fence so it had to be a piece of chrome off the Hit and Run vehicle.

That chrome piece was a small clue. Now I had to find the car. My first step was to learn the year; make and model of the vehicle the piece came from. With that important information and a few more details I could proceed to search for a particular vehicle. I took the piece of chrome to several auto body shops and each mechanic assured me, "That came from the grille of a 1958 Buick. It's a piece of a tooth." I asked them to notify me if such a car came in for repairs.

The 1958 Buick was a monstrous luxury car. The outstanding characteristic that made it the number one luxury car in sales that year was its grille. The grille was an attractive design that appealed to the consumers. It had the appearance of a pleasant smile with parted lips and protruding teeth. That was the way the different mechanics described it. All I had to search for was a 1958 Buick with a cavity.

Four weeks passed from the night of the accident and it was still ever present on my mind because of the harsh order the Lieutenant gave me when he barked, "Go forth and solve!" One afternoon I was cruising Lancaster Avenue. I scanned the rearview mirror to check on the traffic behind me. A 1958 Buick was directly behind me and low and behold it had a tooth with a cavity. I motioned for the driver to pull to the curb.

He was a local fellow who was known to drink heavily at times. I showed him my piece of chrome and how neatly it fitted into his grille. He couldn't deny the piece belonged to his car so he admitted he struck the fence one night when he had been drinking heavily.

I issued a summons to him for leaving the scene of an accident without leaving identification. The fine and costs was $25.00. I told him to go face the fence owner and make restitution and he did. He held no malice toward me but rather respected me for being clever and fair.

My Lieutenant accepted my report without commenting on the brilliant investigation. The Superintendent was ecstatic because it got the fence owner off his back and the Police Private Pension Fund was improved by a generous donation.

THE PICKET LINE

Police officers encounter all the inconspicuous activity that occurs in the community that John Q Public never even hears about. He knows all is not as serene as it appears on the surface. His finger is always on the communities pulse. His experiences vary. Sometimes they are dangerous and sometimes they are boring but the 9 to 5 people only knows what appears in the daily papers or what's on television. Most of the news they get has been filtered, however, a police officer is on the spot where the raw event is happening. Here is a case where I was on the front line while the community slept.

It was in 1958 and a local factory was shut down a month by a bitter strike. The men on the picket line became more hostile as the days grew colder. Emotions escalated and the tension manifested itself in acts of vandalism. Malicious behavior against the building and property increased and boisterous threats of violence toward the administrative workers locked inside the factory and their sympathizers mounted.

One serious incident involved a local fellow who had no brains but a lot of moxy. He didn't work for the company nor did he belong to a union. The office workers hired him to slip his truck loaded with food and staples into the plant. Management people were locked inside in an effort to keep the company operating but since the strike has been going on for weeks they were in dire need of necessities. This compassionate fellow cleverly skirted the picket line and delivered the supplies to the management staff. It was a humanitarian act he soon regretted because the following night his truck was fire bombed in front of his home. That served as a warning to everyone that might meddle in the strike.

The police department in the meantime, by law, played a low-key role. The police couldn't be sympathetic to either side. History, and the courts, taught the police profession that lesson. The courts allowed the police to only enforce two specific regulations. One, the picketers must keep walking while on the picket line, and two, a union supervisor must prepare a running list of the names of the people who are on the picket line. This list must be accurate and presented to the police twice a day since different people are assigned to picket duty during the day. That was the full extent of police involvement.

Weeks passed and management and union were at an impasse. Both sides adamantly stuck to their terms. Tempers rose to a boiling point and a lid couldn't be kept on the explosive situation much longer. The Superintendent knew the strike was at a spontaneous combustion point and he couldn't ignore the strike much longer. His department was bound to be drawn into an ugly affair soon yet the law was specific; the police could only become involved after the fact. Until management and the union negotiated a compromise the police had to standby and wait.

The Superintendent grew uneasier as each day passed so he held a brain storming staff meeting with his supervisors. He expected one of them would offer a tactical solution before the strikers resorted to full blown violence. The only shallow idea suggested was to post an officer near the plant to intimidate the picketers. Conceivably, the picketers would see they were under surveillance and would behave.

I, unfortunately, was available at 4:00 p.m. the afternoon of the staff meeting so I was assigned to go to the factory and park my patrol car in a place where the picketers could see me. When I arrived at the factory I parked in a small vacant lot opposite the factory and twenty-five yards from the pick line. I backed into the lot so I would be facing the picketers. They were huddled around a wood fire burning in a fifty-five gallon oil drum. The days grew cold and damp and this small amount of heat was precious but ineffective.

My presence engendered the opposite affect than what the Superintendent expected. When the cold and bitter picketers saw me they immediately conjured up negative assumptions. They suspected the people inside the factory requested extra police protection or I was there to harass the picketers. They were convinced my presence was not in their best interest but was in sympathy with the management people. I could appreciate their animal loathing toward me but I was hoping they didn't know my personal car and where I lived.

Their negative feelings were unmistakable for their protests were loud. They shouted expletives at me. Their fists were raised and their strike posters were held high and shaken to threaten me. Their ugly vindictives demanded I leave the area. They insisted I wasn't needed and by law I shouldn't be there. They bunched together to plan a strategy to get rid of the cop. A delegation was selected to confront me and inquire why I was here and if it was management who requested I be here?

Frankly, if they quizzed me I hadn't any answers that was convincing or could soothe their violent disposition. I wasn't coached by my superior therefore I didn't know why I was here other than there was a strike. I couldn't cleverly make up a falsehood on the spur of the moment like some men can yet I was in the middle of a very intense predicament that needed a fast thinker. There is no way I can explain how my safety and police authority was on the line, but it was.

As the delegated picketers walked to within ten yards of me a man from inside the factory bolted out of an unguarded door. He saw the picketers' attention was focused on the cop across the street so while they were distracted he dashed from the building. He ran to his car and was about to drive away. He panicked and revved the engine too fast. The rear wheels spun out of control. At such a fast revolution the tires were unable to get a grip on the driveway. The burning tires smoked and the car refused to move. The front of the car rose into the air like a stallion ready to charge. The screeching sounded like chalk drawn across a blackboard yet the car wouldn't get into motion for the driver. He accelerated even more and that only caused the wheels to spin faster.

The whining tires attracted the picketers and the delegation. They saw the car wasn't moving so they forgot about me and took off toward it hoping they might catch up to the driver before he got away. Lucky for him the tires finally took a firm hold of the macadam and off he went leaving a cloud of smoke and a trail of burnt rubber. The car fishtailed down the street and out distanced the maniacal pursuers.

This gave me an excuse to get away too. I turned on my emergency lights and took off after the speeder like a bat out of a cave. My wheels weren't spinning and my car wasn't fishtailing so I soon overtook him a hundred yards down the street. In full view of the picketers I signaled for the driver to stop.

The driver was crying hysterically. He told me he could no longer endure being cooped up inside the factory. His nerves were frayed and he was on the verge of a nervous breakdown. His wife was pregnant and on the phone all the time demanding he come home. Being able to escape the picketers was a triumph but to be arrested was the final straw that could send him over the edge. I assured him I wasn't arresting him for anything. However, I pretended to be writing on my clipboard. This was an act I was performing for the benefit of the picketers up the street although I had no idea how it might affect the outcome of the days' events. After I finished pretending to write a traffic ticket I sent the man on his way. I assured him he wasn't getting a ticket so he better get a grip on himself and drive home carefully.

I returned to where I had been parked and acted like nothing unusual happened. I began writing a fictitious report from the notes that was supposed to be on my clipboard. The delegation of picketers got up the nerve to approach me a second time. This time they were even more ferocious because I distracted them and allowed an office person escape. I saw them coming to confront me and I could tell it wasn't to ask me the baseball box scores. Before they arrived I got out of the patrol car and stood tall to face them head on.

"What did you say to him?" they demanded in a tone expected to menace. I glowered into the eyeballs of the spokesman and with my uniform fortifying my false courage I barked, "I gave that fellow a ticket for reckless driving and I'll lock you up if you don't return to the picket line! Furthermore, get those men who are lounging around up on their feet! They are picketers and are supposed to act like picketers! They are to keep moving! You better keep them walking or I'll lock you up!"

This delegation was typical union goons, a bunch of brutes. I was scared but I learned from the State Police sergeant that one good officer in a clean uniform could control strikers. In spite of my fear I projected I was the boss of this situation and I wouldn't be bullied and I was capable of carrying out my threat. They were taken by surprise and didn't know how to respond. They didn't expect to have to face a fearless cop so without another word they backed away and returned to the rest of the picketers.

They clustered together to hear what the policeman said. While they were discussing their next move I was considering calling for backup support. My other option was to drive out of there but before I finally decided on what to do the strangest and most unexpected thing happened. The picketers let out a wild cheer. They felt since I gave a ticket to a management person I was not siding with them and since I threatened to arrest their boss I had to be neutral. In other words I would be just as quick to protect their interest because I showed no bias.

Their attitude shifted. I was now a working cop and not a spy. They picked up their placards and marched up and down the sidewalk like cadets marching on a parade ground before a gallery of generals on Mother's Day. Their spirit was uplifted and there was rejoicing.

I waited ten minutes more then figured I better not press my luck. Maybe it was best to let what transpired simmer while I took an extended dinner break. I knew the picketers would be happy to see me leave so they could cut out their marching and get back to their heater. As I slowly pulled out of the lot they gave a sophomoric cheer of respect, friendliness and trust. Some of the goons whistled, some applauded and others fluttered their union posters. I pretended not to notice.

My subterfuge worked just as the State Police sergeant guaranteed. All the situation needed was a smart cop with a gimmick.

After dinner I deemed it prudent not to return to the plant. I might provoke a change of heart.

The picketers became friendlier about their task. They were happier because someone in management got the short end of the stick. They now had reason to believe the local authorities weren't against their cause. The strike lasted three more days and then peacefully negotiated.

No one ever knew that a speeding ticket that was never issued produced so much safety.

WHAT A HORRIBLE SMELL

One scorching July afternoon my partner and I received a radio message, "Go to the Churchill Apartments and meet the building superintendent." From past experience it meant only one thing. "Damn!" my partner said. "Probably been dead ten days before the stench oozed through the building and arouse the other tenants. In this heat it could putrefy in less than a week." I asked, "I wondered if the person died from a heart attack, suicide, or a murder?" "Doesn't make much difference they all smell the same," he answered.

The building superintendent escorted us to the apartment. "God! The smell is awful. What took you so long to report this?" He said he and his wife just returned from a vacation. Walking down the hall toward the apartment door we noticed a rope was tied to the doorknob and went over the top of the door and into the apartment. This was a strange new experience. The superintendent unlocked the door but it was wedged tight against the doorjamb by the cord. My partner put his shoulder to the door and gave a hardy shove that broke it loose and it swung freely inward and banged against the inside wall. The stench of the decomposed body intensified.

A young girl committed suicide by tying the cord to the doorknob on the outside of the door and then brought it over the top and tied the other end around her neck. She stood on a low stool and jumped. It was an ingenious plan. She hung there for over a week. The heat of the apartment acted rapidly on the cadaver. Her skin, stretched by the confined gases in her body, bloated her beyond recognition. When my partner freed the stuck door it flew open and slammed against the inside wall where a coat hook on that wall pierced her swelled skin. After the hook punctured the skin all the pent-up body gases gushed out.

The pungent odor was intolerable yet the local undertakers summoned to transport the corpse to the morgue casually went about cutting down the body and placing it into a rubber body bag. I marveled at how they tolerated the foul odor without flinching.

The effluvium from the decomposed body lingers on the uniform and skin. Even after a change of clothes and several showers the scent remains for days in the nostrils and lungs.

It is strange but people who suffer severe chest pains usually become nauseous and retreat to the bathroom where they have an urge for a bowl movement. A person having a fatal heart attack usually does this. Most apartments have small six by eight bathrooms and I never understood why a person living alone had to have additional privacy and close the bathroom door but they do. It is behind the closed door, while on the toilet, the person dies. Such was the case that same summer when the same officer and I were dispatched to meet the superintendent of a different apartment complex.

"Here we go again," he laughed. I chuckled, "I don't mind because this uniform was going to the cleaners tomorrow anyway."

The superintendent led us through a hallway to the apartment but we smelled it long before we got to it. We wouldn't have located it without him because the odor permeated the whole hall. The person died sitting on the toilet and then fell to the floor. Getting the bathroom door open was a struggle because the body lay against it but after a lot of pushing it opened wide enough to squeeze through. The open window wasn't enough to let the stench out so I borrowed a smoke ejector from a nearby firehouse.

From outside of the building I threw the electrical cord through the window and adjusted the ejector fan securely in the window frame. Just as I got the fan secured but before I moved away my partner plugged in the cord. The blast of air drove the fumes up my nose and into my lungs. It was a horrible dose. The same undertakers came to remove the body and again they didn't seem to mind inhaling the foul air.

Around this time my foot doctor was treating my troublesome blister. While he was examining my foot I apologized if my foot smelled even though I took a shower before my visit. He assured me he couldn't smell feet and he never did even during his intern days. There was nothing wrong with his sense of smell. He could smell flowers and cooking food but dirty feet he didn't smell. This was a strange phenomenon. Maybe the undertakers didn't smell decomposed bodies.

The next time I met the undertakers I asked, "How come you're not offended by the smell?" He said, "I put Noxzema Medicated Cream in my nostrils before I get to a scene and then I can't smell anything." That sounded logical so I purchased a small jar of the cream and stored it in the glove compartment of the police car. A week or so later I was sent to a house where a defective refrigerator was leaking gas. Refrigerators today don't break down the way they used to. The coils frequently sprung a leak and let the refrigerant escape. Those fumes were worse than the fumes from a decomposed body and they could be lethal. It stung the eyes like tear gas and pricked exposed skin like a tattoo artist's needle. The only solution was to carry the refrigerator out of the house and let the gas escape into the atmosphere.

Before I left the car I stuffed my nose with Noxzema. Another officer and the homeowner and I wrestled the heavy appliance out the kitchen door. The three of us were terribly stressed because juggling a heavy awkward refrigerator isn't easy. I couldn't breathe at all through my nose because the cream clogged my nostrils. It was impossible to inhale or exhale through my nose and when I snatched a gulp of air through my mouth the refrigerant burned my lungs. I never used Noxzema again.

I've worked with the undertakers since then and unobtrusively check their nostrils. I didn't see any cream. I suspect he was pulling my leg but I never let on that I took his suggestion seriously.

THE SUGGESTION BOX

In the 40's and 50's every police headquarters in the country was a beehive of activity. The lobbies were cluttered with people anxious to read an investigation report. Everyone involved in an incident; the injured, witnesses, relatives and the victims all waited to see the official report. Automobile Insurance Company agents were the most numerous and the most troublesome because they gathered around the reception desk. Representatives from Aetna, Allstate, State Farm, AAA, Keystone, etc. queue at the counter for priority service. Nobody waited patiently and quietly until a clerk could secure the file they needed.

Loud private conversations disrupted regular police business. Telephone messages were difficult to hear and urgent radio messages had to be repeated. A clerk was kept busy sorting through the records for the Automobile Insurance agents. However, several occurrences unfolded in the summer of 1958 that eliminated this congestion overnight. The clutter vanished and tranquility settled upon the office and clerical staff.

The first link in the chain of events occurred when the township hired a new Treasurer who was full of ideas relating to economy. He had the parking meter coin boxes emptied every day instead of every other week. The money was immediately deposited into a bank account to draw interest. He believed other employees had ideas on how money could be saved or how a task could be performed more economically.

The second link occurred when the new Treasurer created a Suggestion Box System. Prizes would be awarded for the best ideas every few month.

The third factor: I was on the department's pistol team and one weekend the team traveled to Hempstead, Long Island to compete against other police teams. At this match all the shooters congratulated a fellow competitor who was just promoted to the rank of Captain. In a private conversation I asked the new Captain to what he attributed his promotion. He said it was due to his success at the Oral Board phase of the elimination process. The Oral Board asked him for an idea he would initiate if he were promoted. He shared the idea he presented to the Oral Review Board with me.

The Captain's idea was for the department to purchase a XEROX machine. This was a new technology recently developed to copy a document. He said the Automobile Insurance agents do not have to appear at headquarters anymore. They telephone the records clerk in headquarters and request a copy of a particular report. The clerk will XEROX that report and mail the copy to the agent for a five-dollar fee. The machine will pay for itself but the major benefit would be the elimination of the congestion at the reception counter in headquarters.

Note how these events entwine: the noisy crowded headquarters, the new Treasurer, the Suggestion Box System, the pistol team, the Hempstead Pistol Match, and a shooter's promotion.

I slid the suggestion to purchase a XEROX machine into the brand new Suggestion Box and waited. A month later I received a reply. *"The committee was dubious about this idea but it is worth an experimental try so a machine will be purchased. The Township Manager and the Superintendent of Police doubted a report could be worth five dollars so they suggested a one dollar fee."*

The congestion in the lobby vanished overnight after the reports were obtained by telephone. A year later an upgraded machine was purchased and the fee was raised to two dollars. There never was an objection to the cost or the raise.

First Prize was given to two men for their suggestion. They were truck drivers who suggested an automatic shutoff valve be installed on the nozzles of the gasoline pump hoses to prevent an overflow and waste of fuel and to eliminate a fire hazard. They both received a $25.00 Treasury bond.

Second Prize went to the Township Manager's secretary. She suggested a trashcan be put in the employee's parking garage to keep the area clean. She received $10.00 in cash.

Third Prize I received. It was a $5.00 bill, but no promotion.

NOTE: In 1975 the police department had three state-of-the-art copy machines. The fee for a report was fifteen dollars and in 1983 the machine in the headquarters' Record Section collected $35,000.00 for the Township General Fund.

FIVE DOLLAR FACES—Five Lower Merion Township employes react appropriately as township manager John J. Scott Jr. (left) rewards them for their suggestions which have been adopted by the township. Far any suggestion adopted under the township's new suggestion program the suggester gets a certificate and $5. From left to right Scott, Bernard A. Loughran, Frances Hantz, James P. Smyth, Joseph A. Cassel, Stanley Novak. —[Photo by Hantz]

THE MODUS OPERANDI

While making notes in my journal I didn't omit the embarrassing incidents and those that went the wrong way. There were foul-ups too. One serious blooper occurred when a partner and I were assigned to a Burglar Detail. We were to concentrate on apprehending the gang who was breaking into the men's clothing stores located in shopping centers. These thefts occurred after the shopping centers were closed for the day.

Our department exchanged liaison reports with the surrounding police departments because they had similar burglaries. Four men's clothing stores were already robbed in Lower Merion. The MO was the same in each case. The burglars waited until the shopping center was closed and all the customers and employees had left and the parking lot was empty. They'd break the glass in the front or rear door and rush inside and grab armfuls of suits off the racks. They'd pack them into a van and race off. The robbery was accomplished within minutes.

My partner and I drove into the rear parking lot of a shopping center after all the stores had closed. In an obscure corner of the lot was a parked car so my partner drove toward it to check it out. As we approached the car we saw a young frightened couple release their romantic embrace. That was the usual reaction when police approached lovers in a parked car. Characteristically the scared boy started his car and nervously flick his headlights on and off in his excitement.

When our patrol car stopped abreast of the car I informed the boy the police department discouraged parking here and to please cooperate. As I expected he said, "OK Officer" and he drove out of the lot. We rode off in the opposite direction.

Suddenly my mind clicked and I said to my partner, "Something was wrong! Go after them!" My partner wasn't in the mood for guessing games and said, "No. It's coffee-break time."

He and I worked together on many burglar details and we followed up every hunch no matter whose intuition it was. All those follow-ups produced nothing so now he decided he didn't want to go on another wild goose chase because it was coffee-break time. I insisted something was drastically amiss and we argued. I didn't know what was out of focus but something wasn't right. It finally dawned on me what was out of place but by then the couple got lost in the night traffic.

What disturbed me was the couple was crummy dirty. It wasn't fresh dirt or dirt collected after a hard day's work but crusted dirt like the grime that accumulates on vagrants. That couple was the most unkempt lovers I ever saw. I argued with my partner that lovers at the least wash to make a decent impression on each other. Their clothes may not be the latest fashion but they are clean. I insisted, "They weren't lovers!"

That wasn't sound logical to my partner. He wouldn't even acquiesce and drive by the men's clothing store to see if the glass was

173

intact. He wanted a cup of coffee and he had control of the steering wheel so I stopped arguing and went along.

The next day at roll call the sergeant informed the squad the men's clothing store in that shopping center was burglarized. The same MO was used as in the previous burglaries. Racks of men's expensive clothing were stolen. Then the sergeant read a liaison report from a neighboring police department concerning these burglars. *"This gang uses a young couple as a lookout. The couple will park in a corner of the parking lot far from the store that's being burglarized. When the couple sees a patrol car cruising in the lot they signal their accomplices inside the store that the police are around. They signal by flicking the headlights on and off."*

I don't know if it was because they were almost caught but there were no more of these burglaries after that evening.

This photo was taken in 1962. I was a sergeant and on the pistol team.

SPUTNIK I AND ECHO I

When I read about the extraordinary accomplishments of the space program or see television reruns of a moon landing or hear about a space probe or exploration a chill comes over me. News accounts of a satellite sent into the heavens to orbit planet earth conjure up memories of the bitter nights I spent on burglar details. I have flashbacks of the cold nights I curled into a fetal position just to conserve body heat while lying on a damp estate lawn. My purpose for being at that godforsaken place on those lonely nights was to apprehend a trespasser who conceivably might walk within the proximity of my post.

On October 4th, 1957 I was sitting on a small boulder waiting for a burglar to walk by. It was a frosty night but there wasn't a cloud in the sky that would obscure the brilliant stars. I searched the heaven for the first spacecraft scheduled to orbit our planet. At 2:30 a.m. it came into view. It silently glided from the Southwest to the Southeast. The sun's rays shone on it from the opposite side of our planet. It reflected off its metallic surface the same way the sun's rays shine on the surface of the moon. It was Sputnik I, the Russian unmanned spacecraft.

A hundred and nineteen nights later I was assigned to a different boulder and in the early morning of January 31st, 1958 I followed Echo I, the United States' first satellite to orbit the earth

In the course of history these two accomplishments are recorded as wondrous feats that ushered in the space age. I was thrilled at the time and bragged that I witnessed both events. I knew how important they were and I felt a sincere appreciation for these unprecedented scientific achievements. If I hadn't been assigned to those horrible details and abandoned on the highest vacant lot in the township I would have been snug in bed under warm blankets. I would have missed them and the bitter weather that ushered in my arthritis.

While I sat on those cold stones I applauded the success of the space program but I wished for a scientific discovery that would thwart the proliferation of house burglaries. I wished for a technology that would eliminate the need for the kind of human suffering I was enduring.

Sputnik I was not much larger than a basketball weighing 183-pounds. It looked like any other speck in the sky only it moved fast enough across the skyline to make it stand out from the stationary stars in the galaxy

SAVE THE TOOTH

In 1959 I investigated a routine automobile accident. A car slammed into the rear of a car that was stopped for a red traffic signal. A four-year-old girl, sitting in the front passenger seat, was hurled face first against the dashboard and sustained facial bruises.

Another officer transported her and her parents to a nearby hospital. I remained at the scene to record the details both operators needed for their insurance companies and to direct traffic around the disabled vehicles.

Before the tow truck arrived to tow the cars out of the intersection I received an urgent request from the hospital Accident Ward. The doctor requested I find the child's front tooth. It was knocked out when her mouth struck the dashboard. He suggested it was somewhere in the car and requested if I found it I should rush it to the hospital.

I frantically searched every conceivable crevice and finally located it hidden under the floor mat beneath the dashboard. I had no idea what value it had once out of the mouth but I rushed to the hospital.

The intern soaked the tooth in a disinfectant solution and cemented it back into the vacant space. After the cement hardened the child was discharged and left the hospital with her parents.

I asked the doctor why he reset the tooth. Did he expect it to take root? He assured me that it would never grow another nerve but it would serve as an excellent spacer until her second tooth appeared.

The longer I live the more wondrous things I'll learn.

This 1967 Plymouth Station Wagon was assigned to me. Like the other police cars in the department it didn't have a siren and the only emergency lights were the "bubble gum machine" and two small flashing lights on the roof.

THE BANDANNA BURGLAR

In the late 1950s there was a busy burglar who cleverly entered many homes in the township. His MO differed from the other burglars who plied their skill in the area. This fellow would enter a house after dark and go directly to the master bedroom. He would wake up the sleeping occupants and demand money. This was unorthodox because burglars never deliberately woke up anyone in the house. Traditional burglars didn't want to be seen because of the risk of being easily identified, however, this fellow wasn't concerned with that possibility.

He also threatened the sleepers with a pistol. Most burglars didn't carry a gun because the penalty was harsher if they were caught with a weapon. He was also unique because he covered his face with a bandanna hence the police dubbed him "The Bandanna Burglar". Newspaper reporters picked up on that moniker and used it in their news reports.

Another of his unusual characteristics was his uncanny ability to mollify a watchdog. It made no difference if there was one or more dogs, a vicious dog, or a dog that by nature was a barker. Whatever trick he used on the watchdog it wouldn't alert its owner of an intruder's presence. When he was arrested he refused to divulge how he gained a dog's trust.

He successfully operated for several years in a few other northeastern states before he came to our locality. The police in the surrounding townships were also stymied by this gunslinger. They couldn't predict where or when he would strike. It became incumbent upon my department to take drastic steps to assure our residents they were safe in their beds. Our Detective Bureau responded with the only primitive tactic in their pubescent minds. Ten patrolmen were posted in strategic locations in the area where the Bandanna Burglar might strike. The detectives gambled he would eventually walk by one of these posts when he was on the prowl.

If it weren't for bad luck I would have had no luck at all for I was one of the unfortunate ten chosen for this detail. Every midnight we were taken to our post and deposited there until the same unmarked police cars picked us up at 7:30 a.m.

My post was an open field where there wasn't a house within a hundred yard radius. The first night was a horrible disaster. It was mid-November and an unseasonably cold night. This baron piece of real estate was void of trees, weeds, grass, or even a small boulder to sit on. I stood for fifteen minutes or until I realized I was silhouetted against the sky. I squatted on my hunches but my leg soon cramped. Finally I stretch out on the cold ground because I couldn't sit on your heels any longer. So all sides would be equally frozen I twisted, turned and rolled from side to side but numbness set in and I soon fell asleep.

The flesh becomes weak quick in bitter cold temperatures. I was unconscious almost an hour before the stinging cold air woke me. I was flabbergasted when I saw I was covered with a dusting of snow. I assessed my situation and resolved to use my imagination and creativity to improve my circumstances or I would have to resign.

Before going to bed that first morning I drove to the rear of an appliance store and salvaged a discarded cardboard box. It was a heavy-duty box whose utility was to protect a new refrigerator while in transport. The box was 44 X 44 X 76 inches. It was large enough for me to squirm into and it had a little extra room for comfort. I strapped the box onto the roof of my car and drove back to my post. I cut peepholes on two sides and hid it in a shallow depression. That was my clever solution.

Each night I brought my shotgun, lunch, thermos bottle full of hot black coffee and my navy duffel bag. In the duffel bag I stuffed two blankets, a navy hammock mattress and high altitude flight gear that was issued to me when I flew in high altitudes in a navy bomber.

After I was dropped off I went directly to the cardboard refrigerator box and set up housekeeping. I spread the mattress inside the box and coiled up under the blankets. All night I stared out of the open top and the peepholes and listened for the Bandanna Burglar's footsteps in the same comfort I'd have if I were lying in my own bed.

I was cozy as a bug in a rug in my little bunker; shielded from the sharp wind and rain and snow. In the morning I stuffed my survival gear into the duffel bag and tucked the empty box back into the shallow depression for safekeeping. I carted my duffel bag and equipment home.

It was a frigid winter and the Bandanna Burglar continued to ply his craft. I can truthfully say he never walked near my post for assuredly I would have seen or heard him even if he took his nocturnal walks as stealthily as a black panther. I never once rested my eyes through that horrible ordeal. I did the job I was assigned.

After many successful months his attempt to burglarize another house failed. The homeowner scared him off and called the police. A few hours later he was found cowering in an empty railroad boxcar that was parked in a railroad freight yard. The railroad yard was a half-mile as the crow flies from my refrigerator box but he couldn't get there from where I was. If he ever passed by me I definitely would have apprehended him.

His capture brought an end to the longest and biterest winter my fellow officers and I suffered through. It was a long nasty detail but I couldn't complain because I was dry and toasty warm for a change. Since I wasn't chilled to the bone I was primed and ready to wrestle a bear.

A WOMAN'S DREAM

I steadfastly believed there was a more intelligent way to apprehend a burglar than by falling asleep on frozen ground in a vacant field. I made up my mind. If my superiors couldn't figure out a more practical scheme then I would. My strategy was to consult the greatest thinkers throughout the ages; I'd hit the textbooks. I enrolled in college night classes and took up Psychology to learn how the mind of a burglar worked but that course didn't throw light on the subject. I signed up for Educational Psychology but I didn't cull any information from that course that could help me outwit a burglar. However, I knew two courses didn't an education make.

Logic was my third selection. The college catalog said I would learn the art of thinking. That was what I needed. I had to learn how to think about my problem if I wanted to solve it. The weeks in the classroom dragged on and I quickly had doubts about this course too. There was a strong possibility I was wasting my time and money. There wasn't a bit of information that could be applied to police work. I couldn't sift out any data that would have an application in how to catch a burglar.

Midway through the semester the professor dwelt on the subject of dreams. He said, "St. Thomas Aquinas espoused, in spite of how logical a dream appears we can not make a valid syllogism while asleep." Then the professor added, "Saint Augustine theorized we can't problem solve in our sleep." He continued in a dull monotone to fill the two hours with all sorts of trivia. "Modern scientists and psychologists have through research discovered men do not have the ability to dream in Technicolor yet women can but rarely do." I left the classroom that evening pondering on the useless tidbits he imparted. I might as well discard all of it because I couldn't foresee any practical use.

A few days later I was cruising in an unmarked police car with another officer. Our assignment was to apprehend the burglar who was plying his trade in the afternoon. He was dubbed the Afternoon Burglar. Joe and I were on patrol less than an hour when a radio message dispatched us to a house. A woman telephoned headquarters and stated a black man had just left her house by the rear kitchen door. She had been napping on her living room sofa when she saw a black man walk down the steps from the second floor and exit by the rear door. She pretended to be asleep so the man would ignore her"

We were driving on that very street and arrived at the address before the radio message ended. We both rushed into the house. Joe stopped to talk to the woman and to obtain more details while I ran through the living room and kitchen to the rear door. It was bolted and a chain safety latch was in place. No one could leave a house and hook the safety chain and bolt the door behind him.

The woman repeated what she told headquarters over the phone. "I was sleeping on the sofa that is at the foot of the stairs and a huge black man walked down the steps. He looked menacingly at me and thought I was asleep so I pretended I didn't see him. He walked through the dining room and kitchen and went out the rear door."

Joe asked her a few routine questions that might help us identify the man if we came upon him. He also sought additional information he could relay to all the other officers on patrol and to those responding to the area. "What color were his pants?" he asked. "I don't know," she said. "What color was his shirt?" "I don't know."

Joe and I met outside the house to confer on the facts we had. "Joe," I said. "This isn't a bona fide burglary. Go to a police box and tell headquarters to call off any police cars that are responding. No sense anyone getting into an accident rushing to this house. I'll stay here to tell the men who arrive before your message gets on the air."

Joe fretted, "How do you know this isn't a bona fide call?" "Joe, I said. The rear door was bolted from the inside and the woman couldn't give you a description of the man's clothing because she was dreaming this occurred. Men never dream in color and women can but rarely do."

"How come she knew the man was black?" he asked.

"Don't you think it is easy for a refine matron like her to believe all the criminals are black men? That's her mind set."

Joe accepted my deductions and drove off alone to the police box. Headquarters immediately radioed the message to disregard the message to all cars. When the message went over the air for all cars to ignore the burglary-in-progress message it was also received by the Captain of Detectives. The Captain was upset because a lowly patrolman took it upon himself to make this important decision without supervision.

Via radio he instructed Joe to standby the police box because he wanted to talk to him. Joe detected from the Captain's enraged tone that he was in deep trouble and he had to prepare an alibi. This was no sweat because Joe was one of those rare individuals who could expeditiously come up with an acceptable rationalization for anything.

The Captain confronted Joe and demanded to know why he took it upon himself to report this was not a bona fide home intrusion. He wanted to know how Joe arrived at his deduction. "Captain, the woman was napping in her living room on the sofa that is at the foot of the stairs. She had a nightmare and dreamt she saw a black man come down the steps and leave by the rear door."

"How can you claim positively she had a nightmare? How can you be sure she didn't see him?" the Captain shouted.

"Well, she couldn't give a description as to the color of his clothing because people don't dream in Technicolor and the rear door was bolted from the inside."

"Didn't she say he was a black man?'

"Yes, but, she is an older refine woman and it is easy for her to believe all criminals are black men."

The Captain drove off but still very peeved that Joe acted the role of a supervisor. Nevertheless, he was satisfied Joe reasoned the situation through to a logical assumption. When Joe returned to pick me up he was trembling from the intimidating interrogation. Joe would prefer to face a burglar than confront the Detective Captain. He told me he repeated word for word what I said and it got him off the hook.

Joe and I never mentioned that incident again but a few months later he was promoted to the Detective Bureau. That had been my secret goal ever since I joined the force. The Captain of Detectives had the final say as to who would be assigned to his command and I know Joe made a favorable impression on him months before. I realize that this one incident didn't have everything to do with his promotion because Joe always had the potential to be a great detective.

Yet, I can't help believing that conversation about the woman's dream was an influencing factor. It might have given Joe an advantage over other qualified officers. After that incident the value of a college education was forever enhanced in my mind.

This is a photo of me in 1961 a few weeks
after I was promoted to Sergeant.

THE PERTH AMBOY PISTOL MATCH

I conscientiously practiced shooting my target pistol every day. Every free moment the empty gun was in my outstretched arm. I dry-snapped it while reading the newspaper and while watching TV. I held the gun at arm's length to strengthen the muscles in my trigger finger, forearm and shoulder. After years of practice my pointing finger became part of the trigger action.

My target pistol was different than most target pistols in several ways. It was heavier than most guns because it had a very thick solid steel barrel. That was why it was called "a stovepipe". State-of-the art guns have a tapered barrel that made them several ounces lighter than my solid steel pipe but I always believed my heavy stovepipe was more stable when an unexpected gust of wind blew.

The trigger "pull" on my gun was illegal for competitive shooting but no one knew it but me. The regulation squeeze or pull on a target pistol trigger couldn't be less than four pounds but the pull on my trigger was two and a half pounds. This gun might be difficult for most shooters to use because of the heavy barrel and the sensitive pull unless they practiced with it as much as I did.

My attention to practice paid off because I could compete with the best police target shooters on the east coast. Unfortunately I wasn't a consistent high scorer. Sometimes I finished with a high score and other times I wound up with a score lower than my potential. My problem was my inability to concentrate. At a critical moment a shot or two would go astray because my mind was on unrelated worries. Family affairs often slithered into my thoughts at a critical moment. I should have worked on my concentration while I was strengthening my muscles.

My coach recommended a solution that worked well for him. He suggested I drink a few ounces of liquor before the match to calm my nerves. He suggested I only drink the amount necessary to create a gentle buzz in my head. That buzz was supposed to keep my mind from wondering. Because I was young I had to consume a few ounces too many to start up the buzz. By the time the buzz was faint I was close to intoxication. Some of my best scores were shot when I was slightly inebriated. I'm sure if my coach had stressed meditation exercises I might have been more reliable. An intoxicated man isn't dependable.

Every year our team attended a Police Pistol Match at Perth Amboy, New Jersey. It was there I almost shot my head off.

It was on a weekend when the east coast was braced against a severe hurricane. It rained in torrents and the gale-force winds blew steadily. Future weekend matches were already scheduled so this one couldn't be postponed. There was no shelter on this range. The contestants sat for hours in their parked cars waiting for their turn to be called to the firing line. The car windows were shut tight or the driving rain would enter the smallest crack and soak the occupants and the interior of the car. Inside the car the cigarette and cigar smoke was so thick it could be cut with a cake knife.

To past the time we took turns telling our favorite joke or police experience and stuffed ourselves with sandwiches and beer. After three hours in this torture chamber our team was called to the firing line just when the storm was at its peek. The wind blew at hurricane speeds and the raindrops stabbed our face and eyes like pine needles. A sailor couldn't function in this weather yet I was standing on the firing line with a skin full of rum.

By rote I loaded my gun two times with five bullets each time. I shot ten bullets within 3 minutes at a target 25 yards away. It was the SLOW FIRE phase of the match. Three minutes isn't enough time for an average shooter in ideal conditions and not enough time for expert marksmen in this fierce storm. In spite of the driving rain causing me to blink and squint I had a perfect score. The scorekeepers double-checked because the ten holes were tightly clustered. It was inconceivable a score could be so perfect in this weather. The scorers used a magnifying glass to measure the hole to make sure ten bullet were fired.

The second phase was TIME FIRE. That's two strings of five shots each shot in 25 seconds from 25 yards away. This phase separated the boys from the men. The buzz in my head got louder and a heavy nicotine film veiled my cataracts yet I shot another perfect score. Again, the scorers couldn't believe the impossible tight grouping. My twenty bullets entered that single hole that was slightly enlarged. The third and final phase; RAPID FIRE, two strings of five shots, each shot in 11 seconds from 25 yards away. This phase is the eliminator. This is when champions spit in their palm before taking a firm hold on the gun grip.

I knew I was the only shooter with a perfect score up to this point. Tension defeats the average competitor but what was defeating me was the loud ringing in my head. It sounded like the bells of St. Mary ringing the Angeles. I braced against the horizontal rain that pelted my jaundiced eyes. My body was perpendicular to the target, taut as catgut in a tennis racket. I was depending on my years of practice and the stovepipe resting on my shoulder.

The Range Officer boomed his rhythmic commands over the public address system. "Are you ready on the right? Are you ready on the left? Are you ready on the firing line? Commence firing!" With the final command he pressed an electrical switch and the targets turned to face the shooters. I lowered my gun and sighted in on the bulls-eye. Calmly I squeezed the trigger five times. I had a full second left, which was enough time to look over the barrel of the gun. I saw that each bullet entered that big hole that grew a smidgen wider.

On this day the best shooters were pleased if their bullet entered any part of the target even if it landed out of the scoring rings. They were thrilled their bullet didn't fly out of the pistol range altogether.

I reloaded my gun for the last five shots at Rapid Fire. Forty shooters waited for the commands from the Range Officer. The buzz in my head now sounded like an air-raid siren. I was cognizant of it but at least I wasn't thinking of my family. My gun was loaded and resting on my right shoulder waiting for the countdown. The Range Officer started, "Are you ready on the right? Are you ready on the left? Are you ready on the firing line?" Every shooter was poised to react to the final command to lower his gun and sight on the target. My concentration broke. I was thinking about how wet I was. I thought of my water-soaked raincoat and the cigarette smoke irritating my eyes. Many inconsequential thoughts came to the forefront of my mind. At the same time I didn't realize I was exerting pressure on the hair trigger. The gun exploded while it was resting on my shoulder and the bullet whizzed by my ear. The explosion blasted my eardrum. Burnt powder and hot lead filings stung my cheek. I pulled myself together and realized I almost shot the side of my face off.

The Range Officer didn't know who fired prematurely and it was too late for him to stop the rhythmic countdown. He gave the final command "Commence firing!" I brought my gun down slowly and aimed it on the target. Annoying raindrop tickled my eyelash. One shot, then the second, the third and the fourth. The gun was empty but I kept it at arm's length pointed at the target. I squeezed the trigger again pretending I had a fifth bullet to shoot and I even gave the gun a false recoil to throw off any scorer who might be counting.

When the smoke cleared I wound up with a perfect score. It was impossible for the scorers to determine if there were 29 or 30 shots in the bull's-eye. My grouping was so tight there was but one large hole. All the bullets went through it and made the hole as large as it was. Nonchalantly I returned to the smoke filled car. My score was a perfect 300 out of a possible 300.

That score won the two-foot tall first place trophy. I never confessed I only shot 29 bullets because our team would have won the trophy anyway. Our score was far higher than the second place team. I never heard a buzz in my head in any of my future matches because I discarded my coach's instructions.

I am the first person on the left on the South River, New Jersey Police Range. This range is similar to the Perth Amboy Police Pistol Range.

THE YANKEE AND THE REBEL

May 1959 I responded to a simple one-car accident where the driver ran off the road and plowed into a tree. Another officer arrived at the scene minutes before me and took the driver to a hospital for First Aid treatment on a few superficial bruises. I stayed behind to write the investigation report.

I made a copy of all the details for the driver and arranged for the car to be towed off the private property and taken to a garage. A neighbor walked up to me and said she witnessed the accident. She also saw the driver hide a whiskey bottle in her shrubbery before the first officer arrived. I thanked her for the information and for her help and went to the bush and retrieved the half empty whiskey bottle.

My investigation report would not be complete until I knew how seriously the driver was injured and found out from him exactly how the accident happened. I drove to the hospital to question him. The accident ward staff had just discharged him after treating his minor abrasions and contusions. He was sober by the time I talked to him. For privacy we left the hospital and sat in my patrol car.

He was a respectable, personable, thirty-five year old salesman from the Deep South who attended a sales conference at a nearby hotel. He rented the car soon after he arrived at the hotel. He gave me an acceptable account of how the accident occurred except he failed to mention he had been drinking and intoxication was a contributing factor to the accident. When he finished his fabricated version I told him what my investigation suggested. I mentioned a witness saw the accident happen and that she said he was intoxicated. She also showed me where he hid the whiskey bottle in the bushes. I let him know I knew liquor contributed to the accident. He admitted he was drinking and agreed I was correct but he didn't plead for leniency. My objective was to let him understand he didn't pull the wool over my eyes.

I handed him a copy of my notes and told him he'd need them to explain the accident to the car rental company, his employer, and his insurance carrier. My notes included the time, date, day, location, damage to the vehicle, damage to the property, the garage that towed the car and where it was stored. I included my name and the department's name and telephone number should any of those agencies require more information. I made no mention of his intoxication on my report.

He didn't expect to be treated like a VIP so he asked, "Aren't you going to arrest me up for drunk driving?"

"No," I said. "You have a carload of people to face and explain what happened. If you were a local resident I would do my duty and arrest you but I feel it would be unreasonable to force you to travel back and forth from your home to attend a Hearing and a future Court Trial."

"I can't believe it," he said. "If the situation was reversed and you were in my hometown the Southern Sheriffs would get a great deal of pleasure out of throwing the book at a Yankee for the same charge. Thank you very much."

Six months later the salesman returned to the same hotel to attend another conference. He went to great lengths to locate me through headquarters. The switchboard operator told him I was patrolling somewhere on Lancaster Avenue in Car #16 so he cruised Lancaster Avenue until he located Car #16.

I never expected to see him again and this time he was a totally different person. His whole demeanor and outlook changed. He stood tall and confident and his former defeated appearance was gone. He was happy as a lark and wanted me to know of the many changes in his life that took place since the accident. He told me he hadn't taken a drink of alcohol since then and he would never drink again. He received a promotion and a substantial raise and his relationship with his wife and children has changed and is fantastic. He was ecstatic and insisted it was I who was responsible for his attitude adjustment and success.

He said my compassion was the turning point in his life. He sees things clearly now and as a result his life and career has expanded. He wanted to reward me for bringing about this change and offered me a monetary gift but I staunchly refused and added, "No thank you. You would take the pleasure out of being a service." He wasn't the first person I flabbergasted with that statement.

Christmas arrived soon after our second meeting and by then I had dismissed him and his accident as another fleeting moment in my police career. There were so many accidents that they overlapped and blurred into one gigantic accident. Each one was important only until I completed a thorough report. His accident was erased from my memory along with the others. However, I was reminded of him and his accident when I open a Christmas card he sent me. He wrote a sincere thank you note and inserted twenty-five dollars. I suppose it was important to him to demonstrate his appreciation in more than words.

It wasn't the card or the money that meant a great deal to me it was the difficulty this fellow from the south faced to obtain my home address. He didn't get it from headquarters because department policy forbids giving out personal information of that type.

In all the hundreds of motor vehicle accidents I investigated or was involved in to some degree this was the only gratuity I ever received. It was his sincere appreciation for the good I brought into his life that assured me I was doing my job right. I was thrilled as he much as was because he made an important change in my life. He didn't know it but his sincere appreciation was the genuine unsolicited affirmation I needed to convince me I was learning and improving.

THE WINDOW WELL

It was the department's inconsiderate practice to assign men who already worked an eight hour day, 8:00 a.m. to 4:00 p.m., to return and work a Burglar Detail from 6:00 p.m. to 9:00 p.m. that same evening. There was no overtime pay or any other kind of compensation and that made it all the more irritating. The department insisted it was the nature of the job and expected of the men in that era. One such assignment was The Evening Burglar detail that dragged on for a winter month.

I was lurking after dark behind several houses one cold evening searching for shelter from the cold 15 mph wind. Every time I thought I found an ideal location to overlook the neighborhood a homeowner would suddenly open the kitchen door and dump the supper scraps into the garbage pail in the rear yard. The kitchen light would flood the area and I feared the person might have a serious heart attack if I startled him.

The worse case scenario was when a dog was put outside and it suspected something was amiss. It barked incessantly until he aroused his owner's attention. The homeowner switched on an outdoor floodlight that was brighter than any overhanging streetlight and came outside to investigate. I narrowly escaped being spotted.

I moved from one location to another. Continuing all the time to pussyfoot around in the dark avoiding anything that made a noise. I didn't want to arouse anyone's attention or shake up another watchdog when suddenly something grabbed my ankle. My heart leaped as far as my Adam's apple. My mind raced helplessly through the possibilities. I was nervously keyed for defensive action if a burglar should attack but if this wasn't a burglar it had to be a dog snapping at my leg, or a rat, or a raccoon, or worse yet a rabid fox. I whirled around to see what had a tight hold on my foot. I was doubly shocked to see my brother Tommy's hand. He was a policeman and also assigned to this detail.

He found shelter in a below-ground-level window well. The well was three feet by four feet wide and four feet deep and it was enclosed on three sides by brick walls. In a whisper I asked him how could he possibly stand in that hole in the company of spider webs, and all kinds of insects but he assured me it was warmer than where I stood.

I couldn't quarrel with his logic. I climbed into the infested window well that was a few feet from the one he occupied. I had to compromised a great deal only because it was definitely warmer and out of the winter wind.

Whenever I get lost in memories of my police past I can't imagine how desperate he and I had to be to bring us to climb into those filthy window wells.

STROKE, EPILEPTIC, DIABETIC, HEART?

When I was a neophyte policeman I was often trapped in situations where I hadn't the faintest idea of what I should do to help a sick person who needed immediate aid only because I didn't have the special training that was needed. I was always hoping and groping for the right thing to do.

In the spring of 1948 I was only on the job five months the evening I walked by a movie theater. The manager rushed out of the theater yelling, "Officer! Officer! A boy inside is having a fit!" I had no idea what I should do for the boy but I followed the manager into the theater anyhow. By the time my eyes adjusted to the dark I saw a well-built college boy lying on the floor in the main aisle. He was flailing his arms wildly and thrashing his legs. Fortunately, for me, a phone call had been made to headquarters and a senior officer came on the scene seconds after me. The officer glanced at the boy on the floor and turned to his friend and ordered him to run to the grocery store next store and bring back an orange.

The friend raced off and within twenty seconds he returned with an orange. The senior officer tore the orange in two with his bare hands and placed a half at the semi-conscious boy's mouth. The boy went at it like a hog after slop. He was like a famished infant seizing nourishment from its mother's breast. He quickly recovered and returned to his seat and watched the remainder of the movie. I was impressed that the officer knew what to do. He knew exactly what the boy needed. I was equally impressed at the effectiveness of the orange.

Six months later a man dropped to the sidewalk a few yards from where I was standing. He wiggled and shuddered like he was having a similar fit. I thought of my previous experience and perhaps the man could benefit from my expertise. I asked if he could use an orange and he said his attack was the result of having too much sugar in his system. He needed to go to a hospital. I flagged down a passing car and we rushed him to a hospital. The symptoms looked the same.

A year went by and this time I was dispatched to an office where a businessman took ill. It was his receptionist's first day on the job so she had no idea what ailed him. She called for the police when he first started thrashing about on the office floor. A gripping sensation came over me because I was without the scholarship to know what First Aid to administer in this case. I found out later the man was having an epileptic fit, and of course, the treatment is totally different from the two previous cases yet the patient's behavior resembled the others.

As the years went by there were similar incidents but each was unique in their own way. I became more at ease with each encounter and came to accept there are many illnesses and no two are exactly alike. I knew that some day there would be a case with unprecedented characteristics that will not be in my arsenal of experiences.

For instance: A hospital nurse and doctor requested I remove an annoying drunk. She claimed the man was intoxicated but he looked sick to me and I told her so. She was adamant so I deferred to her judgment and took the man to the lockup. Overnight he died in the cell.

As I accumulated experiences I became as competent as any police officer can be when diagnosing a person suffering from a stroke, epileptic fit, diabetic shock, insulin shock, heat stroke, heart attack, etc., however, the unusual always popped up to strike me square between the eyes just when I felt the most confident.

It happened the day I responded to an ambulance assist call. An older man was having a fit of a kind I didn't recognize. He was lying in bed moaning in pain. He tried his damnedest to get the other officer and myself to focus on his mouth but he could only mumble and barely move. He was furious because we were too stupid to understand what he wanted us to do. His wife was in the bedroom cowering in a corner.

She finally spoke up, "Officer he is deathly afraid he will swallow his tongue. He wants you to put a safety pin through his tongue and hold it so he wont swallow it." She handed me a three-inch horse blanket safety pin. Her husband probably insisted she do the deed before we arrived but she cringed from the very thought.

I couldn't do it either. There was no way I could jab that pin through his tongue. I handed the pin to the ambulance driver and he too refused to do the deed. Without acknowledging him or his wife we quickly strapped him onto a stretcher and raced to a hospital.

I rode in the stretcher compartment of the ambulance and on the ride to the hospital I tried to hold his slippery tongue between my fingers. It was the most repulsive task I was ever asked to perform.

A year later the ambulance was equip with a gadget that served that purpose. It came in two sizes, a child's size and an adult size, and it was inserted down the throat to prevent the patient from swallowing the tongue.

THE VACUUM CLEANER SALESMAN

One evening I pulled my cruiser off the highway and parked in the shadows. My intention was to take a brief rest. I was only there a few minutes when a car sped by at an outlandish speed. I never saw a vehicle go that fast at this location. I thought the driver must be intoxicated or be fleeing from a crime scene. If he was on an emergency he threw all caution to the wind. But if he was in his right mind this would be an easy speeding ticket to issue. He couldn't dispute the speed or rationalize his lack of good judgment. This was a business district where the vehicle and pedestrian traffic was heavy and the speed limit was posted 25 mph. I shifted into gear and took off in hot pursuit.

I followed him to where the traffic thinned out and where there are no pedestrians. He and I would be safe and away from staring eyes. I signaled for him to pull to the side of the road and slid my vehicle behind him. That maneuver was procedural but it really didn't make the conditions any safer. My emergency light was an insignificant small red bubble gum machine on the roof of the patrol car.

In my most professional bearing I walked up to him and said "Good evening, sir. May I see your cards please? I stopped you because you exceeded the posted speed limit through the business district." He jumped out of his car even after I emphatically told him not to but I wasn't going to argue with him just because he didn't obey my instructions. Instead I walked him to the sidewalk at the rear of his car where it was safer for us both. He was a youth in his early twenties. He wore a business suit, white shirt and tie. That made him different because he wasn't in the dress code of the hippies of the day. He was articulate, gifted, excited and inspiration struck.

"Officer, you are so right! I am so hyped up! I just left a high-pitched sales meeting! I listened to Go-Go lectures. I sang praises to the company. I waved the American flag and the company flag and I sang the company jingle over and over. It was an amazing pep rally and it got me all fired up. Officer, you are so right. I didn't realize I was speeding because my mind was still at the sales meeting and I was still singing the company jingle and shouting Hallelujah and Rah! Rah! Rah!"

I should have known better but like a dunce I asked, "What do you sell?" Without hesitation he blurted, "Obic Vacuum Cleaners!" Again I demonstrated my stupidity by saying I wasn't familiar with that brand. He proceeded to tell me about the inventor and the history of the machine. "It is the best vacuum cleaner on the market! New technology! Terrific suction! Light weight! Whole new concept! Let me show you!" He talked like he was in overdrive.

Before I could say, "No. Not now and not here." he had the trunk lid of his car open and the vacuum cleaner out of the demonstrator's kit. There on the dark roadway under the dim glow of an incandescent streetlight and with traffic zipping passed us he began to demonstrate the accessories. If he could have plugged the cord into the overhanging streetlight he would have given me a demonstration by vacuuming the street between our cars.

He was captivating. I marveled at his sincerity. I was overwhelmed by his enthusiasm more than by the product. Twenty minutes flew by before I could break the spell he cast upon me. I said harshly, "Do me a big favor Pal. Collect all your tools and get out of here fast! Don't bother to put the tools back into their assigned niches in the demonstrator's kit just put them into the trunk and get out of here." He hypnotized me. He charmed me with the sales pitch he learned at the sales meeting.

"Thank you Officer for letting me demonstrate the cleaner." He gathered up the machine and the accessories and quickly put them in the trunk and closed the lid.

I didn't write up the citation for speeding because I wanted to get away from him as quickly as possible. I sensed I was the lucky one because I escaped without purchasing a cleaner from him. I bet the last message the instructors drilled into those salesmen was, "Go forth and sell a cleaner to the first person you talk to!" He tried.

He is destined to be an incredible salesman. Actually he can consider that was the most potent sales pitch he'll ever make because he talked himself out of a speeding ticket.

I am in the police car writing an accident report.

THAT'S NOT THE WAY IT'S DONE IN MY COUNTRY

For the first eight years on the job I listened to everything a senior officer wanted to teach me but there was one thing even the veterans never learned. They were unable to teach me how to tell a motorist he or she violated a traffic regulation and then expect the driver to gracefully accept my judgment call. Not one officer I knew could say he never had an argument after issuing a traffic ticket.

I concentrated on developing a technique that was perfect. The solution didn't come to me overnight but took eight years of trial and error. I analyzed what brought about a favorable result and what caused discord. The rewards were worth the trouble it took to obtain an ideal outcome every time. I called my technique 'my act'.

In my act I was an ideal Pennsylvania State Trooper. I selected each word like a jeweler sorts through a bench full of diamonds to find the perfect ones. I never deviated from what I had planned to say.

Before I even approached the violator I first checked my appearance. How I presented myself was extremely important. I made sure my uniform was as trim as a tuxedo. I guarded my diction and infliction. I examined how I stood, I never slouched, I never clinched my fists, I never had a smirk on my face, I wore my gun belt straight and my holster never hung low over my hip like a wild west gunslinger. I made sure my initial impression didn't intimidate. There were dozens of small details that had to be attended to first or my act would backfire and cause a sour response.

Around 1959 several developing and third world countries sent representatives to the United States to study the latest advancements in police work. These representatives studied several police organizations in the United States and then returned to their home country with ideas that could be adopted to improve their own system.

There was an official from a Middle East country assigned to patrol with me for a day. My Lieutenant instructed me to show him how a small suburban department functioned on patrol. As we cruised the streets our conversation was casual. He explained he has been in this country six months and when he first arrived he had no knowledge of the English language. I was amazed at how well he spoke our language.

The first police department on his itinerary was San Francisco for a month. His second department was Los Angeles for a month and then a month with Oakland, California. Three months were shared with the Secret Service, the Alcohol-Firearms-and Tobacco Agency and the FBI to learn police administration and organization on a grand scale.

His final three days would be with the Lower Merion Police Department to learn how a small department utilized all he learned in the previous six months. His experience in Lower Merion would complete his education in this country. He was riding with me on his last day and in the evening he would fly home.

During our conversation he said his position in his government was similar to a United State cabinet post. He was Secretary of Interior Defense and Public Safety Director. I was impressed by his important position. We leisurely cruised along enjoying our tête-à-tête when a vehicle sped through a red traffic signal. I could have ignored the violation but I figured since he was here to witness a police officer in action I would give him a demonstration. I caught up to the violator and motioned for him to pull to the side of the road. I instructed my guest to stand close by so he could overhear how I handled this kind of situation.

I walked to the driver seated at the steering wheel and tipped my hat and said, "Good afternoon, Sir. I am Officer Bernie Loughran. I stopped you because you failed to properly obey the traffic signal. May I see your driver's license and owner's card, please?" The driver handed his cards to me and I said, "Thank you." I copied the information I wanted and returned the cards to the driver and said, "You shall receive a summons in the mail. Please return it with the prescribed fine and cost. In the future please cooperate with my department and me in our efforts to make the highways safer and slower. Good day, sir." I tipped my cap again and he drove off.

I was pleased with my example of proficiency. There was no mess, no fuss, no disagreement, no argument, no discussion and no denial. My act had been satisfactorily tested once again and I felt I impressed our country's guest.

We returned to the patrol car and I continued to cruise the streets. Neither of us said anything for a long few minutes. I had a feeling he had a criticism to offer but I couldn't see how he could find fault with anything I said or did. He certainly couldn't find fault with the final outcome. I patiently waited until he chose the words he needed to form the English sentences that would put across his thoughts. He finally spoke up.

"That's not the way it's done in my country." Maybe there was something I did or said that left much to be desired. Perhaps an outside observer could further refine my technique. I asked, "How is it done in your country?"

He articulated his answer in perfect English. "The police in my country are quasi-military. The men wear army uniforms and patrol in an army personnel carrier. There are four men assigned to each vehicle. One man is a 'driver', one man is a 'radio operator' and two men are 'rifle bearers'. When they come upon a motorist who has violated the law they signal for him to pull to the side of the road. All four men leave the personnel carrier and walk up to the driver. They ask him to step out of his car. Then they beat the hell out of him."

MY HEART!

I stopped two motorists on Belmont Avenue at Rock Hill Road for failing to stop for a red traffic signal. They pulled to the curb and I parked behind them with half of my car up on the sidewalk. I went to the operators and obtained their cards and instructed them to stay seated until I returned. I walked to the rear of the cars and stood on the sidewalk out of harms way. I knew a policeman distracts passing motorists and often causes them to forget to pay attention to where their car is headed.

I was copying the information when both drivers bolted from their car hoping to reach me before I started writing. They were eager to rationalize why they went through the red light. One fellow failed to check if it was safe to step out of his car. He blindly rushed to me but when he got as far as his rear fender an intoxicated driver misjudged the clearance and brushed against him. He man was rolled between the two cars as you would roll a #2 pencil between your palms to the front of his car. There he flopped like a wet towel.

He lay on the road screaming he was having a heart attack. He yammered on about his heart yet he refused to go to a hospital. His heart medicine was home and that was where he wanted to be taken. I radioed for assistance and my supervisor and another officer arrived.

My supervisor drove the man home and the officer followed in the man's car. I placed the intoxicated driver under arrest and took him to the lockup. I heard no more about the man's heart condition nor did I inquirer about it. I didn't mail a summons to him for the traffic violation because I didn't want to rub salt into the wound. He might get mad and sue me for causing his injuries and any damage to his car. I never heard of him or the intoxicated driver again.

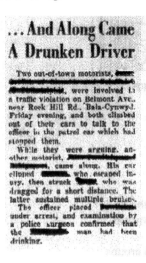

... And Along Came A Drunken Driver

Two out-of-town motorists, ▆▆▆ ▆▆▆▆▆▆▆▆, were involved in a traffic violation on Belmont Ave., near Rock Hill Rd., Bala-Cynwyd. Friday evening, and both climbed out of their cars to talk to the officer in the patrol car which had stopped them.

While they were arguing, another motorist, ▆▆▆▆▆▆▆▆ ▆▆▆▆▆▆, came along. His car elloped ▆▆▆▆ ▆▆ who escaped injury, then struck ▆▆▆ who was dragged for a short distance. The latter sustained multiple bruises.

The officer placed ▆▆▆▆▆▆ under arrest, and examination by a police surgeon confirmed that the ▆▆▆▆▆▆ man had been drinking.

194

WALTER LIPPMANN*

I have a pecking order when it comes to choosing whom I want in my little world. I value my wife and children the most then it's my extended family. The friends whom I socialized with before I became a policeman comes next and at the very bottom of the totem pole are the people I met while on duty.

It makes no difference how influential, wealthy or intellectual an individual is I discouraged a relationship with those I assisted while on duty. I didn't care to have them in my private life. I felt strongly that everyone who crossed my path left an indelible influence on me and as a policeman I dealt with some very dubious people. Some possessed weak characters or flaws that I didn't wish incorporated into my personality. I avoided those who couldn't solve their own problems just to prevent being corrupted. In so doing, I admit, I shut the door on so many people who may have enriched me.

One super individual was Walter Lippmann, the greatest investigative reporter/journalist of his day. Unfortunately, I didn't know of his genius when we met on a foul evening in 1968 on Lancaster Avenue in Haverford. He stepped off the sidewalk into moving traffic to flag down my patrol car. It was drizzling so I stopped and invited him to sit in the passenger seat to discuss why he needed to talk to an officer.

He was short in stature. Like most men who at seventy-nine years of age he lost the battle with gravity and shrank a few inches yet he was still impressive. He introduced himself to be a retired reporter for The New York Herald Tribune and a lifetime member of the Washington Press Corps now living in New York. He produced identification cards to verify who he was and included a newspaper photograph of himself interviewing the Duke of Windsor. He told me he always conferred with local police officers when he had a question indigenous to the area. That sounded like blarney so it didn't impress me. He was just another person drawing me into a time consuming problem.

He went to the heart of his problem quickly. He spoke about a wealthy friend in New York City and to put the man's wealth in perspective he said this friend owned a seat on the New York Stock Exchange worth $350,000. His friend has become heartsick and depressed over the loss of his runaway son. His son disowned him and left home without leaving a trace of his whereabouts. The loss of his son distressed his friend so intensely he was losing his ability to function and on several occasions mentioned suicide.

Mr. Lippmann said that watching his friend deteriorate affected him to a point he had to get involved so through his investigative skills he learned the son was an alcoholic who frequented the bars on the "Main Line". He never met the boy nor did he have any knowledge which bars he frequented. He didn't know where the Main Line was but was given the names Ardmore, Haverford and Bryn Mawr. He arrived by train and got off at the Ardmore station and roamed aimlessly not knowing where to start looking so he asked me to help him.

This was an astronomical challenge I didn't have the time to devote to because I was recently assigned to supervise a squad of men and that involved many new duties and responsibilities. There are a dozen saloons on the Main Line where a person can lose their class and identity and there are a dozen alcoholics hanging in each one. It was like looking for a needle in a haystack but obviously this fragile little old man still had the tenacity that was the hallmark of his reputation.

I questioned him as to his motive and concern. Why did he take on this monumental task? He repeated he couldn't bear to see his dear friend suffer mentally and physically. The loss of his son might soon be the death of him. When I asked if his friend was going to reward him he was deeply offended because he didn't expect me to even entertain such a thought. He replied his friend didn't know of his search and he would not have approved if he did.

Mr. Lippmann thought he could be helpful since he himself is a recovering alcoholic. His plan is to meet the boy in a saloon and sit at the bar with him. Maybe, he hoped, a friendship and bonding might develop. He wouldn't mention his association with his father or the boy's alcohol addiction but hoped during a casual conversation he might twang a chord that would send the boy home.

That was how his conversion came about. It was a casual conversation at a bar that gave him a new slant on life. At the time he was drinking heavily. As usual he was in the Washington Press Club on a beautiful Sunday morning in the company of a fellow alcoholic reporter. Sundays were exceptionally dull days for the Press Corps. Startling news was seldom made on a weekend. Dignitaries rarely visited Washington on Sundays and the President's family and staff preferred privacy on the weekends. There rarely was an international incident to pursue on a Sunday.

He said he was a hyper fellow who didn't know how to enjoy his free time. His only pleasure was chasing after volatile issues so in a moment of depression he asked his drinking companion, "What else is there to do on a Sunday but to get drunk?" His friend walked him to a large picture window and pointed to all the people strolling by outside.

"See those people out there? Some are going to church, some are going to play golf, some are going swimming and some are going to visit their relatives. Some are going to wash their car; some are going for a hike in the park. Some are going horseback riding and some are going fishing. There are so many things to do besides drinking and getting drunk."

Those few words struck him like a bolt of lightning. Suddenly he realized he was missing out on the good things in life. Instead of participating in social activities he was devoting his free time to drinking until he was ossified. His friend's few words had brought about an immediate conversion. He hoped a few well-chosen words at the right moment might affect the young man's outlook. His plan seemed simplistic but who was I to discourage him.

Alcoholics hang in seedy taprooms so it took nerves of steel for a stranger to enter them and ask questions. I drove him to the closest taproom and he went inside without a moment's hesitation while I waited for him in the car outside. It was imperative I stay in the patrol car and wait for the next radio message for at any moment I might be sent to supervise an emergency situation. Luckily he returned within a few minutes. "He's not in there but the bartender said he does drink in there on occasions."

We repeated this at a second bar with the same results. I was thinking this could go on all evening and I didn't have the time to spare. I promised myself there would be only one more taproom and then I'd point him in the right direction and send him off on his own. He could take a cab.

He entered the third taproom and within minutes returned to the car with good news. He was euphoric; the boy was sitting at the bar. After thanking me we parted. I expected it was the last time our paths would ever cross. I was happy he found the boy and it only took asking sensitive questions in three sleazy saloons. I was thinking how close he came to be given the bum's rush because the bartenders in those bars didn't welcome strangers who asked questions. I was glad I didn't have to pick him up off the sidewalk and rush him to the hospital.

That was not to be the last of Mr. Lippmann. He somehow learned my name and my work schedule so the week I was working in the evenings he returned to Ardmore. From New York City he telephoned headquarters and left the message he was arriving on such and such a train and requested I meet him at the train station. This was an imposition because I was a busy supervisor. I had responsibilities that required my presence and time. Nevertheless I met him even though I was apprehensive and didn't appreciate the imposition.

After meeting him few times we became friends to a limited extent. He insisted I go with him to the Washington Press Club where he is a lifetime member. He said he was eager to introduce me to his friends in high places. I refused. I told him I didn't possess the verbal skills necessary to hold a conversation on a high intellectual plateau but he assured me I would be very comfortable with his friends.

From New York he often telephoned my home. He'd plead with me to visit him in New York City so he could introduce me to his friends there. I never accepted his invitations. Undoubtedly he liked me and was impressed by my professionalism.

Five years after our first meeting he died. I never asked him who the alcoholic son was and if there was a possible recovery.

Mr. Lippmann's obituary appeared in all the national magazines and newspapers. Pages and pages were printed of his accomplishments. His peers revered him. The journalism methods he developed were still taught in every university in the country.

It was only after reading his obituary notices that I had regrets. He was a fantastic individual. Our paths crossed for a fleeting moment and I failed to seize that moment to get to know him better. I denied myself the opportunity to be enhanced by a great caring individual who shaped this country's foreign policies and influenced the decisions of world leaders. In my ignorance I avoided him.

*Walter Lippmann was the Dean of American newspapermen. Born in 1889, he was educated at Harvard and taught philosophy there. He joined the staff of The New Republic at it's founding in 1914, interrupted his career to serve as assistant to the Secretary of War--doing special work on peace negotiating--then moved to an editorial position on the New York World. In 1931 he joined the staff of the New York Herald Tribune. His writings were syndicated in newspapers throughout the country, and his column "Today and Tomorrow" won him the Pulitzer Prize in 1958 and 1962. The 1958 award cited the "wisdom, perception, and high sense of responsibility with which he has commented for many years on national and international affairs." He received numerous honorary degrees and such foreign decorations as the Legion of Honor from France and the Order of Leopold from Norway. His books include The Coming Tests with Russia (1961) and Western Unity and the Common Market (1962).

The Borzoi College Reader, edited by Charles Muscatine, Alfred A Knopf: New York, 1967, P 379.

REALLY REALLY

I was in the accident ward completing a follow-up accident investigation report. I had visited a patient on the third floor that was seriously injured in an automobile accident the previous evening. This accident ward had three spare rooms where patients were stacked until the intern had time to finish the first aid treatment he had started on them. Police officers used these rooms when they are vacant to write their reports. I was sitting on a chair in one of these rooms with my notes spread out on the bed when a young nurse entered. Thinking she was going to wheel in a patient I gathered my papers and was about to leave but she entered the room carrying a tape recorder.

"Officer," she said sheepishly, "I saw you come in here and I noticed you frequently bring accident cases to this hospital. I was hoping I could interview you. I'm taking an advanced college course and I must submit a research paper. I chose for my thesis *The Anatomy Of An Accident* since I am currently assigned to the accident ward. You have experience with accidents. May I tape your comments?"

"I have first hand experience with accidents after dealing with them for fifteen years but I am not qualified to discuss the subject."

"Why not?" she asked.

"I'm trained to investigate and report the facts regarding an accident. I'm as sterile as a drone bee because I must be objective and I'm not supposed to have opinions. For example my report will read '#1 operator was traveling east and made a left turn into the path of westbound #2 Vehicle.' Those are the facts and they will satisfy my supervisor, insurance company, lawyer and judge but they don't say why the accident really happened. My report doesn't mention what was on the minds of both operators moments before the accident. Actually #1 operator was thinking about his nasty wife at that precise moment and he didn't care if he lived or died. #2 operator could have taken evasive action but instead wanted to show that road hog he couldn't get away with cutting in front of him."

"I don't understand what you mean. Can you explain yourself differently?" she asked. "Nurse I'm not an ideal person to interview, besides, you took me by surprise so I'm not prepared to share my thoughts on such an important subject. I've thought about this many times but I never shared my ideas with anyone before therefore my ideas are disjointed. But since you asked I'll put it another way.

"You worked in this accident ward and saw odd accidents or you heard about odd cases from the other nurses or you've read about weird accidents. How about the professional singer who accidentally drank a caustic fluid and permanently injured his vocal cords? Or the seeded tennis player who accidentally cut off a toe while mowing his lawn? Or the professional pianist who inadvertently cut off the tip of his finger while working on a woodworking project in his basement?

"I've heard the laments of their friends and relatives. They are *'really sorry'* that an outstanding career was ended by a freak accident. But I wonder, "Is the victim, and for that matter an interested party, really *'really sorry'* the accident happened? Is it possible the victim was caught up in an all-consuming career from which he wished he could escape? Would he rather be doing something else with his life? Is it possible someone earlier in his life recognized a latent talent or skill and forced him to hone it to perfection? Was there no way out of his trap except by a freak accident?"

I only confused the nurse even more and she said, "I don't understand the statement, is the victim, or the interested parties, really *'really sorry'* the accident happened?" I said, "Nurse, I don't want to come across as being callous and uncaring. At an accident scene I can go about the task of helping an injured person. I can soothe and reassure friends and relatives with calming words. I can delicately elicit facts from horrified witnesses but if one professional can't share ideas with another professional, no matter how shocking or whether they are right or wrong, how is either profession expected to grow?

"Let me try once more to make myself clear with this example that happened a year ago. A man came home from work early one evening and found his wife in bed with his friend. He didn't argue, instead, in a rage he snatched his two infant sons from their crib and put them on the front seat of his car and sped away. He raced off into the night with vengeance in his heart. He weighed many questions. Where will he and the children spend the night? If there is a divorce will he lose the children? He loves his wife but he can't live with her again?

"Then there is a horrible accident. I investigate and put the pertinent facts on a report. '#1 operator was passing a vehicle traveling in the same direction. He entered the lane of oncoming traffic and struck #2 vehicle head-on. #2 operator and the two passengers in #1 vehicle were killed on impact. #1 Operator sustained contusions and abrasions.'

"In the accident ward the man wept uncontrollably. 'I'm really sorry I caused the accident. It's my fault. I'm sorry. I'm really sorry.'

"Do you think this fellow is really *'really sorry'*? Or, is he sorry his suicide attempt failed? He can't face the future without the woman he loves and he can't bear to live without the two children he just killed. This type of suicide is accepted by society as an accident. Friends, relatives and insurance companies accept it was an accident. Do you think the man was really *'really sorry'* he had the accident. Maybe it was a failed suicide attempt."

The wheels of the tape cassette were whirling. I wasn't getting my idea across. She expected something else, something traditional. I'm not an articulate person and this is a multifaceted subject. She could present

200

a research paper that was unusual and informative but I wasn't verbalizing my ideas right.

She said, "I can't grasp this 'Are they <u>really really</u> sorry the accident happened?" I responded, "Examine what I am saying and not how I say it. When you approached me I warned you I'd be a poor subject to interview, especially now, I'm emotionally shot."

She asked, "Why is that? You seem relaxed." "Well I'm not. You may be like me. I am emotionally destroyed by a sad love story. All love stories have a lot of sadness. Someone dies or is seriously injured. I call it the Romeo and Juliet syndrome. There are many variations of that love story. The moment you entered this room I was busy writing the facts of an accident that happened in a true love story. A love story with a very sad and yet a happy ending.

"Last evening I assisted other officers extricate a seventeen year old boy from his car. He drove head-on into a tree and was unconscious at the scene. His body was intact except for his lower face. The roof of his mouth was shattered, his lips were chopped liver and his jaw was fractured in several places. His teeth were either knocked out or were embedded in his tongue that had a piece bitten off. When he hit the tree his jaw struck the rim of the steering wheel and that was what caused the facial damage.

"The accident occurred at 11:30 last night. He was unconscious so this afternoon I visited him in his hospital room on the third floor. He is still unconscious or under heavy sedation but his girlfriend is alone in his room. She is so pretty, so delicate and so petite. Her mascara ran from her eyes. Her uncontrollable crying swelled her eyes and face. Her lipstick was smeared over her mouth and there were traces of it all over his forehead.

"After some soothing talk I asked her if she knew how the accident happened and she said she had no idea. 'Tyrone and I loved each other all through school. Our parents knew how deeply we loved each other but they were afraid we are too serious and too young. They tried to discourage us and they did everything to keep us apart. My parents enrolled me in an all-girl college in New England and I will be boarding there for the next four years. Tyrone received a four-year scholarship to a music conservatory in Paris. He was to leave next week. Except for an occasional vacation we might never see each other ever again. We considered running away and getting married. Other kids our age had. We are so much in love.

'My parents insisted Tyrone bring me home by 10:00 o'clock every night. I would lie awake all night thinking about our future and how unhappy and bleak it looked. He did a lot of thinking too while driving the streets for hours every night before going home. He'll never be able to play a trumpet again and after me he loved it dearly. His instructors said he had great potential.'

"After talking to her my investigation was complete. Where the accident occurred the road was winding and poorly lit. Where the tree stood the road has a sharp right curve. If the tree had been located twenty or thirty feet farther into the curve I would have written that he was driving too fast for conditions and centrifugal force thrust him into the tree. But there were no skid marks to indicate that was the case. The boy was familiar with this road. He dropped the girl off at 10:00 o'clock sharp and then cruised the area until the accident at 11:30 p.m.. He pondered the big questions, how could he thwart their parent's plans to separate them and how can they escape the four-year separation?

"He was so distraught and befuddled he cried and his eyes filled with tears. He followed the painted white center line that outlined the bends and curves. The sign read SLOW and he saw the yellow sign with a black right angle arrow and a 10 mph speed limit. He followed the centerline but he never slowed down. That tree was huge. It didn't budge an inch but the damage to the car indicated he was speeding.

"Would I be so presumptuous to say he deliberately drove into the tree? No. But I'll never be sure. I ask you, is he, or his girlfriend, really *really sorry* the accident happened or did it solve their problem? He definitely isn't going to Paris to pursue music. He played a trumpet and now his mouth and lips will never work a trumpet mouthpiece. His girlfriend is at his bedside hour after hour. Do you think her parents might be less adamant considering there was almost a death?

"Isn't that a sad love story? It is sad because there is so much suffering yet it does have a happy ending. He won't be going abroad and they may now go to a co-ed college together. I ask you once more, are these lovers really *really sorry* there was this horrible accident?"

She said, "Your *really really* theory is a little clearer. I'll have to listen to the tape. Thank you."

I wonder if she used anything I said in her research paper.

THE POLICE RECRUITING DRIVE

The complement of the force dropped sharply in 1957. Two recently hired men didn't cut the mustard and were dismissed during their probationary period. Another fellow quit to be an electrician. The department needed ten more men. The job opportunity was advertised in the local and city newspapers but no one responded. In desperation the Township Manager offered a $50.00 bonus for each applicant an officer got who was hired. The incentive was spicy so I became a recruiter. The prevailing negative police image discouraged young men. Here is a sample of the kind of opposition I faced.

It was a harsh winter and the night I'm referring to was bitter. It snowed all day. By 3:00 a.m. there were many motorist stranded without snow chains or with broken links. Some motorist made it to the only all night gas station for service. I pulled into the gas station to check on the attendant. He was a healthy twenty-three year old man.

When I pulled into the gas station he was lying on his back in the slush under a rear fender. He was struggling with a tangled snow chain that became wrapped around the axle. That was the worse thing that could happen to a chain because it was so difficult to untangle. He was very busy taking care of this customer but he had already assisted many other get back on the road. There were others waiting patiently for their turn.

I bent over him to say hello and to assure him the police were close by if he had an emergency such as a personal injury or a holdup. His coveralls were soaked and covered with dirty slush. Gloves were useless doing this tedious work so his fingers were chapped and near frostbitten. I seized the opportunity to offer him a better job with a future.

"Joe," I said. "You would make a fine policeman how about I bring around an application and help you fill it out?" He eyed me like I was affected by the snow and said, "No thanks. I don't ever want that dirty job." That defined the limits of his mentality so I didn't pursue it.

It turned out I was the only officer who found promising applicants. I sponsored two fellows who were hired but they lasted less than a year. They couldn't get used to the shift work and the night work so they quit.

I received my $100.00 bonus anyway.

THE FOSTER CHILDREN

This particular automobile accident left a lasting impression not because it was an unusual accident but because the occupants of the car were so unusual.

The front wheel of their car fell off and the car continued on a hundred feet and into a tree. Luckily no one was injured. The driver was a male African-American and his passengers were his Caucasian wife and their four foster children ranging in age from thirteen months to ten years. The adults were old beyond their chronological years. He was a southern gentleman and she was an elegant lady. They were dressed in their Sunday best. He wore a suit and tie and she wore a delicate lace dress under a frail coat. Their clothes were old and threadbare but they were clean and the children were spotless.

Their very old car was totally destroyed. It was a relic waiting for its last ride to a junkyard. The body was rusted and bruised all over and the cloth covering the seats was worn so thin the cotton padding and a spring had already burst through.

The adults can best be described as 'Lil ole folks'. They were bent from a life of toil and misfortunes that burnt them out and turned them into meek old people. The old man said the four beautiful children were his foster children. An African-American boy, ten years old, was the oldest and he stood close to the old man's side to brace him. He listened to my every instruction. "Don't worry about anything father, I'll explain everything the officer said when we get home."

The nine-year old Asian girl supported the old woman. They stood so close together they reminded me of mourners over a casket. "Come mother, we will sit in the warm police car." On the rear seat of their car an eight year old Oriental girl was changing the soiled diaper on the multi-racial infant.

I made a carbon copy of the details of the accident and as I was handing it to the old man the boy spoke up. "I'll take that officer, thank you. I'll explain everything you said to my father when we get home and I'll call the insurance company too." They climbed into the police car and I drove them to their home.

What made this incident unusual was the fact an agency placed these four young children in a home where the foster parents was responsible for their care but in this case these children were taking care of the foster parents. The children bore the heavier burden in this relationship and they were capable of the task. The way they cared for the adults was heart warming. They reassured and assisted their foster parents in a loving and courteous way. Several times they lovingly called them 'mother' and 'father'. The old couple provided a love some children never receive.

I wonder if the agency placed these six people together by error or was it a deliberate plan.

THE TOWNSHIP DUMP TRUCK ACCIDENT

On a summer day in 1962 I was on routine patrol when the Lieutenant had me paged via radio. I was to report to him at once in headquarters. From past experience I learned when he summoned I was to respond pronto.

"Sergeant, a township dump truck was involved in a fatal accident yesterday. The truck was coming off the eastbound ramp of the Schuylkill Expressway. The driver said his brakes failed so he couldn't stop for the red traffic signal at Belmont Avenue. A couple from New York was traveling south on Belmont Avenue and was struck broadside by the truck and they both were killed outright."

"I heard about the accident and that Sergeant Rogers investigated it. He reported the truck's brakes were defective so what more can I add to his report?" "I want you to go to the garage where the truck was towed and find out why the brakes failed. The township is involved in this accident and we must be thorough because there will be a civil law suit."

I wasn't anxious to improve Sergeant Rogers' investigation because he might take offense to it. I told my Lieutenant I thought Sergeant Rogers' was an exceptional investigator and I didn't know what else I could uncover.

"Sergeant, I want a follow-up investigation and a report from you. So get going." "Yes Sir," I reluctantly responded and drove to where the dump truck was stored.

It had front-end damage and was 'totaled'. A total in police jargon and mechanics' vernacular means it would cost more to repair than the vehicle was worth. Even though this truck was twenty years old it had been functioning satisfactorily. Up until now it was a valued piece of township equipment but because of the extensive damage it had carried its last load of dirt.

I met the garage owner and we discussed the accident. "Sergeant Rogers and I both pumped on the brake pedal and got no response. The brakes are definitely faulty and they were the cause of the accident." He, more or less, was exonerating the truck driver.

"Thanks Ed." I said.

As an after thought I asked, "Ed, will you please get your tow-truck and lift the front end of the truck up as high as you can. I want to get under it and examine the brake pedal from underneath."

"Sergeant is that necessary? That's a lot of work." He balked.

"Ed, I know it is an imposition but humor me, please. I have to write a follow-up investigation. Please lift up the front end."

There was no argument. It was extra work for him and I could appreciate that but he knew he had to comply with my request. If he didn't cooperate it could mean the loss of any future contracts with the township. He maneuvered his tow truck around and lifted the truck high enough for me to look under it with ease. It didn't take me five seconds to locate the cause of the brake failure. Resting on the I-beam, a brace or part of the chassis that holds the truck together, was the pin that held the brake parts together. This pin is an unthreaded bolt approximately 1/2 inch in diameter and three inches long. On the end of this bolt is a small hole in which is inserted a cotter pin.

The brake had only one moving part. After the brake pedal goes through the floorboards it makes a 45-degree bend and where it bends it goes between a rod shaped like a musical tuning fork. A hole is drilled in the ends of the tongs of the tuning fork and a hole is drilled where the brake pedal bends. Through these three holes a steel pin is inserted and acts as a fulcrum. A cotter pin holds the pin in place. However, after twenty years of constant use the cotter pin rusted and wore thin and it dropped away leaving the pin to work its way out of tuning fork.

I used the Department's Graph Flex camera to document my find on film. It took less than three hours to complete my written report. I was proud of myself when I submitted it to my Lieutenant.

"Here's my report, Lieutenant."

"You can't be done already. I hope it is thorough.

"I think you'll like it."

I don't know if he liked it or not. He never commented when I submitted a report, however, if it wasn't satisfactory I'd been told about it in harsh terms.

This 1959 photograph was taken for the personnel files.
I was thirty-three years old that year.

THE FLIM FLAM

In 1960 I was a sergeant one month when headquarters dispatched a patrol car to a gas station. The attendant told the responding officer a customer attempted to flim-flam him out of a tank of gas. The officer was as confused as the teenage attendant. He didn't know how to resolve the problem so he called for the sergeant to assist him. I responded and met him. Two additional officers out of curiosity also showed up at the gas station. I was disappointed that together these three seasoned officers couldn't handle this simple assignment.

The attendant pointed to the customer parked at the gas pumps and repeated his complaint to me. "Sergeant, she wants a full tank of gas but she hasn't the money to pay for it." She promised to mail the money to him but he suspected she was after a free tank of gas. I talked to the young lady to get her version. She was twenty-six years old, well groomed and well spoken. She was with her mother and her two children, five and six years of age. She told me her predicament.

She said she is driving to Norfolk, Virginia from Houston, Texas to be with her husband who was in the navy and recently transferred. Behind her station wagon was a rental-trailer with all her possessions. They stopped at a turnpike restaurant to eat dinner and after paying her check she believed she left her purse, with all her money, on the cashier's counter. She telephoned the restaurant manager from this gas station and he assured her no lost pocketbook was turned in to him.

She asked this attendant for a tank of gas to get her to Norfolk. She promised to mail the money to him as soon as she arrived there. She and her mother were so innocent looking and so distressed I knew they couldn't be con artists. Besides con artists would go for more than a tank of gas. But, the three officers and the attendant weren't convinced they were squeaky clean.

I ignored their words of caution and instructed the attendant to fill her gas tank. The heavily loaded trailer was a burden on the station wagon's motor so it needed two quarts of oil and a pint of transmission fluid. I paid the bill and handed her an extra $20.00 for gas farther along on the trip. The total out of my pocket was $35.00.

The three officers hassled me for two months and let the whole squad know a pretty face took me in. Soon after I received a letter from Norfolk. It was a Thank You note with a check for $35.00. She explained that after they left the restaurant the children were playing in the rear of the station wagon. One child stuffed her pocketbook into a shopping bag that she didn't examine until they arrived in Norfolk. She again thanked me to the high heavens.

My faith in people was vindicated. Until I received the letter my ability to make a wise character assessment was in jeopardy in the eyes of the men in my squad.

THE INSURANCE POLICIES

I was the last person dispatched to investigate an accident where the scene was congested with fire apparatus, rescue equipment, tow-truck, ambulance and police cars. My job was to take photographs and write the investigation report. The accident involved a tractor-trailer and a passenger car. The tractor-trailer had been separated from the wreckage and driven to a vacant lot nearby. The woman passenger had been removed from the crushed car after a tremendous effort and transported to a hospital. Her husband, the driver, was unconscious and was still encased in the twisted metal of the car.

I recorded the pertinent facts. I didn't get involved in the rescue effort. That was for those with the tools that could handle an emergency of this type. While the rescuers went about their work I did mine. It didn't take long to get the information but the rescue operation was slow.

The truck driver was a gentle man who was emotionally upset. His nerves were frayed and he had to be relaxed because after the injured driver was extricated from the car he was needed to drive the big rig away. I kept him engaged in small talk. He said he was a wildcat truck driver. In the trade he was referred to as an Independent. He didn't work for a particular company but obtained his jobs from the union hall. The union hall dispatched him from one company to the next depending on who needed a truck driver that day.

He was taking this particular load to Pittsburgh where he would leave the trailer and load and return with a different trailer and load for another company. There was no reason for him to know who owned the truck or the trailer he was assigned that day. We talked while I recorded unnecessary information just to keep him distracted. I wrote down the name of the owner of the truck, the insurance company and the policy number even though it was not procedural.

The rescue crew worked cautiously to extricate the driver from the mangled car because they didn't want to exacerbate his injuries. The truck driver was beginning to calm down. As I casually examined the trailer he pointed to a small metal box welded to the body. He said the box held the owner's card and insurance company information of the trailer. The company who owned the tractor didn't own the trailer so I recorded that superfluous information too.

The injured driver was finally freed and rushed to a hospital. The intersection was open to traffic and the truck driver proceeded to Pittsburgh with his trailer.

A week later I received a frantic telephone call from a Judge. He said it was his sister and brother-in-law who were involved in the accident. His brother-in-law was seriously injured and his brother-in-law's attorney asked him to obtain from the police the name of the insurance company who insured the truck and the policy number. The

Judge knew it wasn't information routinely secured by the police but he was hoping I had it. We both were pleased that I did have the information but I never told him why I had it. I let him think I was the most through accident investigator in the county.

Two days later the Judge telephoned again. He said his brother-in-law was still in critical condition but there was a slight improvement. He said the information I gave him on the tractor was useless. He needed the same information on the trailer because it was the trailer that was involved in the accident. I didn't ask him to explain that technicality. He needed the information I obtained from the cards in the little metal box.

Like it was common knowledge I gave him the trailer owner's name, insurance company and policy number over the telephone. He was impressed. It was a lucky break for him the truck driver pointed out the little metal box for I would have never noticed it.

This is me in 1960.

THAT'S A GOOD ONE TEX!

If I could choose between patrolling in a car alone as opposed to patrolling with a partner I always opted for being by myself. Most officers preferred the company of a partner for the added protection and safety. Two men together naturally were safer than a man by himself.

If you enjoy the company of your partner the eight hours roll by effortlessly but sometimes it takes a great deal of sacrifice and tolerance. Problems arise when your partner is hungry and you prefer to eat later or if in the middle of the night your partner wishes to rest his eyes while you would rather cruise. A vicious discussion can develop over the slightest inconvenience if the two officers are incompatible.

There are numerous preferences that cause arguments. One man may enjoy puffing on a cigar for hours while his partner is a nonsmoker or has allergies. Raw nerve endings are exposed.

If one officer is a fresh air freak and his partner has a head cold there is real trouble. The man who prefers fresh air will roll down the window on his side of the car but the air enters that window and circulates around inside the car and strikes his partner on the back of the neck. The partner's fever elevates and the quarrelling escalates. "Close the window!" "Go to hell!" "Put out the cigar!" "You go to hell!" It can be a long tedious eight hours for the two men who can't agree.

There is the legendary tale about the two policemen who had no love for one another. They were assigned to patrol together in a car on a snowy winter night. The driver rolled down his window for a breath of fresh air. His partner took it as a spiteful act and lowered his window. The driver sensed his partner's vindictiveness so he lowered his rear window. His partner did likewise. To get back at each other the canvas roof was rolled back on the roadster and the windshield was folded down. After their eight hour tour of duty they returned to headquarters frozen stiff and with an inch of snow in the car and on themselves.

For a month two officers and myself were assigned to a burglar detail. The three of us cruised for eight hours a day in an unmarked patrol car. Fortunately we enjoyed each other's company and overlooked the stress that comes automatically from being confined in tight quarters for eight hours. At the end of the month we were still very good friends. We respected each other on the last day of the assignment even more than on our first day together.

Bill and Tex were terrific policemen. They were proud of the profession and could handle any situation. They had confidence in their ability to tackle any problem. I was eight years their senior and their sergeant yet I felt they respected me personally than for my rank. But they had a fault.

Bill and Tex socialized together when off duty. When they socialized they spent long hours in local saloons. They guzzled beer by the pitcher and when they drank they developed a gluttonous appetite. They ate any food that was displayed on the bar. They consumed peanuts, pretzels, and hard-boiled eggs. They swallowed raw eggs in their beer and devoured hot dogs smothered with relish, onions and sauerkraut. On top of that a sausage sandwich, beef jerky and more beer. Their off duty antics never dulled their enthusiasm or their performance on duty the following day.

I was behind the steering wheel the day after Bill and Tex had an extended night on the town. It was the long night of self-gratification that caused Tex's stomach to be very queasy. He couldn't prevent an uncontrollable escape of insufferable stomach gas. It wasn't on purpose at first because that wasn't his nature. He and Bill were gentlemen on every occasion but anyone who ever ate hard-boiled eggs on top of beer can tell you the combination generates a noxious uncomfortable gas in the stomach. The foul odor escaping from Tex's insides could suffocate an army mule.

I bellowed facetiously, "Tex! Roll down the window! You rotten pig!" They both snickered at my display of annoyance. Bill thought Tex's plight and my annoyance was hilarious so he purposely let loose and expelled his gas. It was equally overpowering. They laughed hysterically at my discomfort. Tex slapped his knee and said. "Bill you're dead. You should roll over and lie down until the undertaker comes for you."

I screamed an order, "Cut that out! I can't breathe. Do you guys want to stop at a restroom?" I made the mistake of pretending I was more annoyed than I was. It encouraged them to compete with each other. They began to judge each other's releases on loudness, offensive odor, and, for the duration of the noise.

There wasn't enough fresh air entering the car even with the four windows wide open so I drove down a back road with my car door wide open and me hanging half out of the car. Back and forth they continued just to see how far they could rile me. Each time there was knee slapping, back patting and uproarious laughter. I couldn't be mad at them because they were behaving like children.

"Can you top that, Tex?" Bill asked Tex after he presented a challenge.

Tex in his Texan drawl responded like he could outdo Paul Bunyan. "Hell yeeeea, Bill."

"Woweeee! That's a good one, Tex!"

TRAFFIC WARRANTS

In 1963 I was the sergeant in charge of the four men in the Traffic Squad. My Lieutenant handed me a hundred Traffic Warrants that had to be to served. This was a highly unusual assignment because serving warrants is the responsibility of a constable and not a task a policeman performs. But it was the sign of the times. "If a job has to be done assign it to a cop because he has nothing else to do." I accepted the warrants and divided them among my men and myself.

A Justice of the Peace employs Constables and they are the ones who serve his warrants. Maybe the constable was inundated with warrants that were difficult to serve because the individual named on the warrant couldn't be located. There are individuals who make themselves impossible to locate by using a fictitious name and address even on legal documents. These people are always on the fringe of the law and a white lie is helpful when they don't want to be located.

This is a brief explanation of a Motor Vehicle Warrant. It is a writ issued by a Justice of the Peace for the arrest of a person who was given a citation for a traffic violation, such as, a failure to stop for a STOP sign or a red traffic signal or for speeding or illegal parking or any Motor Vehicle Code violation. The violator is given a reasonable time to pay the Fine and Cost but should it be ignored a follow-up procedure is begun. A warrant is given to a constable who is authorized by law to apprehend these scofflaws. He is to arrest the person and bring him before the Justice of the Peace for a Hearing. At the Hearing the scofflaw pays up or goes to the county prison.

My men and me were to carry out the assignment but we weren't given instructions on how to accomplish the task. I can't fault my Lieutenant because he never served a warrant himself and since there were no precedents to guide us we had to use our own ingenuity.

At the end of each day we got together and shared experiences. Each of us benefited from the successful tactics or the pratfalls of the other men. It took stealth to serve a warrant on these individuals who were practiced in avoiding detection. One officer said it was best not to boldly walk up to a front door and ring the doorbell. It was wiser to knock gently on the door the way a neighbor does when visiting to join in a coffee klatch. Another officer suggested we should never be in full view of the people inside the house when knocking on a door. It is better to be shielded by the wall beside the door. Another said never carry papers in the hand because it is a tip-off you are a bearer of bad tidings.

Lou told us about the man who was surprised to see a policeman at his front door. He asked the man if he was John Brown and the man denied he was. The man asked Lou, "Why do you want him?" Lou thought fast. "Headquarters got a phone call from a New York lawyer requesting we locate a Mr. John Brown. A relative passed away and left

John Brown a lot of money in a will. Do you know a John Brown?" The man blurted out, "I'm John Brown!" Lou proceeded to tell the man he had a warrant for his arrest. That tale got a round of applause and we complimented him on his genius. It demonstrated the resourcefulness that was required.

The first warrant I selected from my twenty was addressed to a local automobile garage and not to a home address. On my arrival at the garage I was surprised to learn the warrant was issued to a mechanic known only by the nickname "Wimpy."

"Wimpy," I said, taking a gamble the name on the warrant was his, "You got a citation three months ago for going through a red light and you didn't pay the Fine and Cost. Now I have a warrant to arrest and lock you up." Wimpy trembled, "What can I do to avoid going to jail?" he asked. I said, "Give me the $65.00 the Judge wants." Wimpy said, "I don't have $65.00 on me."

I could accept that because the average Joe doesn't walk around with that much money in his pocket. "Tell you what I'll do, Wimpy. I'll pay the $65.00 and you reimburse me when you get paid." Wimpy was thrilled he wasn't going to be locked up on the spot so he agreed. Of course I had no intention of paying. I placed the warrant back in the pile and went about my business.

The following payday I received a radio message to go to the garage and meet a man named Wimpy. Wimpy greeted me and handed me $65.00. "Thanks Sarge. Thanks for paying the fine and for not arresting me. I'll never forget the break you gave me."

Wimpy never did forget that break. He became my best public relations man. Mutual acquaintances told me Wimpy claimed he knew the greatest cop in the world. "What other cop would pay a $65.00 fine to save a person from going to jail? Only Sergeant Bernie Loughran."

Lou had a warrant for a man that caused Lou's frustration to turn to anger. After weeks of many visits to the man's home no one would answer the door. Lou made his visits during the day, in the evening and on weekends. It was like the house was vacant. He decided to try early in the morning before anyone was out of bed. At 7:00 a.m. he knocked on the front door and a sleepy fellow in his pajamas answered. Lou demanded $55.00 or go to jail. Naturally the man didn't have that much money in the house so Lou placed him under arrest. The department procedure forbids transporting a prisoner by oneself but to call for assistance. This was a safety measure so he called for the sergeant to assist with the transportation of his prisoner. I entered the house as the fellow was dressing and preparing to go to jail.

On the mantel I saw the photographs of three teenage girls. I recognized these girls as the kids I often saw either waiting for a school bus or shopping in the local business district. These kids stood out above all the other children because they were so friendly. They were unlike the other teenagers of the day who were skeptical of police officers. Most children avoided even a casual friendly glance from an officer but these girls on the other hand always had a wave and a cheerful hello. "Hi Cupcakes," they'd call out. There was always a friendly greeting.

"Are these girls you daughters?" I asked.

"Yes they are, Sarge."

I turned to Lou and said, "I know these ladies and I know they would be sorely embarrassed if their father went to jail. Let him have until payday to make good on the warrant."

"Sarge, I already placed him under arrest."

"Well unarrest him."

"Sarge you know I can't legally do that. He's arrested and only a judge can discharge him."

"Lou," I said. "Only you and I know he was arrested so I say he is unarrested. He'll give you the money on payday. He will call you. Now don't pester him anymore. Good day Sir."

Lou and I successfully pulled off that charade because the following Friday Lou received a phone call from the fellow and he had the $55.00.

I had a warrant for a Charles Aber, address unknown. I crossed that one off as unserviceable and placed it under the pile, however, that morning I was directed via radio to assist an old woman who fell out of bed. After a young girl and I helped her grandmother get back into bed I asked the girl her name for my report. "I'm Darlene Aber, you know my brother Jason. All policemen know Jason. He works in the garage next door to the police station." "Sure I know Jason." I said. "But isn't Charles his right name?" "That's right, but no one calls him that."

Out from the bottom of the remaining stack of warrants came the one for Charles Aber. I went to the garage and greeted him. "Hi Charles, I have a warrant for your arrest. You owe the judge $55.00."

"How did you know my real name?"

"Routine investigation."

Serving warrants wasn't easy because the names were aliases and the addresses were false and that's why the Justice of the Peace gave them to the police to serve. We deserved a Gold Star for locating the right person and then extracting the money. All the judge wanted to see was the warrant returned with a note saying, "Fine and Cost attached." No one wanted to hear the story how the capture was brought about.

One warrant took years off my life. It was for an African-American at a time in history when black people and the police were poles apart. Because of this hatred and distrust I had to be extra cautious.

I couldn't always get people to answer the front door so this time I decided to go directly to the rear door. The rear door was a solid wooden door, which I considered a break because I couldn't be seen from within the house. I gave a gentle knock and the door swung inward even before

214

I finished knocking. I put my shoe in the door to prevent it from being slammed in my face and surveyed my surroundings.

This was a seven by sixteen foot shed that was added to the rear of the original house. A young black man wearing only dungarees and slippers stood before me. He was about thirty years old and he was alone. There was a gas stove up against the doorjamb. My mind was clicking at a phenomenal speed. I was thinking of the poor engineering job by whoever was foolish enough to install a gas stove near a door. The slightest breeze when the door was ajar would blow the flame or the pilot light out. On the stove was a frying pan with two eggs sizzling sunny side up. They had just been dropped into the pan for they were frying on a moderate flame but they were not ready to be flipped. On an adjacent burner freshly cut potato slices with a mixture of chopped peppers and onions was frying briskly in another pan. This fellow was preparing his breakfast.

Also in my peripheral vision I saw a sharp culinary knife in his hand. It was the same knife he used to slice the potatoes and chop the pepper and onion. In a flash he thrust the knife forward at full strength and speed at my stomach but stopped short of cutting my skin. It was summertime so only a cotton shirt was between that blade and my skin.

I wondered what was this fellow's intention? I thought the swing was more of an uppercut if he had boxing gloves on. It was obvious he had complete control of his muscles and he may be a boxer. From my experience boxers were clean fighters who wouldn't deliberately throw a dirty punch. I had to postpone any more trivial ruminating. There was no way I could deflect the blade or defend myself. My mind whirled like an oscillating cooling fan on high speed. I had no forewarning this would happen and I dared not cause my predicament to worsen. Time stood still for this was a moment of truth.

I stood frozen but my mind was doing gymnastics. I stared into his eyes waiting for him to telegraph his next move and his was locked on mine. I sensed his trainer gave him the same instructions I received when I wore boxing gloves. When facing an opponent in the ring you don't look at his gloves to ascertain which one he will throw next. You don't look at his feet to determine if he will bob to the right or weave to the left. You stare into his eyes and he will telegraph the message to you through his eyes."

I dared not show any fright in my eyes and I couldn't transmit a daring intimidation either. A blink of an eye might cause his pectoral muscle to twitch and I would be dead meat. A smirk might flex his biceps or dumb words from me like, "Get that knife out of my gut, you fool!" would only result in getting him mad enough to drive it home.

There we stood like two fighting cock birds staring each other down. We were poised to strike but waiting for the other to pounce first. Unquestionably he had the advantage so I had to act not react. The solution to this dreadful situation was for me to put on a good act and I couldn't in anyway react out of fear. I knew I had to act but I had no idea what the appropriate act should be.

I consciously ignored the presence of his knife like it was never there and I never saw the thrust. I could see him telegraphing messages faster than I could intercept them. His self-assured stare became full of doubts. "Did the cop see the knife? If he did he would have hightailed it out of here. I'll opt that he saw the knife, now, how can I get out of this mess? I'll wait for the officer to make the first move." The threat was ever present and both futures depended on my next move. Without releasing my penetrating stare I pleasantly said, "Good morning sir, I am Sergeant Bernie Loughran. Are you Johnny Mack?" "Yea! I'm Johnny Mack!" he snarled. "What do you want?"

"Six months ago you were stopped by the Pennsylvania State Police for speeding on the Turnpike. You were given a ticket but you didn't pay it and now the judge issued a warrant for your arrest. The judge wants me to collect $35.00 from you or lock you up. If you have the $35.00 it won't be necessary to put you in jail."

There weren't many greater surprises than this in the history of police work but the fellow took only a snap of the fingers to weigh his alternatives. I'm sure he even calculated the possibility that if he went before the judge I might bring up the nasty subject of an attack with a deadly weapon on a police officer performing his duty. He took a step backward and placed the knife on a table. He poked his hand into his pocket and brought out a wad of money and peeled off $35.00.

I graciously accepted the money and said, "Thank you, Mr. Mack. You won't have to be concerned anymore over this warrant." I took a step to the rear and was out of the doorway pulling the door shut behind me. That incident took less than three minutes because the eggs were ready to flip onto a dinner plate when I closed the door.

It is said that time passes in slow motion when a person is faced with the possibility of death. So slowly a whole lifetime can be reflected upon. I saw a potential for death but I took no time out for thinking about my past. The question looming in my mind was, "What was a good act I could use at this precise moment and why was my life in such jeopardy for a lousy $35.00 that wasn't even mine?"

I have faced my demise before and after this incident and I can assure you I never walked away laughing nor did I ever go away unscathed. Whether or not this man was capable of killing me at that moment is a moot question. I returned to the patrol car and as I drove off I had a sudden pang in the pit of my stomach. An electrical current raced up the vagus nerve to my frontal lobe. It induced a blinding shock and a much too late shot of adrenaline.

Every time I encountered a stressful moment like this one the acids ate away a little more of my stomach lining. I knew the cumulative effects of the insidious ravaging of my body would certainly make my retirement difficult to enjoy. The hypertension was accelerating my arthritis and the resulting pain disfigured my skeletal joints.

A PARKED CAR INVESTIGATION

Until 1965 a vehicle that was parked overnight in the township had to have a tiny overnight light on a fender on the left side so the officer patrolling the area would know the car belonged to a resident. Lower Merion's major crime problem was Burglary so the overnight light was an excellent aide. If a car had a nightlight the police officer could assume it belonged to a resident and all cars without a light warranted an investigation. Every out of town car was deemed suspicious and was investigated.

I didn't know any textbook with a chapter devoted to the subject: "How to investigate an unoccupied parked car". My instructors never discussed a safe procedure yet it is the most hazardous task a police officer performs. Usually an officer is alone when it has to be done. He can't call for assistance from an adjacent beat officer because that officer was busy with his own investigations.

I eliminated some apprehension by studying the parked car as I coasted toward it. I peeked through the rear window to see if it was occupied. I checked under the vehicle to see if there was debris. A collection of leaves and trash was a clue the car wasn't moved for days.

If I came upon an unoccupied car after it started to rain and the macadam under the car was bone dry I knew the car was parked there before the rain started. Conversely I'd know the car was parked after the rain started if the road under it was wet. As I approached a car I examined the glass. If the glass was foggy on the inside then the car was occupied or someone just left the car. If lovers weren't occupying the car then it could be a burglar stalking the neighborhood.

If the glass was foggy on the outside it was condensation and the car was parked there for sometime. If the glass and metal was frosted on a cold night then the car hadn't been moved for hours. Frost and fog wont collect on a moving vehicle. I saw signs that revealed much about the parked car.

Before I left my patrol car I noted on my pad the license number, time, date, and location of a suspicious car. If a burglary was reported later at a nearby address my notes might assist the detective bureau. I kept these notes for weeks and matched the license number with a car that was in the township several times but at various locations.

I would check the doors and if they were locked I'd assume it wasn't a burglar's getaway car. If the car was unlocked the contents of the glove compartment would have answers. There may be a registration card, driver's license or correspondence with the name and address of the owner.

The more I studied the subject the more interesting and less threatening it was. I saw signs that gave up telltale secrets before I even got out of my patrol car. I'm referring to a car parked on a dark lonely rural road.

After I left the security of the police car I was without any means of contacting anyone for help. I was out on a limb relying on my wits. As I cautiously approach the car I'd glance about the area to see how safe or unsafe I was. I'd check all the glass. If one was shattered, usually on the driver's side, the car might be stolen.

I felt the radiator to ascertain if it was still hot, warm or cold. The radiator temperature would indicate how long the car had been parked. If there is snow or dew on the ground I followed the footprints to see where they led. If the car was parked in front of a house that had lights on in every room then the car belonged to a legitimate visitor.

At 2:00 a.m. one night I drove into a train station parking lot. I circled the lot and saw in an isolated corner the familiar six cars that are left there at the beginning of every week. They belonged to businessmen who took the train to the city or to New York and stayed over until the weekend. This particular night these cars were laden with a heavy frost on the glass and metal. I checked them the first night but ignored them on this trip. I went into the station waiting room to check if there was any vandalism. All was well so I continued on patrol.

At 6:00 a.m. I rode through the lot again for a second check. Those six regular cars were intact. A seventh car was parked among them and it had a fog on the inside of the glass but no frost on the metal. I assumed a person who caught an early train to the work parked it there.

At 7:00 a.m. I was ordered by radio to check on the report of a suicide in a car parked in the train station parking lot. The suicide took place in that seventh car. There was no way I could rationalize to my Lieutenant that I checked that lot twice.

That incident taught me one more aspect of a parked car investigation. I learned there was one more item I had to examine when giving a parked car a cursory inspection. I had to check the exhaust pipe and make sure a vacuum cleaner hose was not attached. That was how the man committed suicide.

WHERE ARE THE NOSES?

One winter evening in 1964 I responded to an auto accident. The accident occurred where the highway takes an unexpected dip like a roller coaster. A confused motorist at the lowest point of the downgrade foolishly attempted to make a U-turn at the same time an eastbound motorist barreled over the crest of the hill and rocketed down the slope.

The road was covered with a thin layer of snow and ice; the remains of what had been plowed and cindered several hours earlier. The slippery surface made it impossible for the eastbound motorist to stop on a dime. Instead, he slid at the same speed he was traveling before he applied the brakes and slammed into the turning car. The momentum propelled the eastbound driver and his female passenger crashing face first through the windshield.

What made this accident memorable is that the eastbound driver and his passenger had their noses sheared off by the shattered windshield. Neither of them received any other injury beside the flat blank face with two cavernous holes that made them look like Grim Reapers. There was no blood but compresses were applied to keep the wounds clean. Without the compresses there were those morbid looking dry black holes.

The injured were quickly placed on stretchers and rushed to a hospital. A few minutes after their arrival at the hospital an urgent message was relayed to us at the scene over the police radio. The hospital requested the officers at the scene find the tips of the noses and bring them to the Accident Ward quickly. There was a remote possibility the plastic surgeon could use the flesh to repair the disfigurement.

Three officers and I combed the road for the two noses. After searching randomly for a while we formed a line and slowly searched the area grid fashion. "How about that over there?" It was a pebble. "How about that?" It was a clump of cinders. It was difficult to locate anything in the dark but we preserved and finally found both pieces of flesh. It was sheer luck under the circumstances.

The two pieces were rushed to the hospital but the plastic surgeon said they weren't serviceable. They were pulverized beyond salvaging. They had been ground into the cinder and salt mixture lying on the road. The tow-truck driver drove over them when he was aliening to hook up the cars. The ambulance drove over them and we officers kicked them around several times before they were found.

I'M TIRED AND I WANT TO GO TO BED

I was patrolling on City Avenue one cold damp morning in November. It was 4:00 a.m. and the temperature was in the low 30s. I came upon a man wearing only a pair of under shorts. He was staggering up and down the sidewalk like he was very confused. It was such a baffling sight I couldn't believe my eyes. I wondered what transpired that caused this fellow to be walking the streets without any clothes at this early hour? Naturally I stopped and asked him a few questions.

He was shivering uncontrollably and was in a drunken stupor. He was near comatose and only knew he was freezing. I sat him in the patrol car and turned the heater fan as high as it would blast so he could thaw out. At first the chronological events were vague but as his body warmed his brains unscramble and he recalled some of the specifics.

He said he and his wife went out for the evening to celebrate their wedding anniversary. They had dinner and a few cocktails and then went to a movie. After the movie he insisted they have a nightcap at a cocktail lounge a few blocks from where I found him. While at the lounge he became intoxicated and argued obscenely with his wife because she wanted to go home too early. He was enjoying himself and refused to leave. In a rage she stumped out of the lounge and drove their car home. He didn't worry because he knew she'd reconsidered and return for him. However, there was a time lapse before she finally changed her mind.

She returned to pick him up but by then he had consumed so much liquor he still stubbornly refused to go home. Finally he had to leave because the lounge was closing for the night. By this time he was totally besotted and abusive. She drove only two blocks from the lounge when she realized she made a dreadful mistake. She decided it would be wiser if she didn't take him home. He was too obnoxious and he would be worse in the house so she deposited him on the sidewalk and left him.

In his inebriated state he believed she drove all the way home. When she stopped the car he got out and staggered behind a hedge. He was so intoxicated he thought he had walked into his bedroom. He removed all his clothes and snuggled up under a blanket of damp leaves. He assumed he was nestling in his own chilly bed. The near freezing temperature woke him after he snoozed for an hour. Half asleep he wandered aimlessly up and down the sidewalk not knowing where he was. That was when I came upon him.

Together we searched for his clothes and found them behind the hedge neatly placed over a low shrub. When I first talked to him he still thought he was home but as he sobered he realized what his wife did and why. After he finished dressing in the warm patrol car I deposited him into a taxi and gave the cabby instructions to take him home.

THE G.I. BILL

When I joined the police force I was entitled to the benefits the government offered while I was in training during four grade levels. A provision of the G.I. Bill stipulated World War II servicemen could receive financial assistance while learning a trade. I applied for this benefit at the Veterans Administration and was given a form that my employer was to complete and verify I was in training.

The Township Treasurer was to complete the form but because he was lax I received nothing from the government. He frustrated other veterans on the force and they didn't receive their entitlement either. He believed policemen were over paid for the little they did.

Even Police Chiefs didn't think policemen were worth their salt. They never requested a pay raise for their department because it would mean higher taxes and he might be asked to forfeit his job.

When I was assigned to the Staff and Inspections Unit in 1970 I became aware of the attitude of the Police Chiefs. The Treasurer's duty regarding the veterans' benefit became my responsibilities. I completed the VA forms and verified the man was in our training program. I made sure the veterans received their G.I. benefit.

By 1972 the G.I. benefit given a police recruit had increased. He received three hundred dollars a month for thirteen months. Several recruits complained they didn't get the same amount other servicemen received who chose a different career. Those who entered another field before choosing police work knew of whence they spoke. An apprentice carpenter said he received three hundred and fifty dollars a month. An apprentice bricklayer received three hundred and twenty-five dollars a month and a fellow learning to be a baker received three hundred and twenty-five dollars a month. They wanted to know why they weren't getting the same amount while learning to be a policeman. There was a disparity between careers and the lowest was the police profession.

It wasn't equitable and I didn't have the answer so I telephoned the Chief Administrator at the VA. I asked him to explain the reason for this discrepancy. I asked him why the police trainee received less than a man in another career? This was his answer and it reinforced my belief that the public and the police chiefs had little respect for the profession.

He said, "In the months before the end of WWII the government saw the end coming so it got prepared. It decided the veterans were removed from the work force and should be compensated for the time they lost improving their skill and for the advancement opportunities they lost. A committee approved the compensation in the G.I. Benefits Bill.

A veteran could choose a free college scholarship with a subsistence allowance or financial assistance in a trade until he attained first class certification. To help design a fair formula the committee consulted trade unions, educators, professionals, Police Chiefs and others. Each was queried as to what length of time was necessary to train a man and what was the pay scale at each grade. Most union leaders told the committee it took four years to become a skilled artesian.

"The bakers' union said it took thirty-six months to become a baker and the difference in pay from apprenticeship to first class was three hundred and twenty-five dollars a month. The bricklayers' union stated it took forty-eight months to become a first class bricklayer and there was a three hundred and fifty dollars difference a month from start to finish. The carpenters' union wouldn't accept less so they claimed it took four years to become a carpenter and a three hundred and fifty dollars difference a month. Union leaders, educators and professionals assured the committee it took time and money to train a man to be proficient.

The Police Chiefs advised the committee a policeman didn't need to learn anything. Training wasn't needed to help a child cross the street, walk a beat or drive a patrol car. A patrolman learned everything he needed to know in three months. The Chiefs said they had to be fair to the taxpayers so six months training and a few bucks were sufficient.

"The wise government committee knew six months was not fair or equitable. They didn't want a vast gap nor did they wish to contradict the Chiefs. Even one year didn't seem long enough so they compromised and established a thirteen-month training period for the police recruit and an allowance much less than but closer to the other trades."

This explanation offended me. I was indignant and would prove police officers were professionals and not stupid robots but I couldn't change the G.I. Bill because the expiration date was near at hand. I sat at my typewriter and typed a list of over one hundred and fifty skills a police officer must learn. Some skills he must have more than a cursory acquaintance for it could be the difference between life and death. He was required to know the laws and the latest court decisions or he could lose a case in the courtroom. Each skill mastered became a component of an over-all superior police officer.

Many more demands on a police officer have been added since I held that conversation with the VA administrator. Today an applicant with a college education is preferred because so much more is required of a modern police officer. In 1981 there were 376 Training Keys published for police officers. Each one dealt with a subject every officer must know and understand.

Since I joined the force in 1947 I heard the cliché, "A police officer must know the law before he makes an arrest but a lawyer only needs to know what law book to go to and find the law." I couldn't fathom how an officer was to know all the laws and current court decisions if there wasn't any way for him to obtain the information. I supposed it was like his sex education; he had to learn it on the street. However, there is a major flaw in this method, police officers usually patrol alone. He's without a partner with whom he can exchange ideas and share experiences.

In 1967 the INTERNATIONAL ASSOCIATION OF CHIEFS OF POLICE appointed a committee to develop training material for the patrolman on the front line. The deeper the educators delved into what a patrolman had to know the greater number of subjects they had to clarify. From 1968 to 1983 educators wrote over 375 TRAINING KEYS in a language the men could comprehend.

The Keys covered a variety of subjects and helped propel the police officer toward professionalism. They were informative and helped the officer realize he had a complex job. He realized his job functions were endless and that the public expected him to be cognizant and trained to a professional level.

This was the first reading material made available for patrolmen since I joined the force in 1947. It was a complete reversal of how the Chiefs thought twenty-five years earlier when they advised those who were designing the G.I. Bill that all a police officer had to know was how to drive a car and how to help a child cross the street.

THE TRAINING KEYS

1. Felony-in-progress calls
2. The traffic violator
3. Principles of investigation
4. Crime and its prevention
5. Gathering information from people
6. Causes of juvenile delinquency
7. Hit-and-Run investigation
8. Testifying in court
9. Searching arrested persons
10. Crime scene protection
11. Basic problems in delinquency control
12. Rescue breathing
13. Stopping the traffic violator
14. Stopping the felony suspect
15. Professional police ethics
16. Handling disturbance calls
17. Burglary
18. The effects of alcohol
19. Auto theft
20. Safe driving techniques
21. Aggressive patrol
22. The accident scene
23. Shock
24. The use of handcuffs
25. Principles of reports
26. Adolescent growth and development
27. Sketching techniques
28. Principles of arrest
29. The preliminary investigation
30. Intersectional traffic control
31. Mechanics of the car search
32. Mental illness
33. How to be supervised
34. Burglary prevention
35. Controlling serious bleeding
36. Recognizing the stolen car
37. Field inquiry
38. Physical fitness
39. Introduction to interviewing
40. Driving under the influence
41. Robbery
42. The police image
43. The prowler
44. Transporting a prisoner
45. Tool marks
46. Field note taking
47. Skid marks
48. Juvenile gangs
49. Diabetes
50. Counterfeiting
51. Interviewing techniques
52. Crowd control
53. Under the influence?
54. The nature of prejudice
55. Rules of evidence
56. "The Beats" – Nonconformity
57. Investigative resources

58. Effective report writing
59. Severe mental illness
60. LSD
61. Search and seizure
62. The suspected homicide call
63. Traffic engineering and the police
64. Democratic guidelines of interrogation
65. Dactyloscopy
66. Practical aspects of the service revolver
67. Witness perception
68. Suicide prevention
69. Determining speed from skid marks
70. Guide to evidence collection
71. Organized crime
72. Fingerprint evidence
73. One man car patrol
74. Principles of organization
75. The investigator's report
76. The police baton
77. The Miranda Decision
78. Robbery in progress
79. Estimating the time of death
80. Moving the injured
81. Narcotics
82. The use of firearms
83. The Exclusionary Rule
84. The follow-up investigation
85. Environmental factors in delinquency
86. Physical evidence: blood stains
87. The child molester
88. The incendiary fire
89. Collecting latent prints
90. The family and delinquency
91. Skeletal injuries
92. Pursuit driving
93. Emergency care of fractures
94. Improving the officer/citizen contact
95. Photography An investigative tool
96. Traffic enforcement
97. Dangerous drugs
98. The training discussion
99. Crime and crime statistics
100. Uniform crime reports
101. Legal aspects of Scientific evidence
102. Tool & tool mark identification
103. Police vehicle maintenance
104. Driver observation
105. Vehicle Identification Numbers
106. Tools of the auto thief
107. Auto Theft Investigation
108. The broken home
109. The Runaway juvenile
110. The Polygraph and its use
111. Firearms identification
112. Firearms and related evidence
113. Emergency calls
114. Emergency traffic control

115. Policy
116. Rules, Regulations and Procedures
117. Juvenile vandalism
118. Police courtesy
119. Telephone courtesy
120. Physical description
121. Common driving emergencies
122. Disposition of the juvenile offender
123. Blood analysis
124. Artificial respiration
125. Frustrations and adjustments
126. Handling and transporting firearms
127. Water safety and rescue
128. Rape investigation
129. The Ku Klux Klan
130. Radio procedures
131. Building search
132. Preparing for promotional examinations
133. Tactics of militant demonstrators
134. Pursuing suspects on foot
135. Informants
136. Probable cause
137. Physical evidence – semen
138. Factors in accident investigations
139. Narcotics investigation
140. Community involvement – enforcement
141. Foot patrol
142. Policing Expressways
143. Laboratory instruments
144. Traffic engineering changes
145. Danger and the police role
146. Meeting the threat of danger
147. Missing persons
148. Chemical agents
149. Tactical use of chemical agents
150. Shoplifting
151. Prostitution
152. Police and the New Generation
153. Routine calls for service
154. Arson investigation
155. Roadblocks
156. Fraudulent schemes
157. Hair and fiber
158. Impressions and plaster castings
159. Planning
160. The accident diagram
161. Crime scene and photography
162. Interpersonal communications
163. Basic supervisory principles
164. Motivation
165. Shooting fundamentals
166. Principles of unarmed defense
167. Department-wide planning
168. Assault t cases
169. Bomb incidents - procedures
170. Bomb incidents - searching buildings
171. Bomb incidents - searching vehicles

THE TRAINING KEYS

This photo was taken at my desk. It was 1982 and I was 56 years old.

PROMOTIONS

In 1960 a sergeant retired and forty men took the Civil Service test to fill the vacancy. I was thirty-four years of age with thirteen years experience and still considered too young for the responsibility. Nevertheless, I passed the tests and was promoted.

Two years later a Lieutenant died and five sergeants competed for that position. The Superintendent arbitrarily opted for the oldest sergeant. His rationale was that sergeant was fifty-two years old, on the force thirty years, a sergeant fifteen years and that longevity and loyalty should be rewarded. The Superintendent placated me by saying I was young and there would be another opportunity.

The years flew by and several opportunities came along. The last one was when I was fifty-two years old with thirty-one years experience and eighteen years as a sergeant but the administrative philosophy had drastically changed.

It was now the era for the young men to be promoted so they could be groomed for higher positions while they were still young. Loyalty and longevity were no longer assets or even factors considered. In the current thinking I was too old.

Lower Merion Raises 5 Policemen's Ranks

Lower Merion Township Commissioners last night announced the promotions of five men on its 140-member police department.

Robert B. Miller, 52, was promoted from lieutenant to captain; Felix J. Falconi, 43, and Joseph E. Shea, 46, from sergeants to lieutenants, and Bernard Loughran, 34, and Patrick Joyce, 27, from patrolmen to sergeants.

THE TEXAN AND SODA JOE

I was creeping behind a soda delivery truck whose driver was a friendly salesman known on his route by the nickname Soda Joe. His truck was a huge cumbersome vehicle with side panels that rolled up like a garage door when the driver loaded or unloaded the soda cases. When the side panels are closed the truck converts into an outdoor billboard advertisement on wheels.

As the truck moved slowly passed a shopping center's exit driveway a car leaving the parking lot came to a jarring stop just before it entered the street. The driver intended to drive onto the street after the truck and I passed. I saw the car come to a sudden stop and I also noticed the driver was a large man wearing a Texas Ten Gallon Stetson hat. I also saw, unbeknown to the driver, a Boxer dog squeezing through a partially open rear door window.

I was mulling over the fact the foolish dog was much too large to fit through the narrow opening but to my amazement it did after a great deal of wrenching. It landed on its feet on the move but before it got its balance his momentum propelled him headlong into the soda truck's billboard. There was a loud rumbling thud against the hollow sheet metal but the dog bounced off unaffected and dashed down the street like he was chasing a jackrabbit. The large portly Texan leaped out of his car and galloped after the dog faster than a quarter horse.

Soda Joe, jolted by the thump, bolted out of the cab to inspect the damage to the side paneling and to find out what he struck. He had no idea what happened and only heard the loud slam. I stopped short to avoid a rear-end collision with the truck. "What happened? What happened?" he screamed and I told him. He inspected the side panels and saw they were not damaged but even so Soda Joe was hysterical. He said he would have to submit a report about the injured dog to the company. He was so upset he quivered.

"This means my job. I have so many accidents charged against me and none of them were my fault. Some happened when I was parked properly and away from the truck. One person backed out of a parking space into the side of the truck as I drove down the street. My supervisor said he wouldn't tolerate another accident and there'd be no exceptions. He swore he'll fire me on the spot if I have another accident."

There wasn't much I could do to console Soda Joe although I assured him my report would indicate he had no advance warning nor could he have initiated evasive action. I suggested we get into the police car and go help the Texan find his dog.

A quarter mile away we came upon the Texan. We were happy to see he had the dog by the collar. He was exhausted and accepted my invitation to get into the police car with the dog. I drove the three of them back to their vehicles.

Along the way the Texan breathed heavily and in short quick gulps but he could still tell us his story. He said, "I'm from Texas and I'm visiting friends here. I'm their houseguest for a month. Today my hosts asked me to baby-sit their dog because they had a business appointment. They love this dog and treat it like it was a child. If I lost it or it was hurt they would be devastated. They would never forgive me. I could never be able to compensate them for their loss."

He was the stereotype Texan; about 72 inches tall, 250 lbs., portly and from the appearance of his clothes he exuded wherewithal. He said to Soda Joe, "Please, don't make a report of this accident. Here's a hundred bucks to forget the whole thing." He said to me, "Here's ten bucks for your help. Please, do not write a report."

Soda Joe and I had to swear we wouldn't write reports even after we adamantly refused to take his money. His insistence grew louder and he was about to draw inquisitive spectators. His face grew scarlet so we accepted the money gracefully before he became more vociferous and embarrassing.

Soda Joe and I watched as the Texan and the dog drove off into the sunset. We stared at each other in bewilderment. Finally Soda Joe asked me, "What are we going to do with all this money?" I said, "Joe, the fellow made us swear we would keep silent about the incident and that is what we promised him we'd do. We can't tell anyone about the money or how we came by it."

We returned to our vehicles and drove off into the sunset.

THANKS FOR YOUR HELP

Chief John Litzenberg of the Radnor Township Police Department was one of my favorite policemen. I first met him when he was a detective and I was a policeman for only a few months. Radnor Township borders Lower Merion Township but in spite of the close proximity the two departments rarely worked hand in hand. We were two separate entities that seldom coordinated efforts except to exchange liaison reports. The Villanova Campus Police and the Radnor Police were capable of controlling and expediting the large crowds that attended the football games, track meets, basketball games, and public lectures.

One evening in the mid 1960's Reverend Martin Luther King, Jr. appeared at the Villanova University Field House. He was to present a lecture on the Civil Rights Movement to the university students and the public was invited. The Reverend was a controversial person who drew opponents and hecklers out of the woodwork. The times were tense and the Civil Rights Movement was one of several sensitive issues ongoing during this era. It was a period in American history that had several revolutions going on at the same time that turned good people evil. The Reverend's life was in constant danger.

His goal was honorable and his campaign was passive but his opponents were hostile and vicious. The least little provocation could ignite a riot on the evening of this lecture. There were belligerent forces present on both sides of the issue so if the crowd became physical assuredly many people in the auditorium would be seriously injured.

Chief Litzenberg had only six men available to control this electrified crowd of thousands. The only tool his department had to avert a riot was a movie camera. The strategy recommended by the FBI was to film the audience before, during and after the lecture. The theory being that whoever intended to initiate a disturbance would be deterred by the thought they were on film and easily recognized and identified.

Two of the Chief's plainclothes officers energetically trotted up and down the aisles making their presence obvious. One was scanning the spectators with the camera glued to his eye while the other focused a floodlight on the faces in the crowd. At best this was a futile method of crowd control.

The Chief justifiably expected any errant act would set off a spontaneous riot. There were those in the audience waiting for the right moment to provoke a disturbance. Others were willing to fan the flame once a clash began.

My brother Tommy and I attended the Reverend's lecture. He was a detective and I was a sergeant on the Lower Merion Police Force. We both took an interest in currant events. We wished to be knowledgeable about the Civil Rights Movement and what better way to obtain accurate information than to get it first hand from the Movement's leader.

The hundreds who arrived early occupied all the seats inside the Field House while the overflow crowd outside listened to the public address system. Tommy and I expected an overflow crowd so we arrived at the Field House early; we were still too late to get a good front row seat. Luckily we found the only remaining vacant seats at the very top of the bleachers in the nosebleed section. We were so high up we could touch the steel roof girders, nevertheless, we had a clear unobstructed view of the podium and we overlooked the whole auditorium audience.

Reverend King faced hostile crowds before in every part of the country so he wasn't intimidated any more than usual. He never changed his stance to accommodate the hecklers who were prepared to attack him on every point he made. He stood his ground before many out of control mobs.

There were moments when my brother and I wished we didn't come to hear this lecture because we placed ourselves in a quarrelsome environment. At one moment or another everyone in the building might have regretted attending this lecture. Luckily, except for frequent boos and catcalls, his message ended without an incident.

The grumbling audience filed slowly and cautiously out of the auditorium. The assembly was so tense the slightest shove or bump might start a brawl that could rapidly escalate into a riot. Tom and I took our time and waited until the last of the crowd filed out of the hall and it was safe for us to leave. As we approached the exit door we ran into Chief Litzenberg. It was obvious he was relieved and happy the evening was almost over.

He stopped us and said, "I saw you brothers enter the building and I was so glad you came to help me out if anything tragic started. I was so relieved when I saw I had two extra good men to help me. I'll be forever grateful you came. Thanks a lot."

Since the evening was over we were glad we attended the lecture and learned so much more about the Reverend and his Movement. We were thrilled the evening turned out to be uneventful for the Chief. As we drove home Tom asked, "Bernie, here we are in civilian clothes, no badges, no guns, no batons, no identification and out of our jurisdiction, what could we have done if an uprising did flare up?"

I answered, "Tom, my mind was working on every contingency. My first reaction to a commotion would have been an evasive tactic. I would have slid under my bleacher seat and coiled up in a fetal position until the riot subsided."

My brother thought for a moment and said, "Don't tell that to Chief Litzenberg because he was so happy to see he had extra manpower to back him up."

REARING CHILDREN OF GOOD WILL

From July 20 to July 31, 1964 I attended a conference on Rearing Children Of Good Will. It was held at the Baptist Conference Center, Villanova. The conference was specifically arranged for educators from all over the northeastern states. Among them were school system superintendents, school principals and schoolteachers. Beside the educators there were six high school students, two clergymen, three housewives, three civic association leaders and a dentist and his wife. I was the only police officer.

I hesitated to enter into discussions with all these intellectuals because I expected they'd know so much more than me about race relations or why society was in chaos because of racial prejudice. But, like me, they hadn't a clue and were at the conference groping for answers. There were no solutions offered, yet, we learned a great deal.

On the final day we were bused to the Fellowship Farm, Phoenixville, Pennsylvania where we were escorted into a dining hall and lectured on the anatomy of a 'sit-in'. A 'sit-in' was a Civil Rights Movement maneuver. The lecturer said the people who participated in the sit-ins in the south were hand picked. They were trained not to react in any way toward the spectators or the police. They were to accept whatever abuse was showered upon them because the basic tenant of the Civil Rights Movement was passive resistance.

After a few instructions we were to act out a skit depicting a hypothetical sit-in situation. The instructor set the scene. She said, "This sit-in we were to act out was taking place in a restaurant in the south where the restaurant's policy was not to serve black people. Ten black people entered this all-white restaurant and sat at a table. They ordered a meal but the waitress politely refused to serve them. She told them they could order their meal at the drive-through window and eat it on the patio table but they could not eat inside the restaurant because that was the company policy. The demonstrators adamantly refused to leave the restaurant until they were served inside. They insisted they wanted to eat it inside with the white people and stated they would sit at their table in protest until they were served."

Every one of us knew these situations happened often in the south because we read about them in the daily newspapers and saw them on the TV news. The media portrayed the sit-in participants negatively and spoke of them as radical troublemakers.

Our instructor selected twenty-two people from our group to play in this skit. Ten were to sit at the table and act the role of the protesters who insisted on being served inside the restaurant. Ten were to act the part of those who were already eating in the restaurant. They were to become involved as sympathizers with the manager and the waitress.

The rest of the conferees took seats at a distance and watched the play unfold.

I was chosen to be one of the protesters seated at the picnic table. Five protesters sat on each side of the table facing each other. Half of us were white and half were black.

The (white) waitress politely explained the company policy to us but we insisted on being served inside the restaurant. She called for the (black) manager and he politely but stubbornly adhered to the company policy. Not one of us in the skit had any first hand experience at this so we were confused. We weren't sure how we were to play our part. The waitress and the manager pretended they couldn't understand why we wouldn't abide by the restaurant rules. The patrons, (black and white) who were already served and eating chimed in to help explain the policy to us protesters.

The make-believe manager and waitress and those already in the restaurant vehemently objected to our staying. They became emotionally drawn into the skit and argued with us. They walked slowly in a single file around our table explaining the company policy and chanted obscenities and gauche clichés of the day.

Those who sat with me at the table didn't take it seriously and thought it very silly behavior for educated individuals. We felt ridiculous and giggled. None of us were ever in this type of situation so we didn't know how to behave except we were to do nothing. Some of us laughed while the patrons blurted out harangues. A patron shouted out the first vicious remark. "Why don't you leave where you are not wanted?" That fanned the embers that brought others into the spirit of the theme.

I was surprised how quickly their emotions rose. A black female school principal yelled half-heartedly, "Yea, nigger leave!" The white dentist's wife said sheepishly, "You get your white ass out too you nigger lover!" Another black female superintendent yelled, "Go back to Africa you black sonavabitch!" Someone yelled out loud by not wholeheartedly, "Get the hell out of here or I'll kick your black ass!"

Around the table they stalked the third time. The pace picked up each time they circled. Emotions escalated and they began to get seriously involved and the role-playing mounted to a feverish pitch. The embers were fanned into a flame that rose to a blazing inferno. They vigorously chanted obscenities and tasteless cliché rioters used.

Schoolteachers, black and white, male and female, who never uttered a foul word in their life were shouting, "You black mawtafuckers!" and "You Oreo cookies!" or "You Uncle Tom!" and "Get the hell out of here and don't come back you blackass troublemakers!" It was unbelievable how this skit reduced these good Christian people to behave like a crazed out of control mob.

I was scared so I stared at each person parading around the table to see how far they were going to go with their role in this charade. These brilliant people were behaving like hoodlums. They weren't acting anymore. It had become the real thing.

Their eyes, filled with hatred, bulged from their sockets. Their teeth were now fangs. Beads of angry sweat wet their foreheads. They became fierce animals. The metamorphose before me was indescribable. It was like an orchestra percussion section increasing the tempo to a rushed crescendo.

This skit was taking place in a dining hall. There was only one object on the picnic table, maybe it was left there intentionally and maybe not, but it was a full ketchup bottle. I remind you this was a racially mixed group of educators with high scholarships and academic credentials. Seated with me was a black woman and next to her was a white woman. The same mix held true for the hypothetical customers and the waitress and the manager.

I followed the faces of our tormentors. None of us at the table spoke a word because we were following instructions. We were to demonstrate passive resistance but now I was fearful of our safety. Per instructions we offered no resistance even though we were showered with hostility and verbal vilification. It was no longer a delightful skit.

I watched one large black woman closely because she had become feverishly involved and bordered on hysteria. The perspiration dripped from her forehead but she ignored it as it ran down her cheeks and off her chin. Suddenly, as though she and I were the only people in that hall, she stopped behind me and shouted, "You better leave this restaurant you mawtafucking nigger lover or I'll ---" and in a flash she reached over my shoulder and grabbed the ketchup bottle by the neck. She raised it above her head and was about to crash it down on my skull.

My mind spun rapidly. "How far was I to go with this passive resistance?" My ears ached from a sharp stabbing pain. My head whirled and my heart beat out of control. I heard a penetrating high-pitched noise and I felt the vibrations in my head. I thought she crushed my skull and I was having a near-death experience.

As my mind reeled into focus I realized the source of the screeching noise came from a whistle the instructor blew. She whistled an end to the role-playing just in the nick of time. It brought us all back to reality. That woman, a Superintendent of a school system was exhausted. She sat down beside me and cried her heart out. Others couldn't believe they would ever get caught up in the madness of a riot and loose complete self-control. Each person believed they were too educated and too intelligent to be entrapped by mob psychology. I wanted to comfort her but I was too distraught myself.

I thought of that lifesaving whistle. I recognized that ear-piercing shriek. It was an Alarmer-Thunderer.

Without a word from the instructor we filed from the room. There was no evaluation. The point was made and there was an enormous amount for all to think about. I was psychically drenched and wished for the conference to end. I had suffered so many traumas in these eleven days I couldn't handle any more. Only the ceremonial luncheon remained and it would be over. I hoped I could hold up for one more hour.

At the luncheon I sat with the six high school students and a seventh teenage boy who joined us. He was a sixteen years old black youth with a painful expression. The instructor introduced him. She said he was a trained activist who participated in many sit-ins in the south. He had to flee to this farm to recover and rest from his ordeals because they took him to the verge of a nervous breakdown. I could believe that.

The boy seated beside me was a white student. He excitedly told us he had just received a phone call from his parents and they told him the West Point Academy had accepted him. We complimented him on his good fortune and wished him the best of luck. In passing I said, "You are to be envied for your good fortune."

The young activist looked at me and asked, "Why should we envy him?" He was serious and that was a serious question that took me off guard.

"I envy him because he has his pins in order. He knows what the future has in store for him at least for the next eight years. I envy him because he will obtain an excellent education in a prestigious college and it will be free. I envy him because he comes from a family that has the clout to persuade a U.S. Senator to sponsor their son to be a cadet in West Point. After all, a State Senator has the privilege of only sponsoring two candidates out of the hundreds of applicants vying for his sponsorship. For these reasons and many more I envy him."

The activist spoke up. "Well I don't envy him."

"Why not?" I asked.

"I've thought about this many times in the past few years. I have planned my future and some day I'm going to establish my own academy. It will compete with Annapolis and West Point. My academy will teach peace. My students won't learn how to fight wars or how to kill. They will go to the far corners of the earth spreading peace."

That was another traumatic moment among so many that bombarded me during this conference. My nerves were frayed. I couldn't handle anymore. I had to get back to the security of my home where racial issues were never discussed.

MICHIGAN STATE UNIVERSITY CONFERENCE

iday, May 20, 1965

OFFICER WINS SCHOLARSHIP--Sgt. Bernard A. Loughran (right) of the Lower Merion police department, receives a scholarship from Daniel B. Michie Jr., chairman of the police community relations committee of the National Conference of Christians and Jews. Sgt. Loughran is participating in the 11th annual National Institute on Police and Community Relations being held through tomorrow at Michigan State University, East Lansing.

I attended several conferences and seminars that concentrated on the subject of race relations and I arrived at the point where I had my full of them. Each course was more distressing than the previous one. It amazed me that one subject could be so complicated. It was so difficult to dispel the old mores in which we are entrenched. The nuns, our parents and friends didn't mean to do us a disservice but only repeated the fallacies they were taught.

White policemen are no different than any other group in a community. We attend the same all white schools, marry a white girl from our all white community and we send our children to the same all white schools. We socialize in the same all white bars and attended the same all white fraternal meetings. We respect and repeat one another's stupid beliefs that in turn only perpetuate erroneous ideas.

If I accepted an opposing point of view I couldn't discuss it with anyone. I'd be shunned at social gatherings and lose my membership in my fraternal organizations. My friends would ostracize me.

It takes more than a week at a conference to make the slightest adjustment in a person's views on racial issues. There was so much chiseling to be done on my old granite influences. In this effort I attended one more conference, the 11th Annual National Institute on Police Community Relations, Michigan State University, Lansing, Michigan May 16 to 21, 1965.

On the flight to Lansing I became friendly with two black representatives from the Philadelphia Police Department. One was a member of the Community Relations Unit and the other was a Deputy Commissioner of the Police Department. He was second in command in the Philadelphia Police Department. The Deputy Commissioner was a guest speaker and a moderator on several panels.

When the first class was to assemble the three of us arrived at the auditorium together in civilian clothes. The usher at the door said, "Please wait until all the guest speakers are seated at the head table." The Community Relations Officer spoke up, "He is a guest speaker. He is the Deputy Commissioner of the Philadelphia Police Department." The usher was embarrassed, "I'm, sorry, sir. Right this way." and he took my arm.

That gesture demonstrated the prevailing beliefs. The usher didn't think a black man could possibly attain the high rank of Deputy Commissioner in a Metropolitan Police Department. It was stereotype thinking in its purist form.

Attending this conference were high-ranking members of police departments throughout the country and white and black leaders of community organizations. In the first hour it became obvious these influential men, leaders on both sides of the issue, needed this training as much as me. Those who assembled the people for this conference wisely selected each of them for a reason.

In attendance was the Chief of Police from Selma, Alabama. Only a few years earlier he was involved in the infamous Civil Rights March led by Reverend Martin Luther King, Jr. The Chief of Police from Chicago who had experienced the Democratic National Convention riot where the legendary slogan "The whole world is watching" originated.

236

A Captain from Watts, California the city that had undergone the worse race riot in the country's history was present and the Captain of Police from Birmingham, Alabama where Reverend Martin Luther King, Jr. was confined when he wrote his celebrated letter *"A Letter From A Birmingham Jail"*. These men were major players from cities that experienced this country's recent race riots.

There was the Chief of Police of a department in an affluent community that didn't have a single black resident but because minorities were excluded he could expect a confrontation in the near future.

Men from every corner of the country took a turn expressing their views and venting their emotions. They spoke about personal dilemmas. There were black pastors from the south who had their beautiful churches fire bombed and their parishioners killed.

A police Captain from Chicago rose and said, "I'm being sued for a million dollars and my department won't support me. I am accused of police brutality. All I did was arrest one of those animals." He was so stressed he couldn't express himself between the sobs.

A police official from another city quivered as he spoke. "There are five lawsuits pending against me. My life and health has been destroyed. All I did was do my duty as I was trained and as I saw it. The ignorant ghetto trash can't be controlled or contained except by force."

Church leaders and civic association presidents spoke the same way only with an opposing point of view. "The cops are "pigs". They are prejudice and get great pleasure out of beating up us black folks."

I sat silently and took mental notes. My heart bled for those who were affect the most. These were respected individuals in high positions and now they were on the verge of insanity. Another Captain said his department wouldn't defend him in a court case. He was suspended with the intent to dismiss and he may go to jail. Two Chiefs stated their job caused them to have a heart attack and a stroke. They wept as they unloaded their hatred toward black people.

I tried my best not to shed a tear. My throat was sore from continually swallowing my Adam's apple. I couldn't turn off the tears but shunted them through my tear ducts and they poured out of my nose. My hankies were drenched the whole week.

By the time the conference was over I heard enough. I wasn't the only policeman confused by the times and current events. I learned there were so many complex elements to the racial problem and that no one had all the answers. I reached my lowest ebb. I left for home feeling I'd rather be an ignorant gravedigger than wander through life as bewildered as I was and knowing how much suffering racial prejudice caused.

The three of us returned to Philadelphia on the same airplane but we avoided discussing what transpired during the week because we were too distraught.

THE KID IN THE DINER

When I was assigned to patrol the western end of the township I ate my meals in The Mari-Nay Diner because I liked the food and the fast service. I also liked the diner's name. Two young boys were drafted to serve in World War II; one went into the Marines and the other went into the Navy. After they were discharged they joined forces and opened this diner. They named it The Mari-Nay Diner (Marine and Navy).

One evening I entered the diner and took a quick glance at the counter. Only one stool was unoccupied and sitting next to it was a nine-year-old boy. He was bored with his dinner so he twirled on his stool. His space and my counter area were splattered with bits of food. His mother tried to get the boy to control himself without disturbing the other customers but obviously he was undisciplined and unmanageable.

My primary concern was my uniform. I feared the boy might spray it with food because before I sat down I had to dust his crumbs off my stool with a napkin. The waitress joined in with a wet towel and scooped up the food he spilled in my counter space. The ogling eyes of others at the counter and those in the nearby booths were focused upon me. They were wondering how the cop would cope with this bad situation. I saw a fellow jab his elbow into his friend's side and mumble, "Watch this." I was losing my appetite before I even ordered my meal.

As I took my seat I thrust my hand toward the boy to suggest we shake hands. Our hands were below the countertop and out of everyone's view. Intuitively he placed his palm into mine and as we exchanged a firm handshake I said in a gentle respectful tone, "Your mother must be very proud of the way you sit up and eat like a gentleman when she takes you out for dinner."

That did it. He confirmed what I was taught one night in an evening college class; "If you treat a person as he is he will remain as he is but if you treat that person as he should be or as you would want him to be he will be as he should be or as you want him to be."

The boy rose to the high plateau where I placed him. He spun around to face his dinner plate and picked up his fork and held it properly. His back went ramrod straight and between small mouthfuls we talked about everyday events. He asked sensible questions and gave mature answers to my questions. He was an excellent dinner companion.

When I was on duty there is always the possibility an emergency would draw me away from my meal so I was in the habit of eating quickly. It wasn't unusual that I ate my dinner before the boy and his mother had finished. Beside, I wanted to leave him just in case he had a short attention span.

I signaled to the waitress for my check and said my good-byes to him and his mother. Before I left I again shook his hand, under the counter, and quietly said, "Good-bye, sir. I enjoyed my dinner with you.

You are an excellent dinner companion. Your mother must be proud of the way you behave like a gentleman when you are out together."

The waitress gave me a sly wink. The wink meant she noticed I accomplished the impossible and was thankful I calmed the boy down for everybody's sake. Her second wink and nod said, "Bernie, you're slick".

A week passed before I returned to the diner and I sat on the same stool but this evening the diner was almost empty. The same waitress waited on me. She wasn't busy so she had time to stop and chat.

"Bernie," she said, "I don't know what you said to that kid the last time you were in here but his mother would sure like to know. She told me the boy has had a major attitude adjustment. She has been in here three times since that evening wanting to thank you. She said the boy has been a completely changed child. His transformation is so unbelievable his schoolteacher telephoned her and asked if he was ill or on medication because he has become an ideal student. At home where he was the most mischievous his behavior is the complete opposite from what it had been. She wanted to know what you said to him."

I kept my secret from the waitress but if by chance I ever saw the kid's mother again all I could tell her was that simplistic cliché that I had to pay to learn. It probably was the only worthwhile note I took in class that evening.

In this publicity photograph I am kicking off the "School's Open. Drive Carefully." safety program for the 1969 school year.

BEAT IT OR ELSE

Many situations backfired on me because I didn't follow department procedure. I lost sleep over foolish mistakes that wouldn't have happened if I only followed the tried and true method. My problem lay in my belief that it was best to bring an incident to a quick resolution before it escalated into a major catastrophe. My reprimands often came when I was helping another officer who couldn't handle the situation on his own. Maybe another sergeant would have handled the problem differently.

One such case happened at 1:00 a.m. when I was the only supervisor on duty. A motorist telephoned headquarters and reported a fight was in progress on Belmont Avenue at the Schulykill Expressway. Only one patrol car was available to handle whatever the problem was. Officer Zolly responded but he didn't have the where-with-all to deal with the situation so he quickly requested the sergeant assist him.

When I arrived I saw Officer Zolly cringing near his patrol car. He was watching one driver chase a second driver around their cars. The driver doing the chasing swung a crowbar above his head and was seriously threatening the second fellow. I stepped between them even though I knew this was a high-risk situation and in my deepest falsetto I demanded to know, "What's going on here?"

The fellow with the crowbar was built like a blacksmith and I didn't think he needed a weapon to accomplish whatever he purposed to do. The second fellow looked just as huge and just as healthy. If it was a fair fight the guy with the crowbar might have bitten off more than he could chew. The only thing a little guy like me had going for him was the uniform and there was no outward indication that either fellow respected a police officer's uniform. I definitely didn't look menacing and Officer Zolly couldn't be relied upon for physical support.

I growled like I had a Marine Drill Sergeant's leather throat, "Put that crowbar down and tell me what happened!" The crazed fellow shouted with his arms flailing in the air, especially the one he used to twirl the crowbar, "That sonavabitch cut me off on the Expressway! My wife is about to have a baby and he could've killed the three of us! He ran me off the road!" With that he went after the other fellow again. The second fellow gave a burst of speed to ensure the cars were between them at all times.

I had to convince them both I was in control so in an authoritative tone I asked the one without the crowbar where he was going and he said Altoona. I ordered him, "Get in your car and beat it!" At first he hesitated but he saw the fire in my eyes so he didn't ask questions. He was happy to be rid of both madmen. He was happy he didn't have to confront the lunatic any longer. He rushed to his car and drove away without even saying good-bye.

This infuriated the fellow with the crowbar all the more. I read the thoughts behind his wild eyes and saw that for a brief moment he fancied attacking me because I let the other guy get away. I scowled right into his eyes and snarled, "Pal, get into your car and beat it across that bridge before you get yourself into deep trouble."

His wife in the meantime instead of helping matters was spurring on his seething insanity. She was in the car shouting, "John! John! Get in the car! I'm having pains! Get in the car! I'm having pains!" I don't know if he was following my advice or his wife's henpecking but he reluctantly got into his car and drove across the Green Lane Bridge into Manayunk.

Another job well done by your reliable Street Sergeant in action? Not!

A week later I was standing at attention in front of the Superintendent's desk. The fellow from Altoona telephoned him and wanted to know the name and address of his attacker. He intended to file a civil suit against him. Naturally, I had no names.

The Superintendent was furious because I didn't follow procedure. He shouted, "What do you mean you didn't get their names and addresses?" I had to do some fast explaining because when his face turned scarlet it meant he was going to nail me on a cross. His complexion was brilliant brick red and he wasn't going to be the fall guy this time.

I told him the circumstances. I said I was certain if I didn't take drastic steps immediately someone might be killed and it could've been me. There was no way I could placate those two men long enough to collect pertinent information for a report. I told him the fellow with the crowbar was so hysterical he could have easily killed Zolly, the fellow from Altoona and myself. If his wife was about to give birth I couldn't take care of that while dealing with him. I told him the fellow from Altoona should be thankful I stood between them and saved him from getting a thrashing.

The Superintendent accepted my explanation but I had no idea what he would say over the phone to satisfy the fellow from Altoona.

I never asked him how he made out. There were a few sayings I always embraced like, "Let sleeping dogs lie." "Don't ask questions."

SOMETIMES YOU LOSE

A lady entered headquarters to ask for information. I happened to be walking by the reception desk at the time so I greeted her. She asked if I knew the whereabouts of a certain seventeen-year-old boy and I told her where she might find him. Being nosy I asked why she wanted to meet him and she said she was going to shoot him dead because he got her daughter pregnant.

The woman was noticeably troubled so I patiently listened to her. She spoke of many problems beside her pregnant daughter and the lack of communication between them. Her husband left her and filed for a divorce and she admitted she was a stoned alcoholic. She talked on and on about her misfortune and how her life was on a downward spiral. I listened and then asked for the gun. She went into her pocketbook and handed it to me. She assured me she was relieved after sharing her problems with a compassionate person.

But that wasn't to be the end of her. Night after night she returned to headquarters to talk to me and unburden. I didn't have the time or the expertise to help her. I couldn't solve her affairs so I suggested she seek professional counseling. I was preoccupied with supervisory duties and besides the men were spreading ugly rumors like, "Sarge, your girlfriend is here to see you."

She visited headquarters almost every evening when I was on the evening shift just to talk to me. No matter how helpful I may have been her visits became a serious embarrassment. I insisted she get professional help so she joined Alcohol Anonymous. She stopped drinking and as a result the communications with her daughter improved. A month later she brought her husband to headquarters just to meet me. He traveled from Connecticut to thank the officer who brought about a positive change in the most important things in his life. He stated his wife was a different person and he was considering returning home and living together again.

Her visits to headquarters continued and I didn't know how to put an end to them. The men kept spreading the vicious rumors about us. At first the remarks were amusing but after they were repeated over and over they became a fact. I had to make myself unavailable when she appeared at headquarters for her dose of counseling so I gave the men specific orders to tell her I was on an emergency assignment. She became a thorn that I schemed every evening to avoid. Hiding from her became a game I didn't have time to play. It was tough escaping her.

Because I was unavailable she reverted back to the person who couldn't cope. She drank heavily again so her husband changed his mind and returned to Connecticut. One evening she garaged her car and remained seated in it after she shut the door. She left the engine running and inhaled the automobile exhaust fumes until the carbon monoxide poisoned her. That was how she committed suicide.

SIBLING RIVALARY

A young reporter from the local newspaper was chafing at the bit. He had a burning desire to write an award winning exposé on the shortcomings of the police profession. If he had an opportunity to ride with policemen he was sure he could uncover their weakness, misbehavior, aggressiveness, prejudices, lackadaisical attitude, brutality, foibles and poor training. He expected to use the Lower Merion Police Department to build a case against the whole profession.

He asked the Superintendent for permission to ride in a patrol car but his request was denied because the department policy didn't permit anyone but a Lower Merion police officer to ride in a patrol car. The Superintendent didn't want to set a precedent. The reporter went to the Township Manager and the Manager informed the reporter that a civilian wasn't covered by insurance if he was injured. In the past civic minded citizens and the clergy have been denied this privilege but this reporter was not to be denied. He took his case to the owner of the newspaper and the owner conferred with the Manager. The newspaper owner, Manager and Superintendent agreed that the reporter wouldn't let go his quest. He'd use the denial to confirm his belief there was a lot of wrongdoings swept under the carpet and hidden from the public.

The Superintendent finally allowed the reporter to ride with the sergeant starting on the midnight to 8:00 a.m. shift. I happened to be the sergeant on the midnight shift. I didn't protest or object to having company and I didn't see him as an antagonist. I was looking forward to giving him an insight into the positive side of police work.

For his safety and mine I laid down a few ground rules by which he was to abide. He was to obey all of my orders and he was not to become involved in any incident. He was to be an observer and just listen. He wasn't to leave the patrol car but to do all his observing from within the car or standing beside the car. He wasn't to leave its side unless I directed him.

The first night started out uneventfully until I was dispatched to assist three officers who were sent on a family disturbance call. A family argument escalated to a pitch beyond their control. On the way to the house I reminded the reporter he was to stay by the car and observe.

I entered the house and found two brothers duking it out toe to toe. It was a fight between siblings but when these two bears fought to the death. These fellows fought regularly over nothing after they had been drinking. They didn't verbally quarrel but faced off like two enraged hockey players. They were thirty-year-old men who once were stellar athletes in high school.

The three officers dealt with this family before and knew their widowed mother used the rouge of feigning a heart attack to direct her sons away from fighting but her performance this night had no effect.

I entered the front door without knocking and saw the brothers blindly flailing away. Blood was drawn, furniture was upset and broken and their mother was lying on the floor clutching her breast and shouting, "My heart! My heart!" The three disheveled policemen were standing back waiting for the brothers to burn themselves out. They gave their best effort to separate them but failed and now it was time for the sergeant to take over and get beat up.

I blew an ear shattering blast on my Alarmer-Thunderer and followed up with the booming voice of a displeased football referee. "OK, break it up! Knock it off! Let's go!" These brothers were former high school football players and were conditioned to obey a referee so they released their grip on each other. "OK you guys, pull yourselves together and straighten up this place. Help your mother get into bed and you both get to bed!" They respected authority. The adrenaline was still pumping in their veins but it was time to quit. "OK Sarge", they said.

The other policemen knew from experience that once they stopped fighting they never started up again that same night so they said good night and turned to leave the house. Low and behold we all were surprised to see the reporter standing inside the room taking notes. Simultaneously, the brothers saw him and in one voice demanded to know who he was. I fumbled for an excuse but couldn't think fast on my feet. I said, "He's with me. He's a detective."

"No he isn't, he's a snooping reporter. He's not going to put our names in the paper." With that they pounced upon him and pummeled him with their best punches even though they were a little weaker now. It was a frightful sight to see the reporter as helpless as a ladybugs lying on the floor in a fetal position not knowing how to defend himself. My Alarmer-Thunderer didn't work the second time. We pulled and tugged until we got the two apes off him. All seven of us had bruises. Their mother offered her contribution again, "My heart! I'm dying! Help!"

I snatched the reporter's notebook and pencil from his hands and threw them to the brothers but I would have preferred to throw the reporter to pacify these lions. "Here, they're yours. Nothing will be in the papers." We turned and made our retreat; thankful we hadn't any broken bones.

I drove straight to headquarters and took the reporter into an office. I'm not sure if I acted composed and calm, "Mister, you are done for tonight! In fact you will never ride in another Lower Merion patrol car because you can't obey orders! You got four policemen injured and you almost got yourself killed. Good night and Good-bye."

The following morning I reported to the Superintendent that I dismissed the reporter and he concurred with my decision. I never heard another word about him and I don't know if he quit the local newspaper or was fired. Maybe that experience convinced him his profession was hazardous because I never saw him again.

EIGHT HUNDRED DOLLARS

This incident began on a weekend when there was only one receptionist on duty in headquarters. I was seated at a desk checking the reports the men submitted when a fellow, about forty-five years of age, walked into the building and explained his problem to her. I couldn't overhear their conversation but it was obvious she was confused and since I was the officer-in-charge she lateral the hot potato to me. I wished she were more capable and hadn't got me involved. She should have advised him to return on a weekday when the regular office clerks are on duty. Instead she ushered him to a chair in front of my desk and left to get the report pertaining to his case from the files.

The fellow was remarkably different from anyone I ever met. He had a strong odor of liquor on his breath and considering it was before noon he either was an alcoholic or he took on a few drinks to fortify a shy personality. He had a strange southern accent and at times was difficult to understand. I couldn't tell if he was from the back hills of West Virginia or a remote part of Georgia because I never knew the accents indigenous to various parts of the country.

He wore a beautiful suit that fit him well. He was solidly built and in prime physical condition. His complexion was the color of dark red wine or the color of a highly polished mahogany coffee table. He wasn't a black man. His flesh color was noticeably odd with a pronounced red tone but he wasn't an American Indian either. He respected authority so I classified him a southern gentleman.

The receptionist handed me the man's file and a prisoner's personal effects envelope without a comment. As he talked I glanced at the pages of his file to verify what he was telling me. He said two days before he went to a local used car lot with the intention of buying his wife a secondhand car for her birthday. He selected the car she would like and had the eight hundred dollars to pay for it outright, but first, he explained to the salesman he wanted to take it for a test ride.

Any anxious salesman would let a potential customer take the car for a test ride provided he went along but this fellow insisted he test drive the car alone. He wanted to thoroughly examine the car without the watchful eye of a salesman but this salesman wasn't about to turn a car over to a total stranger for he might not return with it. Besides, this fellow had been drinking.

An argument flared up on the lot and several more salesmen became involved. Voices mounted and a sparing match ensued. The police were called and four officers responded. This fellow was subdued and arrested for Disorderly Conduct and placed in the jail overnight to sober up.

There is a detailed procedure on how a person is to be searched before being placed into a cell. Everything must be taken from the

245

prisoner and placed into a "prisoner's effects" envelope and sealed until the prisoner is released. The only thing a prisoner is permitted to keep is his paper money. This is to avoid an accusation that the arresting officer stole it. The arresting officer in this case made a detailed report of the body search. He recorded what he placed in the "prisoner's effects" envelope and what he let the prisoner keep.

The fellow told me he didn't have his eight hundred dollars the next day. His recall was murky and he vaguely remembered the officer let him keep the paper money but he was hoping it was taken from him and placed in the envelope. He made no accusations only hoped his memory was flawed.

He wasn't positive but said that during the night, as he lay on the hard wooden bench in the cell, he had a Vision. "The Lord appeared before me and scolded me for misbehaving. God told me if I didn't stop drinking He would take my wife and two children from me. God ordered me to change my ways or I would be condemned to damnation. The Vision was real. God was in the cell with me and He was very angry and threatening. I was frightened and I got down on my knees and begged for forgiveness and mercy.

"I promised God I would change my ways. I cried and pleaded with Him not to harm my family but He was not satisfied with a promise. He wanted a sign, some proof of my sincerity. God said if I was truly sincere I'd take that cursed money, the eight hundred dollars that got me into trouble in the first place, and I'd flush it down the toilet. I'd flush it out of my life and begin anew."

The fellow dimly recalled flushing the money down the toilet but he was hoping it was only part of an alcohol-induced nightmare. He was hoping the officer confiscated the money and placed it into the prisoner's personal effects envelope. I showed him the officer's report that stated the money was never taken from him and that the prisoner signed the report. He examined the prisoner effects envelope himself hoping to find the money in it but it was empty and his signature was on it too. He thanked me for my concern and sympathy and left. He was dejected, unhappy, poorer but satisfied he had a bona fide Holy Vision.

A few weeks later a plumber was digging up the driveway in front of the jailhouse. He said to me, "Guess what was in the trap, Sarge. Paper money. Hundreds of dollars; lots of ones, fives and tens. Can you top that?" I wanted to tell him about the prisoner who had a Holy Vision but I let him enjoy his bizarre find.

I reported to my superior how the money got into the sewer trap and every attempt was made to locate the owner but he had disappeared. He returned to the mountains or hills where the people have a red mahogany complexion. He wouldn't have recovered the money anyway because it was used to pay the plumber's bill.

THE HUMAN RELATIONS COURSE

TO: Captain John McComb   May 17, 1968
FROM: Sergeant Bernard Loughran
SUBJECT: In Service Training

Recent upheavals, Supreme Court decisions and changes in public attitude have created an urgent need for a revision in police training. This department has taken a major step in the proper direction with the establishment of its own Police Academy. This step, when first recommended, undoubtedly was ambitious but has proved unequivocally successful.

I recommend a second major revision in our department's training. That is, that certain new subjects are included in the curriculum.

Today's policeman is puzzled about his place in society and he is bewildered by the demands upon him. If he is to find answers he is forced to turn to the sciences concerned with human conduct.

I suggest he look to:

Psychology - The study of individual behavior. A look at the world through the eyes of one individual and learn how he perceives policeman and conversely the policeman will understand his own evaluation of others.

Sociology - The study of groups to learn the effect they have on the individual. The policeman will learn how his own associations have influenced his own attitudes.

Cultural Anthropology - The study of different societies that exist today and their unique variations. He will learn to accept deviation from his own approved norms.

Ethics The study of the policeman's relationship with his fellowman to allow him to compromise with his own conscience.

History - Just as it relates to the police profession from its origin up to how the public views it today.

Political Science - A comparative study of governments.

On the surface, this list may appear weighty or far removed from the police profession but reflects, in fact, the difference between a job and a profession, that is, a profession requires training. It is no longer sufficient to know **how** to do a job but a policeman must know **why** he is doing it in a particular way.

It is not enough to tell a rookie to "use common sense." Common sense has too many fallacies. Common sense assures us the earth is flat. Common sense is based on unquestioned observation such as all crooks are shifty-eyed. Common sense jumps at conclusions; for example, if a person refuses to talk he is guilty. Common sense acts on prejudice, such as, all redheaded women are hot tempered.

It is not enough to instruct a rookie to "treat everyone the same or as equals." Self-discipline without reason is expecting the impossible. Any other course already conducted, such as Human Relations, Public Relations, Community Relations would not conflict or be repetitious. Rather they would affirm, support and fortify each other.

To convey enough thoughts to have meaning I recommend a minimum of 40 hours of instructions.

It must be noted that the ideas that will be transmitted are not personal philosophies but excerpts from lectures from various Professors at Temple University, St. Joe's College and conferences. (See transcript enclosed)

At present there are no sample lectures for your inspection. You can appreciate that at this initial stage it would take a minimum of 5 hours preparation for every classroom hour.

If this recommendation is acceptable it should be instituted at the in service training level. I also suggest the course be related to as "Psychology For Police Officers."

Sergeant Bernard Loughran

In today's climate this doesn't seem like a noteworthy news item but if the tension in the decade when this course was recommended was fully explained and understood then it would rank up there with Robert Peel's recommendation to form the London Constabulary or the establishment of the Pennsylvania State Police.

It was an era when numerous sensitive social issues drew the police into physical combat with the public. The police were trained to respond with force so they used batons, tear gas, vicious dogs, fire hoses, rifles, cattle prods, and mass arrests.

A combat soldier in World War II would have envied the equipment that protected police officers. They wear helmets with face shields, gas masks, and a shield equal in size to a Romans soldier's, a shotgun and a baton as long as a baseball bat. All this threatening equipment and much more just to subdue a group of people who wished to protest an obvious injustice. That is how the large city departments dealt with civil dissidents therefore the small departments acted in kind.

The FBI approved this "meet force with greater force" philosophy. Obviously the profession hadn't advanced beyond the tactics used by the tax collectors of the Feudal Lords.

I had attended a number of college courses, seminars, conferences and lectures. When the department became aware of the demonstrations and riots in other cities I felt that most of what I had learned could be adapted to thwart a major conflagration in our own backyard if the men on the street knew how to handle the situation properly.

After I made the recommendation I didn't really expect it would be accepted because there was no precedence. No police agency ever had such a training program and the Lower Merion Police Department in the past only accepted tried and proven methods. The administrators in the past tread only on solid ground but now the Township Manager and Township Solicitor saw which way the social winds were blowing and wanted the Township to be legally protected. They foresaw Civil Rights Groups attacking the Township on all fronts because it hadn't prepared the police officers with up-to-date Public Relations training. The men hadn't been trained to accept social changes and contrary ideas.

Believe it or not my recommendation filled an immediate need and may have saved the Township from being razed because it has happened to other municipalities. At first the students resisted my lectures. They preferred to emulate the big city police approach "use the baton, meet force with force". It took many painstaking hours of rebuke but eventually they grasped the purpose and wisdom in the course.

The Sunday Bulletin
PHILADELPHIA
Sunday, July 14, 1968

L. Merion to Give Police Human Relations Course

By JOSEPH D. McCAFFREY

Of The Bulletin Staff

The Lower Merion Police Department will soon start in-service training in human relations for every member of the 117 man department.

According to Captain Patrick J. Joyce, officer in charge of training, the township just adopted a plan to train every man in the department in a series of courses approved by the International Association of Chiefs of Police and the President's Crime Commission having to do with human relations.

The training will start in September, he said, and by the end of 1969, "we will have finished up with the whole d partment," he said.

42-Hour Course

The courses themselves w be in police-related psycholog iology, cultural anthropology, ethics, history and police ience and administration, pt. Joyce said. The entire man relations program will 42 hours of classroom work, he added.

Capt. Joyce added that Superintendent of Police G. Andrew McLaughlin approved the overall in-service training program, of which human relations is only a part, on May 24.

Human relations training for Lower Merion policemen, has actually been given to new men entering the department since February, 1967. It was started then as part of the basic training program for new recruits on a much smaller scale. Capt. Joyce said they started with four hours and gradually increased it until now the recruits get 42 hours. The entire basic training for Lower Merion policemen is a 390-hour course, he added.

249

Some to Have 84 Hours

This will continue, he said, along with the in-service training for the rest of the department. In fact, some of the relatively new men who have received their 42 hours will receive an additional 42 hours when the rest of the department goes through the training, he said.

The men to be scheduled first are men who will be coming up for promotion soon, he added. A group of 14 men will be scheduled to be completed before February, 1969. Also, he said, a group of new men will be given the training in September.

Capt. Joyce said the whole course is concerned with human conduct.

"It's the study of individual behavior to understand one's evaluation of others. And it's the study of groups to better understand the effect the association with groups people and how it influences their attitudes."

Study of Variations

Also, he said, it's the study of different societies and the unique variations between societies to better understand the deviations from one's own standards.

"The benefit to the men is to know how to do the job and why," he explained.

Capt. Joyce said that Sgt. Bernard Loughran will instruct the course for the department. Loughran, he added, has just received an associate degree in police science and is working toward the bachelor's degree in social welfare.

Joyce said the course being started this fall for the men who have been with the department for some time is being used as a model to determine how much money will be required to continue it for the remainder of the department.

1969 Budget Item

Once that is determined, he said, then it can be put into the 1969 budget and the entire rest of the department can be scheduled for 1969.

He said that the program is part of the police department's continuing training for men.

"In a nutshell, it's a program that is trying to better prepare our people to deal with today's society," he said.

YOUR HONOR I'M INNOCENT

If I was pressed to help a friend in need I often found a loophole to save their neck. Case in point: I received a panic telephone call from a friend. She was distraught over a traffic citation she received in the mail. The charge was, *"THE OPERATOR FAILED TO YIELD THE RIGHT OF WAY TO AN EMERGENCY VEHICLE"*.

Between sobs she explained she was driving home late one night when she noticed a police car was directly behind her. The emergency lights were flashing but the officer made no attempt to pass her. There wasn't any room or a soft shoulder to pull over on because it was a narrow two lane rural road. There were so many sharp twists and hidden curves she assumed the officer didn't pass because it was too risky. He stayed behind her for a mile until she reached the driveway to her house and pulled into it. He continued on down the road at a relaxed speed. She forgot about the incident but several weeks later she received a citation in the mail notifying her she committed a serious violation.

This type of violation has a fine and cost plus "points" that go against a driver's record. The points are more penalizing than the financial loss. Should she accumulate six points her driving privilege is suspended for six months and she must attend driving classes. A violator of this section of the Motor Vehicle Code is assessed three points or half of the total allowed.

During our conversation she expressed the unfairness of the officer's actions. He never stopped her to inform her she was in violation and would receive a citation in the mail. Three weeks later the mailman delivered it. She arranged to have a Hearing before the District Justice and was hoping for leniency. Except for the unfairness angle she had no defense. In desperation she asked me for an alibi she could hang her hat on and she got one from the best Defense Lawyer possible.

At her Hearing she stood before the judge and repeated word for word what I had suggested. She told the judge she believed the police officer was escorting her home. She asked the judge, "If the officer was on a dire emergency why didn't he blow his horn? Why didn't he give a blast on his siren? Why didn't he blink his headlights? He never indicated he wanted to get by me."

The judge turned to the officer in the witness box and asked, "Officer, did you blow your horn?"

"No."

"Did you blink your headlights?"

"No."

"Did you sound your siren?"

"No."

"Case dismissed!"

She was so thrilled she won the case she called to tell me about it and to treat me to lunch.

The two officers who shared my office overheard both telephone conversations. They overheard my advice and her success in the courtroom. They were furious and loudly branded me a "Cop Hater". "You enjoy making a cop look like a fool! You've done that many times in the past. You are a Cop Hater!" They yelled and demanded to know where was my allegiance to the Brotherhood even though this incident occurred in another jurisdiction.

Inwardly I was pleased with myself because I found a way to thwart the misery a stupid police officer inflicted on an innocent person by not clearly thinking out his own behavior. I hoped the judge's decision would be a lesson to all officers in the future.

I calmly said, because I knew I was right, "I'll make a fool out of any police officer after he has first done it to himself."

This is a photograph of me at my desk working on an accident report.
It was taken in 1966 when I was 40 years old.

REVEREND MUHAMMED KENYETTA

The 1960s and '70s were turbulent times, especially for police officers on the front line. It was a very distressing two decades for everyone concerned with America's future but the police bore the brunt of the rebellions. After weathering all the hysterical social storms the police weren't given a pause to relax and recuperate. In the late 1960s along came Mohammed Kenyetta a young black minister who widened the breach between the "whites" and "blacks" even more. His intention was to improve the black peoples' condition in America but he only singed the already frayed nerves and tore the races wider apart.

He demanded the "white" churches contribute reparations for the wrongs perpetrated on black people since the beginning of slavery in this country. He claimed the white churches supported slavery and condoned the prejudices that prevailed against black people. He insisted the white churches profited from slavery and demanded a sum of five hundred million dollars reparation from them.

Naturally, churches of every denomination objected to this extortion and unequivocally refused to cough up a dime. To attract media attention to his cause he performed offensive acts. He would enter a church during the most solemn moment in the service and cause a shocking disturbance. He interrupted sermons and took over the pulpit to explain his purpose. He entered Roman Catholic churches at the moment of the consecration and shamelessly strutted to the altar with his entourage and spilled the wine and the hosts on the floor and trample on them. To Christians that was an unforgivable and sacrilegious crime but to him no denomination was sacrosanct.

At the same time he was attracting the attention of another group organized specifically to incite. This ad hoc group generated a great deal of attention with their own retaliatory acts. Under the leadership of Rabbi Kahanne the Jewish Defense League was formed. This was a militant group of young Jewish men and their objective was to take revenge on any individual, group or organization that harmed or offended a Jew or a Jewish cause in anyway. Jews would no longer passively accept insults and abuses like their forefathers. The JDL quickly gained respect and fear with violent counterattacks. Many young Jewish men joined the JDL ranks and if Reverend Mohammed Kenyetta offended Jews during a religious service they would retaliate.

It was about 1969 when a Jewish congregation invited Reverend Kenyetta to their synagogue to explain his demands at a peaceful forum. The congregation wanted to know his rationale as to why their Temple should be assessed a large sum of money? I made it a practice to be present when a controversial leader was going to explain his cause. I listened to those who jeopardized, or wished to improve, the status quo. I had to hear Reverend Kenyetta speak because his cause was extremely controversial and ultimately would somehow involve police.

I entered the synagogue early hoping to get a seat but the assembly room was already filled to capacity. Several ushers conferred and then select me from among the people who were queued as far as the sidewalk. They led me down the center aisle to the last vacant seat in the auditorium. It was between two young Jewish men. I thought it odd to be ushered to a seat when it was a standing-room only crowd. Many of those in line were members of this congregation and should have been given a seat before me. Of course I wasn't lucky at all because I was deliberated placed between two militant JDL fighters to serve a purpose. A JDL member was sitting behind me.

Mohammed was never given an opportunity to explain his demands. Every time he began to speak these three fellows interrupted him with shouts, catcalls, derogatory remarks and flailing arms. The fellow behind me rocked my chair every time he got up and he thumped on the back of my head with a folded newspaper. The two on either side of me jabbed their elbows into my ribs and smashed the side of my face with their forearms when they stood up to shout over Reverend Kenyetta. They stomped their feet to make additional noise and every time they brought their foot down heavily they purposely dug the heels of their shoes into my calves and insteps. They intended to hurt and bruise me so I'd get raving mad.

Twice I tried to leave but when I got up to leave they blocked my path. Their noise and commotion was noticeable to everyone in the auditorium. It stirred up interest within those who would have otherwise been passive spectators. The members of the congregation knew whom these men represented and their reason for being at the meeting was obvious. Their physical abuse on me was anything but subtle yet the ushers didn't object to their boisterous conduct.

These three rugged individuals were dedicated to a mission designed by the Jewish Defense League. They were planted antagonist whose purpose was to draw someone into a fight. The auditorium was salted with JDL fighters waiting for a reason to begin. If I fell for their ploy a riot would have erupted. Many people, most of them old and fragile, would have been injured so I took their manhandling until the meeting ended. It was a long torturous hour.

A detective was assigned by the department to attend the meeting as an observer. He noticed what was going on around me and grew nervous because the atmosphere was explosive. He and I worked together many hours in the past so he slyly gave me a few quick hand signals from his position in the far corner of the room. He slowly moved his head from side to the side, placed his finger to his pursed lips then clasped his hands together as in prayer. "I gotcha. Don't say or do anything, please." There was no way for me to return a message. I wanted to reassure him I

already had basic training for this; (read Rearing Children of Good Will).
The ushers selected the wrong Irishman to start a brawl for them.

OBITUARIES

Tuesday, Jan. 7, 1992
The Philadelphia Inquirer

Rev. Muhammad Kenyatta, activist

By Andy Wallace

The Rev. Muhammad Kenyatta, 47, the militant civil rights preacher who confronted Philadelphia-area white churches with demands for reparations in the late 1960s, died Friday at home in Buffalo.

"He was a fierce fighter for the rights of others," said the Rev. Marshall Lorenzo Shepard of Mount Olivet Tabernacle Baptist Church. "He could be depended upon to be in the forefront of the struggle of people for their rights and self-determination."

Since 1988, he was a visiting associate professor at the University of Buffalo Law School, teaching courses in civil rights and constitutional law.

Mr. Kenyatta, who had diabetes, was awaiting a kidney transplant when he died of heart failure.

On May 18, 1969, the 25-year-old Mr. Kenyatta, a Chester native, walked into St. Anthony's Roman Catholic Church in Chester and presented demands for reparations from St. Anthony's and other white churches.

That demand for $500 million, called the Black Manifesto, had been presented by the Black Economic Development Conference two weeks before. It set off intense debate over what, if anything, was owed black people for the years of slavery and what churches should do about it.

Over the next few years, in demanding reparations, Mr. Kenyatta and his followers from the Black Economic Development Conference spilled blood on the altar of a Main Line church and wrestled with an outraged parishioner there, hammered through double oak doors at the Philadelphia Presbytery and took over the offices and dumped a collection plate at Holy Trinity Church on Rittenhouse Square.

Although few churches paid any reparations, they did debate the issue and in some cases contributed to minority organizations and causes.

"He made a major contribution in forcing churches to practice what they preach," said Inquirer associate editor Acel Moore, who reported on Mr. Kenyatta.

Mr. Kenyatta not only confronted the churches, but also took on social concerns. He commandeered a SEPTA bus to protest a nickel fare hike, took over a community center in Chester and led a sit-in and hunger strike at the office of then U.S. Sen. Hugh Scott over Vietnam.

From 1972 to 1981, Mr. Kenyatta was vice chairman of the Pan African Skills Project, an educational program involving the United States, Tanzania and Ghana. He also was a permanent representative to the United Nations nongovernmental organizations section from 1972 to 1978.

For several years in the early 1970s, Mr. Kenyatta was in and out of Philadelphia. He attended Harvard Divinity School in 1971 and 1974, then ran for mayor of Philadelphia in the Democratic primary of 1975. He returned to Williams College and earned his undergraduate degree in 1981, then received a law degree from Harvard Law School in 1984.

In the 1960s in Mississippi, Mr. Kenyatta was trailed by the FBI for his activities and chased out of town by a threatening letter later found to have been forged by FBI agents and approved by J. Edgar Hoover.

In 1974, law enforcement agencies said he had been marked for death by the Black Mafia for stirring up opposition against heroin trafficking in North Philadelphia, and for a time he carried a gun under his shirt.

While studying for a law degree at Harvard, he became a member of the Black Law Students Association and was a leader in a boycott to press for more minority professors.

The struggle, said his wife, Mary Kenyatta, was to "help make the world a place where people could be free to love." The only change over the years, she said, was that he had become "a little more mellow."

Mr. Kenyatta was born Donald Brooks Jackson in Chester, where he attended segregated schools.

"I was a serious kid," he once said in an interview. "My mother taught me to read before I started school, and I got the nickname Socrates. But I was also tough. You had to be. In seventh grade, I was suspended six times for scrapping."

He was very bright, energetic and motivated. He was also a religious prodigy. When he was 12, he first heard the call to preach. Two years later, he delivered his first sermon.

Drawn early into the civil rights struggle, he joined the Chester NAACP at 15. He resigned after two meetings when he found the members still arguing about whether blacks were ready for integration.

During high school, he was billed as "The Boy Wonder Preacher," and he preached nearly every Sunday at Philadelphia at the Solid Rock Baptist Church, his uncle's church.

He attended Lincoln University for a year, then joined the Air Force when money ran out. He was assigned to Altus Air Force Base in Oklahoma and honorably discharged at 18.

For three years, he attended Williams College, but left in 1966 to work for the Mississippi Freedom Democratic Party, which encouraged blacks to join the political process.

It was while he was in Mississippi that he gave up his "slave name" and took on the names of two of his heroes — Elijah Muhammad, founder of the Black Muslims, and Jomo Kenyatta, president of Kenya.

When he burst onto the Philadelphia scene to confront churchgoers and take over community centers, he did it with a new black image that frightened many whites — dressed in fatigues and dark glasses, and a militant attitude. It got people's attention, he said in an interview later.

"People will always tell you they disagree with your methods, but they agree with your goals. The truth of the matter is, very often, had there not been some way to engage people's attention, there would have been no serious debate about goals."

Bishop Robert DeWitt, then the Episcopal Diocese bishop, credited him for "a stunning feat of public education" that "significantly shifted the focus of concern in civil rights, for quite a period of time, from 'What do blacks want?' to 'What are our (white) responsibilities?'"

Mr. Kenyatta is survived by his wife, Mary; sons, Malcolm and Muhammad Santiago; daughter, Latina; mother, Ernestine Bagley; grandmother, Carrie Jackson; three brothers and three sisters.

A memorial service will be held Jan. 18 at 1 p.m. at Mount Olivet Tabernacle Baptist Church, 42d and Wallace Streets, Philadelphia.

By ACEL MOORE

The recent death of the Rev. Muhammad Kenyatta, the black militant civil rights leader, shocked and saddened me. His demands in the late 1960s and early '70s for reparations turned this city's religious establishment on its altars. He forced white religious leaders to rethink their mission and role in the black community.

Kenyatta was only 47 when he died of heart failure brought on by diabetes and kidney failure. He died in Buffalo, N.Y., where he was an associate law professor at the University of Buffalo.

Kenyatta hadn't lived and worked in Philadelphia since 1975, but I have kept up with him through correspondence and telephone calls. I visited him when he was a law student at Harvard, and he would call me whenever he came back to Philadelphia for a visit.

He leaves behind a legacy of civil rights and social activism that will long be remembered. The demonstrations that he led in area churches had an impact that is lasting and ongoing.

Researching Kenyatta's life has caused me to reflect on my own life. As a young reporter, I covered his activities for The Inquirer. I first met him at a demonstration at the Cookman United Methodist Church at 12th Street and Lehigh Avenue in the summer and fall of 1969. Kenyatta was one of eight people arrested for occupying the church, which had been a leading church in the city when the area was all white.

Kenyatta and the others accused the church and its leaders of being hypocrites and of abandoning the concerns of those who now lived in the community around the church. The church had an indoor skating rink and other facilities that the demonstrators said were not open to the surrounding community, which by the '60s was predominantly black.

After the protest, the church opened up the facilities to the neighborhood children.

It was an exciting time in the city.

Muhammad Kenyatta in 1969

The problems and issues were more clearly definable and less complex than they are today. James H.J. Tate was mayor and Frank L. Rizzo was the police commissioner, and black political empowerment had not come to fruition. Demonstrations and marches were the mainstays for protesting grievances.

Among the black community leaders were attorney Cecil B. Moore, U.S. Rep. Robert N.C. Nix Sr. and Clarence Farmer, who was on the city's Human Relations Commission, and the Rev. William H. Gray Jr., pastor of Bright Hope Baptist Church and the father of the former member of Congress.

Charles W. Bowser was a young deputy mayor, the Rev. Leon H. Sullivan was opening Progress Plaza on Broad Street, and the Rev. Paul Washington was establishing himself and his Church of the Advocate as the meeting place for all segments of the so-called black movement.

Before he burst on the scene in Philadelphia as head of the Black Economic Development Conference, which demanded $500 million — called the "Black Manifesto" — in reparations from white establishment churches, Kenyatta had worked in Mississippi in a project that encouraged blacks to vote and get involved in the political process.

Kenyatta — usually dressed in khakis and sporting an Afro and dark glasses — was a black militant's militant. He disrupted church services in the city and in the suburbs in demonstrations that included spilling blood on the altar of a Main Line church, banging down the doors of the Philadelphia Presbytery and dumping a collection plate at Holy Trinity Church on Rittenhouse Square.

At 25, Kenyatta was not only one of the youngest of civil rights leaders when he headed the Black Economic Development Conference (BEDC), he was one of the brightest. White church leaders, as well as members of the black establishment, were intimidated or offended by his style. But once they got to know him, they found a sensitive, highly intelligent man of substance. He also was an urbane, witty speaker who presented logical, well-thought-out arguments in his demands.

I will never forget the press conference that Kenyatta held after documents stolen from an FBI office in Media confirmed that he and his organization were among many black civil rights groups that were infiltrated by undercover and double agents working for the FBI.

At the press conference held at the BEDC office at 18th and Somerset streets, Kenyatta drew belly laughs from reporters when he made a tongue-in-cheek comment about FBI Director J. Edgar Hoover.

"I want you all to know that we have been conducting an investigation of Mr. Hoover. For the past six months we have been looking into Mr. Hoover's sexual conduct. But we haven't come up with anything yet."

Through his organization, Kenyatta took on issues beyond church reparations. He counseled young blacks on how to avoid the draft during the Vietnam War. He challenged black heroin dealers, and, as a result, they marked him for death.

Born in Chester, Kenyatta was a child prodigy. An ordained minister since the age of 12, he preached regularly at the Solid Rock Baptist Church in Philadelphia.

His social activism forced him to delay his education but he returned to school in the 1970s, earning a undergraduate degree from Williams College, a law degree and a divinity degree from Harvard University. He had also attended Lincoln University.

He was a full-time law student at Harvard at age 38. He was elected president of the Black Law Students Association and led a boycott that resulted in more black law professors at the school.

I would say that most of the former church officials and establishment figures who were targeted by the reparations movement learned to respect Kenyatta and sing his praises.

Although the reparations were never paid directly, the churches were spurred to pay indirectly, doing all kinds of things to help the disadvantaged in the inner city. A lot of the programs that resulted exist today.

I am going to miss "Mu," as he insisted on being called. He fought the good fight right up to the end.

Acel Moore is associate editor of The Inquirer.

The
Philadelphia
Inquirer

Thursday, January 9, 1992

HELL'S NOT HALF FULL

The Superintendent assigned me to assist a National Safety Council Defensive Driving Instructor present a Defensive Driving Course to members of a church. Because the media had been promoting this course it became a popular driver's education program.

A hundred people enrolled in the course. Two instructors are needed to conduct each course. The professional instructor presented the course layout, form completion and the general benefits that could be expected. It was a dull hour and the students were restless and disappointed. The instructors alternated each hour so the second hour was my turn. If we were to hold the group's interest I had to be more informative about defensive driving.

This community has narrow two lane roads so I opened with a question. "What would you do if you were driving at a prudent speed and a hot-rodder came up behind you at a reckless speed? He raced his motor to emit a loud muffler noise. He blasted his horn to intimidate you and in general made you very uncomfortable. How would you react to that situation?"

A lady spoke up. She said, in an uncompromising tone, "I'd fix him! I'd drive in the middle of the road and I'd not let him pass. That would infuriate him and it would make me feel good." The class loudly agreed. "Yea! Yea!" I quickly countered, "You would be wrong. What you must do is slow down and drive as close to the side of the road as possible. You gently wave him by. You give the gentleman room to pass, however, as he sped off you wave after him and yell, 'The highway's all yours, Pal. Help yourself. Hell's not half full.'"

The lady and the class were shocked that I suggest you wish a person be condemned to hell but before they could complain I explained. I reminded them I was here to teach defensive driving techniques and not how to teach a stupid jerk good manner. My job was to teach them how to avoid accidents. This brought a round of applause.

We argued feverishly at times and when they presented me with unacceptable behavior I quoted the law. Everyone participated in the discussions. "Everyone drives that way!" they protested. I quoted the Motor Vehicle Code. They continued to argue. We were at an impasse. Back and forth we tugged wasting valuable time. I held up my outstretched arms and in a quiet reverent voice said, "If it were not so I would have told you." This might have fallen on deaf ears at another place but in a church it cracked them up. All was well again.

The instructor who conducted the second hour opened up the following evening's program so on the second Tuesday I had the first hour. I was about to start when a woman raised her hand and asked if I would help her complete an accident report. She said on her way home from the previous week's lecture she and her passengers were debating a point I made. She was distracted and drove off the road and knocked over a STOP sign. The class broke up with laughter. My hour opened up with a laugh and closed with an ovation.

On the last evening I had the final hour. To summarize the course I told a fabrication. I told them about an experience I had on a rainy night. I was patrolling on my police motorcycle and I had stopped a carload of kids. I asked the driver for his cards and he gave them to me. I asked, "Do you know you were driving too fast for the conditions of the road? The road is wet, the traffic is heavy, it is raining and the visibility is poor due to headlight glare. Do you realize you were driving too fast for the conditions of the road?" The kid grunted, "Nope."

I asked him, "Do you know you were driving too fast for the conditions of this car? The windshield wipers aren't doing a good job, the windows are fogged up on the inside, you have only one headlight and the tires are bald. Do you realize you were driving too fast for the conditions of this car?"' The kid grunted, "Nope."

I asked him, "Do you know you were driving too fast for the conditions inside your car? There are too many passengers in the front seat and they are crowding you. There are too many passengers in the rear seat and they are obstructing your view out of the rear window. Do you realize you were driving too fast for the conditions inside your car?" The kid grunted, "Nope."

I was annoyed and said, "You're not too bright, are you?" The kid grunted, "Well I aint standing in the rain." They enjoyed my joke. Those were my closing remarks and they summed up the course.

Five years later I telephoned a sign manufacturers for a price quote on a particular highway sign. The company's owner answered the phone. "The Lower Merion Police? Sergeant Bernie Loughran the Defensive Driving Instructor? You will never know how many times I have yelled under my breath to rude drivers, 'The highway's all yours, Pal. Hell's not half full.'" That was proof positive that some people listened and subscribed to what I taught.

258

MOVEMENT LEADERS' LECTURES

The years I spent as a police officer were terribly harsh on the profession. The mores of the country were rapidly changing. Old traditions were discarded without acceptable replacements. It was a time of upheavals and like most revolutions they were violent. The tactics used to bring about change included boycotts, sit-ins, marches, demonstrations, riots, bombings, campus riots, etc. A new lexicon came into being; prejudice, stereotype, ghetto, bigotry, minorities, ethnic groups and others that explained every problem.

The revolutionist soon learned they couldn't throw stones at the system because a system is an intangible. The stones had to be aimed at the system's representatives and who might they be? The policeman on the beat.

If the rioters were protesting against the school system or school segregation they focused on the cop on the beat. If the water purification system was ineffective blame the cop. If the judicial system moved too slowly blame the cop. Policemen were blamed for the poor conditions in a housing project, the ghetto, the homeless and trash collection. Even though the police played no role in any of these functions they were blamed because he was the visible ever-present representative of the ugly bureaucratic system. His uniform identified him. No one knew the president of the School Board, or the Councilman, or the Water Commissioner or any Planning Board member.

Before 1950 people respected and depended upon police. They respected authority until there was a complete turn-around. Authority came to mean oppression. The young policeman became involved in events they didn't understand. Senior officers couldn't give advice because these were new phenomenon to them too. The social scientist had no answers because it was new to them. The only known police response to the new revolutionary moments was to meet aggression with force. Overcome the anarchist with manpower and weapons. Dispatch them with a show of force.

The younger generation and their rebellious attitude toward the traditional way of life dispirited me. I knew my career choice had something to do with my loathing but I didn't know why we were poles apart. Since my associates were policemen and my instructors were police officers I came to realize I was wearing blinders. It was best if I listened to what the opposition preached and interpret their philosophy for myself. I took it upon myself to attend lectures given by every front line spokespersons of the era.

This is a partial list of leaders I heard speak:

Judge Walsh - Founder of the John Birch Society.

Pennsylvania Supreme Court Justice Judge Musmano.

The U.S. Attorney General in the 1960s.

Reverend Martin Luther King, Jr. - Civil Rights Movement.
Dick Gregory - Civil Rights and Anti-Vietnam War Activist.
Jane Fonda - Actress and Vietnam War Opponent.
Reverent Muhammed Kenyetta - Reparations advocate.
Vice-President Hubert Humphrey - Presidential candidate.
Mr. LaRousche - Socialist Party Presidential candidate.
President Richard Nixon.
FBI Director J. Edgar Hoover.
Roy Wilkens - NAACP president.
Transcendental Meditation teachers.
Washington, DC Anti-Vietnam War protests.
Bishop Fulton J. Sheen, Second Ecumenical Council.
Conferences, workshops, seminars and University courses.
Lectures presented at grassroots meetings.

I adjusted many of my old beliefs but now I was out of sync with my peers. Fellow officers and friends thought I went over the edge and joined the radicals but to the radicals I was still a policeman and a potential enemy. I was in a quandary.

Former Vice President Hubert H. Humphrey mingles with students after delivering an address at the Field House at St. Joseph's College.

I am the guy to the right of former Vice President Hubert H. Humphrey.

VIVA PAPA!

In the fall of 1979 Pope John Paul II visited the United States. His itinerary included New York City, Philadelphia, Chicago, an Idaho family and Washington, DC. In Philadelphia the preparations for his visit were elaborate. His route was published in the newspapers so people of every religious persuasion waited to see him wheeze by.

The Lower Merion police were involved because he was visiting the St. Charles Seminary Chapel that is in the township. Lower Merion's role was negligible. The full responsibility for his protection rested on the Secret Service, since he was a State dignitary, and the Philadelphia police department because they had unlimited manpower.

A celebrity doesn't impress a policeman assigned to the dignitary protection detail. It's just another routine that places an officer in jeopardy. A sniper may be off a millimeter in his gun sight and shoot the officer instead of the dignitary. An officer knows he will be held accountable for the death of a dignitary if he is guilty of a dereliction of duty for a single moment. Two buses loaded with Philadelphia police officers accompanied the Pope. They leapfrogged from one stopover to the next for thirteen straight hours. Most of that time they stood at attention. They boarded the bus and driven from on location to another just to stand and wait. It is no wonder an officer looses his interest no matter how important the dignitary.

My assignment was to make sure the media people stayed corralled within a roped off area in front of the St. Charles Seminary Chapel door. These were professionals who by the nature of their profession worked aggressively to out-scoop their competition. The local TV crew demanded a better position because another TV channel crew had a slight advantage over them. The United Press Corps TV team insisted they come from behind the ropes because their coverage would be for the international media. Local newspaper reporters expected a favored position because this was a local story. They all asked for extra privileges and pressed for something more than I could give.

I ignored them for a half hour because it was too early to take action. At the proper time I faced them and issued a firm impassioned warning. Forcefully I said, "Ladies and Gentlemen if you cooperate I will make sure no one stands between your cameras and the Pope. If you do not cooperate you shall be treated according to the way you conduct yourself." Not a word was uttered. Each person waited for the other fellow to protest first. I stared them down then nonchalantly turned and walked away. No one dared move out of the pen until the Pope left.

An hour later he arrived. His limousine stopped directly in front of the media people and me. I was ten feet from him and not a soul was in front of me. It was just another assignment to me. It was no different than a parade, house fire, riot or whatever attracted a crowd. I was

261

desensitized. A policeman never asks a celebrity for an autograph but when I saw him he was electrifying. I didn't believe anyone could hold me spellbound but this extraordinary person transfixed me.

He stood upright through the sunroof of the car and blessed the waiting crowd lined up on both sides of the driveway. For a heartbeat he gazed into my eyes and I was mesmerized. They were innocent crystal blue eyes that pierced me like laser beams. I felt he was inquiring about my arthritis. Under the overhead spotlight his white cassock and cape were iridescent. I was spellbound. He was not like the rest of men.

He entered the Chapel and talked to the seminarians for twenty minutes then returned to the limousine and was whisked away. No one immediately turned to leave because we had become accustomed to instant TV replay and we were waiting for a replay of his arrival and departure.

There was no Hollywood glitz except for the TV camera lights and the powerful light shining down from the helicopter yet everyone was in awe. I saw the spotlight shining on him when he broke through the darkness and I saw the television crews spring into action and click on their bright klieg lights. A night baseball game could have been played under those brilliant lights. I knew the lights made him glisten but even so he wasn't just lit up, he blazed angelic. Words cannot describe him other than to say he was saintly. I never expected to see a Pope yet I could have reached out and kissed his ring.

After his limousine drove away I turned to the media people and said, "Thank you for cooperating."

I opened the door for the Cardinal getting out of the limousine.

262

The Pope's limousine stopped in front of me. He was only ten feet away when he got out of the car and walked into seminary chapel. In the above photo he is walking into the Chapel. In the photo below he is coming out of the Chapel. A Lower Merion Police photographer took these photographs.

THE WYNNEWOOD POST OFFICE

It was because I admired Officer Jim Wentz, my instructor the first four months on the job, that everything he said I embraced as the Gospel Truth. I absorbed every word he spoke never dreaming his wisdom would help me solve important problems. This time it was when the Wynnewood Post Office became a major police problem.

In 1947 the Wynnewood Post Office occupied a converted house on E. Wynnewood Road, however, the population of the community multiplied so rapidly that location created a massive traffic tie-up in the morning and evening. Residents double-parked in front of the building to collect their mail from their personal P.O. Box.

During the construction of the Wynnewood Shopping Center in the early 1950s a post office was built in a corner of the spacious parking lot. For fifteen years the community continued to swell and the volume of traffic around the new post office created problems within the Shopping Center. The traffic congestion caused shoppers to by-pass the Center.

In 1966 the Center's management pinpointed the reason for the decline in the overall sales. They claimed the loss of revenue was due to the confusion generated by the post office traffic. They conferred with postal authorities and advised them to prepare to relocate elsewhere because their lease would not be renewed when it expired.

Post office officials combed the Wynnewood area for a parcel of land suitable for a new post office. The only available vacant property was on the south side of Lancaster Avenue between Morris and Cloverhill Roads. Even though this lot would be a tight squeeze plans for a building were submitted to the Township by an engineering firm. They sought approval and a permit to build.

On the first Tuesday of every month the Township Manager chaired a staff meeting with all department heads, including the Superintendent of Police. At this meeting the latest projects and permit applications are discussed and if there are no objections they are approved. If there is an objection or a flaw detected in a plan this was the time and place to discuss it. The plans submitted for a new Wynnewood post office was presented and the Superintendent adamantly objected to the location because he foresaw the makings of an automobile and pedestrian death trap.

The Township Manager accepted the Superintendent's objection but before he could refuse a building permit he had to have solid reasons to support his rejection. The Superintendent couldn't present any solid reasons without an in-depth study.

The Superintendent called his own staff meeting. All superiors and supervisors including me (a sergeant) were gathered in his office and he explained where the Post Office proposed to build. Everyone agreed this was not the place for a business that relied heavily on vehicle traffic and pedestrian movement yet there was nothing concrete to support our opinion. A check of the accident statistics indicated there were no accidents at this location. That was because there was nothing but a vacant lot at this location. He asked us to report back as soon as possible with valid objections. I decided to submit at least one idea he might hang his hat on.

I slaved over the problem for a week and drew a blank until I recalled Officer Jim Wentz's conversation. In 1947 he gave me a township history lesson. He explained why the wealthy Philadelphia families chose to settle in Chestnut Hill, a Philadelphia suburb, rather than in Lower Merion. He said, "When the Philadelphians decided to move from their 'brown stones' to the suburbs they studied several locations including Chestnut Hill and Lower Merion. They decided on Chestnut Hill because Lancaster Avenue, the main highway in and out of Philadelphia, was due east and west. The blinding sun rising directly over the horizon in the east in the morning spooked the horses that pulled the carriages. On the return trip home at the end of the day the blinding sun lowering in the west also spooked the horses. Even the chauffeurs of the gas driven limousines complained they were blinded by the sun and found driving unsafe and difficult on Lancaster Avenue."

Armed with a compass I drove to Lancaster Avenue between Morris and Cloverhill Roads and found, as I expected, this location lay due east and west. There were no trees or high-rises to shade the bright sun in the morning between 7:00 and 9:30 a.m. or in the afternoon between 3:00 and 6:30 p.m.. These were the hours when most residents did their business with this post office.

I submitted a written report based on what Jim told me. I stated the automobile drivers would be blinded during the critical peak hours, twice daily, when the sun was rising and when it was setting. I explained no amount of traffic enforcement or warning devices could alleviate this condition. The number of accidents resulting from drivers making rash left turns into the path of oncoming drivers who were blinded by the sun would be astronomical. The number of accidents due to vehicles leaving the post office and entering the traffic flow when it was not safe to do so, again because of the blinding sun, would be predictably high and some of these accidents would be fatalities.

I never heard if anyone else submitted a valid argument against the new post office location and I don't know if my report was helpful. But I'm sure the Superintendent knew I tried.

The Post Office officials never followed-up on their request for a permit to build and I never inquired why. Maybe the Shopping Center owners used the threat to cancel their lease as leverage to boost the rent. Whatever, the Wynnewood Post Office is still in the corner of the Shopping Center's parking lot.

THE TRAFFIC SAFETY MEETING

In 1968 my Lieutenant, the Traffic Safety Officer, was promoted and I was assigned to his desk. He held the position for twenty-five years and secretively guarded it. No one knew exactly how he occupied his day but whatever he did was important because he was the Superintendent's right-hand-man. Clerks were envious because he came to work two hours late and took a two-hour lunch break but he stayed for an hour after everyone left for the day. That compensated for coming to work late and for the extended lunch break. His telephone was glued to the side of his head all day. It was assumed he either made numerous personal calls or had the phone unplugged at the wall jack.

When I was assigned to his desk I quickly learned he was the liaison man between the Superintendent, Commissioners, Township Manager and the public. This was the era when people became involved in their community. Every resident was a traffic engineer. Through him the taxpayers took pot shots at the police and the other township departments. He definitely earned his two-hour lunch break.

It also was the time when the U.S. Government joined with other countries to initiate uniform motor vehicle laws, especially traffic signs and signals. The purpose was to aid tourism. Tourists from all over the country and the world complained they were confused by a hodgepodge of regulatory signs. There were many incongruities between traffic signs in our own forty-eight states.

One simple example; in the east a STOP sign was black letters on a round yellow background while in the west the STOP sign had white letters on a red octagon background. The Government ruled that red signified danger so therefore, universally, all STOP signs had to be white letters on red.

Europe already adopted a uniform sign program. A NO TURN sign was an angled black arrow with a diagonal red line through it. A red diagonal line meant 'NO'. Road signs no longer had words indigenous to the country but uniform symbols that foreigner recognized.

There was such a proliferation of new regulations pertaining to the vehicle, road signs and highway construction that once a month all Traffic Safety Officers in the county were obligated to attend a traffic meeting held in Norristown, the county seat.

The first meeting I attended in my new assignment was quite informative. The purpose of the new regulations was explained and why every community must conform or lose all future Federal subsidies. I learned of futuristic plans that I would never have heard or read about in the newspapers. The guest speaker spoke of legislation that applied to the U. S. Uniform Highway Safety Act and I absorbed every word. 'Uniform' in this context meant 'identical internationally' not just in

Pennsylvania or in the United States. There were two other specific areas he impressed upon us.

He said the Pennsylvania Legislators established a new cabinet post. Since the United States had a Department of Transportation under a Secretary every state should create their own department of transportation cabinet post. Pennsylvania was the first state to establish such a department to regulate the use of the highways and to steer all the municipalities into acceptance and compliance with the Uniform Traffic Code. This new department would be named the Pennsylvania Department of Transportation or PENNDOT. This speaker was appointed the first Secretary of Transportation to launch this cabinet post. In my new position I often had to consult PENNDOT.

The other subject he mentioned was also to become an integral part of my workload in a future assignment. He emphasized there were millions upon millions of Federal money available to every police department for improvement in all aspects of police work. These millions had been laying unclaimed waiting for the picking. All a police department had to do was submit an application to the Governor's Criminal Justice Commission and ask for it.

I returned to work and went directly to the Captain in command of the Staff & Inspections Unit, the person who would submit a request for these funds. During our conversation I mentioned the availability of money through the generosity of The Governor's Criminal Justice Commission. He dismissed me with a superficial "I already know about that money but I don't want to become involved because I'd have to lie too much on the application." That took the wind out of my sail so I didn't pursue it any farther.

It is difficult to describe how irrational the public was in their demands. Every mother demanded a WATCH CHILDREN sign in front of her house. Homeowners band together to demand their street be designated one-way to reduce the noisy traffic. For strength and solidarity neighbors established Civic Associations. Through them they threatened their Commissioners to obtain whatever they demanded. Businessmen formed Businessmen's Associations for clout in their fight for more parking lots and less parking meter enforcement. Schools demanded a policeman be assigned to every intersection to protect the school children so civilian School Crossing Guards were hired at a reduced salary. Residents demanded the speed limit be reduced on their street so speed limit signs were installed. Civic Associations demanded traffic signals and four-way-stop intersections.

The demands were unending and they were all funneled to the Traffic Safety Officer. It was a totally new generation that discarded old traditions and old customs. I was unable to follow the presidents set by my predecessor. It was a totally new world. I quickly learned that the residents of the township had clout and every department head better listen to them.

ROAD SIGNS AND MARKINGS

It was in the late-50s and I was at a desk completing a complicate accident report when a young girl at the reception counter let out a frightening bloodcurdling screech. She was venting her venom on an innocent clerk. She splintered my concentration over a parking ticket she received the night before. The clerk remained calm. She put forth her best effort to convince the girl no one in the office could dispose of the violation at this stage of the legal process. She finally ushered the girl to the Traffic Safety Officer's desk because he had a reputation for handling sensitive issues with finesse. He would delicately explain her legal options. I put the accident report aside so I could hear how he'd appease the raving-mad girl.

"Officer, it's a dark road and I'm not familiar with the regulations on it!" she said.

"Your car was in violation of the NO PARKING ANY TIME sign and the officer did his duty when he placed a ticket on it." The Lieutenant said.

"I know that! Couldn't he take into consideration the road is pitch black and no one could see that sign!" She shouted.

"He isn't supposed to rationalize a motorist's error. It is your responsibility to see the sign." I thought that was a clever response.

She grew more frenzied and added dramatics. "I challenge anybody to see that sign because it is so dirty and it is hidden in a tree.

The Lieutenant suggested she make arrangements for a Hearing before the Justice of the Peace and explain to him why she didn't see the sign. He told her the JP was the only person who had the authority to discharge the ticket.

She screamed, "I'll get no satisfaction from him either. He'll stick up for the stupid cop. He won't drive down that street at night to see how dark the street is and how the sign is impossible to see."

After beating the dead horse the Lieutenant finally lost his patience and snapped, "Do you think the township should put a light over every No Parking sign?"

The girl was as mad as an African-Hornet because he couldn't show some compassion. She left a bitter foe of the police for life.

Six months later the Traffic Safety Officer called me to his desk to show me a unique advertisement he received in the mail. It was a cardboard box 3 x 3 x 15 inches long. He told me to hold the box tightly against my eye and look through a small peephole. I put the box to my eye and blocked all light from leaking in. It was pitch black inside and I saw nothing.

I asked him what product could the company be marketing since I saw nothing. He handed me a tiny three-inch long pen flashlight that came with the advertisement and told me to insert it into a small hole on the side of the box. When I peered into the box and flashed the beam inside at the same time a dazzling bright world came to life.

I saw a typical blacktop road with bright white lines defining the sides of the macadam. Down the center of the road was brilliant yellow line sharply dividing the opposing lanes. Posted on the berm were a variety of signs, STOP, NO PARKING, ONE HOUR PARKING, INTERSECTION AHEAD, WATCH CHILDREN, SLOW, SPEED LIMIT and other information signs. These signs and road markings loomed as bright as the neon signs on Broadway.

I asked him for the meaning of the advertisement and he said the company developed a reflective paint that snares the light from a vehicle's headlights and reflects it back to the driver. Every sign and road marking painted with the new paint will blaze at night and can't be missed. He said the new paint is expensive therefore these signs would be costlier than the present signs. He doubted the township would ever consider installing them.

Ten years later the U. S. Government rigidly enforced every aspect of the Uniform Traffic Code including replacing all old signs with these new reflective ones. Every municipality had to conform with the Code and to help defray a portion of the expense the Government made funds available. The Township Commissioners had to update or lose Federal financial assistance in other areas so the Manager applied for funding for the new signs, including new posts and the salaries of additional laborers that were needed to help the present sign crew.

The installation had to be completed within a time limit or the Grant would lapse. The sign crew worked feverishly to complete this monumental task. Hundreds and hundreds of signs were removed and replaced. Some old signs were erected around the time the first automobile took to the road. Most of them were rusted, corroded and didn't conform to the Uniform Code.

The restoration started around 1970, years after I peeked into the magic box. The Traffic Safety Officer didn't live to see the futuristic advertisement become a reality. Today, when I drive at night toward highway signs and markings and I see how brilliantly reflective they are I can't help but recall the day when I looked into that cardboard box and saw nothing. I'm also reminded of the furious young girl who stormed out of headquarters because she had no retort to the Traffic Safety Officer's sarcastic question, "Do you think the township should put a light over every No Parking sign?"

A motorist driving in the dark might imagine each sign and road marking has its own personal spotlight focused on it.

THE WAY OF ALL FLESH

When I first became a member of the police force I looked around to see what I was getting into and I was appalled to see many healthy senior officers were assigned to menial tasks. I didn't know anything about the Lower Merion Police other than it had amassed an untarnished and excellent reputation. The citizens of Manayunk knew its superior performance and that it was politically unapproachable. Politics could resolve most problems in Philadelphia but not so in Lower Merion.

My friends and I never wandered into the township for fear if something was amiss the police would scoop us up in one giant dragnet without sympathy or political assistance. However, after I was hired I noticed the officers who were only forty-five to fifty years of age discarded like tattered old shoes. These were the men who established the laurels the younger officers proudly wore on their uniform sleeve. It troubled me that these virile men were rapidly drifting toward oblivion without the recognition or the applause they earned.

The three Sergeants who lead the department through the transition from the days of the night watch to the present were assigned to turnkey duty. They wasted away in a gruesome, smelly, dreary, empty cellblock shunned by their peers and their replacements. They were prisoners who sat outside the bars never to be consulted or asked to share the wisdom they accumulated during a lifetime of dedication.

Their days oozed by slower than a slug on a cement sidewalk. Without respect or responsibilities they grew sullen and bitter. They approached the day when they'd be forced to retire because of their age. Some of these pitiful souls might serve in this limbo for fifteen years before their passing would go unheralded. No gold wristwatch, no retirement celebration nor a token handshake from the Township Manager or a Commissioner.

At the same time there were a half dozen senior officers assigned to all day work. Their only duty was to pound the sidewalk and assist children at a school crossing. In a flash these first-rate police officers lost their dignity and their will to carry on. They struggled to bear up under this indignity until their retirement age. Justifiably they became so crotchety that when a stranger asked for directions they rudely shirked them off with their surly stock "Straight ahead" no matter where they were headed.

After my first five years on the job I noticed some of my beloved mentors removed from the squad and placed on all day work. To me these brilliant healthy men hadn't crested yet. I couldn't understand why their superiors looked upon them as 'old'. If they thought they were rewarding these men for years of sacrifice they weren't. It was more like a sentence to a slow death. These men frantically fought to remain with their squad and to continue the round the clock routine. They went pleading and kicking into semi-retirement at the youthful age of forty-five and fifty years of age.

I worked diligently to ease into a soft day work position and it came only when it was my turn to be taken off the street. I was assigned to the Staff and Inspection Unit. This new assignment was thrust upon me just after I had overcame all the obstacles a street cop confronts. I learned it all and conquered the monster. There were no more errors for I had made them all. I was improved by experience. I felt in my heart that I soared with the most accomplished police officers who ever wore a badge.

However, May 1970 at forty-four years of age I was plucked from patrol duty and never told why. Nagging questions loomed in my mind. Was I assigned to a desk because I reached 'that age'? Was I taken off the street because I wasn't as efficient as I thought? Was I to be assigned to a desk until I retired or went insane, whichever came first?

There were many men my age who were left on patrol duty but then I rationalized there wasn't a 'get lost' niche for all of us. It seemed peculiar that some men who weren't assigned to these dead-end positions vociferously begged for them. They pleaded with their superiors and even sought the intercession of their neighborhood Commissioner. Their argument was they 'paid their dues' and deserved an all day work assignment so they could spend their evenings home with their wife and family. They argued they were too old for rigorous patrol work.

I read the book *PARKINSON'S LAWS*, by Professor Parkinson. One of his interesting Laws is, *"every man regardless of his position and responsibilities starts to count paper clips five years before he retires."* I had to accept my retirement was approaching by leaps and bounds. I had to get used to removing paper from the IN tray to the OUT tray. As time passed I decided not to ask why I was transferred. I reasoned it might be best I didn't know and in that way the decaying process might be less loathsome.

May 1970 was the beginning of a whole new way of life. I suffered through many harsh phases and adjusted without rebelling so I could survive this one too. Without any forewarning I reported to a support unit, the Staff & Inspections Unit. I didn't just enter a strange office I entered a totally alien world.

After twenty-two years of honing my skills to a point where I enjoyed going to work I was now thrust into a position with entirely new duties and responsibilities. I had to learn a whole new side of police work. Now I was a quartermaster, caregiver and instructor. This wasn't a routine I could gently slide into. This unit was only a year old under 'the new look' reorganization. It was without precedents. I worked from scratch and it was painful.

If I was purposely taken out of the Patrol Unit and relegated to a desk so I could ease into retirement it turned out that I wasn't placed into the soft lap of ease. My transfer was not into limbo. I went straight forth into hell. I reflect upon my mentors and how lucky they were to be given a no-brainer position and I asked myself why did they protest?

To compound my misfortune a new Superintendent was appointed. He was a man from the ranks with whom I never patrolled so I didn't know his personality or temperament. He turned out to be a hyper person with energy to burn. His mind was constantly on new ideas. He pushed himself and expected others to work just as energetically.

Almost every day he telephoned my desk with orders, "Sergeant draft another General Order! Sergeant draft another procedure! Sergeant draft an Ordinance I can present to the Commissioners! Sergeant write another Grant for the Criminal Justice Commission! Sergeant work up a new work schedule for the Patrol Unit!" He didn't ask, he ordered. I often responded, "Superintendent my pen can't write as fast as your mind can think."

May 1970 was the beginning of thirteen years in hell.

This is me at my desk in June 1983 six months before I retired.

THE LOWER MERION ANNUAL INSPECTION

Every June the Commissioners chartered a bus and toured the township to inspect all township buildings, parks, playgrounds, sewage pumping stations, firehouses and fire vehicles, highway maintenance equipment, libraries and the police department personnel and patrol vehicles. The police personnel and fleet were the last on the agenda. The tour included a lunch and lasted over eight hours.

The Police Department inspection was conducted at an hour when most of the men were off duty or they had just finished an eight-hour shift. Some men loss sleep time before going on the midnight shift. For some it occurred on their precious day off and a few others who were on vacation had to appear if they were not out of town.

The men vehemently objected to having to stand in the sweltering sun for over an hour in their dress blue uniforms while waiting for the tour bus to arrive. The long lunch and extra cocktails might have caused the delay.

The grumbling became so contemptuous it soon reached the Commissioners' ears but they ignored the protests until the men demanded they be paid for the imposition on their off-duty time. The Commissioners didn't want to budget for that so the annual inspection of the Police Department personnel was discontinued in 1965.

This is the Annual Inspection in June 1963. I am the fourth man from the right. The Superintendent is taking my pistol to inspect it. The civilians are the Commissioners. The one in the light jacket is the Chairman of the Police and Fire Committee.

The men in this photograph are waiting for the tour bus to arrive for the June 1955 Annual Inspection. I am the second fellow from the right. The officer on my left and the three officers on my right are assigned with me to the motorcycle squad and that is why our uniforms differ from the other men.

In case you couldn't find me in the above photograph I am the second one from the right.

BY THEIR CERTIFICATES YOU'LL KNOW THEM

Society divides its workers into two classes: white collar and blue collar. White collar workers are the professionals; doctors, lawyers, dentists, judges, professors, etc.. Blue collar workers are the tradesmen; plumbers, electricians, carpenters, bricklayers, etc.. What segregates the classes, or, sets them apart are their certificates.

Professionals have their certificates adorning every office wall. They are hung there to authenticate the person is educated. They are displayed to instill confidence in their owner's competence. Every certificate is exhibited for their clients or patients to inspect. The larger certificates make the statement, "The larger the document the more prestigious the educational institution and all the more cerebral the professorship." The blue-collar workers perform just as valuable a service in the community but they don't receive recognition because they don't possess the all-powerful certificates.

The police have been slow to catch on to this phenomenon. They submissively accepted the public's low esteem. They lack pride in their profession and acquiesce to negative stereotyping. The first joke a child learned was, "Does your father work? No, he's a cop." His first rhyme is, "Brass buttons, blue coat, can't catch a nanny goat."

In the early 1950s there was a major change in police leadership throughout the country that brought about a sweeping switch. The new leaders espoused that education and certificates curried self-confidence, respect and a higher salary. Police departments spurred a campaign to transform their personnel into professionals. Training programs sprang from several sources. Seminars were conducted by the FBI and at the completion of each seminar or conference a proof of Attendance Certificate were awarded.

My first certificate came in 1951 from an American Red Cross First Aid instructor who taught a three hours course. We received a certificate verifying we received First Aid training. I recall how little the course meant to the senior officers. The instructor asked one old timer what was the first aid treatment for a snake bite? The cop said, "Get two shots of liquor. Rub one on the snake bite and drink the other." The class roared. Another seasoned cop held up his certificate and said sarcastically, "This is a pretty piece of paper. I'm going to frame it and hang it in my bathroom - right over the toilet." That explains how resistant pre-1950 police officers were toward training.

As I collected certificates my salary increased and my position improved. However, within the ranks young men held fast to the idea they belong to a paramilitary organization. "We wear a uniform and carry a gun just like soldiers so we are mere soldiers." Others insist they were public servants, no different than field hands. "We are security guards and the public can order us about and vilify us." These men were locked into that mentality and argued theirs is a menial job. They weren't interested in going that extra mile toward self-improvement or toward raising their career choice to a professional level. They didn't believe in the power of a collection of certificates. Mr. Anonymous was correct when he said, "You can't teach an old dog new tricks."

This is a sampling of the certificates I merited after attending formal classroom instructions. Several others are filed in my Personal File and several more were lost in a shuffle.

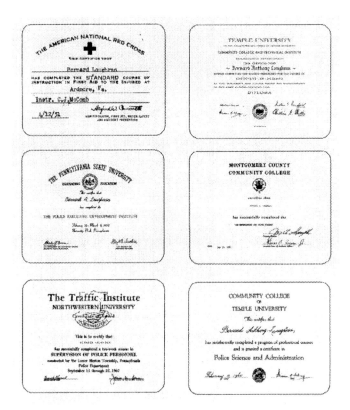

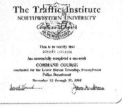

A TELEPRINTER SYSTEM GRANT

The Superintendent gave me a stern order, "Barney write a Grant Application to the Governor's Criminal Justice Commission requesting funds for a Teleprinter System." I hadn't the foggiest idea what he was talking about but I gave him a reassuring "Yes, sir."

I looked in all the police magazines for the article he read but only located an insignificant advertisement with an 800-phone number. I made the necessary phone call and the company sent me literature that informed me it was a typewriter that operated on radio waves. A transmitting typewriter was located in the Communications Room and when headquarters wished to relay a sensitive message to a patrol car it was typed and transmitted via radio to a receiving typewriter in the patrol car. The officer read the message instead of hearing it over the radio.

I contacted the Governor's Criminal Justice Commission office and asked for several application forms and for a representative to come to my desk and assist me complete my first application.

A recent college graduate, who had less experience than I, came to my desk the following day with the forms. I discussed what I was going to request and he told me it was impossible to obtain money for a Teleprinter system. He explained the Commission's funds were created to improve police officers and departments but weren't for purchasing "bricks and mortar". He emphasized, "If the money was for self-improvement there would be no questions asked."

I asked him what was meant by self-improvement and he said, "If an officer wanted to go to college his tuition would be funded because that's self-improvement. Even if the officer took violin lessons that would be considered self-improvement." He also said the Federal Government would only provide 80% of the cost of the project, the State would kick in 10% and the township had to foot the remaining 10%.

I thought for sure I was off the hook so with a relaxed mind I entered the Superintendent's office with the representative's information. "Superintendent, the Governor will not fund bricks and mortar but will pay for violin lessons." "Sergeant, I told you to write an application?" When he called me Sergeant instead of Barney I read between the lines.

I obtained the cost of the system and placed an advertisement in three newspapers requesting bids from retailers. I advertised again to obtain bids from three electrical contractors interested in installing the equipment in the Communications Room and in each of the patrol cars. The difficult part was rationalizing in narrative form on the application why the Teleprinter System was a vital necessity.

For days I labored over this question. After years of experience I had perfected a stilted and bland narrative to explain how an auto accident occurred but now I was asked to elucidate why a Teleprinter had to be in every patrol car. I had patrolled the streets for twenty-two years without one so I didn't know a valid reason for such a foolish piece of equipment. Night after night I lost sleep thinking of a good reason. One morning when the memory of World War II flashed in my vanity mirror I recalled when anyone who owned a short wave radio tuned to the police radio frequency was suspected of being a spy. Even volunteer firemen were discouraged from monitoring police radio messages.

That morning I sat at my desk and wrote excellent reasons why the Teleprinter System was an absolute necessity. I stated every cub newspaper reporter had a short wave radio tuned to our police radio frequency. Every newspaper dispatcher monitored our radio messages. Every TV station knows about a major crime the moment a cruiser or detective car was dispatched over the air. News reporters would dash to the scene and even be there before the police arrived. They could easily compromise a major investigation.

I poured the molasses on extra thick. I concluded with the fact no radio message warranting secrecy until a thorough investigation was completed would be private. Too many indiscreet people would hear about an on-going major incident on their short wave radio or police scanner. Newspaper reporters would clutter the location to badger valuable witnesses. TV cameramen eager to photograph a crime scene and the victims could jeopardize an arrest and a conviction at a trial. Ordinary citizens attracted by what they heard on the radio or saw on TV would require a vast number of crowd control personnel to prevent contamination of a crime scene.

I finished my request by explaining there was little likelihood any agency or individual would possess a Teleprinter with the capabilities of intercepting our signal. To my surprise we were granted the funds. My point of view impressed the Commission.

Six months later my Captain submitted a Grant for a Teleprinter Interface Machine. This machine would receive the answer to an officer's inquiry from the C.L.E.A.N. and N.C.I.C. Systems and automatically relays it to the officer's Teleprinter. The radio operator was relieved of the relaying task and thereby save a great deal of delay.

This Teleprinter System put a secretary in every patrol car. A message is sent once, quickly and accurately. Misinterpretation is eliminated. It is a new way for officers to get the message when they are too busy to listen to the radio.

THE COMMUNICATIONS ROOM GRANT

The Superintendent returned from an out-of-town police convention chock-full of new ideas. He toured a police facility that had state-of-the-art equipment so as soon as he returned to his office he made a beeline to my desk. "Barney, I want the Communications Room updated. I want you to submit an application and get sufficient funding."

I wasn't on the same tour bus so I hesitantly asked him what he specifically had in mind. "What do you mean? What do I have in mind? That room is a disgrace! That room is loaded with so many noisy gadgets a patrol car can't receive a clear radio message. Because of the high decibel count in that room all you hear on the car radio is background voices, whistles, bells, sirens and garbled conversations. I want that room sound proofed. Get carpeting for the floor and carpet the walls to absorb the noise. Put an extension on the communications room that will house the radio operator exclusively. Install an endless belt track to take the messages from the switchboard operator into the radio room." He was on a roll but left the rest to my imagination. However, I had no mental image of an ultra modern Communications Room.

I asked, "Superintendent, will the Criminal Justice Commission approve all this brick and mortar?" "Don't you concern yourself about that! You write the application!" I was so confuse and had no idea where to begin yet I gave him a confident "OK, Sir."

Again, what I considered the most difficult phase was writing a reason that would convince the Commission this department was desperately in need of these improvements or we would become impotent in our fight against crime. Every morning I hoped for an idea that would bring a tear to every eye on the Commission.

Out of the blue I had a flashback to my first day on the job when Officer Jim Wentz taught me there was a Penn Road and a Penn Street, an Indian Creek Road, Indian Creek Lane and Indian Creek Drive and a W. Wynnewood Road, E. Wynnewood Road, Old W. Wynnewood Road and Wynnewood Avenue.

I prepared my narrative after studying the 280 streets on the township map and saw numerous duplications. Many street names sounded alike but were spelled differently. I saw over 200 names that had to be spoken distinctly and without voices or radio static in the background or the emergency equipment would go to the wrong location.

I explained in my application that the Communications Room was 12 feet x 25 feet and cluttered with three switchboard/radio positions that often interfered with one another. There was a Teletype machine continually spewing out messages and a Teleprinter and Interface Machine with inherent noises. Fire alarms, bank alarms, private home security alarms and neighboring police radios monitoring neighboring activity that frequently interrupted or clouded an emergency message being transmitted over the air by our radio operators.

The Governor's Criminal Justice Commission approved my application and I was elated. There were no questions or discussion. My ego was inflated and I believed I was a genius with a pen after batting back-to-back home runs. Now I had to advertise for bids from electricians, radio installers, carpet installers, partition installers and conveyor belt installers. When the submissions poured in I evaluated them and selected people that could do the job economically. It was incumbent on me to accept the lowest bidder or my head would be on the chopping block. When the renovations were completed three months later I collected the receipts and filled out the forms required by the Commission.

Now I had time to process the backlog that was piling up on my desk. I was hoping that was the last time-consuming Grant Application.

The photograph on the left shows the three switchboards that are in close quarters. The radio operator is situated in a small room behind the glass enclosure at the far end of the room. The photograph on the right is the C.L.E.A.N. machine that added to the pandemonium that offended the senses and cause chaos in the communications room.

THE POLICE LIBRARY GRANT

The Superintendent paid a visit to my desk before I could relax. He was fuming. Evidently his hyperthyroidism kept him awake all night. He was so hyper the words shot from his mouth like bullets from a machine gun. "Barney, get started on a Grant for a library."

This was a shocker because our police library consisted of a dozen forty-year-old-never-read textbooks. Headquarters hadn't space for a bookcase so I couldn't imagine where a decent library could be squeezed into the building but then I didn't have his fiercely driven energy. If Ritalin had been available those days I would have recommended he take a daily dose. I asked him, "Superintendent where will this library be located? Beside books how shall it be furnished? How much money should I ask for?"

"Barney, there is a storage room on the third floor in the rear of this building, throw all that junk out. Get the walls painted, lay a rug, install fluorescent lights, get a conference table so the room can be used for training, get stacking chairs with folding desk arms, get shelving for hundreds of books dealing exclusively on police subjects, hang a blackboard on a wall, etc., etc.. Request a double digit figure at least."

I could approach this application because it was character improvement and not solely 'brick & mortar'.

Again there was newspaper advertising for bids on every item. I went to the local library and searched the shelves for the names of police books but there were none on police subjects. I went to the libraries in three local Universities and they had nothing on police subjects. Even police magazines had only a few books to recommend to its readership. I ran out of places to search for police publications.

One morning I went to the Superintendent's office to obtain his signature on a handful of papers, not related to this project, but he wasn't in. I flopped into his padded leather executive chair and the strength that comes with authority enveloped me because at the moment I was at my lowest ebb. I spun 180 degrees like a child left alone on a soda fountain stool and savored the exhilarating glow a padded leather executive's chair can cast. I considered taking a second spin because it was so exhilarating.

I spotted a magazine laying loosely on his cadenza. It was a new police catalogue I never saw so I picked it up and leafed through it. Just by luck it flipped open to a directory of all the latest publications dealing with every police subject imaginable. It was this catalogue that planted the idea for a library into his cranium. I snatched the catalogue and gave it to my typist and she typed every title, author, printing house and the price of each book into my Grant Application.

At the next Criminal Justice Commission meeting my request for a police library was approved.

To make my grant palatable I promised every book in our police library would go through the township public library system and would be given an official Dewey Decimal code number and it would be included in the library's card files. This turned out to be an extra burden on my staff and me. College students began to use our library as frequently as the officers and it generated another time consuming task of keeping track of the books.

The very first college student who wanted to use our library was assigned to research the anatomy of a suicide. She checked several public libraries and they had no literature on the subject. She visited several University libraries and found nothing. As a last resort she contacted my office and we had five recent publications on the subject by five different authors.

These are two of the six shelves and a few of the hundreds of books I purchased for our Police Library.

THE POLICE FILM LIBRARY GRANT

After my success with the Library Grant I hoped the Superintendent would take it easy but relaxing wasn't part of his makeup. "Barney, write a Grant requesting funds for a film library. Include a 30mm projector, a screen to hang on the library wall over the blackboard, a portable screen and a 35mm slide projector with remote controls for changing the slides. Purchase the latest police training films and include shelving for the films.

I asked what parameter should I stay within because the township might begin to rebel against spending all these ten percents. He snapped back, "Your job isn't to worry about the money! Your job is to write a persuasive Grant and my job is to get the funds from the Criminal Justice Commission, the State and the Township Commissioners! The 30mm projector will run in the neighborhood of eight hundred dollars, each film will cost two fifty to three hundred dollars, the screens are a couple hundred, the slide projector, remote control and slides will be over a thousand. Shoot for eighteen thousand."

This Grant was simple to write because I plagiarized what I had written in the Library Grant plea. I only chanced the names of the items. The difficult phase was searching through catalogs for part numbers and prices and advertising for bids.

I promised the Criminal Justice Commission the Township Public Library system could place the names of our films in their card files so they'd be available to the public too. It wasn't long before every high school teacher and college professor was borrowing the films to reinforce their lecture. Keeping a record of who had a particular film and when they were to return it was time consuming. Our films were so popular that in most cases I insisted a film be returned in two days.

I received negative vibrations from a women's group. The instructor thought I was deliberately withholding films from her but she never reserved a film in advance. She requested films, HOW A WOMAN CAN PROTECT HERSELF AGAINST RAPE, SELF DEFENSE FOR WOMEN, WHAT A WOMAN SHOULD DO AFTER BEING RAPED, etc.. Often a college professor or high school teacher withdrew the film she wanted the previous day. She'd throw a mean look that made me think she suspected I was hiding it in a closet just to deprive her of it. She didn't believe there were others who wanted to use the same films. She failed to realize there were colleges, high schools and women's groups also borrowing the films. To assure her I was on the up and up I'd give her the name of the school, the teacher's name and classroom number and suggest she retrieve the film herself if she needed it immediately.

The department had over fifty well-used training films and several hundred well-read text books when I retired.

RIOT CONTROL EQUIPMENT GRANT

With all his spur-of-the-moment orders the Superintendent was speedily driving me into the Snake Pit. I stopped answering the phone for fear he was on the line. One of the other five people in the room would pick up the phone to help buffer his calls. He might be making a simple request to run an earn or ask to cull a statistic from our files but when a major project enter his frontal lobotomy he'd snap into the mouthpiece, "Give me the Sergeant!!" The "immediately" was implied. Everyone in the office heard his voice and they'd rolled their eyes toward heaven in a prayer. The officer holding the phone would say, "Sarge, it's the SUPER."

"Good morning, Superintendent, how can I help?" "Barney, there are riots and demonstrations of every type ongoing throughout the country and the police have to wear protective gear. The youth of this country are behaving like anarchist. We must provide our men with the latest protective equipment. Work up a Grant I can present to the Commission. Ask for everything pertaining to this problem and put in for a van to transport a SQUAT TEAM that can be thrown into the breach on a moments notice. I'll select the men for the Squat Team later. Get the paperwork to me as soon as possible. Thanks, Barney."

I never got a "Thanks" before and I didn't expected it because he was always in high gear and anxious to talk to the next person on his list before he forgot why he intended to call them. He wasn't rude, just a hyper guy with too many irons in the fire.

I checked the police products magazines for whatever state-of-the-art gear was on the market that was intended for the protection of an officer who confronted aggression. I included these items in the Grant.

The Superintendent never had the benefit of the lecture given by the Pennsylvania State Police sergeant who stressed one good Trooper could squelch a riot. Years later I attended a lecture where a ranking police official told us about an incident in which he was involved. He said a man peered out of a third floor window of a row house and threatened to shoot everyone in sight. The Squat Team, Riot Squad and officers from adjacent districts responded in full riot regalia. Men were stationed on surrounding rooftops and others barged into apartments on the opposite side of the street and lurked behind curtains poised to shoot their high-powered rifles. Policemen with drawn firearms shielded themselves behind patrol cars and others cordoned off the street. Over the police radio this official gave the order that no action was to be taken until he arrived. When he appeared on the scene he ordered the men to hold their fire because he was going into the building to talk to the man.

He walked up the steps to the man's apartment and knocked gently on the door. He announced he was an unarmed police officer who wanted to find out why he was so upset and mad at everyone. The man opened the door and the official entered the apartment. The man sobbed as he told the official he was sixty-five years old and it was his birthday. He was crying because he never had a Birthday Party and not once in his life did anyone ever wish him a Happy Birthday. That's why he was mad at the world.

The official wished the man a Happy Birthday and together they walked down the steps to the front door. The police officers at the scene were set to shoot at the first hint of trouble but they couldn't believe their eyes when the official came out of the building with his arm over the man's shoulder buddy-buddy fashion singing Happy Birthday. The official ordered the men to put away their guns and they were to join in and sing "Happy Birthday Dear Elmer."

I had to have grounds so in my Grant narrative I stated the "Annual Law Enforcement Casualty Summary" revealed that between July 1970 and June 1971 there were 1,968 police "combat casualties" in the United States resulting in 110 law officer deaths. Police at a local level suffered 80.64% of these deaths. I requested funds for riot helmets with shields and 30" batons for every man in the department. Because of the changes in social attitudes in the past decade the department realized some people came to demonstrate and others came to destroy.

Firearms were responsible for most of the 110 police officers' deaths so I request funds for three bulletproof vests. This equipment would improve the morale, safety and efficiency of the men who may be forced to face a hostile individual. I wrote they would be a defensive garment and not an offensive weapon.

Bombings had increased drastically in the United States over the past several years. Between 1969 and 1970 1,188 bombs were placed within the United States. In a six month period there were 764 bombs placed and 654 actually detonated. Ten people were killed, 82 injured and an estimated $5,913,248.00 worth of property damaged. Of the 764 bombs placed, 120 were in New York, New Jersey and Pennsylvania. The department needed a bomb blanket. It was light-weight material designed to contain the force of an explosion. It would be just another tool that will be used for the protection of life and property.

Frequently situations occur that require extra manpower so the Tactical Unit would be dispatched. Six skilled police officers may work singly, paired or as a group, in uniform or civilian attire, in marked or unmarked police cars. The Tactical Unit needed a van to transport themselves and whatever equipment may be needed at the scene.

I reminded the Commission since the mores of our society rule out the frisking of women by policemen a magnetic friskem baton will be needed where women are involved. It will eliminate objections because the police officer only has to wave the baton over the female form to detect a concealed weapon. After the on the spot cursory check she will be taken to Headquarters and a traditional hand search will be done by a police matron.

I included these tools and a half dozen more in the Grant application and it goes without explanation there were no "line item vetoes". I often questioned the original purpose of the Federal Funding the young college representative gave me, "Bricks and mortar no, violin lessons OK."

THE DICTAPHONE GRANT

The Superintendent called me to his office to tell me to write a Grant requesting funds for a Dictaphone System. I didn't know the meaning of the word and I had no concept of a Dictaphone System and I told him so. This was an opportunity for him to go on a long dissertation on how much he knew about the System and everything else. He enjoyed expounding on his wide range of knowledge so he explained in great detail how the system functioned and how it was to be used.

He said our detectives spend too much time typing reports instead of investigating crimes. "There is a tremendous backlog of cases that will never be thoroughly investigated because the men are glued to their desk writing reports. The Dictaphone is a small hand held recorder he can talk into and record his reports on tape. He won't have to write reports in longhand first and then type a formal final copy.

"He won't need to check his spelling or grammar nor will he waste time with correction fluid to correct his typing errors. If the Dictaphones are utilized properly they will increase productivity and reduce the backlog of cases. When he is finished recording his report he will forward the tape to a clerk who will knock out a flawless and presentable report without misspelled words and smudges.

"You can see how this system will increase the Detective Unit's output. When their reports get into the hands of Lawyers and Judges they will be impressive and reflect well on the department. We will be highly professional. Get on this right away. Request enough funds to buy a Dictaphone for each detective and a transcriber equipped with a remote foot control and several earpieces; a personal one for each typist."

I was thinking about my own backlog when I said, "Yes, Sir."

After researching for this grant I was shocked to learn each Dictaphone cost $650.00 and the Detective Bureau needed ten. Then there was the transcriber, remote foot control and six earpieces. The system was expensive but the narrative was easy to write because I repeated word for word what the Superintendent said. It sounded good to me so my job was to transcribe it in a way it would convince the Criminal Justice Commission.

The Dictaphone System was approved at the next Commission meeting and I advertised and accepted bids. Within a month the Dictaphones were in the Detective Bureau. It took several months for the detectives to break old habits but eventually they liked the idea that someone else was going to do most of their work, the part that was the most difficult. I privately questioned if the Dictaphones increased their productivity.

A week after the Dictaphones went into service a detective was interviewing a petty thief seated in a chair beside his desk. Another detective called him into an adjacent room for a consultation. He wasn't away from his desk thirty seconds but in that short time the thief was left unguarded. He went through the detective's desk drawer and found his Dictaphone. The following day the detective went to use it and discovered it was gone. He couldn't prove the petty thief stole it but he was the only suspect.

I bet that thief traded it with his drug pusher for a $5.00 fix.

When I was the Traffic Safety Sergeant in 1969 the concerned citizens of the township kept me busy on the telephone. Most of their requests for signs and road markings were reasonable and practical.

THE CELL BLOCK SURVAILLANCE GRANT

When the Superintendent's cleats tapped solidly on the asphalt floor tiles they were frightening. This time I had a feeling he was on his way to my desk. I don't know why I feared him because he wasn't a mean fellow. He purposely wore those cleats to forewarn the clerks he had a reason for walking through the building and it wasn't to slink silently and furtively upon someone shirking their work. His visit this time was to order me to prepare another Grant.

"Sergeant, we need a jail surveillance system to eliminate the need for the radio operator to leave headquarters every hour to check on the prisoners. I want you to apply for a system that will do away with the twenty-four hour a day check. Give this grant priority. Check on what is needed and get a ballpark estimate of the coast and submit it as quickly as you can."

These Grants were out of my league and I was juggling a half dozen of them at the same time. The narratives alone required the efforts of a Harvard speech writer preparing the President's State of the Union address. Newspaper advertising was foreign to me and selecting the proper bidder to avoid a lawsuit was over my head. Collecting receipts and getting the bills paid was complicated and the Federal Government, State and township insisted I keep accurate records. They wanted to know how their money was spent. I didn't ask for help from my staff because they were assigned other tasks.

One devious fellow in my office learned through his underground grapevine that the Superintendent had volunteered to sit on the Governor's Criminal Justice Committee. His job was to evaluate the Applications submitted by all police departments and he was in a position to approve or disapprove any requests for funds. I finally learned why all my Grants were approved without challenges. Up until now I thought it was my imaginative prose that won their approval.

Even so I knew I couldn't reach for the stars just because the Superintendent was on the Committee. I had to prove in the application the request was legitimate. I wrote a compelling request for a complicated but basic cell block surveillance system that would cost an estimated $25,000.00. The Grant was approved and immediately I advertised for bids. Just before the bids arrived a ruptured peptic ulcer put me out of work for five months.

The Superintendent, being the impulsive fellow he was, hired an electronics engineer to implement the jail surveillance system before the Grant approval would expire. The engineer he chose completed the installation for the sum of $85,000.00.

My plan was to hang TV cameras from the ceiling. Each camera would pan two cells and there would be six cameras and six monitors. The engineer's plan had a single camera assigned to each cell and these cameras were installed flat against the wall opposite each cell four feet above the floor. For the cameras to get a right-angle view into the cell they had a series of mirrors that acted like a submarine periscope.

Before I returned to work the installation was completed. When I returned to my desk, for my own information, I checked the engineer's camera layout. I thought it was brilliant and his advanced education served him well. I envied him for his expertise and unique idea. He did an exemplary installation but left me with all the paperwork.

The devious officer who informed me of the Superintendent's position on the Criminal Justice Commission told me of an incident that happened in the cell block while I was in the hospital. During the first week the jail surveillance system was in operation the radio operator regularly checked the jail monitors that were conveniently hung above the switchboard. (The cell block and the switchboard are in two separate buildings.) He glanced at the monitors and noticed the screen on the monitor assigned to the cell that held a prisoner was gradually fading and soon the picture went completely blank.

He went to the jail to check on the welfare of the prisoner and learned the prisoner had been given a dinner that included a side order of sweet peas. He used his spoon to slingshot one pea at a time at the mirror on the TV camera mounted on the wall opposite his cell. The mirror was only two inches square and four feet away from his cell. When a shot was accurate the pea stuck to the mirror like it was pasted. Eventually he covered the mirror and blocked the camera's view. His many misses lay splattered on the floor. This was a case of a playful but clever prisoner with a lot of idle time.

That was a bug the engineer never counted on because his education never included awareness of the twisted criminal mind.

In this photograph I am inspecting the TV cameras that were recently mounted on the jail wall opposite the lockup cells.

BANG! BANG!

Almost every working day of my life I wore a gun. First, I was a tail gunner in World War II and received training with shotguns, rifles, .30 and .50 caliber machine guns and 20 mm. cannons. The machine guns shot 800 rounds per minute and at the slightest squeeze of the trigger dozens of rounds exploded from the barrel. I joined the Lower Merion Police pistol team and for fifteen years I shot a .22 cal. automatic pistol and a .38 cal. revolver. I practiced in all kinds of weather in the spring, summer and fall. On Wednesdays and weekends there were competitive matches.

I took a hurried accounting of how much shooting I did and arrived at a conservative figure over a half-million rounds. The astonishing fact is I wasn't a hunter, I never owned a gun, and I never bought a bullet. In the final analysis all I received for my effort was a loss of hearing in the high pitched tones due to the loud bang! bangs!

I attended 30 police pistol matches a year for 15 years and accumulated quite a collection of certificates. Most of my certificates were deposited directly into my Personal File but these should be enough to verify I shot a humongous amount of ammunition.

In this photo I am shooting 5 shots in 11 seconds at a target 25 yards away. I injured the muscle in my left eye when I was six years old and the muscle in my right eye in my motorcycle accident so I had to squint to get a clear picture of the gun sights and the target.

I include this certificate to verify I attended the U.S. Naval Air Gunners School Jacksonville, Florida May 1945. I shot thousands of rounds in the four weeks I was there.

THE PUBLIC SAFETY BUILDING

THE POLICE BUILDING FROM 1952 TO 1980

For ten years my office was on the right on the third floor where the two windows are. Originally this was a General Motors new car sales office that had two showroom windows on the ground floor. It outgrew its usefulness as a police headquarters and was razed after a two-story building was constructed behind it. This site was converted into an enlarged and modernized parking area.

In 1980 Police Department personnel moved out of their former headquarters and into a new facility. The dedication ceremony was held September 10, 1982. The modern two story structure has an elevator and 18,360 square feet of floor space. It houses Police and Fire Department personnel and can boast of a computer system, modern radio consoles and modern telecommunications equipment. The new Public Safety Building was constructed behind the old Police Building, 71 East Lancaster Avenue, Ardmore.

THE NEW PUBLIC SAFETY BUILDING – SEPTEMBER 10, 1982

QUARTERLY REPORTS

The Superintendent made his typical gruff morning telephone call, "Barney, I attended a Civic Association meeting last night and I was told emphatically by those present that they never see a police cruiser in their area. They were furious and accused the department of favoring the minority communities with extra attention. Other members insisted the wealthy neighborhoods received preferential protection. They behaved like children and demanded, 'We want as much protection as the other communities get'. You wouldn't believe their attack upon the department and on me for my dereliction of responsibility.

"I told them I'd have my Staff and Inspections Sergeant prepare a monthly report of the police activity in their community. I want you to produce a report and mail it to the President of that Civic Association before each monthly meeting." With tongue in cheek I gave a reassuring, "No problem." I expected it would be a simple task (this was seven years before a computer was installed in the Police Building).

I never thought the department was looked upon as being prejudice or favoring one community with more attention than another so I proceeded to cull the statistics for one month for that community and found it to be difficult and even impossible.

I returned to the Superintendent and explained a monthly report wasn't retrievable. I recommended a Quarterly Report that I could dress up to make a professional impression and a copy could be mailed to every Civic Association. I suggested maybe the other Associations had similar negative attitudes and this approach might dispel them. I proposed compiling the statistics for three months would be a far better idea and he agreed.

After appeasing the Civic Associations for three years I explained to the Superintendent the Quarterly Reports consumed too many valuable hours to produce. That time could be utilized to advance some of his more important projects. I suggested the Associations could be just as easily assured the police patrols are evenly assigned when they receive our Annual Report.

The Quarterly Report covers were printed on various colored cardboard and that is why they didn't copy well here.

This photograph was taken in June 1983, six months before I retired. I am 57 years old. Obviously I didn't age well. The job took its toll.

THE DEPARTMENT'S ANNUAL REPORT

The Police Department's Annual Report was a labor-intensive task of my own making. In 1970 one of my many assignments was to prepare the Annual Reports for the Commissioners, however, I knew the public was concerned about their community and police activities so I went all out to impress them. The township map had already been divided into 99 political sections and the Police Department utilized these sections for recording police activities.

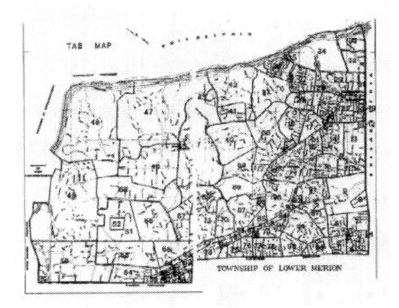

TAB MAP

This is the a map of the Township outlining the geographic location of the
ninety-nine (99) areas used for tabulating workloads within the Township.
Patrol beats are organized by measuring the activity generated when groups
of tabulation areas are combined. Other factors such as type of incidents,
natural boundaries, population and time of day are also considered.

TAB AREAS

The tab area tables show the various categories of activity in each area which require a police response. Analysis of these categories assists police managers in the effective deployment of field personnel.

NOTE

Patrol beats were redesigned after a detailed evaluation of workload and other relevant factors resulting in enhanced ability to provide the most effective police patrol and response to citizens' needs.

Residents of the Township can check the TAB MAP to obtain the Tab number assigned to the area of interest. They then can go to the chart above and get the number a incidents that occurred during the year. This practical use of the TAB MAP was my original inspiration. I culled the Records Section's statistics but left it up to the two officers and their calculator to make my figures jibe. I dissected the Township map so the residents could locate their community.

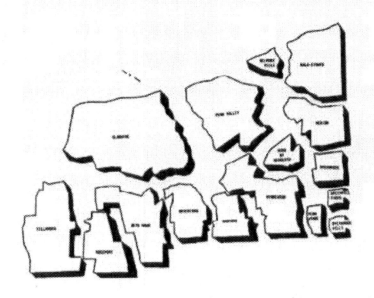

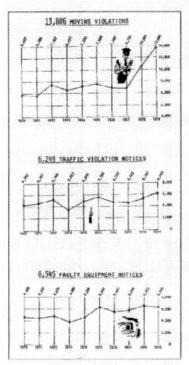

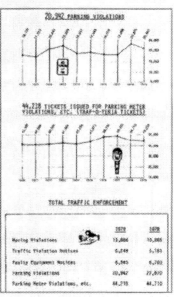

TOTAL TRAFFIC ENFORCEMENT

		1979	1978
Moving Violations		13,886	15,886
Traffic Violation Notices		6,249	6,193
Faulty Equipment Notices		6,565	6,702
Parking Violations		20,962	22,870
Parking Meter Violations, etc.		44,215	44,710

GENERAL INFORMATION

Population	59,600
Area - Square Miles	24
Highway Miles	275
Parks & Playgrounds	38
Schools	30
Fire Companies	6
Post Offices	7
Hospitals	2
Libraries	7
Banks	49
Dwellings	22,521
Houses (17,718)	
Apartments (4,803)	

VEHICLE FLEET

Marked Vehicles	26
Unmarked Vehicles	11
Emergency Vehicles	4
Animal Control Vehicle	1
Multi-purpose Van	1
TOTAL	43

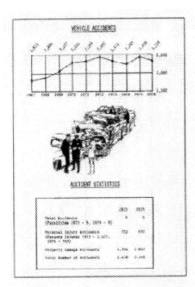

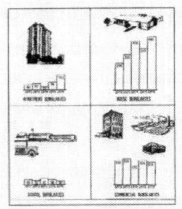

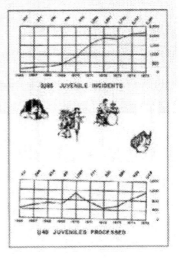

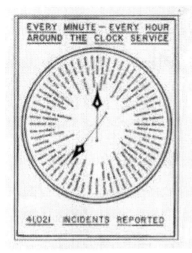

On the preceding pages are samples of the pages in the Annual Reports I produced from 1970 to 1982. No two Reports were the same. I never claimed they were works of art but considering the only tools I had were a typewriter, single-edge razors blades, a 12" wooden ruler, scotch tape, a ballpoint pen, and correction fluid I think I did OK. The pencil drawings I cut out of magazines. Each Report had 25 to 30 pages of pertinent information. It took months of forging and shaping because there was always another project with a higher priority that had to be completed first. I assembled the statistics for the year into attractive grafts and charts to make a visual presentation that would attract the reader's attention.

The office typist went near insane before she got the knack of placing the paper on a slant into her typewriter so figures could be typed in one direction on one graph and at a totally different angle for another chart and another set of figures. Take for example the clock above. Picture her struggling to type in those sixty incidents. The Annual Reports could not have been done without her skill and patience. The two staff officers who guaranteed the statistics tallied and proof read the narratives were worn to a frazzle by the time the Report was sent to the printer. The Reports could never have been printed without their contribution. I never received any criticism from the Commissioners or Civic Associations so I assumed they were acceptable.

Producing these Reports took a great deal of creativity and imagination from a fellow who had just spent twenty-three years on patrol and in all those years never concerned himself with nor had any appreciation for the behind the scenes support system.

304

THE BASIC TRAINING PROGRAM

Starting in 1970 I was responsible for the Basic Training Program for the new recruits and the In-service Training Program for those advancing in grades. The department began its training programs the previous year so I copied the outline that had proved very successful. It was the second year for the basic training program and even though the wheel had been invented there was room for creativity and improvement.

I decided the recruits might benefit from a more memorable introduction to the force than the one I received the night I was sworn in. I conceive a swearing in ceremony that was a royal launching. I eliminated the busy Commissioners and invited a District Justice to administer the Oath of Office. He obliged and donned his robe to accord the solemnity he would dedicate to a wedding ceremony. He realized the value of this ceremony and asked to be included for every group of new recruits in the future.

Upon completion of the sixteen-week course I invited the Superintendent, my Captain, and the Township Manager to the graduation ceremony to give prestige and dignity to the program. They posed for a graduation photograph on the front steps of the Township Building. This wasn't just a superficial act. I intended for it to impart a strong statement to the recruits that they were entering a dignified profession and they were not just beginning a new job.

I introduced many subtle formalities that added nobility to their new career. I wrote a sixteen-page course outline and bound it in a colorful cover for each student. It contained the daily schedule of the subjects to be taught and the name of each instructor. All this effort was to lend credence to each subject and the professional who would teach them. I assembled instructors from every area of law enforcement and from all ranks and expertise so the students wouldn't receive a shallow view from a handful of men. I did all this but with the final approval from my Captain and sanctioned by the Superintendent.

I also invited two Haverford College professors to teach two subjects. Many men in the department protested loudly because they believed Haverford College was a purveyor of communism, draft dodging and Anti-Vietnam sentiments. The Superintendent called me to his office and told me of the loud objections from the men. He suggested, due to the opposition I stirred up, I should reconsider. I told him this was a perfect vehicle by which our personnel would learn that the professors aren't communist and conversely the professors would learn we police are not being taught to harass college students. It might also adjust some of the present bigotry and prejudice against other institutions. He reluctantly agreed with my premise so the professors went on as scheduled.

A Haverford College female student was writing a thesis on the police mentality so she asked me if she could sit in on our course. There was so much paranoia within the department in this era that the men feared she would return to the college with a manual written for the campus protesters about the department's weakness. Again I suggested we should welcome her because she actually would report the objectivity of our training program. She attended the course eight hours a day, forty hours a week, for four months and was so enthralled she returned a second year. Her college councilors recognized our course and she received college credits both years.

In the above photograph District Justice Robert. P. Johnson is administering the Oath of Office to the Recruits. I am standing behind him.

In the photograph below in the first row on the right is the Township Manager, behind him is the Superintendent of Police, behind him is the Captain of the Staff & Inspection Unit, behind him is the Captain of the Detective Unit and I am to his right. A Main Line Times reporter and photographer reported on the new Recruits.

THE POLICE ENTRANCE EXAMINATION

When I applied for the job in 1947 five men applied at the same time. One fellow was eliminated because his IQ wasn't twice his age. A physical examination disclosed another fellow had a heart murmur. The four remaining applicants were hired. One quit after six months to be a plumber. A second had a nervous breakdown and was discharged. A third fellow was so effeminate that when he walked the sidewalk he looked like a female impersonating a policeman. Because of negative flack the department discharged him so I became the sole survivor.

Over the years men were hired in groups of four or five and the department was lucky if half of them stayed two years. At each hiring a few dozen men took the hundred-questions test. When I was assigned to the Staff & Inspections Unit I administered and graded the tests that made no reference to police work nor did it evaluate a person's ability to fill a particular career.

Young men had lost interest in becoming a police officer until the social unrest that prevailed at the time brought about a drastic change. College professors infused students with the idea they should go forth and change the existing system. They taught the students the most productive way to bring about a change was to get involved in politics or join the police force and make social changes through these arenas. They fired up the graduates with the idea they could improve the world by joining the bad guys and chisel away from within.

In January 1975 the Superintendent wanted me in his office immediately. He introduced me to a representative of the Pennsylvania Equal Employment Opportunity Commission. "Sergeant, this man believes our entrance examination is unfair to minorities. Tell him what you think." I had no idea what the Superintendent wanted me to say but I figured if a representative from the EEOC visited the department a complaint was registered about our entrance exam. Depending on my answer a civil action might be forthcoming. All along I thought the test was stupid so I said, "Superintendent it is a dumb out of date test the department purchased in 1932 from a testing agency in Chicago so it has to be biased in some way." The EEOC representative slapped his notebook shut and rose to leave, "Thank you Superintendent and thank you Sergeant." I followed him out the door before I'd get chewed out.

The Superintendent conferred with the Township Manager and Township Solicitor and they advised him to contact a testing agency that specialized in administering police tests. They were apprehensive about a lawsuit. To thwart a court action they decided on immediate safeguards.

I had hundreds of flyers printed and mailed to every college councilor in the Delaware Valley requesting they post our job opportunity on their college Bulletin Boards. Advertisement space was purchased in local and out of town newspapers (black and white) and spots were scheduled on radio stations (two black and one white) that were broadcast several times a day. This was an extremely sensitive project and every sentence was worded to avoid repercussions. All the while there were no precedence for guidance.

A testing agency was hired and their exam was far more difficult than our original test and it had hundreds of questions. The test dealt with police work and was expected to weed out those who hadn't an inclination toward the profession. The agency recommended a sample test with the answers be mailed to every applicant along with a manual explaining how to take the actual test. A week before the test there was a practice run to familiarize the students with the actual test.

Six hundred applicants appeared for the practice drill and six hundred and thirty were present for the actual test. Young men and women of every nationality and religious persuasion came from colleges in eastern Pennsylvania, New Jersey, Delaware, and Maryland. The department utilized the Lower Merion High School cafeteria but it was too small to accommodate the growing number of applicants. The following years the Harriton High School cafeteria was used because it had twice the seating capacity. The Staff & Inspections Unit was responsible for scheduling the written tests, oral examinations, background investigations and physical examinations.

The department emerged unscathed; without a complaint or civil suit. The Superintendent and everyone in my office were ecstatic. Six months later less than half of those who were hired were still on the job so the testing agency didn't perform any better than the old method.

The new hiring process was cranked up six times before I retired. Those who had the job after I left had the advantage of having a format to follow. I handled the laborious hiring procedure plus preparing for the basic training, purchasing uniforms, assembling text books, swearing in, etc. plus writing Reports, Grants, schedules, etc..

The new hiring process was a safe way to proceed. The testing agency was expensive but society was inordinately sensitive toward bias and prejudice so it paid for itself by avoiding lawsuits or scandals.

Only once was the department under the EEOC microscope during this period. A fellow came to my desk just like all the others for an application. He was number five hundred and twenty this particular year so our routine was repeated by rote. He took the test a month later and failed miserably so he went to the EEOC claiming he didn't pass the test because he was prejudiced against the day he filed his application. A representative from the EEOC questioned the Superintendent and again the Superintendent sent for me. I told the representative, "Sir, there were six-hundred and fifty applicants so I can't recall a specific one." The representative snapped, "This fellow was a Peruvian. There weren't many Peruvians. You can't remember a Peruvian?"

Suddenly it struck me. "Oh yes, I remember him. Instead of me insisting he take the application and fill it out at home like I told all the other applicants I permitted him to use my desk to fill it out. That was a mistake because it took him well over an hour. During that time he and his brother-in-law needed to use a restroom. I allowed them to use the employee's men's room instead of sending them to another building that has a public facility. To avoid collusion I asked them to go separately. He also had a three-year-old overactive daughter with him who tampered with everything in the office. She had to go to the restroom too so I had my female secretary take her to the employees' ladies' room. He was the only applicant that made the task cumbersome but no one in the office displayed any annoyance. When he finally left the office we all had a hardy laugh at what a nuisance the three of them were." The complaint was dismissed without any further investigation.

The successful applicants required a background investigation and everyone in the office took part in this. Dozens of candidates were investigated. Parents, spouses and fiancées were interviewed to ascertain if they objected to this person being a police officer. We also checked neighbors, employers, scoutmasters and fellow workers. Very few spoke negatively but if an employer wanted to get rid of a mediocre employee he'd give us an excellent evaluation. We saw through that scheme.

Some interviews were difficult. One chap was so handsome he could pose as a model for a police brochure. Everyone who was interviewed gave a blasé OK. No one was enthusiastic about him being a police officer so I suspected he had a flaw that wasn't surfacing. I visited his parish priest and I asked him if he knew the fellow and he said he knew him for twelve years as a student and as an alter boy. I asked if he thought I should hire him and he gave an unequivocal "No! He's the type of fellow if sent to investigate an auto accident would sit on the curb and cry." I accepted that as a "No" and didn't recommend him for the job.

Below is a newspaper photograph of patrolmen taking a promotional test. The testing agency was paranoid about cheating. I monitored ten tests, entrance and promotion, with a dozen other impartial policemen and never did we ever witness cheating or even suspect someone was peeking at another person's test paper.

THE FALSE ALARM ORDINANCE

Until the mid 1950s the only security alarms in the township were those that protected banks. There were six bank alarms but they were activated so often they became a nuisance. Bank employees giggled when they accidentally set off the alarm and the bank managers dismissed the accident with "What's the big deal? The police haven't anything else to do and it's a good practice drill." Even though the bank employees dismissed their clumsiness as a trivial mistake the responding police officers took the alarm seriously and raced to apprehend the robbers and to protect any hostages. These false alarms were so frequent the police began to feel abused.

At the same time home security companies began to flourish and prosper by selling a wide variety of security alarm systems. Some were intrusion alarms and some were fire alarms. Some were silent and others came with a siren or klaxon horn. The silent alarms alerted a central office and they dispatched their own investigators first and then phoned the local police. The alarms that were equipped with a siren or klaxon horn were intended to frighten away an intruder but in reality they wrought havoc upon the neighborhood at all hours of the day and night. These noisemakers couldn't be shut off except by the owner's key and he was often out of town. The responding officers sometimes cut wires to silence the noise or it would sound off for days.

A high wind or a barrage of hail might disturb a window sensor and set off the alarm. After a few years a tree limb that grew in length would scratch against a windowpane in a gusty breeze and set off the alarm. I've been told by officers that on more than one occasion some alarm owners, when entertaining friends at a cocktail party, would wager on how long it would take the police to knock at the front door after the alarm was purposely set off. The guests wagered on how many minutes it took for the first police officer to arrive. It didn't take long for false alarm activations to be responsible for a tremendous amount of the department's workload. Everything else was ignored when an alarm sounded.

The Superintendent studied the statistics and was shocked by the percentage of manpower hours that was expended chasing after these false alarms. He foresaw the hazard and risk to personnel and vehicles. He couldn't order the men to ignore the alarms but their frequency could be reduced if the owners were penalized every time a false alarm was set off.

He stormed into my office one day, "Barney, the number of false alarms is appalling and must be reduced. One of these days an officer speeding to a false alarm is going to be seriously hurt or he might seriously injure someone else. I must put a stop to them. I want you to work up an Ordinance I can present to the township Commissioners.

Contact other police departments and get a copy of whatever False Alarm Ordinance they may have. Collect whatever material you can and give it to your Captain so he can develop an Ordinance for our department. Get on this right away. Put this project on the front burner." I heard that many times before.

The only local community that had such legislation was Philadelphia and the Court struck it down as invalid the first time it was enforced.

I visited the Villanova University Law Library and went directly to a Purdon's that contained the latest court decisions pertaining to False Alarm Ordinance arrests. There were only a few court rulings because this was a relatively new technology, however, there were the names of six police department that had such an Ordinance.

I dictated a letter and mailed it to the six police departments. I asked them to send me a copy of their False Alarm Ordinance. Within a week I received a copy from the six departments, however, five of them were only one or two brief paragraphs and were totally ineffective for our situation. But the sixth, from a small Texas town, was an in-depth legal document that included every aspect of an alarm system.

Their fines graduated: A $10.00 penalty for the first false/accidental alarm, $25.00 for the second false/accidental alarm, and then the penalty escalated to $100.00, $300.00, and $500.00 each time thereafter. I thought that was steep but without commenting I turned the information over to my Captain. He made a few superficial changes in the proper names and forwarded it to the Superintendent.

The Superintendent, the Township Manager and the Township Solicitor examined it and presented it to the Board of Commissioners at the next regular monthly meeting. It was approved and passed without additions or corrections.

That False Alarm Ordinance stood the test and is probably the same one in effect today. I retired before I found out if it was ever tested in the Courts. Maybe other townships plagiarized our Ordinance the same way my Captain plagiarized the Texas Ordinance.

THE COMPUTER OPERATOR'S MANUAL

In 1980 a state-of-the-art communication center was installed in the new police building that boggled the switchboard operators and brought about another rush order from the Superintendent. "Our communications people don't know how to operate the computers. Neither the salesman or the installer had an instruction manual nor is there a company representative who can train them. Barney, talk to John the switchboard operator. He's taking a computer course in Community College and he can give you ideas for an instruction manual. We go into operations in two weeks so get on this right away!" Front burner again.

Computers were in their infancy and on the market only a few years. I never saw one and I didn't know their capabilities. Until now I had no reason to give them a second thought. A computer was recently installed in the township building and all I ever heard from the operator was the pathetic cry, "The computer's down!" At the same time I'd go to a bank to cash my paycheck and it couldn't be cashed because their computer was down. It wasn't uncommon to be stalled at a department store or supermarket checkout counter because the computer was down. Computers at this time were a public menace.

Nonetheless, it was up to me to produce an instruction manual right away so I called upon John who had a few of night classes under his belt. Without him I wouldn't have been able to start. He turned over his classroom hieroglyphics that were scribbled on loose bits of paper. His notes were in a language that held no meaning for me but together we produced a manual for beginners. I hadn't the slightest idea what the notes meant when I handed them to my typist. She didn't understand them either but typed them without asking.

I used a magazine photograph of a computer for the cover and for the screen examples and produced a manual that looked like it was shipped with the computers. It was simple to read and understand and it carried the department through the transition period. I came up smelling like roses once again.

The Computer Manual cover. One of 20 illustrated pages.

ABSTRACTS OF CERTAIN TOWNSHIP ORDINANCES

One of the first things I did when I was assigned to the Staff and Inspections Unit in 1970 was to delve into the township archives for the records of previous Commissioners' meetings when local Ordinances were enacted. I knew no one had ever codified the Ordinances police officers were to enforce. In 1971 I compiled a police officer's manual with fifty Ordinances. I called my manual ABSTRACTS OF CERTAIN TOWNSHIP ORDINANCES (a summary of the Ordinances police officers must know and enforce). It had a table of contents and a cross-index. If the officer didn't know the Ordinance number he could find it in the cross-reference index.

In 1976 I sorted through the Commissioner's monthly meetings and found twenty new Ordinances and put them in a second edition. Every year more Ordinances were enacted so by 1982 an additional twenty Ordinances could have been added but the Superintendent kept me inundated with other projects. I hadn't the time or desire to indulge in any more of my personal undertakings.

These are the covers on my first and second edition of Township Ordinances that are enforced by police officers on patrol.

APPENDIX

I emphatically and unequivocally state my journal is intended for the enlightenment and enjoyment of my descendants. Should anyone other than a relative take umbrage with what is contained herein I'm sorry about that but I refuse to change a word. I removed all the names in the newspaper articles so no one would be offended just because I wanted to verify an incident.

A skilled writer could tastefully rewrite my material with half the "I's" but it is difficult to write a journal without them. Besides I usually patrolled alone. Rarely was an officer with me but when another officer was present his input was included under a factitious name.

Others may have had similar experiences but I wrote only about my encounters that left an indelible impression on me. Nothing was plagiarized nor did another media subliminally influence me. The dates are not in chronological order because as I was preparing this book I had second thoughts. I'd remove one story and insert another in its place and later have a change of heart. This occurred often.

"Mensch" is Jewish slang for a good man with high ideals, honesty, fairness respectability, compassion, etc. Simply put, he is a man's man. I aspired to be a *mensch* even during the most challenging, hostile and stressful confrontations. To be respected as a *mensch* was more important to me than portraying myself as a blue-ribbon policeman.

I hope my book is interesting reading and I hope everyone in my family who comes after me will be a *mensch*.

My first day on the job was midnight December 1, 1947 and I finished at 4:00 p.m. December 31, 1983.

BL

ABOUT THE BOOK

BRASS BUTTONS was never intended to be a novel, therefore, it isn't a story that connects a series of events and concludes with a case successfully solved. It isn't a Detective Story or a Sherlock Holmes Mystery nor is it a "black book" that discloses negative accounts of the conduct of superior officers and the men with whom I worked.

I didn't start out with the intention of keeping a career journal but my first notation *The Swearing In Ceremony* was so traumatizing I saved it for an after dinner conversation. I added the story about my badly fitted uniform in *My First Police Officer's Uniform* and then the tale about *My First Ambulance Assist* that occurred before I was on the job ten days. That was about an automobile accident where a pedestrian's foot was completely severed at the ankle except for the three inches of skin that held it to the leg. I was ordered to hold the ankle in line with the leg during a reckless ambulance ride to the Accident Ward and while the hospital staff undressed the pedestrian and prepared her for surgery. The horrifying ordeal was too much for a rookie and I suffered a case of dry heaves. Years later, when I believed I was a seasoned Accident Investigator I almost had dry heaves again while in a hospital morgue observing the County Coroner perform an autopsy in the story about *The Autopsy*.

It takes years of on the job experiences to transform a person into a genuine police officer but paying close attention to senior officers and practicing what they taught helped a great deal. In *The Itinerants* I watched an old timer unravel a traffic jam with a kind deed. Instead of yelling orders and wild hand signals he gave the meek frightened driver a few dollars with the instructions "Get the kids (in the car) an ice cream cone." After that experience I was an easy touch for every destitute vagrant passing through town who needed a cup of coffee and a bowl of soup to survive.

In the story *Say A Prayer For The Deceased* I explain how I discovered police officers are actually spiritual and compassionate human beings protected by a hard-case veneer. In *The Perth Amboy Pistol Match* I wrote about the time I almost shot off my head at a police pistol match that was held during a hurricane.

I made arrests too but in *That Man Is Sick* I reluctantly placed a man in the lockup to sober up but overnight he died because he was actually sick and not intoxicated. In *Please Officer, Just One Little Sip,* I expected an alcoholic I locked up to be dead in the morning just because I allowed him to take a sip of Aqua Velva After Shave lotion. On another occasion I checked the records for a prisoner who was arrested for disorderly conduct and intoxication. He needed proof that a Holy Vision visited his cell during the night and ordered him to flush his *Eight Hundred Dollars* down the toilet.

I noted moments in American history, such as, the cold night I waited for President Harry S Truman. I describe it in *President Harry S Truman And Me*. A young reader will not be familiar with the impact *U.S. Senator Joe McCarthy* had on American history and perhaps more than a few senior readers will not recall *Reverent Muhammed Kenyetta* but I'll never forget the afternoon he spoke in a Main Line Synagogue. Then there was my wild and reckless motorcycle ride escorting *Senator John F. Kennedy*.

There were lighter moments among my notes. For example *The Sick Greyhound Bus Passenger* who threw up on my uniform and *The Cattle Truck Lesson* when a senior officer was warning me to beware of cattle hauling trucks traveling through town because a "she cow" might lift her tail and urinate on everyone on the sidewalk. At that very moment a she cow did.

The 1950s, 60s, and 70s were decades of terrifying social unrest and the police shouldered the negative impact of these protests. Unfortunately the police were not prepared for what they had to face. They weren't trained how to properly control the energy of protesters before they themselves were tainted with infamous police brutality charges. Read the *Michigan State University Conference* to understand the point of view of police and well-meaning social workers throughout these hectic years.

My personal proudest moment was when I rose to the occasion and taught *The Human Relation Course*. I wasn't a brilliant teacher but I did have sufficient information to carry young policemen and the department through the turbulent period. The department weathered the threatening social storms without civil suits or ugly blemishes on its glorious reputation. I particularly didn't want to forget the night in *A Barn Is On Fire!* That was the night I learned how to lead horses out of their burning stalls.

These incidents happened in the era before police officers submitted written reports. Except for motor vehicle accident reports officers handled an incident and once it was resolved they didn't submit a written report about it. I had no intention of keeping my own files; therefore, I kept no pertinent information, such as, names, dates, times and places. I unequivocally repeat the only reason I kept a brief account of these incidents was so I'd have bedtime stories to tell my grandchildren.

I accumulated hundreds of these stories because they were too precious to discard. Now in my musing, years after I retired, I relive those moments and I find them amusing but I assure you they were not hilarious the first time around. They were in fact very stressful. After thirty-six years my collection became so bulky I bound my favorite ones to keep them from getting lost. That is why my book BRASS BUTTON was published.

Born June 11, 1926 – Died June 11, 2002